Geopolitics

Making Sense of a Changing World

John Rennie Short
University of Maryland, Baltimore County

ROWMAN & LITTLEFIELD
Lanham • Boulder • New York • London

Acquisitions Editor: Susan McEachern
Acquisitions Assistant: Katelyn Turner
Sales and Marketing Inquiries: textbooks@rowman.com

Credits and acknowledgments for material borrowed from other sources, and reproduced with permission, appear on the appropriate pages within the text.

Published by Rowman & Littlefield
An imprint of The Rowman & Littlefield Publishing Group, Inc.
4501 Forbes Boulevard, Suite 200, Lanham, Maryland 20706
www.rowman.com

86-90 Paul Street, London EC2A 4NE

British Library Cataloguing in Publication Information Available

Library of Congress Cataloging-in-Publication Data

Names: Short, John R., author.
Title: Geopolitics : making sense of a changing world / John Rennie Short.
Description: Lanham, Maryland : Rowman & Littlefield, 2022. | Includes bibliographical references and index.
Identifiers: LCCN 2021020039 (print) | LCCN 2021020040 (ebook) | ISBN 9781538135389 (cloth) | ISBN 9781538135396 (paperback) | ISBN 9781538135402 (epub)
Subjects: LCSH: Geopolitics. | World politics—21st century.
Classification: LCC JC319 .S519 2022 (print) | LCC JC319 (ebook) | DDC 320.1/2—dc23
LC record available at https://lccn.loc.gov/2021020039
LC ebook record available at https://lccn.loc.gov/2021020040

Brief Contents

PART III. REGIONAL REALMS

PART IV. NEW GLOBAL CHALLENGES

Contents

PART I. INTRODUCTION TO GEOPOLITICS

PART II. THE NEW WORLD ORDER

PART IV. NEW GLOBAL CHALLENGES

List of Figures and Chart

FIGURES

CHART

List of Maps

List of Photos

List of Tables

Preface

I had little choice: geopolitics was, and still is, such an integral part of my life. I was not only born during a major conflict in the Cold War; I was the result of it. My father had been called to fight in the Korean War. He was conscripted in 1950–1951 as "cannon fodder" for the U.S.-United Nations (UN) forces sent to beat back North Korean and Chinese troops. He was about to be sent to a country on the other side of the world, for a country he had little interest in and for a cause he did not share. In the working-class mining community where I grew up, the "right wing" only extended as far as to voting for the Labour Party while the left extended into support for more socialist and Communist platforms. My father had no appetite for fighting against "Communism." His mother, my grandmother, whom I adored, would remind us of the Soviet sacrifice during World War II. She remembered Winston Churchill less as a wartime leader than an English class warrior, who hated unions and miners and the working class. Knowing he was about to be called up, my father and mother conceived me. I owe my existence to a Cold War encounter.

At my primary (elementary) school the world map displayed in front of the class depicted the British Empire. In my earliest classes, most of the world, at least as it appeared to my youthful gaze, was colored red to signify that it was British. I did not have the understanding that it was merely a claim to territory, not necessarily the wish of the people of the territory. It had, to my "innocent" eyes, the solid signification of rightful possessions. As the years passed, the seemingly solid turned into air, as the British red was reduced as one piece of territory after another turned another color to signify departure from the imperial grasp. I was a witness to decolonization. The British Empire was disappearing, quite literally, in front of my very eyes. My youthful gaze revealed the ongoing diminution of empire. Those early school years corresponded with the geopolitical decline and cartographic collapse of the British Empire. The Empire disappeared from public view, transferring into discourses of historical memory, memorialization, and occasional site of contestation. There was a sting in the tail of imperial collapse. Years later in 1982, my younger brother, serving in the Royal Navy, was on the HMS *Sheffield* when it was sunk by an Exocet missile off the coast of Argentina during the Falklands War. Twenty of his shipmates were killed. I then realized that geopolitical conflicts are always constructed on the backs of personal trag-edies. My brother was injured but survived and indeed prospered. But for days we had no idea if he was alive or dead, maimed or unharmed. The experience burned home the message that despite my interest in geopolitics, all the screen images I viewed, all the books I read and all the academic papers I skimmed, nothing prepared me for the personal experience of the human costs of conflict.

Images of such geopolitics pervaded my later school years and then my uni-versity years. Television screens broadcast searing images of the Vietnam War and, closer to home, of the Troubles in Ireland. In the early 1970s as a graduate student in Bristol, geopolitical machinations caught up with me: I remember playing football with refugees from Chile, at the invitation of a Catalan friend escaping Franco's Spain. After the matches, at the social gatherings, they would speak about family members left behind, friends and allies who had perished in the murderous thuggery of a regime installed and aided by the United States. The architect of the U.S. plan, Henry Kissinger, was a self-styled, realist geopolitician.

As a young faculty member in the 1980s I remember marching, in Reading and London, against the installation of U.S. Cruise missiles little more than twenty miles from my home in Reading. And then, suddenly, the existential threat was gone. In 1989 came the fall of the Iron Curtain. An icon of the Cold War, the Berlin Wall was soon reduced to memorabilia. Two years later, the So-viet Union was dissolved. The Cold War era, like my youth, came to an end. My life changes seemed be in some sort of crazy synchronization with geopolitical shifts and tumbles. A new chapter of my life opened just as a new world order was emerging. I moved to the United States in January 1990 to take up a post at Syracuse University. Initially, it seemed more insular and more provincial in the very best senses, and thus somehow safer. I no longer had to fear IRA bomb attacks as I had when in London. The whole place seemed more relaxed. Oceans separated it from bad things. Geopolitical conflict happened elsewhere, far from my new home. That feeling was reinforced, surprisingly enough, when the United States went to war. In the first Gulf War (1990–1991), U.S.-led forces quickly and relatively easily defeated Saddam Hussein's army. The war was over so quickly and with so few U.S. casualties that there seemed like a new world order of a United States triumphant, the sole superpower able to wield its power and influence across a unipolar world. Well-equipped professionals, smart bombs, and precision lasers ensured a quick victory, so unlike the quagmire of Vietnam. In and out quickly, objectives achieved, and few U.S. fatalities. The U.S. military had finally vanquished the ghosts of defeat in Vietnam and was now reinforced by the belief that swift military solutions were possible. Later, there were disturbing images of the killing and torture of Shia in the south of Iraq, encouraged by the U.S. president to rise against Hussein. Disturbing, yet far enough away to disappear quickly, like a shout from a long distance. I was watch-ing great power politics play out. It became confusing, however, when it was the lack of great power involvement that led to even more carnage. Mass killings in Rwanda and Bosnia undercut the easy notion that violence was due always to the machinations of great powers.

To have even the most passing of interests in current affairs during my life was to be given an ongoing lesson in geopolitics, indeed, *multiple* lessons with different and questionable prescriptions. A new set of lessons came on 9/11—the blowback that brought new designations and new forms of geopolitics—with the fall of the towers in New York City. The country I was living in now was renamed the "homeland"—the implicit distinction being that there was a non-homeland that was the cause of danger. I balked at the term and do still. The collapsing twin towers was such an easy metaphor to describe the end of an old world order that I always resist the temptation. However, I was as everyone else witness to new forms of geopolitical struggles with networks rather than nations, terrorists rather than soldiers, and pornographic violence as geopolitical "performance art." Then there was the fiasco of the invasion of Iraq, the long war in Afghanistan, and the seemingly never-ending "War on Terror."

I not so much have an interest in geopolitics as geopolitics has an interest in me—shaping, informing, attracting, and repelling me down through the decades. One of my early books, *An Introduction to Political Geography*, first came out in 1982. The rapid change in world events necessitated an enlarged and revised second edition, published in 1993, dedicated to my brother Kevin. Due to changing geopolitics, my book had to be updated: to commit to print in such a rapidly changing world is to risk rapid intellectual obsolescence. My other interests, especially concerning urban issues and the history of cartography, then demanded more of my professional time. It was only around 2010 that I seriously changed directions and began teaching and writing about geopolitics. This was both a change and a reversal. Hence this book.

In order to teach geopolitical courses, I immersed myself in geopolitical writings. I was fortunate that the field, once so barren and arid, now looked like a rainforest of exuberant growth. It was a vibrant field with old theories critically reexamined, fresh ideas, and new perspectives being developed. In 2013, I moved to Washington, DC, and was able to easily access the city's thriving geopolitical community of think tanks, regular meetings, and conferences. I developed a research interest in the South China Sea's geopolitics. In order to make sense of all things, I must write about them. I approached Susan McEachern at Rowman & Littlefield with a proposal to write a text on geopolitics. She agreed and graciously supported my efforts. The book in your hands or on your screen is the direct result of encouragement and guidance from Susan.

THE STRUCTURE OF THE BOOK

This book will introduce you to geopolitics. It will provide an understanding of the basic themes of geopolitics and an introduction to geopolitical issues around the globe. It is divided into four parts. Part I, "Introduction to Geopolitics," consists of three chapters. You have to start somewhere. I begin with an introduction to the evolution of traditional geopolitical thinking, focusing on writings in the West over the past 150 years and on ideas generated during the Cold War and their subsequent elaborations. I introduce the traditional Western discourses that first emerged in the nineteenth century, not only to provide the historical context of this particular intellectual discourse, but also because they continue to have contemporary relevance. I look in detail at the writers of bygone years such as Halford Mackinder (1861–1947) and A. T. Mahan (1859–1914) because their ideas continue to roll through the halls of academe and more significantly along the corridors of political power. It was John Maynard Keynes who reminded us that "Practical men, who believe themselves to be quite exempt from any intellectual influence, are usually the slaves of some defunct economist. Madmen in authority, who hear voices in the air, are distilling their frenzy from some academic scribbler of a few years back."[1] Similarly, political and military leaders as well as popular commentators may be surprised to realize just how much their ideas owe to the long-deceased geopolitical writers of the past. Hitler's invasion of the Soviet Union drew on two generations of German geopolitical writings. The containment policy of the Cold War relied on themes developed by Mackinder a half-century earlier. The current U.S. naval base in Bahrain draws its strategic rationale from the nineteenth-century writings of Mahan. I develop the ideas of geopolitics as forms of geographical imaginations often generated by specific geopolitical moments. The specific nature of their production makes their subsequent and (much) later uses all that more problematic, more ideological than scientific. Theories of geopolitics, while often claiming some form of universality, are always rooted in specific interests from particular viewpoints. Rather than a mere summary of geopolitical thinkers, the chapter introduces readers to the idea of geopolitics as a situated knowledge, not as a set of unvarying rules but as an intellectual response to specific events. Several intellectual contexts will be identified: declining states, rising empires, hegemonic projects, and marginal power-status. For example, the writings of Mackinder (1861–1947) are discussed as a response to the rise of other imperial powers threatening British global dominance.

Geopolitics has a long history as the study of the power relations between states. New perspectives have emerged that provide us with fresh understandings of political space beyond the narrow focus on nation-states. *Critical geopolitics* looks at the social construction of political spaces, exposes the material interests involved in the narratives used to explain this space, and explores the spatial construction of national identity. As part of this more critical turn a lively feminist geopolitics began to take shape. In addition, *popular geopolitics* was exploring the role of popular culture and mass media in structuring national identities and popular geographical understandings of the world. In the conclusion to chapter 1, I make the case for a *hybrid geopolitics* that combines elements of the traditional and these more critical perspectives.

Chapter 2 discusses the spaces of geopolitics, the basic territorial building blocks of the geopolitical order, empire, nation-state, and world order. Through "empire," I explore the notion of imperial overstretch and collaborative elites. "State" includes theories of the state, including imagined communities, banal nationalism, states of exception, and the variety of crises of the state. Then, I describe a series of world orders and introduce the rising, great-power rivalry of the contemporary world order, a theme elaborated in part II.

Chapter 3 adopts a space-time perspective with a discussion of large-scale historical changes of the past five hundred years. The chapter introduces the space-time matrix of geopolitics. I will look at three major processes: the creation and transformation of a global economy; the shifting nature of a global polity;

and the importance of unfolding globalizations. The case study of the East Sea/ Sea of Japan naming issue in this chapter is interesting in its own right, but also introduces the idea of scale and how scalar effects of global, national, and local processes interact and intersect over time in specific places.

Part II, "The New World Order," follows on from the idea of world orders raised in chapter 2 to look in more detail at the three major actors in the current geopolitical world order and their jostling for position. The United States, China, and Russia are ascribed respective chapters as befits their importance in this new geopolitical world order. The relative decline of the United States, a resurgent Russia, and an advancing China are all reconstructing the geopolitical landscape. The United States is the world's superpower, but its hegemony is threatened. Even its own military intelligence agencies refer to the "near-peer" competition from Russia and China. A recent report argues that the threats posed to the United States by these competitors are at their highest point since the Cold War.[2] I look at the geopolitical rise of each of these powers, outline their current configuration, and assess their relative weaknesses and strengths. Chapter 4 explores the rise of the United States from an imperial republic to its present position of global dominance. The republic grew from thirteen colonies to continental domination. Ideas of frontier and empire are pivotal to a geopolitical understanding of the United States. Emphasis is placed on its rise to global presence after World War II, the entanglements of empire, the Cold War, and the issue of imperial overstretch.

Chapter 5 considers the recent rise of China, its deepening influence in East and Southeast Asia, and its growing global reach. After the end of the Cold War, the rise of China as a major power is the single most significant geopolitical event of the past thirty years. The rise of China as regional military power and global economic power, its changing role in the wider world, and especially its geoeconomics significance are discussed. Chapter 6 considers the geopolitical fallout of the collapse of the USSR and the resurgence of Russian geopolitical strategies and tactics.

I am acutely aware that these three chapters of the book sound like an update of *1984*. In his famous novel, George Orwell imagined three great powers, Eurasia, Eastasia, and Oceania as empires based on Russia, China, and the United States. They were in a state of perpetual war. The novel presents a bleak vision of a dystopic of incessant conflict, constant surveillance, and censorship. My own view is more sanguine because while there are elements of all of these in the current world order, there are also countervailing tendencies. But nothing is determined. A world order in the process of becoming can take any number of forms of being.

Part III, "Regional Realms," looks at specific regions of the world, including Africa, Europe, the Middle East, South Asia, and South and Central America. Each chapter provides a historical introduction in order to contextualize present-day issues. Chapter 7 focuses on the rise of a unified Europe, its extensions into more peripheral areas, and the backlash from core countries over the free movement of peoples. I discuss the reasons behind the rise of the European idea and its current discontents. Chapter 8, "Middle East," discusses the politics of oil and religion, the Arab-Israeli conflict, the Iran-Saudi polarization, and the Arab

Spring. The political issues of a demographic bulge and its possible impact on the Arab Spring are examined. Chapter 9 is concerned with Africa. It examines the northern fault line along 10 degrees North, the site of the continuing ethnic conflicts in some countries and of the resolution of long-standing issues in others. Chapter 10, "South Asia," highlights how the conflict between India and Pakistan not only frames the geopolitical concerns of this region but also is a matter of global concern. The ethnic divides across the region are explored. Chapter 11 focusses on Central and South America and outlines how and why decades of social unrest were followed by relative peace and asks whether this is a permanent or transient condition. The rise of Brazil to geopolitical significance is also noted.

Part IV, "New Global Challenges," consists of chapter 12 where I conclude the book with a discussion of two global challenges, pandemics and climate change, that are unsettling and reshaping relationships between the global order and the state.

DEDICATION

My goal is to turn my interest in geopolitics plus a lifetime of entanglements into a text. It is perhaps too heavy a burden for one book to carry. Our largest ambitions are rarely realized; their results always are so much smaller than our dreams for them, so much less than our hopes for them. So, it is with some hesitation then that I dedicate this book to the memory of my beloved brother, Kevin Short (1964–2020). A good man.

NOTES

1. Keynes, J. M. (1936). *The general theory of employment, interest and money.* London: Macmillan, 383.

2. Vergun, D. (2020). *Near-peer threats at highest since cold war, DoD official says.* Washington, DC: U.S. Department of Defense. https://www.defense.gov/Explore/News /Article/Article/2107397/near-peer-threats-at-highest-point-since-cold-war-dod-official -says/.

I

INTRODUCTION TO GEOPOLITICS

1

Writings

At its heart, geopolitics is a form of geographical imagination that highlights the operation of power in, through, and around political space. There are many different types of geopolitics. The oldest encompasses the geographical context and spatial expression of international relations and is especially concerned with power relations between states. This traditional approach highlights the spatial strategies of states and empires as well as the geographical arrangement of imperial systems and world orders. There is also the more recent emergence of a more critical geopolitics that we will discuss later.

Geopolitics is a form of situated knowledge, neither a socially neutral nor a politically innocent form of understanding, but one deeply marked by who is using it, when, and for what purposes. It is a form of knowledge created by specific people at certain points in time for particular purposes. It is also a product of "geopolitical moments." Uprisings, wars, and border clashes are only some of the more dramatic moments that prompt revisions of the geopolitical imagination. There are geopolitical narratives of rising and declining empires and states, of hegemonic projects for major powers, and of regional roles for minor powers. And while some geopolitical ideas have a long life, there are no "laws" or "theories" independent of their creators and the context of their creation.

Geopolitics has a long and global history.[1] Here I will focus on the development of traditional geopolitics in the West in the contemporary era.

GEOPOLITICAL WRITINGS IN THE WEST

Geopolitics in the West first emerged as an academic discipline in the nineteenth century, due, in part, to the rise of the German state and its entry onto a world stage dominated by Britain.

The German Contribution

Professional commentaries and academic contributions arose from an emergent intellectual class eager to explain, justify, and promote Germany's expanding role. One such academic is Friedrich List (1789–1846), who was born in Germany and spent time in the United States. List could see the significance of the vast U.S. market and was impressed by the protectionist doctrine of Alexander Hamilton that provided a model for an expansionist Germany. He espoused an economic nationalism that argued for Germany to have a vast range of territories for economic progress. Writing at a time of a British-dominated global economy, List enunciated the role of national economic interests and especially of German economic interests.[2] He argued for tariffs to protect German industries and for a greater territorial reach to ensure large captive markets. List was an economic nationalist. He theorized that, in the face of overwhelming British economic power, Germany could only advance its economy behind a tariff barrier with protected markets. This was the model of national development adopted in the late twentieth century in the economic nationalism of *development states*, such as China, Japan, and South Korea.

An important intellectual context in Germany and across Europe and North America is Social Darwinism. Darwin's theory of evolution is outlined in *The Origin of Species* (1859).[3] This text was widely influential among social commentators who would now be described as "social scientists." They were observers of the social world who wanted to find a scientific basis of social phenomena. It was the British writer Herbert Spencer, not Darwin, who coined the phrase *survival of the fittest* in 1864. Darwin's theory of evolutionary biology was used to provide a "scientific" justification of social differences. Social Darwinism mapped the theory of natural selection onto the workings of the contemporary social world. Social inequalities were depicted as the result of the blind operations of biological inevitability and by extension perfectly "natural" forces above mere politics. Social Darwinism was used—then as now—to justify existing inequalities and marginalize any opposition to this state of affairs. In this narrative, social inequalities were natural, not the result of power and influence. Social Darwinism laid the basis for eugenics, for fascism, giving a putative scientific rationale for social inequalities and imperialism. Inequality for the Social Darwinists was biologically determined, not socially constructed. Those at the top of the hierarchy were there not through accident or privilege, but because of an innate biological superiority. Comforting news for the affluent and powerful, whose standing was now officially legitimized by "science."

Social Darwinism justified existing social relations as the natural order of things ordained by the impersonal forces of biology. Because societies were seen as biological units above and beyond the operation of mere politics, then revolutionary and reformist movements that questioned the status quo could be marginalized as working against the natural order of things, quite literally as unnatural. This biologizing of the status quo delegitimized critics of existing hierarchies and inequalities by rendering them unscientific. The Marxist counter-critique of the existing order was thus framed as a science of history in order to counter the Social Darwinist monopoly of science and inexorable processes of social change. Marxism was in part a critical response to Social Darwinism in order to identify unfolding natural "laws" that favored the working class.

Social Darwinism was more an excuse for social inequalities than a serious science. It was also a misreading of Darwin, who firmly stated, "it is not the strongest of the species that survives, nor the most intelligent, but the ones most responsive to change."[4] Yet Social Darwinism influenced geopolitics. Nations were imagined less as political constructs and more as "natural" biological units that needed to grow or die, locked into a never-ending struggle for the domination of space. It was the "survival of the fittest" applied to international relations. The international order was seen as a zero-sum game. The world was viewed as a giant cake, fixed in size. One country's slice of the world's wealth was at the expense of all the others.

This Darwinian imagining of the nation-state became an important theme of German political geographers. Friedrich Ratzel (1844–1904) argued that a rapidly growing Germany needed more space, *lebensraum* (living space), in order to grow.[5] States were locked into a competition for territory. The territorial expansion of the German state was a necessity in order for the country to grow and prosper. The need for *lebensraum* became a central tenet of German geopolitics.

The German liberal Friedrich Naumann (1860–1919) coined the term *Mitteleuropa* in 1915 to refer to the idea of pan-German states stretching across Central and Eastern Europe.[6] The region would provide a large market for German goods and space for German expansion with existing societies brought under German control and dominance. You can see where this is going: it leads to World War II. It is also an example of how a geographical description, such as *Mitteleuropa*, the German word for "middle Europe," is loaded with political and economic consequences. It is less a simple geographical description than a geopolitical strategy.

The term *geopolitics* was first coined by the Swede Rudolf Kjellen (1864–1922).[7] He wanted Sweden to align with the Germans against Russia. He saw the contest in Europe as a struggle for dominance between a pan-Slavic movement dominated by Russia and a pan–German-Nordic movement. Kjellen saw Sweden as part of this German empire that should dominate the Austro-Hungarian states and the Balkans. He was codifying a geopolitical theme that stressed the need for rising powers, in this case Germany, to have space and territory in order to compete on the world stage and resist Russian expansionism and British economic domination.

After World War I, when Germany was soundly defeated by Allied powers, geopolitics became even more integrated into German social thought. An influential figure was Karl Haushofer (1869–1946). He served in the army for a while and was seconded to Japan. In 1919 he was appointed to a chair of Geography and Military Science in Munich. Haushofer was very friendly with Rudolph Hess, a leading Nazi and Deputy Fuhrer from 1933 to 1941. Hitler, probably influenced by Hess, appointed Haushofer as the president of the German Academy in 1933. Haushofer was a prolific promoter of geopolitics. He edited the influential geopolitical journal *Zeitschrift fur Geopolitk* from 1924 to 1944 and established an institute for geopolitics that produced maps, books, and atlases to inform public opinion. More than one million copies of the publication *The German People and Their Living Space* were printed and widely circulated.[8]

The geopolitical ideas outlined by Darwin, Ratzel, Naumann, Kjellen, and Haushofer directly fed into the ideologies of the German Nazi Party, its ideas of territorial expansion, and the perceived need for a German Empire to stretch across Eastern and Middle Europe. Map 1.1 is a snapshot of Europe at the height of German power in 1941–1942 that shows an extended German Reich, after the annexation of Poland and much of Eastern and Central Europe as well as areas under direct German occupation. The dream of German geopoliticians since the nineteenth century was finally realized.

Map 1.1. Europe under German occupation, 1942 (Margot Lyautey, Marc Elie. German Agricultural Occupation of France and Ukraine, 1940–1944. Comparativ. Zeitschrift für Globalgeschichte und vergleichende Gesellschaftsforschung, Leipziger Universitätsverlag, 2019, 29, pp. 86–117. ff10.26014 /j.comp.2019.03.05ff. ffhal-02562731f)

The Anglo-American Contribution

Anglo-American contributions to geopolitics are perhaps best embodied in the work of the Englishman Halford Mackinder (1861–1947) and the American Alfred Mahan (1840–1914), respectively generated during a British discomfort at the end of their expansionary imperial age and the U.S. search for strategies at the start of their formal imperial phase.

Mackinder saw the academic discipline of geography as an "aid to statecraft."[9] Geographical understanding was vital to identifying grand strategies of international politics. He was writing at a time when formal imperial annexation was coming to an end. The world of vast open and claimable spaces for colonial expansion was over. The safety valve of territorial expansion through colonial expansion was no more. Mackinder was concerned with understanding and managing international space at this time of closing frontiers. He wrote in 1887 that "we are now near the end of the roll of great discoveries."[10] The world of infinite promise had become a closed world, a giant chess board.[11] For Mackinder the key part of the global chessboard was Eurasia, what he termed the pivot or heartland of the Eurasian "world island." Control of this pivot area was crucial for domination of the world island. And control of the world island gave the opportunity for global dominance.

Mackinder sought to understand the geopolitics of the balance of power in his contemporary world, one dominated by the land powers of Germany and Russia and the more maritime states of the UK and a rising United States. Mackinder's notions were set in the context of Russian land power and UK sea power. In a paper presented at the Royal Geographical Society in London in 1904, titled *The Geographical Pivot of History*, he formulated a threefold division of the world (see map 1.2).[12] The pivot area, the heartland, consisting of Eastern Europe and Russia, was the key to the control of the world island, which was surrounded by an inner crescent and an outer crescent. The pivot area was the seat of land forces. The inner crescent was part oceanic, part continental, while the outer crescent was wholly oceanic.

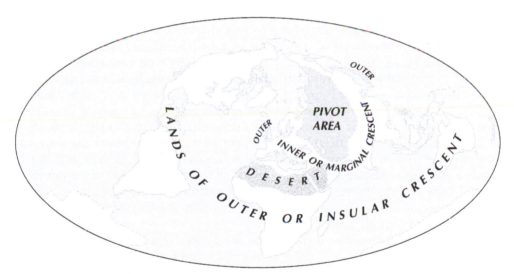

Map 1.2. Mackinder's world view

Mackinder sought to protect the British Empire. He moved from being a believer in free trade to a firm supporter of imperial protectionism underwritten by UK naval power. In his 1902 book, *Britain and the British Seas*, he argued that Britain and its empire was under threat from the land-based empires of Russia and Germany. He noted, with some alarm, the declining UK percentage of world trade as France, Germany, and the United States expanded their overseas commerce.

In his last work, an article published in 1943, *The Round World and The Winning of The Peace*, he revisited his theory in the light of modern warfare, especially airpower. He foresaw a United States pulled into Europe through the use of Britain as a "moated aerodrome" and the rise of China and India.[13]

Mackinder's work was especially popular in the United States, where it was first published in 1942 by the National Defense University Press in Washington, DC, and by commercial presses in 1962 and 1981. With his division of a world that foreshadowed the Cold War and that hypothesized the central strategic role of the USSR, Mackinder became an influential figure for U.S. strategists figuring out how to respond to a new world order at the end of World War II and at the start of the Cold War. Later, his implication that the geopolitical location of Russia, now the USSR, necessitated constant expansion slotted directly into U.S. fears and helped guide some of the hysteria of U.S. Cold War thinking.

In his 1942 book, *America's Strategy in World Politics*, Nicholas Spykman (1893–1943) counseled against the isolationism then prevalent in the United States. Spykman's book was drafted before the United States entered World War II.[14] Drawing on the ideas of Mackinder, he argued that the United States needed to play a more active role across the world especially in containing any Eurasian power. Spykman renamed Mackinder's three categories as Heartland, the Rimland, and offshore Islands and Continents. His ideas were used by postwar strategists during the Cold War eager for spatial strategies to deal with the conflict with the USSR. He is sometimes referred to as the "intellectual godfather of containment," a theme discussed later in this chapter.

Alfred Thayer Mahan (1840–1914) was born into a military family and graduated from the Naval Academy in 1859. He was socially well connected and later became very friendly with President Roosevelt. While much was being written at the time about westward territorial expansion across the continent, Mahan was keen to point out the importance of projecting national power through a large navy. He argued that sea power was a determinant factor in the strength of nations. Expanding states need big and powerful navies to protect the national economy and to police the maritime choke points. The fleet had to be as globally mobile as possible. Mahan saw the command of the sea as crucial to the development of trade and commerce. He argued for a large number of ships and relatively few but strategic bases. His basic argument was that the United States needed a big navy to defend trade routes.

Mahan's 1890 book, *The Influence of Sea Power Upon History, 1660–1783* stressed the importance of sea power in the rise of an empire. Naval power guaranteed a country's commercial use of the sea in times of peace and its control in times of war. He argued for the United States to build up its naval presence in order to compete on the world stage. He made the case for Hawaii as a vital military base to counter rising Japanese power. Mahan's ideas coincided with those of Theodore Roosevelt, who read his 1890 book in one weekend in May 1890 and reviewed it favorably.[15] Roosevelt was in wholehearted agreement with the need to build more and bigger ships and deploy them around the world. Roosevelt especially agreed with Mahan's suggested pressure points of the global maritime routes. Roosevelt saw imperialism as the natural outcome of the responsibility of superior nations to advance progress. Roosevelt and Mahan corresponded, discussed, and promoted a view of American assertiveness through the deployment of an enlarged, blue-water navy. Roosevelt began to turn these geopolitical ideas into state policy as both assistant secretary of the navy and later when he was president from 1901 to 1909.

Mahan propounded his ideas in a series of articles in popular journals of the day, including *Atlantic Monthly*, *Harper's*, *Collier's*, and *Scribner's*. He outlined a new world role for the United States and argued for the U.S. annexation of Hawaii, Guam, Philippines, Panama Canal, and the Virgin Islands. He waged a campaign to induce public opinion toward accepting a greater naval role for the United States to truly become a world power. Mahan fought against the anti-imperialist movement in the United States that argued for less foreign intervention. In direct contrast, he argued that overseas expansion was similar to westward expansion and just as vital to economic growth and national strength.

Mahan's legacy is still evident. Not one but four ships have been named USS *Mahan* and there is an entire class of destroyers titled *Mahan*. Mahan's hopes for U.S. global power underwritten by a big and powerful navy came to fruition: U.S. naval bases are found around the world from Bahrain and Diego Garcia to Singapore and Sasebo in Japan. The United States has the world's biggest navy with the largest collection of the ultimate in naval force projection, aircraft carriers. The U.S. Navy has a total of nineteen; the rest of the world combined has only twelve. Mahan's ideas were influential not only in the United States, but they also formed the intellectual backdrop and justification to the massive buildup of naval power in Germany, Japan, and the UK in the early twentieth century.

These diverse geopolitical ideas circulated around the world as empires and proto-empires looked for strategic doctrines. On the eve of World War II, for example, Japanese military strategists and nationalist politicians had totally imbibed the ideas of Haushofer on the need for territorial expansion and those of Mahan on the importance of sea power. Japan turned these into strategies for winning World War II by invading Southeast Asia and launching attacks on U.S. naval forces in Pearl Harbor.

GEOPOLITICS OF THE COLD WAR

Formal geopolitics waned as an academic interest immediately after World War II. The defeated powers had generated the notion of geopolitics as built on ideas of racial superiority and the operation of brute force rather than international laws. The experience contaminated the basic idea of geopolitics.

Soon after the ending of World War II, the world was divided along ideological lines between the United States and USSR. The Cold War pitted the two former allies against each other. Although formal geopolitics largely disappeared in the academy of the immediate postwar world, geopolitical theorizing continued at the strategic level of statecraft. We can look at two examples, from opposite ends of the ideological divide but sharing global goals.

Containment

The geopolitical strategy of containment has various founding documents and an early guiding doctrine. The American diplomat George Kennan (1904–2005) wrote the first document. He held posts, in order, in the Soviet Union, Germany, Czechoslovakia, Portugal, and London. In 1944 he was assigned again to Moscow. The United States was poised to have a major global role in the new postwar world that was beginning to take shape. A pressing question was how to deal with the USSR on the world stage. Kennan took a view distinct from either an appeasement with the Soviets or beginning World War III with the horrifying prospect of nuclear weaponry. Instead, Kennan counseled in a five-thousand-word telegram he sent in 1946 that the Soviet Union could be contained. For obvious reasons it is referred to as the Long Telegram. Later, in 1947, he formalized his ideas in an article in *Foreign Affairs* under the title "The Sources of Soviet Conduct." He did not sign the piece and it came out under the authorship of "X."[16]

There was an inherent conflict between the United States and the USSR; they were rivals, not partners, but, according to Kennan, the relationship could be managed by neither allowing them to expand their power across the world, nor directly engaging them in war. Rather, the best U.S. strategy was to contain Soviet power by the "application of counter-force at a series of constantly shifting geographical and political points."[17] The USSR was powerful but over the long term, he believed, the United States would win out because of the weakness of the Soviet economy, the underlying lack of legitimacy of the Community Party, and its problems in dealing with the vast multiethnic Soviet Empire. Over the long term, if the United States could provide a model for other countries, the policy of containment would keep Soviet power in check until their system collapsed internally. Kennan, as X, counseled for a long-term, patient but firm and vigilant containment of the Soviet Union's expansionary tendencies. Containment was not simply the use of military and political counter-pressure but also the application of psychological pressure on the Soviet Union to make them assess the risks of future expansionary tendencies. It was an inherently optimistic view written at a time of general pessimism.

There was also the Truman Doctrine. In 1947 President Truman announced in Congress that the United States would "support free people who were resisting subjugation by armed minorities or by outside pressure."[18] It was in the context of perceived Communist threats in Greece and Turkey. In practice, the doctrine was an open-ended commitment to the installation of anti-Communist regimes. Governments, especially in what was then described as the Third World, had to be primarily anti-Communist but not necessarily democratic or progressive.

NSC 68 was a more formal policy document, produced by the National Security Council and sent to President Truman in 1950. This document reaffirmed containment as a policy of neither appeasement nor war. Compared to Kennan, however, *NSC 68* exaggerated the threats to the United States. Once the USSR had a greater military arsenal, the brief asserted, it would strike the United States. It outlined a zero-sum game and laid the basis for the subsequent arms race. It also called for a more muscular response even in distant and peripheral places. The whole world was now the site of containment. It was all-out global containment that lacked the subtlety of Kennan's graduated response. It was an open-ended commitment to a Cold War strategy of global military engagement.

Figure 1.1 is a poster produced by the U.S. Information Service in 1951 that calls for everybody to help in containing Communism. A national personification of the Philippines stands ready with the machete of democracy on the island nation to defeat the looming Communist threat of the hammer and sickle spreading across the islands. The poster presents a plucky Philippines as part of the global war of containing Communism but fails to note that the islands were annexed by the United States as part of its overseas imperial expansion and only achieved independence in 1946. As part of the agreement, the Philippines had to concede twenty-three military bases with ninety-nine-year leases over to the United States. There was a Communist presence in the Philippines, but it was more of an indigenous movement, with a long history of resistance to Japanese and American occupation and to the entrenched political power of the economic elite of the islands. The poster ignores all of this but highlights the envisioning of nations of the world as part of the struggle between two global forces, one good and the other very bad.

Figure 1.1. Containment: The U.S. viewpoint (U.S. National Archives and Records Administration)

Figure 1.2. Containment: The USSR viewpoint (Museum of Political History, St. Petersburg, Russia. Photo by John Rennie Short)

There was a Soviet response in the ideological struggle. Figure 1.2 is a poster produced by the Soviet government around 1950. It depicts a U.S. soldier planting American flags and bases to encircle the USSR. There is an image of an olive branch hiding an atomic bomb. The anti-Semitic Jewish caricature, a gun, and a pile of dollar bills completes the picture of U.S. expansionism. There was also the direct military response to the U.S. buildup suggested by figure 1.2. Photo 1.1 is a Soviet medium-range ballistic missile site in Lithuania. I visited the rusting site in 2007 but was still able to note from the information in the underground missile silo that one of the target sites was Edinburgh, Scotland. The city was an active target all the time I was in my high school barely thirty miles away.

Photo 1.1.   Abandoned missile site, Lithuania (John Rennie Short)

The containment strategy had many parts, not all of them consistent with one another. Kennan's original formulation was a more sophisticated response to a bipolar world that took an optimistic long view that the USSR could be contained without all-out war until it collapsed from its own contradictions. And that is what happened in 1989. The NSC document was a more global militaristic framing while the Truman Doctrine—as it turned out—was a blank check cashed in by any dictator able to describe any local resistance to their thuggish rule as part of a global Communist conspiracy.

Sea Power

Sergey Gorshkov (1910–1988) was a Soviet naval officer for most of his adult life. He saw active service in World War II in the Black Sea. By 1956 he was put in charge of the entire Soviet Navy. He was admiral of the Soviet Fleet from 1967 to1988. Gorshkov was also a deputy minister of defense and thus able to influence debates within the upper reaches of the Kremlin. He was so adept at surviving Kremlin infighting that he was able to use his power and influence to build up the Soviet Navy, arguing that it was vital to securing the Soviet Union from its enemies in the West. Russia was traditionally a land power and Gorshkov, in an argument similar to Mahan's, pointed out that global prominence demanded a global naval presence.

His 1979 book *The Sea Power of the State* echoes Mahan's argument for the necessity of expanded sea power for world power status.[19] Under his guidance the Soviet fleet was greatly expanded and enhanced. Nuclear weapons were part of the growing arsenal carried by ships and submarines. He is credited with creating a blue-water navy that could operate across the world oceans. During World War II, the Soviet Navy was mostly active in the Black Sea but not capable of force projection in the Atlantic or Pacific. Under Gorshkov's influence, the Soviet Navy became a nuclear power able to project Soviet power with operational squadrons around the world in the Atlantic, Pacific, and Indian oceans. In 1968 his portrait appeared on the cover of *Time* magazine. The February 23 article, titled "Russia: Power Play on the Oceans" contains this quote from Gorshkov: "The flag of the Soviet navy now proudly flies over the oceans of the world. Sooner or later, the United States would have to understand that it no longer has mastery of the seas."[20]

Under Gorshkov, the Soviet fleet moved from a small coastal defense to the second largest navy in the world with at one time 385 submarines. He also developed the merchant marine fleet so that it could be easily transferred to military duty. Still, there were geographical limits to Soviet naval expansion. The lack of warm-water ports, the numerous choke points, such as the Black Sea, and the lack of bases in the Pacific and Atlantic all limited the Soviet Navy. Greater parity was achieved with the submarine fleets; they were less constrained in movement than the surface fleet.

Even from this brief introductory analysis, I hope that you can now discern what I mean when I use the term *situated knowledge*. Geopolitics arises from particular junctures, written by specific people with a particular agenda. Ideas generated in a particular context can then sometimes join in the general circulation of ideas, prompting counterarguments as well as validations.

CONTEMPORARY DEBATES

After World War II, geopolitics became an ugly idea associated as it was with German and Japanese plans for ethnic cleansing, spatial annexation, and territorial enlargement by brute force.

Throughout the 1950s and 1960s, strategic studies focused on the threat of nuclear war and how to implement the policy of containment. It saw a bipolar world. But by the 1970s the world was becoming more complex than simply a standoff between the two major nuclear powers. New and emerging world orders required more nuanced understandings.

Things began to change in the 1970s.[21] Henry Kissinger, the U.S. secretary of state under Richard Nixon, explicitly used the term "geopolitics" in his speeches and writings and the term entered the popular discourse. Kissinger used the term with reference to the need for the United States to ensure global equilibrium while advancing its national interest. His argument was in response to a knee-jerk anti-Communism on the one hand and the concern with human rights on the other. It is often referred to as a *realist foreign policy*, in contrast to an idealist foreign policy more concerned with the advancement of human rights. We will explore this realist/ideality polarity in subsequent chapters. We should note, in passing, that Kissinger's geopolitical savviness, while endlessly promoted not least by himself, is also subject to withering criticism.[22]

By the 1980s geopolitics remerged as a distinct academic enterprise and a vibrant *critical geopolitics* also began to emerge.[23] There are now a variety of geopolitics. Let us consider four strands. First, there is a continuation of *traditional geopolitics* concerned with the spatial strategies of nation-states and the changing spatial architecture of international relations.[24] These themes are particularly strong in think tanks and with popular commentators and writers.[25] The books of the former Secretary of State Henry Kissinger, such as *World Order* (2014) for example, carry on this tradition. Robert Kaplan is a popular writer, described by his publisher as a "renowned geopolitical analyst" whose books include *Asia's Cauldron* and *The Revenge of Geography*. In a more recent book, *Marco Polo's World* (2018), Kaplan describes geopolitics as "the struggle of states against the backdrop of geography."[26] Note the similar biological analogies to those used by the earlier German geopoliticians. Kaplan tends to advance a more realist than idealist view of U.S. foreign policy. In the lead chapter of the book Kaplan quotes and builds directly on Mackinder's "world island" notion in an outline of a U.S. role in Eurasia. In later chapters he references explicitly Mahan's ideas for a greatly expanded U.S. Navy. Kaplan's work is a prolonged debate with the basic ideas of Mackinder and Mahan in order to guide U.S. foreign policy in the twenty-first century. Both Kissinger and Kaplan represent geopolitics centered in Washington, DC. It is the American view of the world. There are others. In the subsequent regional chapters, we will note some of the geopolitical perspectives from different regions of the world.

Critical geopolitics also emerged in the 1980s and 1990s.[27] This approach is most commonly found in colleges and universities and is now the dominant form of academic geopolitics. Critical geopolitics sees the world differently from those perched on the upper levels of think tanks in the capitals of great powers. It adopts a wider angle of vision and deconstructs the basic entities of traditional geopolitics. Where traditional geopolitics takes nation-states and national interest as given, a more critical geopolitical approach seeks to discover the social construction of nation-states and to ask whose interests are represented and not represented by the national interest. This more critical approach deconstructs geopolitical categories and sees them less as given starting points and more as constructs that frame the world in ideas and strategies. In this more critical geopolitics, national borders, for example, are not taken-for-given demarcations but constructs that are created, maintained, and justified.[28]

There is also the critical evaluation of the founding figures and ideas of geopolitics. Gerry Kearns's biography of Halford Mackinder situated his work in wider class, gender, and national contexts. Neil Smith also contextualized the work of Isaiah Bowman at a time of U.S. entry onto the global stage of World War I.[29] The ideas of geopoliticians, as these biographies reveal, are not independent of social relations and political power but deeply embedded in existing relations of power. While traditional geopolitics looks to figures like Mackinder, more critical geopolitics looks to figures like Peter Kropotkin (1842–1921). Born into the privilege of the aristocracy of Tsarist Russia, he developed an interest in geography and radical politics. Kropotkin had an alternative version of political organization. He proposed a centralized system of self-governing communities and worker-controlled enterprises. Kropotkin envisaged a politics without the central state.

There is also a decolonization of the geopolitical imagination as the arguments from the periphery are given a wider hearing. Traditional geopolitics, for example, tends to see Africa as a place where Western power is projected and contested rather than as source of geopolitical thinking. The Tanzanian leader Julius Nyerere's Pan-Africanism, in contrast, sought an understanding of the world more reconciled to African concerns than Cold War binaries.[30]

There is *feminist geopolitics*.[31] One strand examines the too-often-ignored role of women. Elaine Stratford, for example, explains how ideas about bodies, gender, and home were mobilized to create healthy populations, vigorous nations, and ascendant empires.[32] The role of women in empires and empire-building, especially their role in sexual exploitation, is explored by Julie Peakman.[33] But feminist geopolitics does more than just acknowledge and question the male gaze that pervades traditional geopolitics.[34] There is the concern with alternative conceptions to a world order dominated by states and the pursuit of "national" interest. The *national* is wreathed with quotation marks here because while it covers the entire national population, it may not serve the interests of *all* the national population. The politics of this geopolitics is concerned with identifying more community-based, progressive movements, such as the rise of a global green movement that stresses sustainability rather than the pursuit of narrow national economic interest; or humanitarian movements that call for the rights of indigenous peoples, undocumented migrants, and the marginalized; or the role of women's activism in the Middle East.[35] It is geopolitics more concerned with nongovernment agencies and grassroots movements than with nation-states imagined as one coherent unit. It moves between different scales of analysis in a globally connected world. The previously easy distinction between the national and the global begins to falter, for example, when indigenous peoples in the Amazon call on international help defend their land against a Brazilian development state.

Finally, there is *popular geopolitics*, which looks at the way that popular ideas of the world, the state, regions, and peoples are produced, transmitted, and consumed. Figure 1.1, for example, is as much rhetorical as cartographic, depicting a Philippines under attack. Figure 1.2, in contrast, depicts the same U.S. foreign policy as an attempt to strangle the USSR. Popular geopolitics elides beliefs with geographical understandings and representations.

Popular religious beliefs often have geopolitical consequences, such as the U.S. Christian right's unwavering support of Israel. Religions that see an apocalyptic end to the world can influence popular understandings of war and peace, diplomacy, and international relations. Video games fashion a popular understanding of threats to the homeland. Movies often contain ideas about the geopolitical world order embedded in images of other nations and peoples. Geopolitical tensions were embodied in the early James Bond movies, for example; many of them were produced as the Cold War was easing. The connections between terrorism and particular regions of the world are a common trope of Hollywood action movies. Popular geopolitics looks at the way geopolitical ideas and images are incorporated, produced, and contested in popular culture. Jason Dittmer and Daniel Bos, for example, explore the relationship between popular culture and international relations from a geographic perspective.[36] From books to movies and television news to games and magazine articles, popular culture is filled with geopolitical ideas. When newspapers provide maps of the world, they are maps with purpose that convey more than just cartographic images of the world to their readership. A popular television series, such as *Homeland*, for example, provides a view of a United States constantly under threat. The heroine, compromised and damaged, saves the United States from evil threats from home and abroad. The title of the series depicts the need for the United States to be a "securitized state" after 9/11. The depiction of other countries in popular media is also revealing in that it can reinforce existing stereotypes of the *foreign other* and of home. Andrei Tsygankov, for example, shows how U.S. newspaper coverage of Russia from 2008 to 2014 was framed around the idea of a neo-Soviet autocracy. Russian politics that did not fit this frame were ignored, and overall, the coverage tended to present Russia as a dark contrast to brighten the image of a democratic United States leading the "free" world.[37]

HYBRID GEOPOLITICS

Geopolitics today is a vital and dynamic field. The divisions of the contemporary geopolitical scene that I have just outlined are rough classifications that bleed one into another. Classical geopolitics in the modern era is more aware of the social construction of their categorizations. Critical, feminist, and popular geopolitics still consider the role of state and its interactions with other states. It is more accurate to consider contemporary geopolitics as a hybrid that encompasses elements of the different approaches with differences in emphasis rather than solid categorical divisions. This book provides an introduction to this *hybrid geopolitics*.

Hybrid geopolitics uses a variety of approaches. Let us end this chapter with alternative ways of doing geopolitics. Two examples: The first is the work of Tiffany Chung. She was born in Da Nang, Vietnam in 1969. Her father fought for the South Vietnamese Army against North Vietnamese forces, was imprisoned for fourteen years, then took his family to the United States in 1975. Chung's exhibition, *Vietnam, Past is Prologue*, is a meditation on the Vietnam War through maps, text, and photographs. In the first section of the exhibition, titled "Remapping History," maps and photographs document the major battles that her father fought in during the war. There is a map of Operation Lam So'n 719 in 1971, in which her father's helicopter was shot down. Another section, "Remembrance of the War," includes interviews with twenty-one former refugees from Vietnam now living in the United States. The final section, subtitled "Reconstructing History," draws on archival material to present fragmented records and half-lived lives, containing drawings, photographs, and flight paths of exiled Vietnamese. Part art, part geopolitics, the exhibition condenses various themes of critical and feminist geopolitics in an aesthetic and personal response to the Vietnam War. It makes no claim to either objectivity or understanding. It nevertheless encourages a deeper response to our understanding of the war and its aftermath.[38]

The second example is the Brazil pavilion at the 16th Venice Architecture Biennale in 2018. Titled *Walls of Air*, it contained ten large-scale maps of the country that depicted borders, migration flows, movement of goods and commodities, the real estate market, and environmental issues. It was an imaginative cartographic depiction that highlighted the walls that both contain and divide Brazilian society. The sheer size of the maps had an impact as well as the imaginative projection of data and information that opens up our thinking of how the political space of Brazil is constructed and how it can be understood.[39]

Both of these projects are as much aesthetic as analytical. But all the better, in that they offer up new ways of seeing and understanding, beyond the conventional formulas and practices of traditional geopolitics. The deployment of paintings, interviews and maps and the use of more subjective experiences of personal involvement provides other and often very powerful ways to imagine geopolitics. And just as we began this chapter, we will end with the evocation that at its heart, geopolitics is a form of geographical imagination.

SUGGESTED READINGS

Agnew, J. (2003, 2nd ed.). *Geopolitics: Re-visioning world politics*. London: Routledge.

Black, J. (2015). *Geopolitics and the quest for dominance*. Bloomington: Indiana University Press.

Cohen, S. (2015). *Geopolitics: The geography of international relations.* Lanham: Rowman & Littlefield.

Dittmer, J., & Sharp, J. (eds.). (2014). *Geopolitics: A reader.* London: Routledge.

Dodds, K. (2014). *Geopolitics: A short introduction.* Oxford: Oxford University Press.

Flint, C. (2017, 3rd ed.). *Introduction to geopolitics.* London: Routledge.

Flint, C. & Taylor, P. J. (2018, 7th ed.). *Political geography: World-economy, nation-state and locality.* London: Routledge.

Jones, M., Jones, R., Woods, M., Whitehead, M., Dixon, D., & Hannah, M. (2014). *An introduction to political geography: Space, place and politics.* Abingdon and New York: Routledge.

Rosenberg, Mike. (2017). *Strategy and geopolitics: Understanding global complexity in a turbulent world.* Bingley, UK: Emerald Publishing.

Smith, S. (2020). *Political geography: A critical introduction.* Oxford: Wiley-Blackwell.

Journals specifically devoted to the topic include *Geopolitics* and *Political Geography*.

NOTES

1. Geopolitical writings have a long history. Moshe Halbertal and Stephen Holmes reach back to show that the Book of Samuel in the Bible is a complex meditation on the problems of statecraft.

Halbertal, M., & Holmes, S. (2017). *The beginning of power: Power in the Biblical book of Samuel.* Princeton, NJ: Princeton University Press. In this book we will focus on the more contemporary era.

2. List, F. (1841). *The national system of political economy.* London: Longmans, Green, and Co.

3. Darwin, C. (1859). *On the origin of species: By means of natural selection or the preservation of favoured races in the struggle for life.* London: John Murray.

4. Ibid.

5. Ratzel, F. (1901). Lebensraum: A biogeographical study [2018]: [translated into English by Tul'si (Tuesday) Bhambry]. *Journal of Historical Geography, 61,* 59–80. https://doi.org/10.1016/j.jhg.2018.03.001.

6. Naumann, F. (1915). *Mitteleuropa.* Berlin: G. Reimer.

7. Tunander, O. (2001). Swedish-German geopolitics for a new century: Rudolf Kjellen's "The state as a living organism." *International Studies, 27(3),* 451–63. https://doi.org/10.1017/S026021050100451X.

8. Two books published in the 1940s provide a critical perspective on German geopolitical thinking leading up to to World War II:

Gyorgy, A. (1944). *Geopolitics: The new German science.* Berkeley and Los Angeles: University of California Press; Strausz-Hupe, R. (1942). *Geopolitics: The struggle for space and power.* New York: G. P. Putnam.

9. Mackinder, H. J. (1887). On the scope and methods of geography. *Proceedings of the Royal Geographical Society and Monthly Record of Geography, 9,* 141–74.

10. Ibid., 141.

11. Mackinder, H. J. (1904). The geographical pivot of history. *Geographical Journal, XXIII,* 421–44. When Mackinder presented this paper at the Royal Geographical Society on January 25, 1904, in London, one of the commentators, Spencer Wilkinson, noted that "whereas only half a century ago statesmen played on a few squares of a chess-board of which the remainder was vacant, in the present day the world is an enclosed chessboard and every movement of the statesman must take into account of all the squares in it," 438.

12. Mackinder, H. (2018). *Democratic ideals and reality: The Geographical pivot of history.* Singapore: Origami Books.

13. Mackinder, H. J. (1943). The round world and the winning of the peace. *Foreign Affairs.* https://www.foreignaffairs.com/articles/1943-07-01/round-world-and-winning -peace.

14. Spykman, N. J. (2007). *America's strategy in world politics: The United States and the balance of power.* New York: Routledge.

15. Mahan, A. T. (1889). *The influence of sea power upon history.* New York: Little, Brown.

16. Kennan, G. F. (1947). The sources of soviet conduct. *Foreign Affairs.* https:// en.wikisource.org/wiki/The_Sources_of_Soviet_Conduct.

17. Kennan, G. F. (2012). *American diplomacy: Sixteenth anniversary expanded edition.* Chicago: University of Chicago Press.

18. Truman, H. (1947). The Truman Doctrine, 1947. *U.S. Department of State Office of the Historian.* https://history.state.gov/milestones/1945-1952/truman-doctrine.

19. Gorshkov, S. G. (1979). *The sea power of the state.* Annapolis: Naval Institute Press.

20. Gorshkov, S. G. (1968). Russia: Power play on the oceans. *Time.* http://content .time.com/time/magazine/article/0,9171,837933,00.html.

21. Hepple, L. W. (1986). The revival of geopolitics. *Political Geography Quarterly, 5,* 21–36.

22. For a wide range of opinion, compare Kissinger's trumpeting self-assessment: Kissinger, H. (1982). *Years of upheaval.* Boston: Little, Brown with the critical Bundy, W. (1998). *A tangled web: The making of foreign policy on the Nixon presidency.* New York: Hill and Wang and the very critical Hitchens, C. (2001). *The trial of Henry Kissinger.* London: Verso.

23. O'Sullivan, P. (1986). *Geopolitics.* New York: St. Martin's Press; Tuathail, G. Ó. (1996). *Critical geopolitics: The politics of writing global space.* Minneapolis: University of Minnesota Press.

24. See Chapman, B. (2011). *Geopolitics: A guide to the issues.* Santa Barbara, CA: Praeger; Cohen, S. (2014). *Geopolitics: The geography of international relations.* Lanham: Rowman & Littlefield.

25. Marshall, T. (2016). *Prisoners of geography: Ten maps that explain everything about the world.* New York: Scribner.

26. Kaplan, R. D. (2018). *The return of Marco Polo's world.* New York: Random House, 235.

27. Tuathail, *Critical geopolitics.*

28. Dittmer, J., & Sharp, J. (2014). *Geopolitics: A reader.* London: Routledge.
Dodds, K. (2014). *Geopolitics: A short introduction.* Oxford: Oxford University Press.
Dodds, K., Kuus, M., & Sharp, J. (eds.). (2016). *The Routledge Research Companion to critical geopolitics.* London: Routledge.
Flint, *Introduction to Geopolitics.*

29. Kearns, G. (2009). *Geopolitics and empire: The legacy of Halford Mackinder.* Oxford: Oxford University Press; Smith, N. (2003). *American empire.* Oakland: University of California Press.

30. Sharp, J. (2013). Geopolitics at the margins: Reconsidering genealogies of critical geopolitics. *Political Geography, 37,* 20–29.

31. Dixon, D. P., & Marston, S. A. (eds.). (2013). *Feminist geopolitics: At the sharp end.* Abingdon: Routledge.

32. Stratford, E. (2019). *Home, nature and the feminine ideal: Geographies of the interior and of empire.* Lanham: Rowman & Littlefield.

33. Peakman, J. (2019). *Licentious worlds: Sex and exploitation in global empires.* London: Reaktion.

34. Dixon, D. (2015). *Feminist geopolitics.* Farnham and Burlington: Ashgate.

35. Pratt, N. (2020). *Embodying geopolitics: Generations of women's activism in Egypt, Jordan and Lebanon.* Oakland: University of California Press.

36. Dittmer, J., & Bos, D. (2019, 2nd ed.). *Popular culture, geopolitics and identity.* Lanham: Rowman & Littlefield.

37. Tsygankov, A. (2017). The dark double: The American media perception of Russia as a neo-Soviet autocracy, 2008–2014. *Politics, 37,* 19–35.

38. Smithsonian American Art Museum. (2019). Tiffany Chung: Vietnam, past is prologue. *The Smithsonian American Art Museum.* https://americanart.si.edu/exhibitions/chung.

39. Americas Society/Council of the Americas. (2019). Walls of air: The Brazilian pavilion at the 16th Venice Architecture Biennale. *Visual Arts Gallery.* https://www.as-coa.org/exhibitions/walls-air-brazilian-pavilion-16th-venice-architecture-biennale.

2

Spaces

Geopolitics is a form of spatial imagination. In this chapter I examine some of the main imaginings that circulate around the spatial units of empire, nation-state, and world order. I explore these key units of geopolitics to provide a spatial context for the temporal approach of chapter 3 and the more contemporary chapters that follow in parts II and III. I also note some of the newer spaces of geopolitics, including outer space, cyberspace, and new impending spaces of concern, such as climate change.

EMPIRE

An empire can be defined as a territorial unit in which a center dominates the periphery to the latter's disadvantage.[1] Imperial expansion is limited by the tyranny of distance. Empires expand through transport improvements from the introduction of horses, the building of better roads, the greater use of sea and transoceanic shipping lanes, and, later, with the introduction of railroads and air routes.

For millennia, empires were the dominant spatial form of political organization. Some of the earliest polities were imperial city-states in Mesopotamia. For example, the city of Uruk emerged around six thousand years ago in the southern part of Mesopotamia. Sophisticated irrigation allowed the high agricultural productivity that underwrote Uruk's power. The city broadened its influence, referred to as the "Uruk expansion," in the upper reaches of the Euphrates and Tigris Rivers. Surrounding peoples were brought under the cultural and economic control of Uruk. The city's elites developed more expensive tastes that generated the need to control exotic goods and materials from ever-more-distant territories. In a process that is repeated over and over again through history, imperial expansion reached its peak and then turned into decline. The Uruk Empire ultimately collapsed, invaders razed the monumental buildings of the temple in the main city, and local traditions reemerged in regions formerly controlled by Uruk.

Subsequent history is one of imperial powers becoming larger and their territorial reach more extensive as space-convergence improvements, such as cavalry and better road networks extend the effective imperial range. In the Middle

East, after Uruk, came the Hittites and then the Assyrians. The Assyrian Empire emerged from an area centered in the city of Nineveh, in what is now northern Iraq. It eventually exerted its control over a region stretching into modern-day Turkey and Egypt and down to the Persian Gulf. This was Empire 1.0 based primarily on military subjugation. Expansion was achieved through brutal military campaigns. Defeated cities were subjected to mass killings, their fields covered with salt, and their orchards chopped down in systematic campaigns of intimidation and terror. Conquered regions provided goods and services to Assyria, providing the basis for massive building programs in the successive capitals of Kalhu and Nineveh.

There was a distinct core-periphery structure of "the land of Assur" (the name of the god of the Assyrians), and a widening territory under its control, the "yoke of Assur," where provincial governments were charged to provide a steady supply of resources and continuing political allegiance. People were moved in mass deportations, leading to ethnic and cultural mixing. By 640 BCE the empire was at its greatest territorial extent as more of the wider region came under the "yoke of Assur." In the peripheral zones, although political allegiance was demanded, cultural and ethnic diversity remained as client states retained their own elites and culture. The cultural relations were a two-way rather than just a one-way imposition of Assyrian culture.

The Assyrians eventually lost control as local resistance to their rule stiffened and as mercenary armies sided with the competing empire of Babylon. By 610 BCE Assyria ceased to exist; some regions of the former empire came under Babylonian control while others regained some autonomy. Nineveh was destroyed.

New imperial powers continued to emerge in the region. One of the most prominent was the Persian Empire. It began in the present-day region of Fars in Iran and peaked from around 559 BCE to 331 BCE. At its greatest extent it covered a vast area, from the Indus Valley in the east to Greece in the west and from Central Asia in the north to Egypt on the southern reaches. It was a well-run empire that practiced religious tolerance yet encouraged a political uniformity of strict allegiance to Persian leadership. The vast territory was divided into a system of provinces. Monumental buildings adorned the capitals of Ecbetana, Persepolis, and Susa, symbols of religious devotion but also as displays of political and economic power at the heart of the empire.

Rome emerged from under the shadow of the Etruscans around 509 BCE and grew to imperial dominance around the Mediterranean. Its rise was due to a ruthless and efficient military machine that overwhelmed its enemies. Roads were fashioned that pulled the territories together with the quick and efficient movement of soldiers, officials, and merchants. Viaducts were built, bridges were constructed, and cities emerged. The political space under Roman control both enlarged and tightened with trade links, well-maintained infrastructure, and at times brutal state violence. By year 1 of the Christian calendar, the Mediterranean became a Roman lake. Under Augustus (r. 27 BCE–14 CE) the republic became an empire. Empire 1.0 based on state violence and forcible incorporation was, if not completely replaced, then softened with Empire 2.0 based on taxation rather than plunder, justice rather than dictates, and the dispensing of Roman citizenship to elites in the periphery. As one writer notes, "the empire ceased to be mechanism of extraction, and became a sort of commonwealth."[2] At its greatest extent the Roman Empire extended across much of Europe, the Near East, and coastal North Africa (see map 2.1).

By the middle of the nineteenth century the dominant imperial power was Britain. Its naval power enabled the empire to extend across the globe. It contained elements of Empire 1.0 of military might, Empire 2.0 with the integration of some subjects into citizens, and Empire 3.0, a flexible, ever-changing constellation of multiple forms of imperial control and management (see table 2.1). Imperial arrangements included self-governing settler societies, colonies, and protectorates. We can make a distinction between *formal empire*, involving direct British military and political control, and *informal empire*, where economic dominance was achieved without the need for military intervention or political annexation. The greatest success story of the informal empire was South America, where Britain had a large market for its goods, services, and capital flows without having to pay the costs of imperial control. In later chapters we assess the claim that the United States is an imperial power.

Table 2.1.   Types of Empire

Type	Characteristics
Empire 1.0	Forcible incorporation of periphery, rule from center
Empire 2.0	Forcible incorporation of periphery, rule from center, extending citizenship to elites in periphery
Empire 3.0	Direct rule: forcible incorporation of periphery, rule from center, extending citizenship to elites in periphery, some decentralization of power
	Multiple forms of center-periphery relations from direct control to self-governing provinces
	Indirect rule: greater reliance on local elites

World history and global geography of the past fifteen hundred years were shaped by the rise and fall, the expansion and contraction of empires. The legacies of imperial geographies continue to structure the modern-day political landscape. Even though we live in an ostensibly postimperial world, we can make some generalization about the geopolitics of Empire and its continuing impact on contemporary geopolitics. In the regional chapters that follow we will track some of these legacies in more detail.

Limits to Empire

Empires increase their territorial extent because they are more able to overcome the tyranny of distance. Compare the Uruk expansion with the size of the Persian Empire and the global extent of the British. While Uruk at its greatest extent was limited to the area of Mesopotamia, the Persian empire stretched across the Middle East into Asia and Europe; and first the Spanish and then the British Empire reached global penetration. Better transport and improved networks enabled empires to extend their spatial reach. But empires, no matter how vast, have territorial limits to their power. As they expand further from their core,

Map 2.1 The Roman Empire in 117 CE (Wikimedia / Tataryn)

the ability to wield effective and overpowering force tends to weaken. There is a distance decay effect in their military power and political reach. Far from the empire's center, borders are more vulnerable. Distance acts as a friction against the operation of centralized power. Empires tend to be most vulnerable when they meet other similarly sized powers, and the easy incorporation of scattered and fractured peripheries is replaced by the resistance of the more durable and cohesive power of a competing empire or an alternative power center.

We can make a distinction between *borders*, the fixed lines of territorial demarcation, and *frontiers*, which are territorial zones of transition between two or more territorial units. The borders and frontiers of empire and states demarcate the effective range of imperial power. Hadrian's Wall ran across northern England from coast to coast in Roman times, marking the northernmost limit of effective Roman control. Large segments are still visible to this day, a testament to the builders. But as recent archeology has revealed, the wall was also a site of interaction between a Roman core and Celtic periphery.

Frontiers can also be *shatter zones*. Anthropologist James C. Scott describes them as places of resistance and refuge to state-making and state rule. They exist where people are displaced or hiding or seeking refuge. He cites Yunnan in southwest China, parts of highland Africa that were safe from slavers, and parts of Amazonia.[3] Robbie Ethridge and Sheri Shuck-Hall describe the frontier of U.S. expansion into indigenous lands as a rolling shatter zone.[4]

Shatter zones can be areas of instability subject to the volatility of competing imperial interests and state powers and perhaps even to a range of local actors. The term is often employed to describe a region in Eastern Europe that runs along the edge of the Russian and German empires. The historian Timothy Snyder describes the area between Russia and Germany that includes parts of Poland, Ukraine, the Baltic region, and Belarus as "the Bloodlands." The region earned this term between 1932 and 1945 due to enforced famine, mass killings, deportations, and ethnic cleansing. More than fourteen million civilians were killed in little more than a dozen years.[5]

The boundaries of Empire can be places of conflict. Those on the other side of the border can pose a threat. The border marks the furthest limit of an empire's power and hence is more vulnerable to attack than the imperial center. That is why empires tend to build walls and garrisons along their borders. The border can also be the dividing line between competing powers jostling for territorial supremacy. We have a record, albeit a one-sided narrative to be sure, of the conflict at the western edge of the Persian Empire. As the Persians extended their reach westward, they butted up against the Greek city-states. Some of them resisted Persian power. At the Battle of Marathon in 490 BCE, an Athenian army defeated an invading Persian army. For some Western commentators, Marathon marks an important turning point for the rise of the West, a victory for humanism, individualism, and democracy over authoritarian slavery. Marathon is now one of the foundation narratives of Western civilization as the west became "the West" and the east became "the East." Anthony Pagden, among many other scholars, describes a 2,500-year struggle between East and West as beginning on the plains of Marathon, an idea that we will explore later.[6] Our knowledge of the battle and its context is entirely from Greek sources, who understandably paint the Persians in an unflattering way and the Greeks in the best possible light. An alternative case could be made that the Persians represented a multicultural enterprise concerned with political stability and cultural tolerance. And Greece, like much of the Persian Empire, was a slave state; so its claim to democracy was always partial and limited.

There are also limits on the capacity of empires to expand or even maintain their control. As they expand, they come across more frontier zones that provide resistance, they generate more borders that need to be protected and maintained, and they have a reputational status that needs to be protected. As they grow larger, they take on more responsibilities and must carry heavier burdens. Paul Kennedy uses the term *imperial overstretch* to refer to the steady extension of imperial powers beyond their military and fiscal capacity.[7] He uses the example of Spain. In 1600 it was the first global power with territory in Asia as well as Europe and the Americas. But its vast reach also involved more responsibilities: fighting the Ottoman Turks and taking on Protestant powers in Europe. The empire extended beyond its limits in part because it felt it needed to do all these things not only to maintain material interests but also to project the image of its power. In a more contemporary example, the United States continued to fight in Vietnam, long after any sort of victory was possible, in part to protect its image as a military superpower. Imperial overstretch is invoked to explain the fall of the Napoleonic Empire and the Soviet Empire. It is also frequently employed to highlight the strains on the global role of the United States. Imperial overstretch for the United States is evident after years of the long war in Iraq and Afghanistan since 2001, in the declining support of the American public's appetite for continued military involvements and the mounting fiscal strains that such a global posture implies for a country losing its relative economic primacy in the world.

Empire as Territorial Integration

Much of the historical geography of the world has been shaped by the rise and fall of empires and the spatial spread of imperial influences. Alexander the Great reversed the flow of Persian influence by extending Greek influence throughout Eurasia, taking over much of the remnants of the Persian Empire. The Roman Empire turned the Mediterranean into a Roman lake and influenced the post–Roman Empire history of much of Europe with a rich legacy of laws, language, and religion. These and other empires, such as the Ashanti in West Africa and the Mayan, Aztec, and Inca in the Americas were also cohering spatial units that in many cases created more homogeneous political surfaces aiding cultural mixing, economic ties, and religious dispersals that diffused creeds and beliefs across space. Empires pulled peoples and regions together in shared experiences of (often forced and brutal) spatial convergence. Empires promoted global integration. English is spoken in countries all around the world due in large part to a legacy of British colonialism and imperialism.

Charles Parker argues that in the period 1400–1800, empire building across the globe, including the Chinese, Ottoman, Mughal, and Safavid as well as the Spanish and British, created international markets and global exchange networks.[8] These global empires encouraged, forced, and facilitated the movement of people, the spread of new technologies, the diffusion of cultures, and the transmission of religion and scientific practices. The result was a tighter integration of global space. Increasing contact between different cultures led to cross-cultural borrowings. For example, a fascinating exhibition of art produced in the interaction and exchange between Portugal and its trading areas in Africa, Asia, and South America in the sixteenth and seventeenth century shows a complex blending and borrowing: West African wooden and ivory sculpture that incorporated Portuguese figures, precious objects produced in Goa using Christian iconography for the market in Portugal, Japanese paintings that depict Portuguese merchants, and the introduction of European firearms and maps into Japan. The title of the exhibition was accurate: *Encompassing the Globe*.[9] Whether it be in intellectual discourses and practices, or in sports, language, religion, and forms of government, modern empires have integrated much of the world: Spanish speaking in South America, cricket playing in India, rugby in Fiji, Catholicism in Goa, and British-inspired representative government in Australia and Canada are just some of the many consequences of the globally integrating effects of modern empires.

Core-Periphery

Empire was undertaken not primarily to promote cross-cultural integration. There was a hard core of material interests. Spain and Portugal laid claim to vast territory in the New World, Africa, and Asia to provide gold, silver, spices, and other raw materials for the home countries. Britain held on to India because it provided a rich source of raw material for British industry as well as a captive market for goods produced in Britain. The king of Belgium grabbed control of the Congo simply to extort and exploit the people and the resources as much as possible. The modern colonial empires of European powers were founded on violence to indigenous peoples. Across North and South America, Africa, Asia, and Australasia indigenous lands were annexed, appropriated, or stolen and local people were subject to new forms of control. Subsequent economic development was shaped and guided by this core-periphery structure, with the periphery used as source of raw materials and as markets for goods produced in the core. The core industrialized while the periphery remained a cheap resource base and a secure market for manufactured goods. The core regained wealth as wealth was drained from the periphery. Take the case of the industrial revolution in Britain. An important early industry was cotton manufacturing; factories in Britain imported cheap raw cotton and exported cotton goods especially to large captive markets, such as India, where the domestic textile industry was destroyed by the British authorities. The industrial revolution in core countries was built on the foundation of unequal exchange between the core and the periphery.

Local Elites

Empire could be costly; much better to have economic control without political responsibilities. British economic interests were pursued vigorously in South America without formal annexation. Latin America was the real success story of British commercial empire because there was market penetration without enacting the responsibilities of formal empire. Direct imperial annexation was, in a sense, a sign of failing to achieve economic ends without direct political intervention. Formal annexation became more common in the late nineteenth century because of increasing imperial rivalries between core countries. Formal imperialism also resulted when the ruling elites of peripheral countries refused to go along with business arrangements.

A key concept is that of the ruling elites, groups that concentrate power in any single country or region. *Collaborative elites* reproduce the imperial center. This was the case of Anglo-Americans in North America before the American Revolution or with the British colonial settlers in Australia and New Zealand. Collaborative elites can also encourage imperial incorporation. Throughout much of Africa and India, for example, the British authorities used indirect rule, working through local rulers who were rewarded for their efforts. Local leaders and existing hierarchies served to secure colonial rule. If and when the collaborative elite lost legitimacy and their grip on power, then the colonial power often had to intervene. Local elites could also remain in power with imperial backing if they could successfully tie their existence to imperial imperatives. Throughout much of the Cold War, for example, local elites in countries around the world, such as the Philippines under Marcos, maintained their grip on power by reminding the United States of their anti-Communist credentials or, in the case of Cuba, informing the Soviet Union of their anti-capitalist policies.

Empire as Ideology

Empire is not only a material practice of incorporation and control of territory but also the basis of an imaginative practice. Empire is often justified and rationalized with a set of validating yet tractable principles. Such rationalization enables imperialists to defend their mission through a range of ideas of racial and cultural superiority that at its extreme declares them as bearers of a divine mission. Whether as pretext or felt beliefs, Empire is legitimized. The British, like the Romans, were convinced of racial superiority that obligated them to rule others. When the Soviets and the Americans faced off in the Cold War, each side believed they were the best and perhaps only alternative for the future of humanity. They shouldered not only vast military responsibilities, but also the ideological weight of Communism and capitalism, respectively.

Imperial ideology was portrayed consistently by popular representations throughout history. Such portrayal was especially strong since the mid-nineteenth century at a time of increasing literacy and increasing political participation. States sought to legitimize their particular forms of imperial rule with appeals not only to elites but also to the masses. Empire was performed in rituals, ceremonies, and staged events and represented in popular discourses in literature, cartographic images, and more recently movies. In order to evoke popular support, imperial adventures often are presented as noble and heroic enterprises. The Bush administration and its supporters in the media portrayed the U.S. invasion of Iraq as a mission to export freedom and democracy. The subsequent carnage, social dislocation, and political collapse could never be justified. It reminds me of the famous quote imaginatively attributed to an early Briton by the Roman historian Tacitus (56–120 CE) who imagines the warrior leader speaking before another losing battle with the might of Rome and saying, "They make a desert and call it peace." Today we would call it *collateral damage*. Empire has a hard time saying sorry, admitting error, or listening to those in their newly made desert.

There were also critics of Empire. Not all Americans agreed with the U.S. annexation of the Philippines in 1902 after a bloody campaign involving U.S. troops and the deaths of up to 200,000 Filipinos fighting for independence. Some loudly criticized the endeavor at the time in words that with a few tweaks could be used for every subsequent U.S. involvement.

> We condemn the experiment imperialism as an inexcusable blunder which has involved us in enormous expense, brought out weakness instead of strength and laid our nation open to the charge of the abandonment of the fundamental doctrine of self-government.[10]

The British writer J. A. Hobson offered a penetrating analysis of imperialism in a study first published in 1902 when the British Empire was at its greatest extent.[11] He identified what we would now call the *military-industrial complex* that benefited from an aggressive imperial policy. He singled out large capital investors looking to secure new areas for profitable investments. He defined the taproot of imperialism as the desire of capital seeking foreign investment opportunities. These capital interests had effectively captured the foreign policy objectives of the British state. Hobson's ideas strongly influenced Lenin's analysis of the economic forces behind imperialism. In a pamphlet written in 1916, Lenin argued that

> To the numerous "old" motives of colonial policy, financial capital has added the struggle for the sources of raw materials, for the export of capital, for "spheres of influence," i.e., for spheres for profitable deals, concessions, monopolists' profits . . . and finally for economic territory in general.[12]

The End of Empire

Empires come to an end. In the early nineteenth century the Spanish Empire in South and Central America began to collapse as local elites sought political freedoms that eventually resulted in today's patchwork of nation-states. The twentieth century was the century of nationalism. As old empires collapsed, new states emerged in revolutionary ruptures and postcolonial emergences to create a tapestry of nation-states across the globe. The world splintered. To take just a few examples: The breakup of the Austro-Hungarian empire after World War I led to the creation of Austria, Bosnia, Croatia, Czech Republic, Hungary, Italy, Montenegro, Romania, Serbia, Slovakia, and Ukraine. The rapid decolonization after World War II meant that former colonies, such as Kenya, India, Pakistan, and Vietnam achieved independence and became nation-states in their own right. The collapse of Yugoslavia after 1989 resulted, eventually, in six new independent countries. The fall of the Soviet Union in 1991 in turn led to the creation of fifteen new states. In 1900 there were 57 independent countries, 70 by 1930, and today the United Nations has 193 members. The retreat from empire began in earnest after the end of World War I. The League of Nations mandated the breakup of the Ottoman and German empires into territories scheduled for independence. The narrative had changed from a prewar commitment to colonial expansion by dominant powers to a postwar move toward national independence by nationalists. Pressure continued to mount after World War II, especially in Southeast Asia.

The retreat from empire gained pace after World War II. From 1945 to 1954 the anticolonial nationalist struggle was strongest in Southeast Asia, where the relatively easy Japanese defeat of the European colonial powers undermined any notion of Western superiority in Asia. In Africa the nationalist movement was inaugurated with Sudan's independence in 1956. Ghana, Kenya, and Tanzania soon followed in, respectively, 1957, 1963, and 1964. At a speech in South Africa in 1960, the British prime minister at the time, Harold Macmillan, spoke of "the wind of change" sweeping across the continent.[13] It was a wind that would sweep away formal colonial power.

The Postcolonial World

We live in a postcolonial world, but one still marked by imperial legacies. There are the economic legacies of colonial countries enriched by their colonies, whose economies in turn were stunted and directed toward metropolitan enrichment more than local development. There are also the political legacies of the national boundaries of postcolonial states drawn by imperial cartographers that reflected inter-imperial claims rather than national coherences. The tiny country of Gambia, for example, owes its existence to a British need for control of the mouth of a river that flowed into French colonial territory. The legacy is also apparent in the form of international legal arrangements that organize the world to perpetuate Western dominance.[14] The former colonial powers of Britain and France, for example, still wield enormous influence because of their vast empires that provided the basis for sustained economic growth, national wealth generation, and foreign bases. The imperial core-periphery structure is embodied in today's international differences in wealth and income.

The world was understood, explained, and narrated from the imperial centers. Colonialism was an empire of cultural signification. The experiences of the colonized were given shape and form and meaning by the metropolitan center. The production of knowledge was like other manufacturing processes; raw materials were shipped in from the periphery for value-added work, then shipped back around the world. Knowledge is produced in place as well as time. That knowledge was created in the metropolitan centers to describe the rest of the world. The social sciences and humanities and especially geopolitics were produced in the context of an imperial system of power. Theory production was part of the imperial project: classify and conquer. It was not just an economic system, but also an empire of signs, a global knowledge system that turned local signification into a worldwide understanding, all from a specific location. The material culture, meaning, and significance of the periphery were annexed as well as its raw materials and commodities. There was an intellectual and economic appropriation. Whether it be in the continuing existence of archives of imperial/colonial domination, such as botanic gardens that house "exotic species," museums that contain treasures from "around the world," "international" universities that narrate the world, or in the form of later human legacies, such as the North African population in French cities, Puerto Ricans in New York City, or Jamaicans in London, the metropoles as much as the periphery are marked by a colonial presence.

A number of writers laid the foundation of what is called postcolonial theory. Edward Said, especially in his 1978 book *Orientalism*, develops the notion that the West describes and defines the Middle East.[15] The discourse of Orientalism is more a product of the Occident than an objective excavation of the facts of the Orient. The Middle East was invented and defined by the West from a position of economic and political dominance. The very definition of the region as well as its broad outlines and precise details were developed in and by and through an imperial Western location. The colonial power relations are reflected and embodied in the ways the world is described, demarcated, and explained. Writers such as Frantz Fanon, Edward Said, Gayatri Spivak, and Homi Bhabha have outlined the negative impacts of colonialism, its capture of discourses; its privileging of certain peoples, places, and ideas; and its creation of the subaltern. We now have a rich body of work that develops the notion of subaltern cultures, otherness as both an identity and a source of difference, and hybrid identities in a world marked by inequalities in power and prestige.

We also have postcolonial reckonings. Photo 2.1 is a photograph of a statue that stands in a public park in the center of Punta Arenas, Chile. It was erected to celebrate the life of a Hispanic landowner. I took the photograph in December 2019 after Chile had experienced months of massive street protests and civil unrest. There was an iconography to the civil disobedience as the walls of public buildings, churches, and statues became the favorite target of protests. You can see this statue has been defaced with pictures of the indigenous peoples, inscriptions of "genocide" and "assassin." A poster on the ground read, in English, "Jose Menendez, the great landowner of the Patagonia, ordered the mass murder of the entire Selk'nam tribe, shooting them. For every dead body, Menendez would pay one pound to the killers." Statues, like systems of organized knowledge, celebrate some but not all. This defacement is a literal postcolonial rewriting of history.

Photo 2.1. A defaced statue in Punta Arenas, Chile (John Rennie Short)

STATE

A postimperial world is one dominated by nation-states, now the basic building block of the global geopolitical order. I look at five elements of this key unit—the rise of the secular state, nations and states, imagined communities and banal nationalism, different types of states, and crises of the state.

The Rise of the Secular State

Canossa is a small town in northern Italy. In 1077, Henry IV, the Holy Roman Emperor, knelt bareheaded in the snow, to ask for absolution from Pope Gregory VII. The fight between the secular and religious leaders had been brewing for a while. The emperor wanted control over appointing clergy. Gregory resisted the king's power grab and sought Henry's abdication. Henry, in turn, was probably responsible for an assassination attempt on the pontiff. According to the legend, Henry, dressed in a hair shirt as a sign of his penance, traveled to where the pope was staying in Canossa. When he was refused entry, he waited outside for three days. Finally, he was allowed entry and he begged forgiveness.

At first blush, it looks like a victory for the pope and dominance of religious power. But in reality, not much changed in their relationship. After Gregory tried to have Henry excommunicated a second time, the emperor invaded Rome, deposed Gregory, and installed a new pope. The "walk to Canossa" has taken on wider meanings. Although Henry knelt, he came to embody a secular nationalism (in this case German resistance) against ecclesiastical power. While some see a nationalist element in the story, with Gregory representing Italy and Henry, Germany, their wider significance is a redefinition of the role of religious authority in the political power of the state. Henry ultimately showed that secular power could be affirmed against religious authority. The road to Canossa, as it turns out, marks the beginning of the evacuation of religious authority from automatic political power. It is the first faltering steps on the notion of a secular state.

In some cases, it involved a curtailment of religious authority. Henry VIII (1491–1547) remade religion in England. In order to gain a divorce from his Catholic wife he established a Church of England separate from the Church in Rome. The new Protestant faith became the state religion, and the king was made the head of the Church. Henry nationalized religion.

Religious and secular power was often combined in the personage of a ruling king or emperor. In dynastic China, the emperor was the link between heaven and earth. Elsewhere, kings legitimized their rule with the notion of their divine right to rule. The idea ran out of legitimation. In England Charles I was beheaded in 1649, found guilty of tyrannical power and attempting to overthrow the rights and liberty of the people. In the next century French republicans guillotined Louis XVI in 1793 for conspiracy with foreign powers. Both regicides mark, in the bloodiest forms, the emergence of a state founded more on popular will than kingly power: they mark the emergence of citizens from subjects.

Sure enough, there are still monarchies: the UK, Norway, and Thailand, for example. But other forms of government have largely replaced kingdoms and more secular states have emerged from religious foundations. The struggle is not a straight-line arc. The rise of religious fundamentalisms across the world, whether it be Zionist claims over land in the Middle East, Hindu claims for India to be a Hindu state, the political role of Buddhist nationalist monks in Sri Lanka and Burma, or Christian evangelicals promoting a religious agenda in the public sphere in the United States, the state remains an arena for competing versions of the state. Does it represent the secular will of the people or does it also represent a more religious element in the form of a covenant between people and their deities? The road to Canossa is as winding as it is long.

Nations and States

We can make a distinction between a *state* and a *nation*. The state, according to Max Weber, is a unit of political authority that has a monopoly of violence over a piece of territory. A nation, in contrast, is a community of people with a common identity, shared cultural values, and an attachment to a particular territory.

The term *nation-state* embodies the subtle and complex relationship between the two. We can identify a variety of forms. There are *nations without states*. After the fall of the Ottoman Empire, the Kurdish nation was divided among a variety of states, including Turkey, Syria, and Iraq. Kurds became minorities in states that were not Kurdish, and for many of these states the Kurds—with their resilient nationalism—remain a threat to national territorial integrity. Most states contain a variety of nations. Belgium, for example, contains two main linguistic nations, one Dutch-speaking and one French-speaking. Great Britain contains a number of separate nations. The rise of Scottish nationalism is a reminder that the British state is a composite amalgam, the result of English incorporation of different national territories.

In postcolonial states there are often a variety of nations. The colonial experience tended to exacerbate differences; colonial powers would often play one group against another. Belgium exacerbated the differences in its colonies between the two main rivalrous ethnicities, the Hutu and Tutsi, in order to keep overall control. In some cases, such as Tanzania, there are so many different tribal groups that centrifugal force outweighs centripetal forces, while in countries with two or three competing groups, such as the Hutu and Tutsi in Rwanda, the conflict can be more intense. In multinational states national coherence can be tested with rivalries and tensions that become particularly marked during economic downturns. After the global economic recession of 2008 created economic insecurity, for example, there was a rise of ethnonationalism in Europe.[16]

In the regional chapters that follow we will discuss in more detail some of the tensions involved in states with more than one nation and nations without states.

Imagined Communities

In an argument of great subtlety Benedict Anderson argued that nations are not so much facts of race or ethnicity.[17] Rather, they are what he terms *imagined communities*. He paid particular attention to the role of print capitalism in creating a national discourse. Anderson identified three institutions of power: the *census*, the *map*, and the *museum*, that together allow the state to imagine the people under its dominance, the geographic territory under control, and the nature of historical legitimacy. We can further Anderson's notion of imagined community by exploring the idea of *national imaginaries*. These are one element in the taken-for-granted geographical imaginaries that connect space and society, identity, place, meaning, and territory in active, constantly changing constructs that move backward and forward from plausible representations of reality to effective constructors of reality. Friedrich Nietzsche noted that imaginaries encompass more than the real world, that they're only interpretations and not facts, and in his widely-cited-but-impossible-to-source quote, that "whichever interpretation prevails at a given time is a function of power and not truth." Imaginaries fill out the world with hopes and wishes as well as facts and observation; they describe and explain as well as affect and influence. They embody, shape, inform, and condense power relations in geographical worldviews. National imaginaries include what I have described previously as "national environmental ideologies" that reference how myths of wilderness, countryside, and city are expressed in the national territory.[18] But they also include images, ideas, and narratives of a nation's place in the world. In the regional chapters that follow, I will draw upon the idea of national imaginaries in the discussion of popular geopolitics.

Banal nationalism is a term used to describe the everyday expression of nationalism from currency to flags to the singing of a national anthem. The term was first employed by the social psychologist Michael Billig.[19] In the United States, for example, the flag is a well-recognized symbol of patriotism and national pride (see photo 2.2). Before every major sporting event many people place their palm across their heart as the national anthem is sung. It is a common ritual, an everyday expression of a shared national identity and experience. Neither overtly militaristic nor xenophobic, the national anthem can be mobilized and/or contested during times of conflict. It plays a role in mobilizing popular support for internal debates but especially in realizing geopolitical doctrines and strategies. A deep and powerful layer of banal nationalism underscores the powerful geopolitical role played by the United States.

Varieties of States

We can distinguish between different types of states by size, economic power, and military might.

They also differ in geopolitical influence and significance. The more powerful may exert an outsized role in world affairs. There is marked asymmetry in global affairs with only a very few countries with the military strength to impose their will across space. We can distinguish between superpowers, great powers, regional powers, and minor powers.

Superpowers have the ability to influence events around the world. Successive superpowers have risen and fallen. In the late sixteenth and early seventeenth centuries, Spain was the first global power with possessions spread across the world. By the nineteenth century, Britain emerged after years of struggle with France as the world's superpower. Britain's global influence was embodied in its

Photo 2.2.   Flag in Washington, DC, office building (John Rennie Short)

territorial annexation across the globe enabled by its naval power, which allowed it to influence events all over the world. Britain's success encouraged emulation. Today the United States remains the single largest superpower with the ability to achieve global military reach and project its influence around the globe, undergirded by an extensive distribution of U.S. military bases and military assets around the world.

Hard power is the ability to coerce others through the superiority of military forces. *Soft power* is the ability to co-opt others to your point of view without the use of force. It involves the export of cultural goods, economic assistance, and the establishment of regulatory standards. The United States also wields considerable soft power in the global cultural economy. The United States thus has both hard power through its military superiority, but also elements of soft power through wide dispersal of its cultural forms and its pivotal role in drawing up international regulatory standards. The political scientist Joseph Nye, who drew the distinction, argues for the use of *smart power*, which combines hard and soft power in successful strategies that weaponize soft power. In recent years the distinction has become less clear. When the United States imposes levies on exporting countries or China promotes the theft of intellectual property of foreign companies, then soft and hard power merge. There is also the weaponization of technology. The role of Chinese companies in the creation of national 5G networks raises security risks for the United States and some other states. Even the cultural economy is affected. When countries ban foreign movies that they deem to be unpatriotic or when the Chinese government establishes Confucius Centers in foreign universities that promote Chinese national policies, we are witnessing the *weaponization of culture*. Many Australian universities now see these Chinese-financed centers as a possible security threat. An easy division between hard and soft power is beginning to collapse with the weaponization of the instruments of soft power.

Table 2.2 lists the top military spenders in the world according to the percentage of global military spending. The United States is by far the largest military spender, buttressing its large military with global reach. China and Russia come in second and sixth, respectively. Then there are a range of regional players, such as Saudi Arabia and India, former imperial powers, such as the UK and France, other European countries such Germany and Italy, and then rich countries. In East Asia, South Korea and Japan are living in a troubling neighborhood.

Table 2.2. Shares of Total World Military Spending

Country	% of World Military Spending
USA	36.0
China	14.0
Saudi Arabia	3.7
India	3.7
France	3.5
Russia	3.4
UK	2.7
Germany	2.7
Japan	2.6
South Korea	2.4
Italy	1.5
Australia	1.5
Brazil	1.5
Canada	1.2
Turkey	1.0

Source: Stockholm International Peace Research Institute

Great powers are a step down from superpowers. They are large enough to impose their weight on world affairs but lack either economic or military power to achieve global dominance. Where they have marked regional influence, they are known as a *regional hegemon* in comparison to the global hegemony of a superpower. China, currently a great power angling to become a superpower, is a regional hegemon in Southeast Asia.

Considerable attention has focused on the *grand strategy* of great powers. We can define a grand strategy as a coordination of multiple actions to achieve shared strategic objectives. Grand strategies may be easy to identify, but they are difficult to pull off; they must contend with rationality crises, blurred vision, competing interests, and a rapidly changing world.

Regional powers, in contrast to great powers, may also have strategies, but they have limited global reach. They can still play a major role in specific regions; examples include India in Central and South Asia; Saudi Arabia in the Arabian Peninsula; or Turkey, Iran, and Iraq in the Middle East. Where strong regional powers operate, there may be regional norms different from global norms. In the South China Sea for example, China's occupation of disputed islands constitutes a new regional order that undermines the global maritime order of the United Nations Convention for the Law of the Sea (UNCLOS).

Then there are the *minor powers*, the vast mass of countries that have a limited role as individual power centers. They can pool their resources to create more geopolitical weight and collectively combine to form alliances such as the Association of Southeast Asian Nations (ASEAN). They can also play a strategic role in competition between greater powers and can influence global events through their role and position in regional issues that engage the global as local events "go global." Vietnam, for example, was a relatively small country that came to play a huge role in the Cold War as the United States interpreted Vietnamese nationalist sentiments as part of global Communist conspiracies. Examples of countries that can condense wider conflicts include North Korea, which has the capacity to widen and involve superpowers (United States), great powers (China), and other powers in the region (South Korea and Japan). North Korea's significance rests mainly in its control over nuclear weaponry and the rationality of their use in its asymmetric relation with the United States. The North Korean leader calculates that with his nuclear arsenal and willingness to use it, the United States has to conclude that attempted regime change will result in the loss of at least one major U.S. city. That cost is too high to topple his rule. This doctrine of *asymmetric escalation* is employed by relatively weak states.[20] Even small states can trigger wider conflicts and invite great-power rivalries.

We can make a distinction among *strong states* where central authority has a measure of significant control over the national territory, *weak states* that have less power, and *failed states*, which lack control altogether.[21] This categorization is fluid as stable states can topple into instability and unstable states achieve greater territorial integration. Libya under Gaddafi was a relatively strong state that became a weak state immediately after his overthrow and quickly descending into failed state status. Afghanistan has traditionally been a weak state where the central government in Kabul often exerts little control over the Pashtuns in the south or the Uzbeks and Tajiks in the north. The dangers of a failed state are obvious in countries such as Somalia, where the lack of central authority creates the space for piracy, local militias, and a variety of bad actors.

Thomas Barnett distinguishes between a functioning core of the world system, outlined by relative stability, rule of law, full integration into the global economy, and a non-integrating gap marked by political instability and social unrest.[22] Barnett's maps show countries as the main unit. A more accurate map would provide a finer mesh that could identify integrating and non-integrating regions. Colombia, for example, is shown as being wholly within the non-integrating region whereas in reality the major cities of Bogota, Medellin, and Cali are part of an integrating world. The rural areas, in contrast, are marked by conflict and instability.

States of Exception

There are also *states of exception*. The term is used to refer to the power of the state to proclaim exceptions to the normal rules of governance, the standard safeguards of citizens, and the usual and accepted limits on state power. State authorities proclaim some kind of special circumstance, such as a security threat that requires exceptional measures. Some states of exception can regularize the exceptional into the permanent. The Third Reich can be considered a state of exception that lasted its entire life of twelve years. In times of crisis—real, imagined, and manufactured—states can increase and extend their power into new forms of imprisonment, expanded surveillance, and more draconian police powers, all justified with reference to exceptional circumstances. In the wake of 9/11, the Bush administration introduced exceptional laws. The 2001 Patriot Act, for example, extended surveillance of citizens. Temporary states of exception can be embedded permanently into accepted powers of the state, long after the exceptional circumstances. In 2020, long after the Patriot Act, the U.S. senate voted to give the CIA and FBI the power to examine a citizen's browser without a warrant. As the theorist Giorgio Agamben has argued, a state of exception can become normalized into a permanent state of affairs.[23] The possibilities of more states of exception are increasing. The background noise of constant terrorist threat, both real and imagined, the growing populisms that are eager to see the "other" as a national threat, the riling up of emotions with cybercampaigns, all create a febrile atmosphere. States of exception are now more likely than at any time in the past thirty years.

The Crises of the State

The state is subject to various kinds of pressure that can be described as a series of crises. An *economic crisis* occurs when the economy fails to meet popular expectations. When lack of jobs, decline in living standards, and reduction in purchasing affects more than a permanent underclass, they create the conditions for a *legitimation crisis*, in which the state loses its ability to reflect the popular will of the country. *Rationality crises* result from the failure to make the necessary number of correct decisions. *Fiscal crises* occur when expenditures exceed revenues.

Economic crises can take a variety forms from short to long term. Daron Acemoglu and James Robinson examine the deeper structural elements in seeking an answer to the question of why some nations are richer than others.[24] Even accepting that the core-periphery structure led to an uneven development, there is still the case that even among peripheral countries there are substantial differences. Acemoglu and Robinson argue that in states where narrow elites rule to their own economic advantage, then national development is stunted. When a few oligarchs become very wealthy, the society fails to provide economic improvement for the majority. They describe *extractive political systems* geared toward the enrichment of few: "Poor countries are poor because those who have power make choices that create poverty."[25] There is a vicious circle of self-enrichment by the few compared with the more virtuous circle where creative destruction of continual economic improving created some very rich people but also allows more people to do well. China's development of the past thirty years has created an increase in the number of billionaires but also raised more than three hundred million out of poverty. In North Korea, in contrast, hunger continues to stalk the land while the leader rules in luxury. Extractive institutions designed to enrich the few do not create the incentives for people to save and innovate. In Zimbabwe, for example, Mugabe took land away from productive farmers and distributed it to his cronies. The result was a decline in the country's ability to feed itself and impoverishment for the majority. Extractive institutions can survive for a while but since they do not allow for creative destruction, they suffer in the longer term.

A *legitimation crisis* occurs when a state loses its popular appeal and its ability to govern. When a state loses the support of an increasing part of the population, its legitimacy is at risk. During the Arab Spring, for example, the governing elites of Egypt, Libya, and Tunisia no longer had the support of the majority of the population. In Syria, the Assad regime lost the support of the majority of the Sunni population. Declining living standards, a sense of injustice, and a feeling of profound alienation between the government and the governed prompt a legitimation crisis. The crisis can take a shallow form when the party in power is highly unpopular or can be deeper when the entire system or regime is unpopular and wholesale change is demanded.

A *rationality crisis* occurs when the state makes enough poor decisions that other crises emerge. The U.S. decision to invade Iraq in 2003 was based on faulty assumptions and led to the death of almost one hundred thousand Iraqis, the displacement of millions more, and the deaths of more than four thousand U.S. troops.

A *fiscal crisis* is when a state has more expenditure than revenue. Military and social spending, either singly or together, can outmatch the revenue from taxes and tariffs. In the short term the state can borrow money, and the biggest economies can borrow more, but ultimately a fiscal crisis turns into a political crisis as debts must be repaid and unpopular cuts in spending must be made. Fiscal crisis is an endemic feature of poor countries but is increasingly a problem for richer countries because they either spend a lot on social welfare and the military (the United States), or they spend a lot on social welfare (Western

European countries), or they have a low tax base and/or rampant tax evasion (e.g., Bulgaria, Italy).

The ultimate political failure is the *collapse of the state*. Varied ideas have been put forward to explain the process. First, there is *modernization theory*, which argues that as states and societies develop economically, the greater the desire for democracy. As societies modernize, according to this theory, pressures for democracy build up. I think this is more a hope than reality. And in many societies people rank security and economic welfare above democracy. Amy Chua takes an opposite view from this modernization hypothesis.[26] She argues that the export of free markets and democracy does not lead to "modern" societies. Rather, it reinforces and exacerbates class differences, especially if wealth initially flows to a tiny ethnic elite, such as the Chinese in many of the states in Southeast Asia. Ethno-nationalism can flower in more democratic societies if minorities are not protected. The unrestrained adoption of neoliberal policies is as likely to generate conflict and disruption as to promote peace and harmony. Incomplete or illiberal democracies can be dangerous.

Samuel Huntington refers to a *development gap*, when people's aspirations rise faster than the state's ability to meet them.[27] In a globalizing world with rapid flows of information, people in connected societies may feel themselves worse off in comparison with others. Ian Bremmer suggests a J curve as explanation (see chart 2.1).[28] Stability is on the vertical axis and the degree of openness is on the horizontal axis. As a country moves away from an authoritarian or totalitarian system toward increased openness, then stability falters, only to pick up again with extreme openness. States move across the curve, but the maximum instability occurs when a previously very closed society begins to open up. North Korea is stable but very closed. South Korea in contrast used to be closed and stable but with a gradual opening up saw a period of instability with military coups and student protests in 1960, 1980, and 1987. South Korea then moved beyond this state of affairs with the election of the first democratically elected president in 1987 and is now both stable and open. Stability depends on economic growth and national wealth.

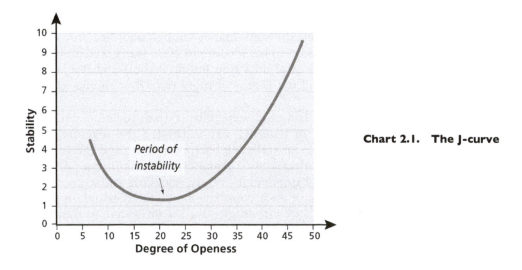

Chart 2.1. The J-curve

The *demographic transition* also plays a role. After a period of high population growth, followed by a decline in death rates and birth rates, most societies experience declining birth rates and thus a shrinking population. The result, at least for a limited period, is a *youth bulge* as the high birth rate ages. A population with many people under age thirty can produce a *demographic dividend* as more people enter the workforce, but if there are few jobs or economic opportunities then there is the explosive growth of young people unconnected to the existing system. In Somalia, two-thirds of the population are aged under thirty and have no job. In the epicenter of the Arab Spring, Tunisia, the median age was thirty with an unemployment rate of 14 percent. The U.S. median age, in contrast, is thirty-seven. A large number of disaffected youth is more easily moved to take to the streets and adopt more anti-establishment and anti-government attitudes than their elders. They have less to lose and more to gain with a radical change in the status quo.

There are also *contagion effects* as events in Tunisia were witnessed, admired, and copied in Egypt, Libya, and Syria. Similar instances happened with the fall of the Iron Curtain when protests in Poland were witnessed and then copied, in rough order, in Hungary, East Germany, Czechoslovakia, Bulgaria, and Romania.

The nature of the regime also has an effect. One variant is the *Dictator's Dilemma*. If the society is completely closed, as in the case of North Korea, there is little space for political dissent. It remains underground. Savage repressions can have success over both the short and longer terms. The Kim family has retained its iron grip and repressive regime over three generations. So-called softer authoritarian regimes that allow some room for protest to act as a safety valve can open up channels for dissent that can overflow into regime change. The Dictator's Dilemma: hang onto power through very hard rule and risk the possibility of an unground eruption or allow some form of safety-valve release that may carry the seed of your destruction. If you are new to freedoms to choose things such as religion or where you live, then it is easier to vent the opinion that you should be free to choose your leaders.

In reality, of course, state collapse can contain different elements of all the forces just outlined.

WORLD ORDERS

We can think of two types of world order. There is the overall structure and then there is the changing cast of principal players in the structure. The dominant structure of the present world can be described as the *Westphalian system*. The system emerged in Europe after the bitter, long, and blood-soaked Thirty Years' War, which lasted approximately from 1614 to 1648. It started out as a religious conflict but soon became a geopolitical contest for dominance in the heart of Europe. More than eight million people died, almost a quarter of the entire population of Central Europe. The devastating conflict was brought to an end with a series of meetings that involved 178 separate participants and a set of agreements now known as the Treaty of Westphalia. This treaty essentially outlines a system of sovereign states free to follow their own ways. The main emphasis was on religious affiliation. The treaty imagines the world as a community of states bound by rules of order and assured autonomy by their neighbors. In effect, the treaty helped create the idea of a modern nation-state with fixed and inviolable boundaries. Religious influence was weakened to such an extent that secular states began to emerge. The contemporary community of the modern nation-state received its birth certificate at the Treaty of Westphalia.

The treaty sought to guarantee the equal sovereignty of states. It was not a total success. It was not employed in the colonial annexation of territory employed by European imperial powers in the eighteenth and nineteenth centuries. Bigger, more powerful states continued and continue to lean, directly and indirectly, on smaller and weaker states. The asymmetries of power between states continue to dominate world politics. Religion continues to exercise a role in the life of the state. And there was and still is the problem of what the community of states could do to protect the rights and even basic safety of minorities in other states. This is a problem that remains and was brought into vivid and tragic relief in such instances as the genocide in Rwanda, the ethnic cleansing in Bosnia, the expulsion of the Rohingya in Myanmar, and all the other all-too-numerous crimes against humanity committed by governments against their own people. But the treaty did codify sovereign states as the basic building blocks of a rules-based, international community. Over the centuries it displaced, if not eradicated, alternative conceptions of a world order such as the religious-based order of a militant Islam, the authoritarian nature of imperial tsarist Russia, or the traditional Chinese vision of world order as a system of governance centered on China, previously embodied in the emperor, that values order and harmony rather than freedom and dissent.

Richard Haas describes the Westphalian system as World Order 1.0, which lasted up to the end of the Cold War, sometime around 1989–1991. Since the end of the Cold War, a new order has emerged. World Order 2.0 involves the understanding that states have obligations as well as rights, the notion of sovereign obligations, a more multilateral world less dominated by just one or two great powers, and a redefinition of national security issues to include the fiscal deficit, democracy deficits, and the challenges of climate change.[29] World Order 2.0 still involves respect for borders but also includes growing international calls to do something about repression inside national borders. Respecting borders while guaranteeing human rights can be tricky. When should states intervene and how? There is also a redefinition of the space of international issues extending beyond the merely territorial to the maritime, cyberspace, and outer space. The new world order involves ideas of the global commons and its management and regulation.

Main Actors

The principal actors of the world order have shifted and changed. The great powers of the world order are constantly shifting. In the eighteenth century, France and Britain fought a truly global war for supremacy with battles waged in Europe, India, the Americas, and across the oceans of the world. By the middle of the nineteenth century, Britain was the undisputed global superpower, but by the end of the century British dominance was challenged by a rising Germany and an expanding United States. Great powers were emerging to challenge British global dominance. Great-power rivalry led to two world wars.

We can briefly characterize recent history: from 1945 the United States and the USSR were the leaders of two competing power blocs as the Cold War waxed and waned over almost fifty years, pitting global capitalism against a form of socialism set in the dynamic background of countries emerging from decolonization.[30] After the fall of Communism in 1989 and the end of the USSR in 1991 there then followed a brief period of U.S. global hegemony. The bipolar world of the Cold War so long dominated by the United States and USSR was now replaced by a single hegemon, the United States. But a peace dividend never fully materialized because the brief calm was ended by the long and continuing War on Terrorism after 9/11, the disastrous invasion of Iraq, continuing involvement across the globe from Djibouti to Philippines, and the recession of 2008. The brief interlude of uncontested U.S. hegemony from 1989 to 2008 was soon replaced by the rise of a great-power rivalry as an ascendant China flexed its economic and political muscles and a Russia financially buoyed with rising oil and gas prices entered the stage as near competitors to the United States. Defeat in Iraq and Afghanistan and global economic crisis meant that the United States was no longer as strong as first thought. And in the United States, there were rising political forces arguing against the U.S. global role, its defense of other nations, and its membership of multilateral institutions and practices.[31]

When a hegemon such as the United States faces great-power rivalry, it is faced with the *Thucydides Trap*.[32] The ancient Greek argued that there is always a competition between the major power of the moment and rising competitors. Serious rivals to the hegemon constitute great-power rivalry. The Trap: If the hegemon avoids confrontation, it encourages appeasement. Too much resistance provokes outright conflict. Graham Allison looked at what happened in world history, from the late fifteenth to the late twentieth century. He found that in sixteen instances when a ruling power was faced with rising power, such as France and the UK in the mid-eighteenth century or France and Germany in the mid-nineteenth century, all but four ended in war. The exceptions were Portugal and Spain in the late fifteenth century, UK and United States in early twentieth century, United States and USSR in the mid to late twentieth century, and UK/France and Germany in the late twentieth century.[33]

Some caveats are in order. In a globally connected world strong ties between China and the United States constitute a platform for continual interaction and shared interests. The globalized economy almost dictates some form of great-power cooperation. The trap can be softened if the hegemon, in this case the United States, uses alliances and multilateral organizations to spread the load, share the burden, and soften the direct conflict between the hegemon and its rivals. But if the United States, in an era of populist nationalism, pulls away from a global order, it may risk more direct confrontation, in which case the trap is set.[34]

The United States is still the dominant power with global reach, but its military is undercut by its relative economic decline, especially after the 2008–2009 recession. China's GDP was only 25 percent of U.S. GDP in 1990 but exceeded it by 2014. As U.S. global influence recedes, the stage is set for the complex regional geopolitics where other great powers and regional powers can and do play a more significant role. A "world in chaos" and a "world disordered" are now common tropes.[35] Perhaps we should use the term world (dis)order.

We are living in a world of change, one in which the older is being replaced by a new order yet to fully crystallize into stability and coherence. The Westphalian system is challenged. The frozen stability of the Cold War, although it was more like a long ice age with periods of warming and cooling, is now replaced by the dynamic context of a relatively declining United States where there is a loss of belief in, and commitment to, the multilateralism of the post–World War II world. The European Union is fraying at its edges and collapsing in the center. Russia and China are seeking a larger role in a world order that challenges the Western liberal model of the dominance of the United States at the center of multilateral connections. Great-power competition strains multilateralism. The United States no longer has overwhelming force and now has near-peer competition, especially in the Indo-Pacific. China and Russia are back on the global stage. There is a reemergence of great-power competition and the proliferation of various regional powers, such as India, Saudi Arabia, and Turkey. A rich variety of regional orders constitute this dynamic world (dis)order. In part III, "Regional Realms," I will look at these regional orders in more detail and how they connect with the emergent world order.

NEW GEOPOLITICAL SPACES

The space of traditional geopolitics was the surface of national territories spread out across the globe. Nations-states jostled and cooperated across this surface. Geography was an aid to statecraft in Mackinder's formulation because it allowed a geographically informed imagination to be employed. Contemporary geopolitics, in contrast, extends the notion of political space.

Outer Space

In June 2018 President Trump directed the Pentagon to create a new space military service branch to add to the existing ones of Army, Navy, Air Force, Coast Guard, and Marines. While many criticized the idea as a gimmick, it did awaken wider public interest to a new theater of international conflict and cooperation. Just as the establishment of the U.S. Air Force in 1947 signaled the growing importance of air power in global and regional conflicts, this new branch highlights a new arena for geopolitical strategy. Since 1958 with the launch of the first satellite capable of orbiting the earth, space has become an important realm for commercial and military purposes. The deployment of satellites is now a vital part of our modern lives, providing such essential services as global positioning, weather forecasting, and telecommunications that we all rely on. Modern economies rely on satellite deployments in the flow of everyday life. And that makes them especially vulnerable. The orbiting hardware is a target-rich environment of indispensable assets. China, Russia, Iran, and North Korea are only some of the countries that pose a threat to the space assets of the United States.[36] Space threats take a variety of forms from a direct attack on satellites from space or the ground. There are weaponized satellites and projectiles as well as lasers and electromagnetic pulses. Satellites can also be attacked electronically with radio frequency signals.

The struggle for the mastery of space is heating up. China has major aspirations. In 2018 China launched thirty-eight orbital satellites, the most of any country in the world, including the United States. Its goal is to deter U.S. attacks, to have the ability to attack U.S. satellites, and to deny the U.S. hegemony in space. Space is the arena for a new arms race. And just as we could identify seafaring nations as key players contesting power in the fifteenth, sixteenth, and seventeenth centuries, we can now identify spacefaring nations, such as the United States, Russia, and China, as key players in the struggle for dominance of outer space.

Cyberspace

We are linked by the flows and connections across the internet. A new space has emerged, *cyberspace*. It provides for incredible connections and flows of information and knowledge across national boundaries. But it can also be a source of disinformation, propaganda, and bad intent. Cyberspace is another space that is being weaponized. *Cyberwarfare* involves actions by nation-states or other organizations to damage national networks in the form of espionage, sabotage, propaganda, and economic disruption. *Cyberoperations* are now an integral part of statecraft. In 2014, the North Korean states, angered by an unflattering depiction of their leader in the movie *The Interview*, hacked the files of the parent company, Sony, and released damaging and embarrassing emails.[37] This is a frequent ploy of the Russian state, which uses clandestine campaigns on the internet and social media to undermine political institutions at home and abroad. The leak of confidential emails of the U.S. Democratic National Committee in 2016 was a typical Russian state-sponsored tactic. From 2017 Saudi Arabia weaponized Twitter in order to damage the reputation of those Saudis critical of the increasingly authoritarian rule of the crown prince. Dissidents were placed on a public blacklist. One of them was Jamal Khashoggi, killed in 2018 in the Saudi consulate in Istanbul on the orders of the Saudi state. Another example: during the demonstrations in Hong Kong in 2019 the Chinese state mobilized social media to demonize protestors. Cyberspace is also breached to provide information. The 2018 cyberattack of customer information of Marriott hotels was a Chinese intelligence-gathering campaign.

We now live in the age of the Internet of Things (IoT) in which people-to-people, people-to-machine, and machine-to-machine connections are increasingly seamless. But this also creates a threat environment for data mining and a threat potential to critical infrastructure vulnerable to hacking, malware, and ultimately to ransom or direct attack. Even just the reconnaissance of critical infrastructure provides crucial information for possible later use. The vulnerability of data files, financial markets, national security information, and vital services, such as water supply, sewerage, and emergency response systems, is heightened with the development of the IoT. A city's, a country's, or indeed a nation's functioning is now based on the IoT. The national digital infrastructure is vulnerable to manipulation, control, and attack by both state and non-state actors. Cyberspace is a new space of contestation as well as cooperation.

Cities

Cities are important political units in their own right. One study, for example, looked at how cities in Europe are not simply nested within and beneath the regulatory immigration frameworks of nation-states but play an important role in their own right in border control and in the monitoring, exclusion, and control of migrants.[38]

Cities house more than half the world's population: they consume 75 percent of the world's energy and emit 80 percent of the world's greenhouse gases. But cities are not just areas of problems; they are innovative sites for policy solutions.[39] Cities are responding with both mitigation and adaptation. Mitigation focuses on reducing the concentrations of greenhouse gases by using alternative energy sources, encouraging greater energy efficiency and conservation, and through the promotion of carbon sinks through planting trees. The city of Curitiba in Brazil is the showcase for many successful policies. The city of Chicago has developed policies anticipating a hotter and wetter climate by repaving with permeable materials, planting more trees, and offering tax incentive to green office roofs. There is a bottom-up movement from urban residents for a better quality of urban life. Global climate change issues, such as the shrinking polar ice sheets and the perilous state of polar bears, are real but distant, long term, and difficult to solve for the urban residents of today's megacities. But the residents have an immediate experience of poor air quality in their city and a more immediate and greater ability to leverage local policies that effect change. The global issues can seem distant yet still pressing, creating a sense of anxiety without any form of immediate political response. The nation-state can be both too big to deal with urban issues and too small to affect global affairs. National legislatures, such as the U.S. congress, whose debates are shaped more by big monied interests than the everyday needs of local citizens, can too often lock into ideological disputes and paralysis. The city is the sweet spot of climate change issues because it is small enough to connect with citizens and tailor specific policies, while large enough to affect a real difference. Cities are the ideal stage for developing policies and practices of sustainability compared to the global and the national. There is also growing competition between cities. As the world globalizes, cities are assessed by international standards in the competition for investment, skilled people, and creative industries. Cities need to respond to the demands of an increasingly mobile and ecologically aware capital and global talent pool. Cities are now ranked, compared, and assessed by the greenness of their environment and their success in moving toward more sustainable policies. Cities are nodes in a global network of flows of people, ideas, and practices. While the world is often described as separate national surfaces of nation-states, it is increasingly visualized as a global urban network. Cities are learning from each other, as policies are tested in cities with the more successful ones diffused, adopted, and adapted around the global network. By 2020, the U.S. Conference of Mayors Climate Change Agreement included 1,066 mayors representing a total population of over ninety million citizens. The organization helps cities with policy formulation to accelerate energy efficiency and adapt infrastructure to meet international standards through discouraging sprawl and encouraging urban greening. Many U.S. cities have initiated environmental legislation that exceeds EPA standards, in the absence of national leadership. The C40 group is a consortium of the world's largest cities committed to tackling climate change to reduce carbon emissions and to increase energy efficiency. Forty cities signed up in 2006 (hence the name), but by 2020 membership increased to ninety-six cities, representing a tenth of the world population and a quarter of global GDP. The cities of the world are where adaptation and mitigation policies are being most tried and tested. The cities are the cause of many of our environmental problems but also, as it turns out, the solution.

Bodies

The body is an important geopolitical site. Our movements are defined, for example, by our citizenship, which limits and regulates the mobility of our bodies. The nature of our body—whether male or female, straight or gay, White or Black—structures both our access to power and the how, why, and when power is imposed on us. There is biopolitics at the intersection of human biology and politics. The theorist Michel Foucault wrote about the state regulation of bodies. He argues that life is enmeshed in politics. He wrote of a "power that exerts a positive influence on life, that endeavors to administer, optimize, and multiply it, subjecting it to precise controls and comprehensive regulations."[40]

Power is expressed in control and regulation of bodies, whether it is assigning or not assigning citizenship, issuing passports, recording births and deaths, encouraging or discouraging high birth rates, pursuing or not pursuing certain public health measures, regulating women's bodies, and adjudicating the legality of sexual behaviors.

Embodied geopolitics is concerned with how bodies are shaped, constrained, managed, and damaged by politics. National security in this perspective is primarily about the regulation and monitoring of different bodies. War is about not just the projection of power but the impact of this power on the human body through maiming and killing. Feminist geopolitics foregrounds the regulation and management of human bodies. Maria Boikova Struble, for example, reconsiders politics as the incorporation of bodies in an era of disasters and threats. A recent edited collection looks at how bodies are subject to chemicals to coerce and suppress in war and at times of civil unrest.[41] An embodied geopolitics considers the importance of bodies as sites of politics and politics as the regulation and control of bodies.

New Spaces of Concern

There are new spaces of concern apart from the classical geopolitical concern with the protection of borders and the maintenance of national territorial integrity. If we take a look at the United States, while some may worry about the threat posed by a rising China or a belligerent Russia, there are also other concerns that rarely make the formal geopolitical agenda. The borrowing weakness of the United States is undermined by its relative economic decline. It has gained easy credit because foreigners have been willing to buy U.S. dollars. But if the United States weakens enough so that people do not hold dollars, then the U.S. deficit would mount and there would be less money to pay for the social peace at home through Social Security and Medicare, while also maintaining a vast military. The fiscal crisis is a geopolitical crisis. Similarly, the rising infrastructure deficit, a huge backlog of deferred maintenance, weakens economic growth and national security. The infrastructure deficit is also a geopolitical issue. Climate change, which is generating more fires in the West, droughts in the South, and mounting storm damage along the coasts, also poses a threat to the national space. Fiscal and infrastructure deficits and climate change all pose "national threats."[42] They may be nonmilitary, but they still present existential threats to the nation.

GEOPOLITICAL HOTSPOTS: BLACKHOLES AND WORMHOLES

In this chapter we looked at empires, nation-states, and world orders. For the moment, however, we can shift our scale of analysis and consider some of the very small units of the world order that barely figure in great-power politics but play a significant role in global society. They include the blackholes of the global financial community such Panama, Switzerland, Cayman Islands, Bermuda, Cyprus, possibly Malta, and many others that are vital links in the flow of flight capital, dirty money, and the proceeds of corruption and the black economy. They are blackholes because they lack transparency about financial dealings, which attracts people and institutions seeking to stash money from the reach of taxation and accountability. They can be likened to wormholes in the universe, where capital can move more freely and faster than in normal international banking space.

These wormholes allow the rich and connected to escape the friction and gravity that limit ordinary mortals.[43] Malta proposed an Individual Investor Program that offered citizenship for a straight fee of 650,000 euros. The program was effectively selling European citizenship. After much international criticism, the program was placed on hold, and then in November 2013 a revised program offered citizenship in return for 1,150,000 euros. The rich can easily skirt the requirements that restrain and restrict the rest of us.

The Caribbean is filled with tax havens, such as Anguilla, Bahamas, British Virgin Islands, Cayman Islands, Dominica, Nevis, and Panama, that provide a curtain of secrecy that hides the movement of money (see photo 2.3). The Cayman Islands, for example, has no income tax, no corporate tax, no estate tax, no inheritance tax, and no capital gains tax. They have no tax treaties with other nations and no exchange controls; setting up a company might take all of a couple of hours. Little surprise then that this tiny island is home to more than one hundred thousand "companies."

Photo 2.3. The British Virgin Islands: One of the more attractive blackholes of international finance (John Rennie Short)

Researchers at the University of Amsterdam measured the flows of value through these offshore financial centers.[44] Table 2.3 is a list of the world's top tax havens, defined as places where either disproportionate amounts of value disappears and/or moves outward. They are listed in order of value of these flows. Although these places are small and thus often ignored in standard geopolitical

Table 2.3.   The Top Tax Havens

British Virgin Islands (UK)
Taiwan
Jersey (UK)
Bermuda (UK)
Cayman Islands (UK)
Samoa
Liechtenstein
Curacao (Netherlands)
Marshall Islands
Malta
Mauritius
Luxembourg
Nauru
Cyprus
Seychelles

Source: https://www.ofcmeter.org

analysis, these wormholes of global capitalism play an outsized role in global society.

SUGGESTED READINGS

Agamben, G. (2004). *State of exception*. Chicago: University of Chicago Press.
Anderson, B. (2006, revised ed.). *Imagined communities: Reflections on the origin and spread of nationalism*. London: Verso.
Billig, M. (1995). *Banal nationalism*. London and Thousand Oaks: Sage.
Kennedy, P. (1989). *The rise and fall of the great powers*. New York: Vintage.
Haas, R. (2017). *A world in disarray*. New York: Penguin.
Hobson, J. A. (1938, 3rd ed.). *Imperialism: A study*. London: Allen and Unwin.
Huntington, S. P. (2006). *Political order in changing societies*. New Haven and London: Yale University Press.
Jones, B., & Taussig, T. (2019). *Democracy and disorder: The struggle for influence in the new geopolitics*. Washington, DC: Brookings
MacKenzie, J. M. (ed.). (2016). *The encyclopedia of empire*, 4 volumes. Oxford: Wiley Blackwell.
Said, Edward W. (1978). *Orientalism: Western conceptions of the Orient*. New York: Random House.
Short, J. R. (1991). *Imagined country: Society, culture and environment*. London and New York: Routledge.

NOTES

1. Suny, R. G. (1995). Ambiguous categories: States, empires and nations. *Post-Soviet Affairs, 11*, 185–96. For a more general theory, see Galtung, J. (1980). "A structural theory of imperialism"—ten years later. *Millennium, 9*, 181–96. And for a comprehensive survey see MacKenzie, J. M. (ed.). (2016). *The encyclopedia of empire*, 4 volumes. Oxford: Wiley Blackwell.

2. Harper, K. (2017). *The fate of Rome*. Princeton and Oxford: Princeton University Press, 9.

3. Scott, J. C. (2009). *The art of not being governed: An anarchist history of upland Southeast Asia*. New Haven and London: Yale University Press.

4. Ethridge, R. F., & Shuck-Hall, S. M. (eds.). (2009). *Mapping the Mississippian Shatter Zone: The colonial Indian slave trade and regional instability in the American South*. Lincoln: University of Nebraska Press.

5. Snyder, T. (2011). *Bloodlands: Europe between Hitler and Stalin*. New York: Random House.

6. Pagden, A. (2008). *Worlds at war: The 2,500-year struggle between East and West*. Oxford: Oxford University Press.

7. Kennedy, P. (1989). *The rise and fall of the great powers*. New York: Vintage.

8. Parker, C. H. (2010). *Global interactions in the early modern age, 1400–1800*. Cambridge: Cambridge University Press.

9. Levenson, J. A. (ed). (2007). *Encompassing the globe*. Washington, DC: Smithsonian Institution.

10. Brands, H. W. (1992). *Bound to empire: The United States and the Philippines*. Oxford: Oxford University Press, 104.

11. Hobson, J. A. (1938, 3rd ed.). *Imperialism: A study*. London: Allen and Unwin.

12. Lenin, V. I. (1965). *Imperialism: The highest stage of capitalism*. Moscow: Progress Publishers.

13. See https://www.bbc.co.uk/archive/tour-of-south-africa--rt-hon-macmillan/zv6gt39.

14. Pitts, J. (2018). *Boundaries of the international: Law and empire*. Cambridge, MA and London: Harvard University Press.

15. Said, Edward W. (1978). *Orientalism: Western conceptions of the Orient*. New York: Random House.

16. One study of Spain found significant differences between the nationalist attitudes of social classes. Nationalism strengthened in the working class during a recession but weakened among the wealthy.
Hierro, M. J., & Rico, G. (2019). Economic crisis and national attitudes: Experimental evidence from Spain. *Ethnic and Racial Studies, 42*, 820–37. https://doi.org/10.1080/01419870.2018.1432873.

17. Anderson, B. (2006, revised ed.). *Imagined communities: Reflections on the origin and spread of nationalism*. London: Verso.

18. Short, J. R. (1991). *Imagined country: Society, culture and environment*. London and New York: Routledge.

19. Billig, M. (1995). *Banal nationalism*. London and Thousand Oaks: Sage.

20. Allen, M. A., Bell, S. R., & Clay, K. C. (2018). Deadly triangles: The implications of regional competition on interactions in asymmetric dyads. *Foreign Policy Analysis, 14*, 169–90; Pruitt, D. G. (2009). Escalation and de-escalation in asymmetric conflict. *Dynamics of Asymmetric Conflict, 2*, 23–31.

21. Shultz, R., Godson, R., Hanlon, Q., & Ravich, S. (2011). The sources of instability in the twenty-first century: Weak states, armed groups, and irregular conflict. *Strategic Studies Quarterly, 5*, 73–94.

22. Barnett, T. (2004). *The Pentagon's new map*. New York: Berkeley.

23. Agamben, G. (2004). *State of exception*. Chicago: University of Chicago Press.

24. Acemoglu, D., & Robinson, J. A. (2012). *Why nations fail: The Origins of power, prosperity, and poverty*. New York: Crown.

25. Ibid., 68.

26. Chua, A. (2003). *World on fire*. New York: Doubleday.

27. Huntington, S. P. (2006). *Political order in changing societies*. New Haven and London: Yale University Press.

28. Bremmer, I. (2006). *The J curve: A new way to understand why nations rise and fall*. New York: Simon and Schuster.

29. Haas, R. (2017). *A world in disarray*. New York: Penguin.

30. Westad, O. A. (2017). *The Cold War: A world history*. New York: Basic.

31. See https://www.brookings.edu/research/the-purpose-of-multilateralism/?utm_campaign=Foreign%20Policy&utm_source=hs_email&utm_medium=email&utm_content=77390268.

32. Allison, G. (2017). The Thucydides trap. *Foreign Policy*. https://foreignpolicy.com/2017/06/09/the-thucydides-trap.

33. Allison, G. (2017). *Destined for war: Can America and China escape the Thucydides trap?* Boston and New York: Houghton Mifflin Harcourt.

34. Wright, T. (2017). *All measures short of war: The contest for the 21st century and the future of American power*. New Haven and London: Yale University Press.

35. Jones, B., & Taussig, T. (2019). *Democracy and disorder: The struggle for influence in the new geopolitics*. Washington, DC: Brookings; Kagan, R. (2018). *The jungle grows back: America and our imperiled world*. New York: Knopf; National Intelligence Coun-

cil. (2012). *Alternative worlds*. Washington, DC. https://www.dni.gov/files/documents /GlobalTrends_2030.pdf.

36. Harrison, T., Johnson, K., Roberts, T. G., Bergethon, M., & Coultrup, A. (2019). Space threat assessment. *Center for Strategic & International Studies*. https://csis-prod .s3.amazonaws.com/s3fs-public/publication/190404_SpaceThreatAssessment_interior .pdf.

37. Stengel, R. (2019, October 6). The untold story of the Sony hack: How North Korea's battle with Seth Rogan and George Clooney foreshadowed Russian election meddling in 2016. *Vanity Fair*. https://www.vanityfair.com/news/2019/10/the-untold-story-of-the -sony-hack.

38. Fauser, M. (2019). The emergence of urban border spaces in Europe. *Journal of Borderlands Studies, 34*, 605–22.

39. I draw heavily on my paper, Short, J. R. (2015). Why cities are a rare good news story in climate change. *The Conversation*. https://theconversation.com/why-cities-are-a-rare -good-news-story-in-climate-change-45016.

40. Foucault, M. (1976 [trans. R Hurley, 1979]). *The history of sexuality volume 1: The will to knowledge*. New York: Random House, 137.

41. Struble, M. B. (2019). *The politics of bodies at risk*. Lanham: Rowman & Littlefield; Mankoo, A., & Rappert, B. (eds.). (2018). *Chemical bodies: The techno-politics of control*. Lanham: Rowman & Littlefield.

42. Forno, R. (2019, September 10). Don't ignore serious nonmilitary threats to U.S. national security. *The Conversation*. https://theconversation.com/dont-ignore-serious -nonmilitary-threats-to-U.S.-national-security-122444.

43. Warren, K. (2019). The top 15 tax havens around the world. *Business Insider*. https://www.businessinsider.com/tax-havens-for-millionaires-around-the-world-2019-11.

44. OFC Meter: *Offshore Financial Centers across the world*. https://www.ofcmeter.org.

3

Becomings

Philosophers and poets down through the ages have reminded us of the crucial distinction between *being* and *becoming*. Plato saw *being* as the world of ideas and *becoming* as the world we live in. In this division there is a resultant tension between fixed ideas and a changing reality. The notion that the world was constantly in flux has been espoused from the ancient Greeks to the present day. The Greek philosopher Heraclitus said that no man ever steps in the same river twice. The Latin poet Lucretius reminded us that all things are transitory. Nietzsche argued that fixed entities are false concepts in a world of constant change, while writers such as Albert Camus, Martin Heidegger, and Soren Kierkegaard worked to expound an existentialist philosophy of the lived experience.

Fixed categories make it difficult to grasp the complexity of a world constantly in motion. In the previous two chapters I looked at some of the texts and spaces of the geopolitical imagination. I tried to imbue them with dynamism, but they risk intellectual immobilization in a rapidly accelerating world of change. In this chapter I want to look at what I define as the geopolitical processes of becoming and in particular the creation of a global economy, the emergence of a new global polity, and the nature of unfolding globalizations.

A GLOBAL ECONOMY

Let's begin then with the idea of an evolving global economy and its geopolitical implications. A convincing case can be made that we have been living in a truly global economy ever since the European appropriation of the New World in the sixteenth century. Intercontinental trading patterns have been created, maintained, and reinforced as local economies have been connected to world trading circuits and national economies have been interconnected.

The Core-Periphery Model

Immanuel Wallerstein theorized the essential nature of this global economy in a series of books that outlined a *core-periphery model*.[1] The relationship between the core and periphery was one of *unequal exchange* as cheap commodities were imported into the core countries for the more value-added work in the creation of manufactured goods that were then exported around the world. The system was constructed for the enrichment of the core with the consequence of what theorists described as the *development of underdevelopment* in the periphery.[2] It is a model that allows us to move beyond the nation-state as the only unit of analysis, to see transnational structures that guide national and local outcomes and to have a more dynamic framework in which to understand geopolitical events. It is a model that still has relevance. Photo 3.1 is a scene from the docks of Yangon. Much of Myanmar's economy is still based on the export of primary commodities, such as timber and minerals. In this example, timber from old-growth forest is exported to Japan and China where it is manufactured into value-added commodities.

Photo 3.1.   Primary commodity exports from Myanmar (John Rennie Short)

There are of course elaborations to this simple model. Between the core and the periphery there is the liminal space of the semi-periphery inhabited with countries heading in either direction, generating enough growth to enter the core or falling from core position. We can identify semi-peripheral economies, such as Australia and Canada, where an early reliance on primary commodities still allowed for relatively high rates of internal economic growth and high average incomes. As we will see in chapter 11, Argentina presents an interesting case because it had a very similar position to both Australia and Canada at the start of the twentieth century but ended up in a very different place at its end, a reminder that differences in political arrangements can influence economic outcomes. We can also identify the semi-periphery as containing countries seeking to achieve some level of autonomous economic growth in order to take up a more core position. In other words, the core-periphery model is best seen as one of change and flux.

The global economy emerged over centuries. A global trading system appeared in embryonic form in Europe around 1150 with the increase in trade both within Europe and between Europe and the East. The French historian Fernand Braudel, in two magisterial multivolume series, described Europe as the pivotal region in the development of a global capitalism.[3] This region had key ingredients for global expansion, including development of a merchant class, the growth of urban trading centers, such as Genoa, Venice, and Milan in the south and the Hanseatic League towns of Bergen, Bremen, Hamburg, and Lübeck, and the beginnings of money as a means of exchange. The merchant society, the urban trading circuits and the use of money were the essential prerequisites for the development of longer-distance trade between 1500 and 1600, when European went truly global.

It was not just a global economy but a capitalist global economy. Taking a very long view, Giovanni Arrighi argued that we can best understand the world economy as a global capitalism marked by a cycle of crises with cycles of expansion and contraction. Each cycle comes to an end as increasing conflict between competing powers leads to the rise of a new hegemon. Arrighi notes the rise and fall of Genoa, the Netherlands, Britain, and then the United States as dominant hegemons.[4] Are we witnessing the emergence of China as the up-and-coming hegemon? The geographer David Harvey develops these ideas further in his analysis of a global capitalism as prone to recurring crisis. He describes the geopolitical consequences as the new imperialism.[5]

From the sixteenth to the nineteenth century the general story of incorporation of much of the world into the core's sphere of influence and world history is, by and large, the story of its incorporation. When normal trading did not provide the benefits to the core, the means of incorporation employed ranged from crude gunboat diplomacy to colonial appropriations, territorial annexations, imperial conquests, and the sophisticated manipulations of indirect empire. A variety of methods were employed from the colonization of settler societies and indirect control through collaborative elites, to the direct control of formal imperialism. Formal imperialism increased in four decades around 1900 as competition increased between core countries and emerging countries eager to assert a core position and challenge British supremacy.

Armed with understanding of the core-periphery model, we can see the conflicts in Europe and around the world as, in large part, the battle for supremacy of the core. In the sixteenth century Spain and Portugal struggled for global dominance, in the seventeenth century it involved Spain, the Netherlands, England, and France. By the eighteenth century the competition had boiled down to Britain and France for global dominance. The victory went to the British in the Seven Years' War (1756–1763), which was fought on a global scale with British and French forces fighting each other in North America, Europe, and India. By the middle of the nineteenth century Britain was the undisputed superpower in the core, controlling and policing world trade routes. The long cycles in world politics identified in the *Modelski Model* describe the rise and fall of core hegemons from Portugal (1494–1580), the Netherlands (1580–1688), Great Britain I (1688–1792), Great Britain II (1792–1914), and the United States (1914–). Modelski identified four phases for each hegemon in each of these long cycles:

- a global war phase, signifying the end of the previous cycle and the start of a new one;
- the world power phase at the peak of an empire's relative strength;
- the delegitimation phase, when security concerns are replaced by the pursuit of material prosperity; and
- the deconcentration phase, when economic and military supremacy of the hegemon is challenged.[6]

In this model, the United States is currently somewhere between the delegitimation and the final phase of deconcentration.

Incorporation of the periphery involved both collaboration and resistance. Ruling elites in the periphery played an important role. Collaborative elites were those who aided or facilitated economic penetration. Collaborative elites could benefit enormously with little trickle down to the vast majority of people. Strong collaborative elites, such as the landowners of Latin America, meant there was little need for direct political control by core states. Noncollaborative elites fought against such incorporation. Formal involvement by the core countries occurred to install a collaborative elite or to intervene when the collaboration was breaking down or being challenged. The transition from informal to formal empire was often based on the need for the core state to uphold a collaborative system that was breaking down and to forestall the actions of other core states.

Incorporation into the core was often resisted. Again, the geopolitics of world history can also be reimagined as a series of resistances. Photo 3.2 was taken inside a church in the city of St. George's, Grenada. It represents a one-sided view of history. The "horrid rebellion" mentioned in the plaque was a revolt, mainly by Blacks, freed and slaves, against British slave rule. Known as Fedon's Rebellion, it was an armed struggle that sought to overturn British White rule, put an end to slavery, and create a Black republic along the lines of the revolution in nearby Haiti.[7] Rebellions, uprisings, and resistances characterized the era. So rather than a merely local event, the Maori Wars in New Zealand from 1845 to 1872, between the colonial government and local peoples resisting the annexation of their land, was a part of a global resistance that included large-scale uprising against the French, constant rebellions against British rule in Egypt and the Sudan, and the Filipino resistance struggle (1898–1902) against U.S. annexation. Even the xenophobic outbursts against foreigners, such as the Boxer rebellion (1899–1901) in China, were part of the peripheral resistance.

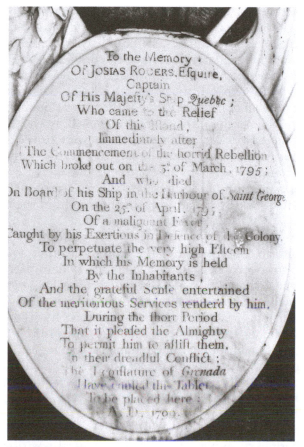

Photo 3.2. Plaque in church in St. George's, Grenada (John Rennie Short)

Global Shifts

The core periphery model is a simple one and like all models is an abstraction from the richness of reality. We can for example highlight a number of trends that do not fit into the simple model. There are at least four global shifts.

The first is the shift in the balance of power toward the primary producers. Newly independent countries all gained a greater control over their natural resources. In the past fifty years, however, some countries, originally on the periphery and semi-periphery, have sought to gain even more control over their natural resources. Collective bargaining power improves their hand and so countries have formed cartels to control the price of a single commodity. The most successful was the Organization of Petroleum Exporting Countries (OPEC). This cartel was created in response to the oil companies' decision in 1959 to decrease the price of oil from $2.08 to $1.80 a barrel. The aim was to increase demand, but this had very negative impacts on countries such as Venezuela, where oil made up 90 percent of its exports. Venezuela held talks with Middle East producers to provide a common front in the negotiations with the oil companies to secure higher prices. The result of these talks was the establishment of OPEC in 1960. As oil became a vital lubricant, literally and metaphorically to the economies and indeed societies of core countries, OPEC's bargaining power increased and in December 1973 OPEC unilaterally raised the price of oil to $11.65 dollars a barrel. In 1979 the price of a barrel of oil was again increased, this time to $30.00 a barrel. There two hikes in oil prices meant a huge redistribution of wealth. Formerly poor oil producers became some of the richest countries in the world. In the case of Iran, for example, the money was used by the Shah to carry out an extensive program of modernization, which, as we will see in chapter 8, carried the seeds of his own destruction. The largest negative impacts were on the poorer peripheral countries without access to oil. The increase in the cost of oil also prompted the exploration for oil reserves in areas previously considered not economically feasible. Oil rigs began to appear further from the coast, and deeper into the Arctic.

Commodity cartels can wield near monopoly power over supply, but their actions may encourage substitution or the search for other sources. Producers' cartels tend to be stronger when just a few countries dominate production levels and weaker when a large number of countries are involved. The nature of the commodity is also important. While oil can be kept in the ground or conveniently stored for long periods, bananas in contrast have to be sold quickly. During economic booms the primacy producers can profit from the increase in demand, which jacks up prices. But reliance on a single commodity in the national economy creates the possibility of the *resource curse*, which we will discuss in detail in their specific examples in chapters to follow.[8] Few countries with rich oil and gas reserves escape the resource curse. One notable exception is Norway (see photo 3.3).

Second, there was the rise of the *development state* devoted to ensuring the shift from semi-periphery to core, or to a more central position in the core. In the nineteenth and early twentieth century, the classic example was Meiji Japan, which followed the Western model of stimulating industrial production and gaining control of overseas territory to ensure continued supply of raw materials. More recently, in countries such as Japan, South Korea, and latterly China, the protection of domestic industries and the aggressive pursuit of a manufacturing export base was a common strategy. The development state model was most effectively applied in East and Southeast Asia. In the early years it was associated with limited domestic consumption and an emphasis on moving up the value-added chain of manufactured products. Then as growth continued economies were reoriented to concentrate on more high-value goods and services.[9]

Third, there is the *global shift in manufacturing*.[10] As an example we can consider the case of Nike, the shoe company named after the Greek goddess of victory. Nike has never made any shoes in the United States. Their original business model consisted of selling Japanese-made shoes at track meets. Then, as Japanese wages and conditions increased, Nike shifted their supply to factories in the cheaper-labor South Korea, and the city of Pusan became the capital of Asian shoe manufacturing. As Korean wages increased, Nike reduced their costs by shifting their supply of shoes to the even cheaper-wage factories of Indonesia and Vietnam. The Nike story was repeated across the manufacturing sectors as

Photo 3.3. An oil rig in Norwegian North Sea waters (John Rennie Short)

companies shifted production to reduce wage costs. Sometimes this was reinforced by the big-box retailers who used their considerable purchasing power to squeeze manufacturers' profit margins, who in turn were forced to shift operations to the cheapest manufacturing areas simply to maintain the business links with the giant retailers.

The net effect of global shift in manufacturing was a restructuring of class relations across the globe. In the rich world the global shift in manufacturing employment heralded a decline in the power of organized labor, and the strengthening of capital in the ongoing capital-labor relations. In the newly industrializing, the shift along with the development of import substitution industries and sometimes increases in commodity prices resulted in the decline of absolute poverty and in some countries an expansion of the middle class.

Fourth, there is the hypermobility of capital. International banking is not new. Early international banking outfits included the family-run businesses of the Medici, Fuggers, and Rothschilds. However, finance markets tended to be national, and financial transactions had to be negotiated through the maze of national and sometimes even local currency regulations. A significant shift in recent decades has been the liberation of financial capitalism and the decline of national control over money flows. Smaller, weaker countries have always been subject to outside financial power but the most interesting change in recent years has been how even the larger countries are now subject to the "market sentiment" to enact policies that send the "right" signals to the financial markets. Flights of capital can affect national stability. Money has achieved its transcendental global capitalist potential of becoming transnational, nonnational, and truly international.

A GLOBAL POLITY

World Order 2.0

In the previous chapter we raised the notion of world orders and used Richard Haas's distinction of a World Order 1.0 based on the Westphalian system of nation-states and new World Order 2.0 still coming into focus. This World Order 2.0 is a world in the process of becoming with a number of transforming and transformative characteristics. It is a more multilateral world less dominated by a few great powers and more cognizant of new forms of geopolitical threats, including fiscal crisis, democracy deficits, and climate change. It is a world dominated by networks and flows as much as bounded space. Radical terrorist groups or nongovernment organizations seeking radical environmental change operate more as networks than the bounded spatial units of the nation-state.

While World Order 1.0 developed rules for both peace and war between nation-states, there is now a large and growing middle zone for state interaction. In the *gray zone*, somewhere between war and peace, states seek advantage over others without sparking armed conflict or outright war.[11] The activities of Russian "little green men" in eastern Ukraine in 2014 is a classic example of a state, in this case Russia, altering the status quo by employing unconventional forces of state power.[12] China's use of its ostensibly commercial fishing fleet to exert control in the South China Sea is another example of gray zone activity. A gray zone is below the level of armed conflict but above that of peace. It is a condition between war and peace. Much of the gray zone interaction occurs in the new and liminal spaces of outer space, oceans, and seas as well as cyberspace. These yet largely ungoverned spaces create the perfect conditions for gray zone activity. Outer space has yet to be fully regulated or brought under agreed-upon standards of behavior and involvement. Even when there are regulations of the oceans, these are flouted by China in the South China Sea at no seeming cost. The anarchy of cyberspace has allowed bad actors and bad actions to flourish.

An intensive and deepening globalization has impacted sovereign states. An economic globalization of transnational capital flowing around the world, and production chains snaking their way across boundaries, have weakened the middle class in the Global North and enlarged the middle class of the Global South. While this has created new spurts of growth in the South, it has resulted in growing discontent in the North and dissatisfaction with traditional political elites. The election of Donald Trump, Brexit, and the rise of right-wing nationalist in Central and Eastern Europe are all part of a broader trend of a new anti-globalist populism. This new global system was in part devised by the ideas of neoliberals in Central Europe, such as Frederick Hayek and members of the Geneva school, who sought a global economy integrated by the international flows of capital but insulated from mass democracy. Organizations such as the World Trade Organization and its predecessor, the EU, and the European Court of Justice were designed to ensure capitalism, not by replacing the state, but by protecting it from democracy.

Neoliberalism and Its Resistances

Neoliberalism began as a reaction to the rise of the Keynesian/New Deal State that was in turn a political response to the Great Depression. Faced with massively high unemployment and the real threat of political instability, economic theorists like John Maynard Keynes and political operatives like Franklin Roosevelt fashioned, almost on the fly, a model of an enlarged state responsible for mopping up unemployment, reducing business downturns, and providing a welfare net so that market downturns did not have such devastating social outcomes. The period from 1933 through the 1970s marks the high point of the Keynesian/New Deal when there was a consensus, in much of the developed world, between capital and labor on the role of government. Government spending stimulated demand so that unemployment would be limited and controlled. There were critics of this dominant discourse. Friedrich Hayek (1899–1992) was a long-standing critic who, in his 1944 book, *The Road to Serfdom*, argued against centralized government planning. However, he was a lonely voice in the wilderness, his ideas only resuscitated in the 1970s and 1980s, praised by Margaret Thatcher and Ronald Reagan and part of the growing revival in the work of classical liberal economists—those who saw the market rather than governments as the solution to social ills. Beginning in the 1970s a new metanarrative was established that sought to limit government spending especially on welfare programs, reduce social subsidies, deregulate markets, globalize economies, and impose limits on tax increases. This neoliberal agenda was promoted by global systems of governance. Both the International Monetary Fund (IMF) and the World Trade Organization (WTO), for example, promoted neoliberal economic policies.

Although the term is widely used and frequently cited as a coherent argument, *neoliberalism* is at times an inchoate grouping of ideas that coalesce around core propositions that deregulated markets and freer global trade will increase economic growth and raise living standards. Around this central ideological core there are subsidiary ideas about accountability, choice, competition, incentives, and performance. Neoliberalism is also a political process that recasts citizens as consumers, reimagines states less as providers of public services and more as promoters of private growth, and shifts governance issues from citizen entitlements to consumer choices. The term is now used so often and so loosely in the literature that it is in danger of losing its sharpness, turned into a blunt category used to signal general intent rather than inform specific analysis. Some invoke the notion of a variegated neoliberalism, its polymorphic character and its path-dependent and locationally specific character.[13] In a full-blown neoliberalism, markets trump the state, capital wins out over organized labor, consumers replace citizens, and market choice replaces citizen rights. The private market and the accompanying individual consumerism are enthroned as the means and measure of success.[14]

There are resistances to neoliberalism with the balance of forces varying by country and even by cities within a country, and so we have differential patterns of greater or lesser degrees of residual welfarism with resurgent neoliberalism. There are also resistances that take a more demonstrative form. Demonstrations at the WTO meeting in Seattle in November–December 1999 galvanized a wide body of opinion. Almost 1,200 nongovernment organizations in eighty-seven countries signed a petition calling for a fundamental reform of the WTO. The official opening of the conference was delayed as almost twenty thousand people blocked the delegates entering the meeting at the Washington State Convention and Trade Center and effectively closed down the center of the city. Over the next few days, protest actions were seen around the world and the WTO, which had been an organization unknown to the wider public, was placed before the harsh glare of media attention. The success of the protest in Seattle led to protests at the joint IMF/World Bank meeting in Washington on April 16–17, 2000. The institutions responded to the criticism. The IMF issued a communiqué that admitted the growing discontent with globalization and that prosperity was not reaching everyone. The IMF announced initiatives for renewed emphasis on debt relief for poorer nations and tighter auditing of IMF loans to avoid abuse. The World Bank issued a statement that pledged to give more money to fight AIDS and speed up debt relief for developing nations. The president of the bank, James Wolfensohn, claimed that the bank was going to focus its energies on small-scale programs aimed at eradicating poverty. The Occupy Wall Street movement that began in New York City in 2011 gave rise to Occupy movements in cities across the country and the world (see photo 3.4). The very broad—indeed too broad—nature of its complaint, lacking a legislative or political focus, meant that it soon disintegrated. The sentiments did not disappear, however; the movement morphed into more specifically targeted policies, such as raising the minimum wage or universal health coverage. The Occupy protest, as the others before and future, raises awareness of the inequities of capitalism and the failures of neoliberalism.

The ideas of neoliberalism are being actively contested—three in particular. The first is the idea of small government. In his first inaugural address delivered on the west front of the U.S. Capitol on January 20, 1981, Ronald Reagan said, "In this present crisis, government is not the solution to our problem; government is the problem." No American president, or indeed any government leader this side of sanity, would use the same or similar words to address the present crisis. There is now recognition that markets left to their own devices can wreak havoc as well as bring economic growth. There is a sense that government is the problem solver of last resort when markets fail to work. Just as in the Great Depression of the past, so with the Great Recession and the COVID-19 pandemic, we discover again that governments are important and have a vital role. The second idea is the notion that deregulation is the cure for our ills. The call for deregulation was always really a demand for an overturning of government over-

Photo 3.4.   Occupy tents in Washington, DC, January 2012 (John Rennie Short)

sight, mandated standards, and systems of control. In the wake of the economic meltdown these now seem like good things. The third idea is that financial globalization, especially the free flow of capital, is a good thing that needs to be encouraged by little or no controls. Unfettered, unregulated flows, especially of the more exotic credit swaps, hedge bets, and futures trading have been creating major problems for years. There is no longer such a clear commitment to unfettered financial markets.

What Do Global Metrics Tell Us About the World?

Over the past thirty years a range of indices have been developed by public and private organizations that measure national performances on a range of metrics, including economic growth, education, health, human development, and political freedoms. These comparative indices allow us to compare, contrast, and rate countries on economic performance, social progress, and political stability. I am fascinated by what these measures could tell us about the world. So, with two colleagues, I sought to combine them to produce a classification of the countries in the world.[15]

The plethora of indices raises a question. To what extent are the indices measuring the same underlying feature? In a provisional attempt to answer this question, we collected data on 15 indices for 145 countries (see table 3.1).

Table 3.1. Description of Indices

Economic Freedom: Heritage Foundation measures economic freedom based on ten quantitative and qualitative factors, grouped into four broad categories, or pillars, of economic freedom: Rule of Law (property rights, freedom from corruption); Limited Government (fiscal freedom, government spending); Regulatory Efficiency (business freedom, labor freedom, monetary freedom); and Open Markets (trade freedom, investment freedom, financial freedom). Each of the ten economic freedoms within these categories is graded on a scale of 0 to 100. A country's overall score is derived by averaging these ten economic freedoms, with equal weight being given to each. *More free=higher value.*

Corruption Perception Index: Transparency International's index ranks countries and territories based on how corrupt their public sector is perceived to be. It is a composite index—a combination of polls—drawing on corruption-related data collected by a variety of reputable institutions. The index reflects the views of observers from around the world, including experts living and working in the countries and territories evaluated. *Less corrupt=higher value.*

Human Development Index (HDI): The Human Development Index (HDI) is a summary measure of average achievement in key dimensions of human development: a long and healthy life, being knowledgeable, and having a decent standard of living. The HDI is the geometric mean of normalized indices for each of the three dimensions. *More developed=Higher value.*

Democracy Index: The Democracy Index is an index compiled by the Economist Intelligence Unit that measures the state of democracy in 167 countries, of which 166 are sovereign states and 165 are UN member states. The index is based on sixty indicators grouped in five different categories measuring pluralism, civil liberties, and political culture. In addition to a numeric score and a ranking, the index categorizes countries as one of four regime types: full democracies, flawed democracies, hybrid regimes, and authoritarian regimes. *More democracy=higher value.*

Freedom Index: In the original index, countries are given a total press freedom score from 0 (best) to 100 (worst) on the basis of a set of twenty-three methodology questions divided into three subcategories and are also given a category designation of "Free," "Partly Free," or "Not Free."

Country Risk: The Fund for Peace's Fragile State Index (FSI) is compiled by collecting thousands of reports and information from around the world, detailing the existing social, economic, and political pressures faced by each of the 178 countries that we analyze. The FSI is based on the Fund for Peace's proprietary Conflict Assessment System Tool (CAST) analytical platform. Based on comprehensive social science methodology, data from three primary sources is triangulated and subjected to critical review to obtain final scores for the FSI. In the original index, *More fragile=higher value.*

Gender Inequality (UN): Index for measurement of gender disparity that was introduced in the 2010 Human Development Report twentieth anniversary edition by the United Nations Development Programme (UNDP). According to the UNDP, this index is a composite measure that captures the loss of achievement within a country due to gender inequality. It uses three dimensions to do so: reproductive health, empowerment, and labor market participation. *More unequal=higher value.*

Quality of Life: Social Watch's Basic Capabilities Index (BCI) looks at basic social indicators, such as health and education. BCI values for 2011 were computed for 167 countries where data are available out of the 193 member states of the United Nations. *Better quality of life=higher value.*

Country Indicators for Foreign Policy Risk (CIFP): The data set provides at-a-glance global overviews, issue-based perspectives, and country performance measures. Currently, the data set includes measures of domestic armed conflict, governance and political instability, militarization, religious and ethnic diversity, demographic stress, economic performance, human development, environmental stress, and international linkages. *More risk=higher value.*

Digital Access: International Telecommunications Union Digital Access Index (DAI) measures the overall ability of individuals in a country to access and use new Information and Communications Technologies (ICTs). The DAI is built around four fundamental vectors that impact a country's ability to access ICTs: infrastructure, affordability, knowledge, and quality and actual usage of ICTs. The DAI has been calculated for 181 economies where European countries were among the highest ranked. The DAI allows countries to see how they compare to peers and their relative strengths and weaknesses. The DAI also provides a transparent and globally measurable way of tracking progress toward improving access to ICTs. *Greater access=higher value.*

State Fragility: Systemic Peace's index is composed of eight component indicators for the most recent year available for 167 countries with populations greater than 500,000 in 2013 (no data for newly independent South Sudan). ***More fragile=higher value.***

Freedom of the Press: Reporters without Borders' index measures the level of freedom of information in 180 countries. It reflects the degree of freedom that journalists, news organizations, and netizens enjoy in each country, and the efforts made by the authorities to respect and ensure respect for this freedom. ***Less freedom=higher value.***

Satisfied with Life Index: The subjective well-being index represents the overall satisfaction level as one number. The index is based on data from UNESCO, the CIA, the New Economics Foundation, the WHO, the Veenhoven Database, the Latinbarometer, the Afrobarometer, and the UNHDR. These sources are analyzed to create a value for subjective well-being: the first world map of happiness. While collecting data on subjective well-being is not an exact science, the measures used are very reliable in predicting health and welfare outcomes. ***More satisfied=higher value.***

Human Rights Index: The Cingranell-Richards (CIRI) Human Rights Dataset contains standards-based quantitative information on government respect for fifteen internationally recognized human rights for 202 countries, annually from 1981 to 2011. It is designed for use by scholars and students who seek to test theories about the causes and consequences of human rights violations, as well as policy makers and analysts who seek to estimate the human rights effects of a wide variety of institutional changes and public policies, including democratization, economic aid, military aid, structural adjustment, and humanitarian intervention. The composite index presented is an average of the twenty measures created by CIRI. ***Fewer human rights abuses=higher value.***

Social Progress: The Social Progress Index, first released in 2014 building on a beta version previewed in 2013, measures a comprehensive array of components of social and environmental performance and aggregates them into an overall framework. The index was developed based on extensive discussions with stakeholders around the world about what has been missed when policymakers focus on GDP to the exclusion of social performance. ***Better social and environment progress=higher value.***

We employed a statistical technique known as principal component analysis (PCA) that allows us to identify underlying dimensions from the original data. A PCA allows us to identify:

- underlying dimensions (components),
- what each index contributes to the underlying component (component loadings), and
- national scores on these components (component scores).

We identified one major component that we termed *Rich, Progressive, and Stable Versus Poor, Regressive, and Unstable* that explains more than two-thirds of the total variance and is associated positively with each of the indices. The loadings of all the indices, apart from *Economic Freedom*, score equally highly and positively. This component reaffirms and highlights the connection between social progress and political stability. It is the fundamental statistical backbone of explanatory variance in our data set. It suggests that economic development and social progress go hand in hand with state stability. This statistical finding reaffirms other work that shows how democratic institutions and rule of law promote economic growth. Acemoglu and colleagues, for example, show that democracies increase economic growth. They suggest democratization increases GDP per capita by about 20 percent in the long run. Democracy increases growth through greater investment in social welfare and education, the encouragement of investment and economic reforms, and the reduction of social conflict. Democracy, social stability, and economic growth go hand in hand.[16]

It is important to remember that this is a statistical technique, and the results must be analyzed carefully. As a form of scrutiny, table 3.2 lists the countries with the highest positive and negative component scores. It is clear from these results that our technique was able to distinguish between the richest and more democratic countries of the world, and the poorest and less free. So, we used the component scores of all the countries to create groupings of similar countries. We used a grouping program that allowed presetting the number of groups based on similarity of component scores. As a first cut, we identified a three-group classification of what we term *Rich*, *Poor*, and *Middle*. These are simple terms but have deeper meaning. *Rich* implies a wealth of not only economic growth but also political freedoms and social stability. The poverty of *Poor* countries is not only in low income per capita but also in the lack of political freedoms and social progress. The *Rich* include northwest Europe, North America, Australia, and New Zealand. The *Poor* world contains much of Africa and Asia. The *Middle* includes those neither very rich nor very poor and includes much of South and Central America, southern Africa, and Eastern Europe. In map 3.1, we get a better sense of the global nature of the Middle. The Middle includes those countries on the way up, such as China and Vietnam, as well as those on the way down, such as Venezuela.

Table 3.2. Top Five Positive and Negative Component Scores

Positive	
Denmark	6.29
Sweden	6.22
Norway	6.09
Switzerland	5.99
Netherlands	5.97
Negative	
Yemen	−5.14
Democratic Republic of the Congo	−5.31
Sudan	−5.48
Central African Republic	−5.59
Chad	−5.60

A five-group classification shown in map 3.2 provides a finer mesh. ***The Very Rich, Free, and Stable*** group consists of the very richest countries that are stable democracies and score high on human development and social progress. They are the rich core of the global economy with the highest standards of living and the freest of societies. It is a relatively tight nexus that covers countries only in North America, Europe, and Australasia. Japan is the only country that makes this group from Asia and there are none from Africa, the Middle East, or South and Central America. This is the very rich core of the global economy and the democratic heart of the global polity.

The ***Affluent and Free*** group is only one notch down from the very rich core. It includes countries from across the globe but is most prevalent in Eastern and Southern Europe and in South America. It includes Argentina, Estonia, and Hungary.

Between the two extremes of very rich and very poor are two groups that constitute a middle ground between rich and poor, free and unfree, stable and unstable. The ***Upper Middle*** is suggestive of a group closer to the top than the bottom. There is global coverage with countries in South and Central America, southern Africa, and Eastern Europe. Asian countries in this category include the Philippines, Thailand, and Mongolia. The ***Lower Middle*** includes countries rapidly developing, such as China, but with issues of human rights as well as poorer countries with more authoritarian, undemocratic regimes and more limited human rights. The geographic spread is concentrated in Asia and Africa and includes countries such as Algeria, Cambodia, and Vietnam.

The ***Poor and Not Free*** are the problem countries with limited economic and social progress and greater instability. The tropical region of Africa is home to many of these countries as well as the cockpit of the Middle East and Laos.

The maps present a static snapshot of an evolving world. Analyses of subsequent iterations of the respective indices, many of them updated annually, will provide a more dynamic picture of a world in the process of becoming.

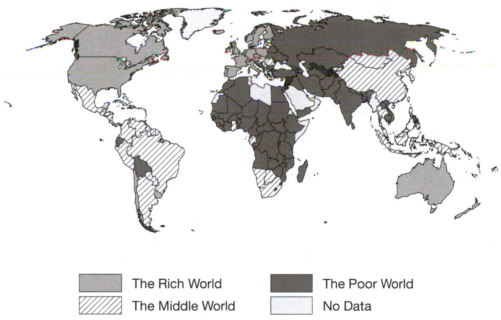

The Rich World   The Poor World
The Middle World   No Data

Map 3.1.   Three-group classification of countries

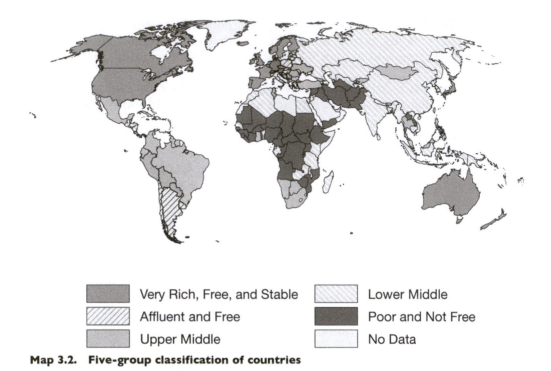

Map 3.2.   Five-group classification of countries

GLOBALIZATION AND ITS DISCONTENTS

Globalization is neither recent nor new. The year 1492 marked the first wave of globalization as the Columbian Exchange stitched the separate hemispheres into a single unit. In the late nineteenth century, another wave of globalization widened and deepened the global connections. New regulatory modes were added as major powers sought to expand their reach and negotiate with their rivals. This second wave from 1880 to 1918 saw the partition of Africa, the creation of international organizations and institutions, and the final wresting of the territory from indigenous peoples.

The sense of rupture involved in the creation of global capitalist economy is best summarized by prescient commentators of the time. Marx and Engels were always infatuated with capitalism and its dynamism and ability to change the world. In the *Communist Manifesto*, published in 1848 and in English in 1888, they outlined a program for revolutionary change. The phrase "Workers of the World Unite" is a reference to the global nature of the industrial capitalism of their day. The *Manifesto* is a biting critique of capitalism but also a form of praise for its revolutionary ability to transform and shrink the world, draw countries into the capitalist orbit, and engender urbanization that rescues people from the "idiocy of rural life." It is world of contrast change, space-time compression, global penetration of capitalism, and the incorporation of the periphery by the core. They note the subjection of Nature's forces to man, machinery, application of chemistry to industry and agriculture, steam-navigation, railways, electric telegraphs, clearing of whole continents for cultivation, canalisation of rivers, whole populations conjured out of the ground.

At one point they describe global capitalism as so revolutionary that "all that is sold melts into air."[17]

In 1910, the Austrian economist Rudolf Hilferding, a keen observer of finance capitalism of the day as well as Minister of Finance under the Weimar Republic, describes how

[i]n the newly opened up countries the capital imported into them intensifies antagonisms and excites against the intruders the growing resistance of the peoples. . . . The old social relations become completely revolutionized, the age long agrarian isolation of "nations without history" is destroyed and they are drawn in the capitalist whirlpool.[18]

The idea of "all that is solid melting into air" and the metaphor of the "whirlpool," I think deftly summarizes the idea of revolutionary change of globalizing capitalism, a world in constant motion, and a shrinking of the globe, as well as a disrupting of old orders with the possibility of something new emerging.

This second wave came to an end in the interwar period of the twentieth century when the Great Depression quickly supplanted economic growth, global trade was reduced, foreign immigration was restricted, and protectionist policies were adopted. The resulting economic chaos paved the way for a new era of global economic regulation. During the closing years of World War II, a new regime of regulation was established to stabilize the international economy. The experience of the Great Depression, when stagnation was reinforced by national governments' pursuit of protectionist policies, highlighted both the dangers of unregulated international trade and the mutual benefits of managed international cooperation. The Bretton Woods agreement was signed in 1944; its general aim was to maintain national economic sovereignty for the capitalist developed world with new rules to foster cooperation between countries. The World Bank, International Monetary Fund (IMF), and a system of fixed exchange rates were all established. The fixed exchange rates, which effectively kept currencies pegged at fixed values with the U.S. dollar acting as a convertible medium of currency, lasted until 1971 when a more liberal and deregulated global financial system emerged, ushering in the present wave of globalization. This third wave of globalization, which I have characterized as Late Modern, is a wave of reglobalization; it courses through the structures created by the previous two waves.

Globalization is under attack.[19] The electoral victory of Donald Trump, the Brexit vote, and the rise of an aggressive nationalism in mainland Europe and around the world are all part of a backlash to a global economic order that was established at the end of World War II. In 1944, delegates from the Allied countries met in Bretton Woods, New Hampshire, to establish a system repudiating prewar protectionism that was the economic backdrop to the Depression and to the rise of Fascism. A "new global order" was imagined as a result of open markets and free trade. New institutions, such as the International Monetary Fund,

the World Bank, and a precursor to the World Trade Organization, were established to coordinate the integration of national economies into an international
system. Behind the agenda was a belief that greater global integration was more
conducive to peace and prosperity than a narrow economic nationalism. Initially,
this viewpoint was more a promise than global reality. Communism still controlled large swaths of territory. And there were fiscal tensions as the new trade
system relied on fixed exchange rates, with currencies pegged to the U.S. dollar,
tied to gold. Capital could be moved easily around the world only with the collapse of fixed exchange rates and with the unmooring of the dollar from the gold
standard in the late 1960s. Dollars generated in Europe by U.S. multinationals
could be invested in suburban housing projects in Asia, mining developments in
Australia, and factories in the Philippines through London. An even wider world
for global capital mobility was created with the collapse of the Soviet Union in
1990–1991 and with China's entry into the WTO in 2001.

Economic Globalization

While capital could now scour the world to ensure the best returns, labor was
fixed in place, so there was a profound change in the relative bargaining power
between the two away from organized labor toward a footloose capital. Instead,
there was a consequent severing of the ties between the national economic interests of labor and global economic interests of capital.

This freeing up of trade restrictions meant that goods once made in the
United States might be made in China and then imported to the United States.
The result of this trade transformation is a global shift in manufacturing as the
industrial base shifted from the high-wage areas of North America and Western
Europe to the cheaper wage areas of East Asia—first Japan then South Korea—
and more recently China and Vietnam. As factories shuttered, mechanized, or
moved overseas, the living standard of the working class in the West declined.
The workshop of the world shifted. The poverty rate in China in 1981 was 84
percent; by 2010 it had fallen to 12 percent. The global shift meant a redistribution of global incomes away from the blue-collar workers in the West to the new
middle-class of East and Southeast Asia.

With the decline of Socialism, there seemed to be no other political or
economic ideology in the West that could compete with this new reliance on
free trade and open markets. No alternative seemed possible against those who
argued that the economy could only be based on free trade, global markets, and
production chains that snaked across national borders. Economic globalization
promised to raise all living standards in the long run. For many, the long run
seemed too long a wait. A growing chasm in living standards emerged between
economic elites and those blue-collar masses who saw little improvement with
economic globalization; indeed, as inequality increased, their relative positions
declined. The backlash against economic globalization was marked most in
those countries such as the United States, where economic dislocation unfolded
with weak safety nets and limited investment for job retraining.

There are calls now for various forms of economic nationalisms. While they
may not unravel the thickest trade ties of economic globalization, they do reframe

the debate about how the national economy may fit into a global framework. We are witnessing a new geopolitical dynamic as economic nationalisms attempt to renegotiate the relationship between the state and the global economy.

Political Globalization

Political globalization involves the smoothing of regulatory systems and legislative structures between states often in order to promote and to further economic globalization. Trading organizations, such as the North American Free Trade Agreement (NAFTA), were established to harmonize and to synchronize regulations and legal frameworks of different nation-states to reduce the friction of cross-border trade. Differences were flattened to smooth international transactions. While economic unions became common, more formal political unions among states are still rare events. A prominent exception is the European Union, an economic and political alliance of most European countries, which we discuss in chapter 7. As a relatively new political union, the European Union dramatically highlights the populist resistance to the political globalization occurring around the world.[20]

We should be careful with the term *populism*. Traditionally, it specified demands by citizens for more political power and greater economic equality. Originally, populism's egalitarian, anti-elitist stance held out the promise of better conditions for ordinary people.[21] In the United States, a high point of populist resonance was Roosevelt's New Deal, which resisted the bankers' demand to cut wages and to restrict public spending during the Great Depression. In the UK, the welfare state was founded after World War II by a Labour Government. It established the National Health System, which has become both an ongoing institutional practice and an enduring national ideal.

More recent manifestations have a more authorization streak. Trump in the United States, Bolsonaro in Brazil, Duda in Poland, and Orban in Hungary are all examples—in different forms—of *authoritarian populism*, which uses an anti-elitist rhetoric to promote an authoritarian agenda. It is not a conservatism, which is opposed to change, but an authoritarian claim that only some people are the "real people" of the nation. This is an ideology that promotes homogeneity rather than diversity, resists the claims of marginalized and minority groups for greater political equality, and flourishes in a time of cultural globalization.[22]

Cultural Globalization

The "flattening" of the world through easier travel, trade, and the movement of people, ideas, and practice creates a more diverse ensemble of cultural forms in cuisine, movies, values, and lifestyles. Cosmopolitanism was embraced by many of the elites but feared by some. The foreign "other" became an object of fear and resentment, whether in the form of minorities seeking greater political rights, in immigrants, or in imported cultures.

The backlash to cultural globalization is evident in the rise of religious fundamentalism and political nationalism.[23] Often the two are intertwined, as in the ruling Bharatiya Janata Party (BJP) party in India. Old-time religion can be a refuge from the "ache of modernity," producing a standard set of simple answers to complex questions. There is also a rising nationalism as "native purity," that is contrasted with "profane foreign." Across Europe, from the UK to Bulgaria and Poland, new exclusionary nationalisms resist the entry of the foreign. And even in those countries that benefited from economic globalization, there is a backlash against cultural globalization. An idealized past is contrasted to the seeming cultural chaos of modernity. The "invention of tradition" grows more strident.[24] Immigration is the most profound form of cultural globalization that also results in dramatic heightening of national and racial identities. In the United States, White, native-born Americans moved from being the default category to a source of identity clearly mobilized by the Trump campaigns.

The linkage between cultural globalization and authoritarianism is hinted at and prefigured in the ideas of Hannah Arendt. She argued that, in a time of change and social dislocation, there is profound need for a sense of both place and belonging that favors homogeneity and order.[25] A world that is rapidly changing and increasingly cosmopolitan has as its "antimatter" the rise of authoritarian nationalism. There is a "seductive lure of authoritarianism" that proffers simple, reassuring answers to complex, disturbing issues, clear demarcations between "us and them," and a return to an imagined past of a happy folk.[26] Compared to the insecurity and uncertainty of a cosmopolitan globalizing world, a populist authoritarianism seeks to create and maintain comfort, order, security, and belonging.

Globalization has become a catchword encompassing a rapid, disquieting, disruptive, social, and economic change of the past twenty-five years. The backlash takes the form of economic nationalism and authoritarian populism. The "globalization project" contains much that is desirable, that is, improvements in living conditions through global trade, reducing conflict and threat of war through political globalization, and encouraging cultural diversity through an ever-widening globalization. Yet globalization in its present form has generated economic inequalities, political uncertainties, and cultural anxiety that is restructuring the relationships between the nation-state and a global order, changing and transforming each in turn.

GEOPOLITICAL HOTSPOT: WHAT'S IN A NAME, EAST SEA/SEA OF JAPAN

It's not a major geopolitical issue—more of a disagreement between two allies. And yet it has the ability to conjure centuries-old enmity, distort decades-old alliances, and undermine current geopolitical strategies. It is also an example of the importance of *scale* and *effect* in geopolitics. Traditional geopolitics focuses on specific territories at specific times. The world of becoming is more complicated. Events in the here and now jump both temporal and spatial scales as they entangle the present with multiple pasts and operate on the regional, national, and international scales all at the same time.[27] As an example, Tanya Heikkila and colleagues looked at the complex hydro-politics of the Mekong River Basin at both the domestic and international levels.[28] Our example examines the naming dispute between Japan and South Korea.[29]

We humanize the world by turning space into place. One of the main and most important ways we do this is by assigning names. To name provides meaning and confers identity. To name is to create order. If names create order, then the fundamental question that a more critical toponymy asks is, *whose order*? Naming is an act of power that privileges some name-giving groups over others. The condescension of history erases some names, while others remain contested.

The Sea of Japan/East Sea debate between Japan and South Korea provides a case study of a colonial/postcolonial naming issue between two sovereign states. Since the early 1990s, a sustained campaign has been waged, in large part underwritten by the Republic of Korea (hereafter South Korea), to promote a global recognition that the East Sea is a legitimate name and that the singular name of Sea of Japan is a toponymic injustice.

Naming and renaming are infused with emotions and feelings. Feelings can run so high that changing names is sometimes only possible after long campaigns. In 1975, the Alaskan Legislature sought to change the name of the highest mountain in North America from Mount McKinley to the indigenous name of Denali. Mount McKinley was named after a politician from Ohio who was president of the United States from 1897 to 1901. A long time ago for a president best known perhaps for being assassinated, but still so important that the Ohio Congressional Delegation resisted the change and blocked its passage as late as 2015 when the secretary of the interior invoked her powers to name geographic features if the U.S. Board of Geographic Names (USBGN) took too long. Place names are not just descriptors; they are emotional connections, filaments of memory, strands of longing. Place names are infused with affective power.

There is a very long history in Korea, dating back at least 1,500 years, of using the term "East Sea" to describe the body of water to the east of the Korean peninsula. By the eighteenth and nineteenth centuries, Western explorers used a number of names, including Sea of Corea and Gulf of Corea. Even early Japanese maps sometimes used the term Sea of Joseon or Sea of Japan to reference the same body of water.

As part of an expansive Japanese imperialism, Korea became a Japanese protectorate in 1905 and was annexed formally in 1910. The domination took many forms, including a toponymic colonialism. A Japanese naming system was applied to all maps, including place names, roads, and natural features of the country in an expression of Japanese power. The singular use of the name "Sea of Japan"—with its erasure of "East Sea"—was formalized in international usage at the 1929 Conference of the International Hydrographic Organization (IHO) when the term "Sea of Japan" was recognized as the only official name, and reconfirmed at subsequent meetings of the IHO in 1937 and 1953. Korea had no independent voice at the initial meeting, and there was little international sensitivity to the colonial context of the new name.

At the end of the Korean War (1950–1953), the Korean peninsula was divided into two countries, the Democratic People's Republic of Korea (North Korea) and the Republic of Korea (South Korea). North Korea defiantly used the name "East Sea." In South Korea, there was little official attention to the Sea of Japan/East

Sea naming issue due to South Korea's history of elite collaboration with the Japanese colonial regime. Some of the South Korean military and economic elites prospered under the period of Japanese control and had little interest in raising issues about South Korea's colonial relations with Japan. However, 1960 marks a change. The brief Second Republic (1960–1961) saw the beginnings of a more critical attitude toward Japan. Military rule (1961–1963) and then a series of authoritarian governments (1963–1987) adopted a more overt nationalism and East Sea became a commonly used term. Then as South Korea democratized, there was an even greater articulation of the colonial experience's negative aspects. In September 1991, both South and North Korea joined the United Nations. A more globalized South Korea could now address the naming issue in international forums.

South Korea initially sought to effect change through formal channels of international organizations. In 1992, Korean officials raised the naming issue at the sixth United Nations Conference of Standardization of Geographical Names (UNCSGN) in New York City. In 2007, the two Koreas combined to submit another naming amendment at the ninth UNCSGN. The official position of the South Korean government is that the correct international usage should be the dual name "East Sea/Sea of Japan." The official Japanese position is to resist either changing the designation of Sea of Japan for East Sea or to adopt a dual name. They argue that "Sea of Japan" is widely accepted in international usage and adopting a dual name would be confusing.

As South Korea became more self-confident and wealthier, with its migrants forming large and successful communities in the United States, the country was more able to address the naming issue. There is a powerful constituency that sees the name "East Sea" as a central feature of Korean national identity. In recognition of this constituency, South Korean official government documents all use the term "East Sea." The South Korean Ministry of Foreign Affairs as well the Ministry of Education, Korean Hydrographic and Oceanographic Agency, the National Geographic Information Institute, and the Korean Culture and Information Service, among other agencies, all promote the usage of "East Sea." South Korea also uses its soft power to influence the change of name. Campaigns are waged through quasi-government institutions, such as the Korea Foundation. The Korea Foundation was established in 1991 to promote a better international understanding of Korea by supporting overseas research and hosting conferences and other events. The official policy of the Korea Foundation is to employ the term "East Sea." Other institutions with similar strategies and tactics include the Society for East Sea, established in 2004, and the Northeast Asian History Foundation, established in 2006. In effect, South Korea has a two-track naming policy. Government bodies more concerned with domestic issues and domestic audiences use the term East Sea almost exclusively while the official policy for foreign consumption is the use of the dual name.

In the formal arenas of naming regimes, there is stout resistance to changing names, using dual names, or being involved in the Korea-Japan conflict. The more the South Koreans have pushed the issue, the more overtly politicized it becomes. The formal place name regimes shy away from entering such a political minefield. The United Nations Group of Experts on Geographic Names

(UNGEGN) and the IHO have largely avoided making a definitive decision, hoping South Korea and Japan can sort it out between themselves. The USBGN persists in the use of the term "Sea of Japan" and does not currently envision the use of dual naming. While the USBGN is only binding for U.S. federal agencies, it exerts tremendous influence in the United States and around the world; many other institutions rely on the board for guidance. The U.S. government has distanced itself from the debate, preferring not to antagonize two important allies.

In the United States, despite lack of success with the USBGN, the South Korean government, in alliance with the large and influential Korean diaspora, has been more successful at influencing politics at the state level. In February 2014, the State of Virginia House of Delegates, after intensive lobbying by the South Korean government and the local Korea-American community of more than 85,000 people, voted to ensure that the name "East Sea" would be used alongside "Sea of Japan" in all textbooks used in Virginia schools. Despite intense lobbying by the Japanese government, the law was enacted when Governor McAuliffe signed the bill into law. In 2019, the New York State Education Department (NYSED) advised all superintendents and principals in the state's education system to use the name "East Sea/Sea of Japan."

The government of South Korea through its formal organization such as the Ministry of Foreign Affairs and state-funded, nongovernment organizations, such as the Korea Foundation, the Society for East Sea, and the Northeast Asian History Foundation have all worked to promote the naming issue in a variety of discourses, including newspapers, textbooks, maps, and atlases. In our study we examined a variety of discourses over an eighteen-month period from mid-2017 to the end of 2018: in journals and newspapers, educational material, including atlases and textbooks and internet sources. For each of these discourses we identified different possible namings: "East Sea," "East Sea or Sea of Japan" and "Sea of Japan." The data that we collected revealed that by 2018, out of a total of 541 citations across all discourses that we examined, only 43 percent used the singular "Sea of Japan" while 48 percent employed some form of dual naming. The singular use of "Sea of Japan" continues to dominate in U.S. journals and newspapers and to a lesser extent in the international English-language newspapers. Dual naming is more prevalent in the educational materials of books and especially atlases and in internet searches. Overall, it is clear that dual naming has gained traction as a third-party compromise to deal with a contested issue.

The Korean effort to have the name formally changed has so far proved elusive. The United States and world organizations responsible for naming have yet to rule in their favor. Their campaign has been much more successful in shifting the discourse away from an automatic and singular use of "Sea of Japan" in the less formal areas of everyday linguistic practice in atlases, journals, newspapers, textbooks, and the internet. Dual naming is now a *de facto* if not the *de jure* reality. More people around the world are now aware that the singular use of the term Sea of Japan is not the only possible designation. The campaign has been successful, not in achieving a universal change or in formal recognition of a dual naming, but in making a change across different discourses and in making the name itself an issue that journalists, authors, and publishers now must address. The contestation itself is now part of the naming discourse. The success of the campaign shows what a concerted national effort by an affluent and well-connected country using its soft power can achieve. Change was affected by one state using its soft power to change the linguistic narrative from an acceptance of a singular name to the promotion and wider diffusion of an alternative renaming or dual naming.

This case study is important in its own right, but also for what it reveals about scale jumping in both space and time, postcolonial toponymy issues, and the national use of soft power to effect toponymic change.

SUGGESTED READINGS

Applebaum, A. (2020). *Twilight of democracy: The seductive lure of authoritarianism.* New York: Doubleday.

Arrighi, G. (1994). *The long twentieth century: Money, power, and the origins of our times.* London: Verso.

Dicken, P. (2015, 7th ed.). *Global shift: Mapping the contours of the world economy.* New York: Guildford.

Haggard, S. (2018). *Developmental states.* Cambridge: Cambridge University Press.

Harvey, D. (2014). *Seventeen contradictions and the end of capitalism.* Oxford: Oxford University Press.

Modelski, G. (1987). *Long cycles in world politics.* London: Macmillan.

Rasler, K. A., & Thompson, W. R. (2014). *The great powers and global struggle, 1490–1990.* Lexington: University Press of Kentucky.

Short, J. R., & Dubots, L. (2020). Contesting place names: The East Sea/Sea of Japan naming issue. *Geographical Review,* 1–20. https://doi.org/10.1080/00167428.2020.1827936.

Short, J. R., Vélez-Hagan, J., & Dubots, L. (2019). What do global metrics tell us about the world? *Social Sciences, 8,* 136. https://www.mdpi.com/2076-0760/8/5/136.

Wallerstein, I. (1988). *The modern world system: A second era of great expansion of the capitalist world economy 1730–1840.* San Diego: Academic Press.

NOTES

1. Wallerstein, I. (1974). *The modern world system.* New York: Academic Press; Wallerstein, I. (1979). *The capitalist world economy.* Cambridge: Cambridge University Press; Wallerstein, I. (1988). *The modern world system: A second era of great expansion of the capitalist world economy 1730–1840.* San Diego: Academic Press. Wallerstein's ideas have spawned a great deal of subsequent interest. See the academic *Journal of World-Systems Research.* They underpin much academic geopolitics; for examples, see Flint, C., & Taylor, P. J. (2018, 7th ed.). *Political geography: World-economy, nation state and locality.* Abingdon: Routledge; Agnew, J. (2005). *Hegemony: The new shape of global power.* Philadelphia: Temple University Press.

2. Amin, S. (2014). *Capitalism in the age of globalization: The management of contemporary society.* London: Zed; Frank, A. G. (2011). *World accumulation.* New York: New York University Press.

3. Braudel, F. (1972–1973). *The Mediterranean and the Mediterranean world in the age of Philip II.* (2 Volumes). New York: Harper and Row; Braudel, F. (1981–1984). *Civilization and capitalism 15–18th century.* (3 Volumes). London: Collins.

4. Arrighi, G. (1994). *The long twentieth century: Money, power, and the origins of our times*. London: Verso.

5. Harvey, D. (2005). *The new imperialism*. Oxford: Oxford University Press; Harvey, D. (2010). *The enigma of capital*. London: Profile; Harvey, D. (2014). *Seventeen contradictions and the end of capitalism*. Oxford: Oxford University Press.

6. Modelski, G. (1987). *Long cycles in world politics*. London: Macmillan. In a similar vein see Kennedy, P. (1989). *The rise and fall of the great powers: Economic change and military conflict from 1500 to 2000*. New York: Random House; Rasler, K. A., & Thompson, W. R. (2014). *The great powers and global struggle, 1490–1990*. Lexington: University Press of Kentucky.

7. Candlin, K. (2018). The role of the enslaved in the "Fedon Rebellion" of 1795. *Slavery and Abolition, 39*, 685–707; Cox, E. L. (1982). Fedon's Rebellion 1795–96: Causes and consequences. *Journal of Negro History, 67*, 7–19; Murphy, T. (2018). A reassertion of rights: Fedon's Rebellion, Grenada, 1795–96. *La Révolution française. Cahiers de l'Institut d'histoire de la Révolution française*, 14. https://doi.org/10.4000/lrf.2017.

8. Brollo, F., Nannicini, T., Perotti, R., & Tabellini, G. (2013). The political resource curse. *American Economic Review, 103*, 1759–96; Sachs, J. D., & Warner, A. M. (2001). The curse of natural resources. *European Economic Review, 45*, 827–38.

9. Haggard, S. (2018). *Developmental states*. Cambridge: Cambridge University Press; Leftwich, A. (1995). Bringing politics back in: Towards a model of the developmental state. *Journal of Development Studies, 31*, 400–27; Wong, J. (2004). The adaptive developmental state in East Asia. *Journal of East Asian Studies, 4*, 345–62.

10. Dicken, P. (2015, 7th ed.). *Global shift: Mapping the contours of the world economy*. New York: Guildford.

11. Mazarr, M. J. (2015). *Mastering the gray zone: Understanding a changing era of conflict*. Carlisle, PA: Strategic Studies Institute and U.S. Army War College Press.

12. "Little green men" refers to Russian soldiers in unmarked green army uniforms carrying modern Russian military hardware who became a decisive force in eastern Ukraine in 2014.

13. Brenner, N., Peck, J., & Theodore, N. (2010). Variegated neoliberalization: Geographies, modalities, pathways. *Global Networks, 10*, 182–222.

14. Chernomas, R., Hudson, I., & Hudson, M. (2019). *Neoliberal lives: Work, politics, nature, and health in the contemporary United States*. Manchester: Manchester University Press.

15. Short, J. R., Vélez-Hagan, J., & Dubots, L. (2019). What do global metrics tell us about the world? *Social Sciences, 8*, 136. https://www.mdpi.com/2076-0760/8/5/136.

16. Acemoglu, D., Naidu, S., Restrepo, P., & Robinson, J. A. (2019). Democracy does cause growth. *Journal of Political Economy, 127*, 47–100.

17. Marx, K., & Engels, F. (orig. 1848). *Manifesto of the communist party*. https://www.marxists.org/archive/marx/works/1848/communist-manifesto/ch01.htm#007.

18. Hilferding, R. (1981; orig. published in German in 1910). *Finance capital: A study in the latest phase of capitalist development*. New York: Routledge. The actual quote is from Lenin, V. I. (1917, first pub in Russian). *Imperialism: The highest stage of capitalism*. https://www.workers.org/marcy/cd/marxlen/imperial.htm.

19. I draw heavily on my previous paper: Short, J. R. (2016, November 28). Globalization and its discontents. *The Conversation*. https://theconversation.com/globalization-and-its-discontents-why-theres-a-backlash-and-how-it-needs-to-change-68800.

20. Agnew, J., & Shin, M. (2019). *Mapping populism: Taking politics to the people*. Lanham: Rowman & Littlefield; Casaglia, A., Coletti, R., Lizotte, C., Agnew, J., Mamadouh, V., and Minca, C. (2020). Interventions on European nationalist populism and bordering

in time of emergencies. *Political Geography, 82.* https://www.ncbi.nlm.nih.gov/pmc/articles/PMC7365071/.

21. Franks, T. (2020). *The people, no: A brief history of anti-populism.* New York: Metropolitan.

22. Jenner, K. (2005). *The authoritarian dynamic.* Cambridge: Cambridge University Press.

23. Norris, P., & Inglehart, R. (2019). *Cultural backlash: Trump, Brexit, and authoritarian populism.* Cambridge: Cambridge University Press.

24. Hobsbawn, E., & Ranger, T. (eds.). (1983). *The invention of tradition.* Cambridge: Cambridge University Press.

25. Arendt, H. (1966, 3rd ed., original 1951). *The origins of totalitarianism.* New York: Harcourt Brace.

26. Applebaum, A. (2020). *Twilight of democracy: The seductive lure of authoritarianism.* New York: Doubleday.

27. Campbell, C. J. (2018). Space, place and scale: Human geography and spatial history in *Past and Present. Past & Present, 239,* e23–e45. https://academic.oup.com/past/article/239/1/e23/2957256?login=true#.

28. Heikkila, T., Gerlak, A. K., & Wolf, A. (2014, July 23–25). A study of conflict and cooperation in the Mekong River Basin: How issues and scale matter. In *Proceedings of the FLACSO-ISA Global and Regional Powers in a Changing World Conference,* Buenos Aires, Argentina. http://web.isanet.org/Web/Conferences/FLACSO-ISA%20Buenos Aires%202014/Archive/e5bb2629-b8c0-4711-889c-b8825baaff77.pdf.

29. The material is drawn from Short, J. R., & Dubots, L. (2020). Contesting place names: The East Sea/Sea of Japan naming issue. *Geographical Review,* 1–20. https://doi.org/10.1080/00167428.2020.1827936.

II

THE NEW WORLD ORDER

4

The United States and Its Neighbors

GEOPOLITICAL CONTEXT

This chapter focuses on the United States of America. The United States provides numerous examples of themes discussed in chapters 2 and 3. It is a *superpower* with global engagements and elements of both *hard* and *soft* power. It is at the very the core of the *global economy* and was a prime architect of the *global polity* that emerged after World War II. From 1945 to 1989 it was one of the pillars of the *bipolar world*. In recent years, however, it is under strain. At home, there are recognitions of the growing costs of its global role, especially in the wake of the disastrous invasion of Iraq and the long war in Afghanistan. The United States has experienced *imperial overstretch*. There is a growing populist resentment against the never-ending wars and a *legitimation crisis* reinforced by the growing inequality exacerbated by *neoliberalism* and *economic globalization*. The backlash to globalization is expressed in cultural anxiety, economic uncertainty, and growing political polarization that were vividly and shockingly expressed in the insurrection at the Capitol on January 6, 2021. Abroad, the United States is still trying to figure out its global role post–Cold War. For a period from around 1989 until 2001, the political elite believed in the untrammeled ability of the United States to shape the world. The belief was subsequently shattered by the 2001 terrorist attack, the failures of the War on Terror, the global financial crisis, the rise of China, the persistent opposition of Russia, and its ambiguity about how to interact with its European allies. The United States is now trying to navigate a complex geopolitical space in facing the challenges of a resurgent China, an intransigent Russia, and European allies unsure of the U.S. commitments.[1] The competition between the United States and China, in particular, is also perhaps the most recent example of the *Thucydides Trap*.

Despite these mounting issues it remains the world's most dominant military power with global reach and unsurpassed interventionist capabilities. It has the strategic advantage of a location between two oceans, considerable soft as well as hard power, and immense economic resources as one of the bigger and richer economies in the world. Since the end of the Cold War, it has emerged as the global hegemon, albeit one faced with terrorist threats and growing competition from other powers in a world order that is rapidly changing. We will consider how and when the United States arrived at this position of global dominance and some of its costs, benefits, and consequences. We will also explore what the future may hold for a global superpower with rising near-peer competitors. Even if a new world order emerges, the United States will continue to play a significant role.

The U.S. status as a global superpower makes neighbors of almost every other country in the world, although some are closer than others in a transactional sense. Later chapters will explore the role of the United States in regional orders across the world. In this chapter, we will only discuss the immediate geographical neighbors of Canada and Mexico in terms of "closer to home" border issues (see map 4.1).

Map 4.1.   The United States and its neighbors (International Mapping)

IMPERIAL REPUBLIC

The United States is the preeminent power of the moment, yet it has been preparing for this role from its inception. Even as loyal colonists, Americans chafed at the territorial limitations set by the UK. In 1763, the British drew a Proclamation Line along the crest of the Appalachian Mountains to restrict settlements. The British were eager to maintain good relations with Native American allies, especially the powerful Iroquois, to counter the French and their Native American allies in the interior. The American settlers, in contrast, saw the land beyond the line as a rich opportunity denied them by a distant sovereign.

Ambitious men like George Washington resisted the British limitation on westward expansion. Regarding the Proclamation Line forbidding settlement west of Appalachia, he wrote to a friend in 1767,

> I can never look upon the Proclamation in any other light (but this I say between ourselves) than as a temporary expedient to quiet the minds of the Indians. It must fall, of course, in a few years, especially when those Indians consent to our occupying those lands. Any person who neglects hunting out good lands, and in some measure marking and distinguishing them for his own, in order to keep others from settling them will never regain it.[2]

The colonists' anger at the restrictions and the issues of taxation without representation led to the War of Independence and eventually to the creation of a new republic. George Washington envisioned the United States as an imperial expansionist republic at its birth. Behind the bright idealism of the declaration of rights and enunciation of principles in the founding of the new republic, there was the hard edge of a compulsive land grab.

The barrier of the Proclamation Line did not last long; ambitious colonials and then the new nation laid claim to territory across the continent. The republic wrested territory from indigenous peoples in a long series of conflicts that led to the territorial annexation of tribal lands and the eventual expulsion and near annihilation of traditional landholders. Land was also claimed from the competing empires of Spain and Britain. In the north, the new United States sought to expand at the expense of the British Empire and in the south and west at the expense of the French and Spanish empires and later the Mexican state.

The United States was both an inheritor of three centuries of European expansion in North America and a new actor on the stage of imperial competition. Through purchase, secession, assertion of claims, military conquest, and annexation, the thirteen colonies, initially pressed up against the eastern seaboard, expanded to become the United States of continental proportions.

Even before the Americans had title to the land, they claimed it in forms of *cartographic imperialism*. In 1816 the Scottish-born, Philadelphia-based mapmaker John Melish (1771–1822) published a map of the United States (map 4.2). Compared to his map made three years earlier, this later map extended the depiction of the country all the way from the Atlantic to the Pacific. Never mind that all this territory was then not part of the nation: the new republic had found its epic continental representation.[3]

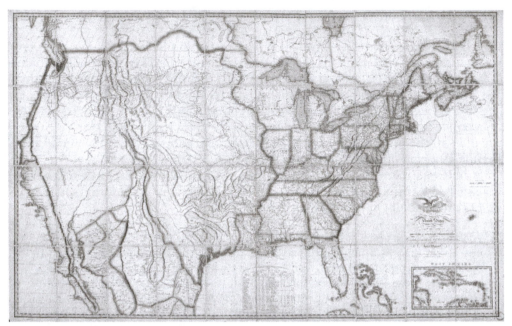

Map 4.2. Cartographic imperialism. Map of the United States of America with the contiguous British and Spanish possessions, John Melish, Philadelphia, 1816. (Library of Congress Geography and Map Division Washington, DC)

The cartographic imperialism was backed up by geopolitical claims. The *Monroe Doctrine* of 1823 warned off any further encroachment or interference by European powers in the Americas. The doctrine announced to the world that the United States had an exclusive sphere of influence in the New World. At the time, the doctrine was more a statement of hope; the United States had limited military power to underwrite its expansive claims. The Monroe Doctrine was reinforced by the *Roosevelt Corollary* in 1904 when the United States had a larger military and naval presence. The corollary stated that the United States would get involved in disputes between European and Latin American countries. It subsequently became a blank check for U.S. involvement in South and especially Central America. U.S. presidents cited the Roosevelt Corollary as justification for involvements in Cuba (1906–1909), Nicaragua (1909–1910, 1912–1925, and 1926–1933), Haiti (1915–1934), and the Dominican Republic (1916–1924).

There were ideologies to support the imperial territorial imperative. *Manifest Destiny*, first announced in 1845, gave theological justification for continental expansion.[4] It was employed to justify the war with Mexico. The frontier's closing, officially announced in 1890, provoked concern that the days of expansionism were ending. In 1893 the young historian Frederick Jackson Turner (1861–1931) saw in an expanding frontier the essential source of a vital democracy.[5] Continual expansion and territorial enlargement became associated with ensuring economic growth and republican democracy. On the other hand, there were also the critics who argued, and continue to argue, that expansion at home and overseas diverts the nation from the construction of a true democracy at home.[6]

THE RISE TO EMPIRE

By the second half of the nineteenth century, the United States joined Western powers in what has been termed the *age of imperialism*, the period from 1870 to 1914 when much of the world and especially Africa and parts of Asia were divvied up by imperial powers as territorial annexations to secure markets, guarantee imports of cheap primary products, and stave off the territorial ambitions of competing powers.

Foreign interventions took multiple forms after the Civil War. The United States expanded its reach across the Pacific toward Asia. Alaska was acquired in 1867 from Russia, and a series of Pacific islands were annexed, including Midway (1867), Hawaii (1888), and Samoa (1889). This expansion was an early pivot to Asia. American business interests were very keen on accessing the huge potential of China that was then being exploited by other foreign powers. Many of the Pacific island annexations were part of a strategy of ensuring an American chain of ports to Asia and especially to China. Other countries were also interested in the vast market of China. The U.S. *Open-Door Policy*, announced in 1885, argued that trade with China should be open to all countries. It was designed to head off any European power's attempts to monopolize trade with China.

Business interests were especially keen on such expansion because it had the possibility to increase the size of markets for both imports and exports. In the zero-sum business mentality of the time, the world's wealth was like a giant cake fixed in size. One nation's slice was always purchased at the expense of others. The idea of endless expansion became part of the nation's DNA. The colonial adventures were attempts to emulate the success of the British Empire, and the closing of the frontier in 1890 created fears that expansion was coming to an end. Business interests and political forces looked beyond the territorial limits to see a larger world beyond the existing borders as a source for endless business expansion.

The decline of the Spanish Empire in the New World provided new opportunities for a rising United States. The Spanish-American War of 1898 lasted only ten weeks. Superior U.S. forces quickly overwhelmed a weakened Spain, and under the 1898 Treaty of Paris, the United States effectively gained control of Cuba, Puerto Rico, Guam, and the Philippines. The rise to empire has a complicated domestic context. There was the muscular militarism of people like Theodore Roosevelt, who saw the military mission as a test of the nation's manhood. There were business interests that saw new untapped markets for American commerce. And even avowed anti-imperialists such as Andrew Carnegie and Mark Twain supported the invasion of Cuba for what they saw as a humanitarian mission to liberate the Cuban people from Spanish oppression. There was also a Social Darwinism, briefly described in chapter 1. In the United States in the late nineteenth and early twentieth centuries, an explicitly racist imperial ideology was a taken-for-granted assumption that legitimized the takeover of countries such as the Philippines. But there was also resistance. In January 1899 the U.S. Senate voted to ratify the peace treaty with Spain. Some senators argued that taking control of the territories was a civilizing mission, a sacred duty, placed upon the United States by its wealth and moral character. Others, such as

Senator Hoar, who spoke for many when he noted that "This Treaty will make us a vulgar, commonplace empire, controlling subject races and vassal states."[7] The treaty ratification passed by only two votes.

Cuba was turned into a client state. Puerto Rico and Guam were incorporated as territories, and the Philippines, after a bitter war, became a colony. The Philippine-American War (1899–1902) was a dirty war with atrocities on both sides. More than fifty thousand Filipino soldiers and civilians were killed and a further two hundred thousand died from consequent famine, cholera, and other diseases. In a precursor of things to come, water torture by U.S. forces became a common interrogation technique. Domestic repugnance at the campaign crystallized in the American Anti-Imperialist League. It would not be the last time that the United States would be involved in what promised to be a "splendid little war" that in reality turned into a "large, inglorious, vicious conflict."[8]

The drift to empire was contested. In 1901 a case was brought to the Supreme Court that questioned whether the United States could rule the occupied territories under martial law. Chief Justice Melville Fuller argued

> The idea that this country may acquire territories anywhere upon the earth, by conquest or treaty, and hold them as mere colonies or provinces . . . is wholly inconsistent with the spirit and genius, as well as with the words, of the Constitution.[9]

He was in the minority in the 5–4 decision. The growth of the U.S. empire was not preordained or automatic: it grew through such pivotal and contested decisions.[10]

The United States gained permanent territorial additions through annexation, sale, and appropriation. In the early years, it was an empire that was embraced in popular culture. Figure 4.1, for example, is from a children's book published in 1900. Later, it was an empire partly hidden through the creative use of designations such as "protectorates" and "permanent territories."[11] Although some became independent, such as the Philippines, Micronesia, Marshall Islands, and Palau, even to this day the United States still officially has five permanent territories: Puerto Rico, U.S. Virgin Islands, Guam, Northern Mariana Islands, and American Samoa.

The United States became a serial interventionist in the affairs of Central and South America. There were the excursions to prop up friendly regimes and to overthrow those unwise enough to provoke the wrath of the United States. Cuba was routinely invaded, first in 1906, then in 1911, and again 1917 in order to quell domestic disturbance. Punitive expeditions were sent to Mexico in 1911 and 1916; Nicaragua became a protectorate from 1903 to 1933; and Haiti was brought under direct U.S. military control from 1915 to 1934. Central America became the U.S. backyard. Nominally independent countries were economically and politically dominated by the United States. And as a last resort, when the *collaborative elite system* broke down or collapsed, the United States intervened. The United States engineered the breakaway of Panama from Colombia in order to ensure the construction and U.S. control of the Panama Canal. Land was annexed in the heart of Central America to build and control the canal.

Figure 4.1. Teaching Empire (Frank Baum, The Navy Alphabet, 1900. University of Florida Baldwin Library https://ufdc.ufl.edu/UF00087056 /00001/20x)

The United States also purchased islands from Denmark—now the U.S. Virgin Islands—to reinforce strategic control over the canal in the Caribbean.

We have an amazing critique of this policy. Major General Smedley Butler served in the U.S. Marine Corps from 1898 to 1931. In a fascinating article first published in 1935 he describes his role:

> I spent thirty-three years and four months in active military service. . . . I spent most of my time being a high-class muscle-man for Big Business, for Wall Street and for the Bankers. In short, I was a racketeer, a gangster for capitalism. . . . I helped make Mexico, especially Tampico, safe for American oil interests in 1914. I helped make Haiti and Cuba a decent place for the National City Bank boys to collect revenue in. I helped in the raping of half a dozen Central American republics for the benefits of Wall Street.[12]

Few military memoirs then or since, have such a devastating insight.

In the global scheme of things, however, U.S. actions were small and limited. The Monroe Doctrine only applied to the Americas and even there the United States respected existing European colonial possessions. The newly annexed territories were small or had limited appeal to the major powers of Britain, France, Russia, and latterly Germany and Japan. An expansionist ideology had to compete with a strong strain of isolationist tendencies in domestic politics. The relatively small military and the existence of other imperial powers with larger armies and bigger navies placed severe restrictions on U.S. projections of power. Hegemony in the Americas allowed the United States to bully small nations in the hemisphere and to undertake small-scale police actions to quell peasant uprisings or put down populist movements against the local elites, but it did not have enough military heft to sustain a global geopolitical strategy. On the eve of World War II, the United States had no military alliances and few troops stationed on foreign soil.

The Rise to Global Empire

In the context of shell-shocked and war-shattered colonial powers such as the UK and France, the United States emerged more fully onto the world stage in the immediate aftermath of World War I. President Woodrow Wilson sought a new world order and in 1918 announced a fourteen-point plan that included a demand for freedom of the seas, reduction of trade barriers, and the establishment of the League of Nations. It was a call for a form of *economic globalization* that only fully came to fruition after the end of the next world war. There were also more specific points, including the establishment of an independent Poland and the breakup of the Austro-Hungarian and Ottoman empires. The United States was now a player in the geopolitical shaping of a new world order. It lasted only briefly, however; the United States soon retreated from the stage of world affairs as the country sank into isolationism and an economic depression.

World War II saw the direct involvement of the United States in global affairs. Its entry to the war was delayed because of strong isolationist sentiment. Although World War II began in Europe and started in 1939, it was only in 1941—after the Japanese attack on Pearl Harbor—that the United States joined the war against the Axis powers. It proved decisive. The United States provided enough money, personnel, and materiel to ensure Allied victory in Asia and Europe.

At the end of the war, the United States began a pronounced deployment of its military forces. By 1948, the number of troops mobilized decreased to just over a half-million in the army and less than a half-million in the navy from a peak of eleven million at the height of the war. The military was set to return to its default position of remaining small with little direct influence on the broad contours of public political debates. But this time would be different as the United States resumed its rise as a global superpower.

The rise started off as a defensive posture. In 1946, a young diplomat in Moscow, George Kennan, sent a long telegram to Washington, DC, outlining a containment policy for a perceived Soviet threat. In March 1947 President Truman announced to the world that the United States would support "free peoples who are resisting subjugation." The *Truman Doctrine*, enunciated during a civil war in

Greece, gave official weight to the notion of *containment*. It was a warning shot against what Truman and many others saw as Soviet expansionism. In a growing climate of postwar paranoia, Congress later that same year passed the National Security Act, which created the National Security Council (NSC) and the Central Intelligence Agency (CIA) and reshaped the Department of Defense as the largest and most influential of government agencies. The world was reimagined as the stage for global conflict in a struggle between light and dark, right and wrong, democracy and capitalism on the one side against, on the other, an expanding Communism bent on world domination. The Bush administration framed the War on Terror as a similarly Manichean struggle between good and evil.

Because it was the largest economy at the end of World War II, the United States was easily able to imagine a global role for itself. The old imperial powers of the UK and France were bankrupt, Japan and Germany defeated. The Soviet Union experienced huge wartime losses of people and resources. A more sober assessment could have depicted the USSR as what Daniel Yergin called a "cruel, clumsy, bureaucratized fear-ridden despotism" just hanging on to power.[13] Yet it was a Soviet Union of formidable power and efficiency that was represented by U.S. analysts instead, all the better to frame the muscular U.S. response. Out of this foundational paranoia emerged the model of an imperial United States. It was never described in those terms. The words and images of Empire and imperialism were tainted because of their association with European colonialism. For domestic consumption the United States was never an Empire, simply a powerful force for good, keeping the darkness at bay, spreading the light of democracy and the unalloyed benefits of capitalism. America stood for democracy, freedom, and liberty. Who could question those ideals? And the obligatory answer is, only those promoting undemocratic regimes, unfree societies, and a totalitarian agenda. The United States was portrayed at home as a force against evil, a knight in shining armor, which allowed the country to be inextricably linked to the rest of the world as a nation permanently at arms. Now, "America's interests and responsibilities were unrestricted and global."[14]

Paranoia increased in 1949 when Communists gained control of China after decades of civil war and the Soviets exploded their first atomic weapon. The response was a fifty-eight-page report produced by the newly established NSC. Known as NSC-68, the report outlined a global strategy for the United States as a massive buildup of military power to achieve "situations of strength." It was an open-ended commitment to an empire of global reach and military dominance. Between the rhetoric of Empire and political realities, there was a large gap filled by caution, uncertainty, and a sober assessment of the costs. Although Truman enunciated his doctrine, U.S. troops were not sent to Greece during its civil war.

The Korean War (1950–1953) changed everything. The sudden advance and stunning success of the North Korean army in 1950 called into question the credibility of the fledgling superpower of the United States. Korea turned a tentative notion and inchoate desire into the hard reality of Empire as U.S. troops were shipped to the peninsula. North Korea was invaded, and permanent military bases were established. Korea crystallized the postwar paranoia, allowing a quadrupling of the U.S. defense budget, the official adoption of NSC-68, and the domestic acceptance that the United States would have a permanent military presence far from home. The war on Korea "occasioned the enormous foreign military base structure and the domestic military-industrial complex to service it."[15]

Using the term *Empire* in association with the United States is fraught with difficulty.[16] The term, as used here, does not signify the formal imperialism of the nineteenth century so much as a system of compliant and satellite states. The system is held together in multilateral agreements, military treaties, and trading arrangements with different and even changing degrees of strength and coherence. But exactly what is this American Empire? It is not like previous Empires that annexed territory and peoples into a singular political orbit. The earlier fragments of U.S. Empire such as Hawaii and Puerto Rico have long since been incorporated. The U.S. Empire was less about annexing territory and subjugating peoples than about sustaining a global order. It did share, however, previous imperial systems' similarly messianic implications of morally sanctioned endeavors against ideologically defined enemies[17]—a role that is embodied in and reinforced by the banal nationalism of popular culture.

The Empire that first emerged from the Korean War became a sprawling archipelago of military bases around the world, a vast military-industrial-security complex backing a pervasive worldview dominated by visions of global hegemony. There are still at least eight hundred bases with a half-million U.S. personnel spread around the world in at least seventy countries.[18] Never before has there been such a military presence of a single power across the globe. From the end of World War II until today, the United States has redefined itself as a national security state with global reach, while war and military involvement has been normalized by a self-fulfilling predisposition to paranoia.

There were critics of Empire, and opposition sometimes came from unusual sources. President Eisenhower (1953–1961), a Republican and former military leader, gave a farewell address to the nation on January 17, 1961, in which he warned his fellow Americans of the political influence of a military-industrial complex of "an immense military establishment and a large arms industry."[19] He spoke of the grave implications of a huge defense establishment. To this day, it remains a remarkable speech. Eisenhower was a professional military man, serving as the supreme commander of allied forces in Europe during World War II. The growing U.S. global military presence was a recurring worry to Eisenhower. He gave a speech in the first year of his presidency in 1953 in which he warned of excessive defense spending and in a striking metaphor described humanity as "hanging from a cross of iron."[20] The farewell speech was not a rushed afterthought: Eisenhower worked on at least twenty drafts. The final version was the result of a decade of rising concern with the emergence of an American Empire. In this final address to the nation, made to a national television audience, President Eisenhower warned his fellow Americans that "only an alert and knowledgeable citizenship can compel the proper meshing of the huge industrial and military machinery of defense with our peaceful methods and goals, so that security and liberty may prosper together."[21]

Despite such criticisms, the empire grew and expanded. There were ebbs and flows in the course of Empire. Plotting the Department of Defense (DOD) budget over time, for example, reveals four postwar peaks. There was the huge spike of the Korean War when annual spending reached $500 billion (in 2002 dollars), two smaller spikes topping $400 billion during the Vietnam War and Reagan's military buildup in the 1980s, and then a huge increase in the wake of 9/11. By 2018, the DOD total budget was $668 billion—a doubling from 2001. Today, defense spending now accounts for around 15 percent of all federal spending in the United States. A complex web of connective tissue links the military with armament manufacturers and political representatives. The revolving door propels former military and political figures into lucrative corporate appointments as lobbyists and consultants. The arms industry provides jobs in congressional districts, keeping politicians in power. The manufacturers promote more value-added technologies to a military eager to spend and to politicians eager to burnish their reputation as hawks with a strong commitment to defense spending. A lethal alliance of politics, economics, and military promotes a continual spending on war despite its designation as "defense spending." The United States is the single biggest military spender in the world, responsible for 40 percent of total global arms spending. Its military expenditure is now greater than the next ten largest military powers combined.[22]

Once the empire was established, it soon developed a self-sustaining expansionary dynamic. A vast military-industrial-security complex was established with a huge and insatiable appetite for expansion and growth and tentacles reaching into every state and congressional district to ensure widespread political support. There was acceptance at home that the United States could, and should, pursue global reach to maintain hegemony. Threats, both real and imagined, included phony missile gaps, a Vietnamese peasant uprising recast as a Communist takeover, national liberation movements perceived as Communist insurgents, a Soviet Empire on the verge of collapse portrayed as an expansionary force. Local events were reimagined as global conspiracies. Even when the Soviet Empire did collapse in 1989–1991, there was no long-lasting peace dividend as the U.S. role was reimagined from a containment of Communism to the global power responsible for global security. The bipolarity of the Cold War was replaced by the unipolarity of American power reaching across the globe. In a stunning twist, the collapse of the USSR signaled not the abatement of the U.S. Empire but its enlargement and expansion.

Empire needs a shadow. To justify the huge costs, an equally large counter-force needs to be imagined, created, or invented. This was easy during the Cold War when an "evil" Soviet Empire fitted the bill. With the USSR's demise came a brief period of uncertainty before global terrorism became the shadow of the U.S. Empire, standing for everything bad against everything good. Empire needs enemies that must be of some consequence to justify and legitimate their counterweights. Acts of terrorism are seen as acts of war, assassins as criminal masterminds. Shadow empires, when absent, are soon manufactured and invented. If no specific animus is detected, then a more general notion of maintaining global order is employed or a vaguely defined global terrorist threat is conjured. The terrorist shadow was invoked strategically. As the war on Iraq failed to show progress and criticism was mounting, the secretary of state at the time, Donald Rumsfeld, circulated a fifteen-point memo on April 19, 2006. "Keep elevating the threat," he noted in point fourteen. The next point went on, "Talk about Somalia, the Philippines, etc. Make sure the American people realize they are surrounded in the world by violent extremists."[23] It is in the interests of many leaders to jack up the level of threat and portray a United States as beleaguered by enemies. Shadow justifies Empire.

Shadow is ever present, whether real or imagined, a permanent threat morphing over time from Soviet expansionism to global terrorism—a never-ending threat that is used to justify American military spending to promote the Pentagon's global footprint and evoke the public's support of Empire. The United States is placed on the path of persistent conflict, recurring national security crises, and a never-ending war. A permanent war, either in process or in preparation, was the tragic outcome of the U.S. Empire.

The Empire varied over time.[24] The U.S. Empire 1.0 was fashioned initially out of a response to the perceived threat of Soviet expansionism. A nuclear arsenal and a system of alliances sought to contain Soviet power and to instigate interventions, military and economic, open and clandestine. It was successful at two levels. Soviet power was contained, and it never did lead to a hot war between the two competing superpowers. Perhaps more by luck than strategy, the Cold War kept tension and fear alive but never escalated into nuclear war. It could have been worse. With the fall of the Soviet Union, U.S. Empire 2.0 emerged, based on the fact that the United States was the sole remaining superpower, the only country capable of sustained global reach, with the support of a domestic polity that encouraged both this military strength and global engagement.

It is now possible to speak of Empire 3.0 as the old military-industrial system concerned with the projection of military powers is now transformed into military-industrial-security-surveillance system. One of the consequences of 9/11 was the buildup of a massive security-surveillance apparatus under the rubric of counterterrorism. The perceived, imagined, and constructed terrorist threat created a bloated "security" bureaucracy accompanied by its offshoots in the private sector. There are, for example, now more than 850,000 people in the United States with top-secret security clearance. Under the cover of counterterrorism, no budget is large enough, no existing staff levels are high enough, and no contract too generous for the legion of private-sector contractors. Largely unregulated and unreported, a vast apparatus—only parts of which are focused effectively on counterterrorism—has emerged since 9/11. Fear drives the growth of this vast bureaucratic apparatus—not just the fear of a repeat attack, but the fear of those in power of the political consequences of such an attack on their watch. No one wants to be the person who is blamed for not spending enough to prevent an attack against the homeland. "Counterterrorism" now replaces "Communism" as the general threat that justifies all sorts of padded budgets, lucrative contracts, and self-fulfilling growth. Just as paranoia allowed the building of the military-industrial complex, terrorist paranoia similarly creates a burgeoning security-surveillance system. As well as in never-ending war, we are in an era of continual counterterrorism. Dana Priest describes it as the rise of the new American security state.[25]

There were also tactical differences as the empire morphed and modified. There was the *realist-idealist debate*.[26] While the realists argued for Empire to be directly connected to material interests, idealists argued for more humanitarian objectives. If the policy is more tightly connected to immediate material interests—the realist position—or if the ends are more noble—the idealist position—then Empire works better. For the idealists, the failure of the United States to stop genocide in Bosnia or Rwanda is often cited as an example of what happens when the United States does not intervene. In this interpretation, U.S. power can be used to stop evil. This is the Empire as a force for good. Of course, realism and idealism are rarely such clear-cut positions and at times they alternate. After the Rwandan massacres were made more public, the United States reflected a more idealist strain; after the debacle of Iraq, the realist was more dominant. Yet both start from an imperial posture; both see U.S. power projected around the world. While they differ in their aims and objectives, the underlying sense of global reach is apparent.

The Costs of Empire

Empire incurs costs.[27] For the United States they come in a variety of forms. For example, there are reputational costs. One of the brute facts of Empire is the association with the ruling regimes of individual nation-states. In a perfect world these collaborative elites would be stable, democratically elected governments committed to the rule of law, markets, and individual freedoms. Canada is the perfect ally, usually compliant, not too critical, with shared values and very stable. Alas, the rest of the world is more complex. Empire has to deal with the collaborative elites that exist rather than the ones that it desires. While regimes in Empire 1.0 enunciated their anti-Communism to elicit support, regimes in Empire 2.0 need to voice their support of the war on terror.

A global presence means that the United States can be entangled by political events around the world. The manager of the global world order may quickly become caught up in national and local situations that confound, confuse, and penalize. The United States is tainted by its association with repressive collaborative elites, undermined by unsuccessful elites, and threatened by non-collaborative elites. War, according to an unverified quote oft attributed to Ambrose Bierce, "is God's way of teaching Americans geography." It is also the way Americans learn the hard lessons of the complexities of the world outside their borders. Much is written of the projection of U.S. power around the world. There is another story yet to be written about the ways that U.S. power is entrapped, appropriated, transformed, and molded by more local centers of power and influence. U.S. global power is not simply projected; it is bent and often undermined as even lofty goals are turned into compromised strategies and murkier objectives on the hard ground of foreign places. The more distant and different the local geography, the longer the engagement, the more the initial intent changes. Empire is the uncomplicated experience not of power projected but of power undermined, sullied, and transformed. Empire is not simply a physical projection of power and influence; it involves an alchemy that changes everything in the process.[28]

There are also personnel limits. These become more obvious during periods of prolonged conflict: just as you need more boots on the ground, more people make the rational choice that a military career is only best undertaken when the risk of active service is limited. The burdens of constant military campaigning can lead to sharp declines in recruitment and retention that create workforce shortages, especially of the skilled and the more gifted. The personnel issues remain partly hidden through the deployment of professionals rather than a citizen army based on conscription. Vietnam was an unpopular war because it was undertaken when conscription was in operation. Young Americans were drafted from their every-day lives to fight in an unpopular war halfway across the world. In 1968, Nixon campaigned on a promise to end the draft: it was a way to undermine opposition to the war in Vietnam. The draft was eventually ended in 1973 when the military moved to an all-volunteer force. Although there are periodic calls to bring it back as a means to generate shared sacrifice, it is unlikely to happen. The military prefers the all-volunteer force; it is easier to train and retain. A modern military requires professionals who are highly trained rather than the simple foot soldiers of earlier campaigns. But an all-volunteer force means that military involvement is not a collective experience, a widely shared rite of passage, but a job and per-haps a career. Only around 1 percent of families in the United States are actively involved in the military. Military engagements thus involve only a tiny minor-ity of Americans. The small all-volunteer force minimizes the domestic impacts of military engagements. When wars are conducted without a shared sacrifice, either in terms of active service or increased taxes—two wars were conducted in Afghanistan and Iraq at a time of massive tax cuts—then the chasm between the political decisions that sustain Empire and the human costs of maintaining Em-pire becomes profound. We honor the military in public discourse. But on closer inspection the yellow ribbons, care packages, and messages of support are small tokens that only reveal the discrepancy between the actual burdens of war and an empty rhetoric of shared sacrifice. The direct military costs of Empire are born by only a very small proportion of Americans, a situation that makes it easier to maintain public support for the imperial posture. One commentator noted "the frictionlessness and invisibility of modern warfare" for the American public that normalizes the condition of America being at war.[29]

Then there are the rationality crises of Empire. There are the tactical errors. An obvious question to ask of U.S. conduct in the Iraq War was why so many mistakes, incorrect troop levels, lack of precise objectives, poor strategy, and failed tactics. It took nearly seven years from the invasion before the insurgency was brought under some form of control. Incompetence. Sure, plenty of blame to go around: Rumsfeld's arrogance; the dumb mistakes of the U.S. diplomat in charge of the country, Paul Bremer, to disband the Iraqi Army and freeze out the technical skills of those associated with the Baathist party, which included most of the country's competent engineers and technocrats. There was no end of arro-gance veiling incompetence and overlying ignorance. Yet, there is the deeper is-sue of a rationality crisis. Imperial forays require lots of decisions made quickly. And there are limits to the number of right and timely decisions that can be made in the unforgiving, brutal, confusing, and confounding real time of war.

Waging a war means centralizing knowledge and information, using a hi-erarchical structure to gather and process information. The military structure tends to be long on discipline and obeying orders, rather shorter on debating alternatives, and assessing different scenarios. Maybe before the war starts, but particularly once it gets going, plans made at home unfold despite changing realities on the ground. Mistakes and errors are endemic to war. But then there is the particular rationality crisis of the U.S. Empire, which is prone to magical thinking, the recurring self-deception that the United States can successfully influence outcomes in other countries. The belief that the United States, *because* it is the United States, can set the world right is a recurring feature of U.S. foreign policy from Korea through Vietnam to Iraq. This magical thinking is reinforced by a lack of knowledge of other countries and the nature of local elites. Strategists of the Vietnam War had no prior knowledge of Vietnam, and the senior leadership of the Iraq War prided themselves in their inability to speak Arabic let alone understand the intricacies of Iraqi society. No, in the land of magical thinking the rest of the world is just like the United States, just not yet, but with a bit of help they can be the United States. This stems from a belief that the United States is the obvious endpoint of social development, political striving, and social progress. Other countries just have to be guided toward the inevitable goal. The world is filled with complex cultures with convoluted history and varied social geographies. The particularities of place undermine the simple projection of U.S. power. The world is complex, yet Empire sees simplicity and assumes plasticity to U.S. power. The long war in Afghanistan was, as an example, a fantasy of nation-building in a dysfunctional nation with a corrupt governing elite. The policies of Empire are often magical fantasies that can lead to disappointment.

At times, the fantasies are revealed for what they are, and a clear-headed rationality takes hold. The *Powell Doctrine*, for example, was one of the most sustained considerations of using U.S. power. The term was employed by a journalist but is associated with Colin Powell in the run-up to the 1990–1991 Gulf War. It calls for some fundamental questions of the military: is there a vital national security threat, a clear objective, a full assessment of cost and benefits, exhaustion of all nonviolent means, an exit strategy, popular support, and international agreement? If the answer is yes, then use overwhelming force to ensure victory. Go big, go long, or go home.

But there are also deeper strategic mistakes of Empire. One is the tendency for global events to be interpreted, understood, and responded to in military terms.[30] The United States, with its vast military power, is like someone who carries around a giant hammer. They look for nails and bash everything even remotely resembling a nail. It is in the nature of the imperial posture to respond on a grand scale with the military solutions always there, just waiting to be mobilized and deployed. Much is made of the difficulty in fighting against terrorism. Analysts speak of the asymmetry between superpowers on the one hand and a vast yet slow-moving military arsenal against non-state terrorist groups on the other—small, nimble, focused, and secret. But the asymmetry is not a fact of nature. Try dropping the big hammer and try a smaller hammer. And maybe it is not even a nail you are dealing with. A flexible imagination is needed as much as military hardware. Yet the U.S. Empire is predisposed toward seeing the world from the perspective of wielding a big hammer that searches only for a nail. The 9/11 attack could have been treated as an issue of law enforcement: "a dreadful crime was committed; let us bring the criminals to justice" could have been a legitimate and appropriate policy objective. Too easily, the military solution, the declaration of war, continues to be employed. Even the conservative columnist

George Will can write, "the more we couch our thinking in military categories, the more we open ourselves to misadventures."[31]

One argument is that the U.S. foreign policy was hijacked during the Bush administration by neoconservatives with their vision of remaking the Middle East and their policy of projecting U.S. power through preemptive strikes. Even if this assertion is true, the deeper question is, why is it so relatively easy to get the United States to go to war? Despite popular resistance, the country inevitably went to war. The Congress gave President Bush the authority to declare war and to initiate a preemptive strike against a country that was not a direct threat to the United States. A willing Congress, supportive press, and persuadable public are all part of the unfolding drama of Empire in this case. In the superheated environment post–9/11, it was relatively simple to get the United States to go to war with evidence that was neither compelling nor actually true as it turns out. The simple conclusion and most threatening structural flaw are that the United States goes to war too easily and too often. Once war occurs, lots of things can and do go wrong. It is the very nature of war.

Wars are elemental. They stifle criticism. Perhaps that is why not only the practice but also the rhetoric of war is so constantly employed in U.S. domestic policy: The War on Crime, The War on Drugs, The War on Poverty. The words are neither accidental nor innocent. War is invoked because it is often difficult to get the government to do things. The Founding Fathers were leery of concentrated government power, so they spread it across different branches and divided it between states and the federal government. The system is designed to support the status quo, not for the government to be an active agent. The evocation of a permanent threat and the declaration of war give the necessary justification and generate support for large-scale government action. There is no more concentrated government action than the prosecution of wars. Declared wars are vehicles for mobilization that have the added advantage of stifling criticism and legitimizing dissent. The loose and fragmented nature of U.S. political organization makes war one of the few ways that governments can get big things done. War works against democratic debate and serious criticism. Employing the rhetoric of war makes it easier to marginalize alternatives and to demonize critics.

There is the growing fiscal crisis of Empire. The total direct costs of the Iraq War are estimated around $3 trillion. Then there are the indirect costs. Before the War on Terror, in January 2001, the Congressional Budget Office was predicting budget surpluses into the future. After a decade of tax cuts and two wars, the budget surplus of $2 trillion turned into an annual deficit of $12 trillion. The War on Terror and tax cuts turned the United States into a credit risk, put pressure on the dollar, and cramped other forms of government spending. Empire comes at a huge price. The United States is running up against the fiscal limits of Empire. Some deny these limits. Defense spending is sacrosanct for many in Congress. The real costs are often hidden by off-the-book accounting and passing the costs on to future generations in the form of borrowing now and paying later. The costs of Empire are unrelated to the threats we face. Costs increase despite, not because of, the threat levels. A vast, global, and expensive military presence must be paid for in blood as well as gold. The military expenditures skew the economic trajectory and lessen the ability of the federal government to build, innovate, and educate. Defense spending, with its many supporters, bears down on the federal budget as a huge weight, forcing expenditure cuts onto the much smaller programs, especially the domestic discretionary spending that accounts for only around 12 percent of all federal spending. Programs that feed hungry kids are cut while bombers and rockets continue to be purchased. The USS *Gerald R. Ford*, introduced in 2017, cost close to $13 billion, part of a program to replace older carriers, with a conservative cost of $37 billion. Even the mid-life overhaul of one of these older Nimitz class carriers, USS *George Washington*, cost $3 billion in 2016 (see photo 4.1). The United States reigns supreme in military spending as it slides down the table of economic competitiveness, educational access, infrastructure spending, and the quality and equity of its social programs. The fiscal limits become more pronounced as imperial overstretch bumps up against the fiscal crisis of declining relative economic power.

Photo 4.1.   The projection of power: The Nimitz-class aircraft carrier USS *Harry S. Truman*, 2018. (U.S. Navy)

There are also collateral costs of the fixation on Empire as revealed by the events of January 6, 2021, when thousands marched to the Capitol and around eight hundred people illegally entered to threaten the political chambers to deny Biden's election victory. It constituted a massive security failure. The security surveillance apparatus and those who fund, control, and manage it had devoted far too much time, money, and effort looking for foreign conspirators, hunting down Islamic terrorists, and the like while ignoring the growing and deadly right-wing extremism that formed the backbone to the Capitol insurrection. The fears of Empire meant that genuine internal threats to the republic were ignored or downplayed with almost catastrophic results.

The Retreat from Empire?

There is now less support for the imperial posture. The twenty-first century did not start well for the United States. There were the terrorist attacks of 9/11 that unleashed a global War on Terror and the resulting fiasco of the Iraq invasion, all against the backdrop of a major recession and the squeezing of the middle class as rampant inequality divided the nation. The longest U.S. war in Afghanistan will ultimately end with the Taliban regaining control. At a time of relative economic decline and fraying polity, the Empire is losing its appeal. In his speech to the graduating class of West Point on June 13, 2020, President Trump said,

> We are ending the era of endless wars. In its place is a renewed, clear-eyed focus on defending America's vital interests. It is not the duty of U.S. troops to solve ancient conflicts in faraway lands that many people have never even heard of. We are not the policemen of the world.[32]

There is growing distaste with an establishment that had predicted that Hussein had a smoking gun, that the Iraqi people would welcome U.S. troops, that Afghanistan could be won, and peace brought to the Middle East. Small engagements became unwinnable wars that never seemed to end. The United States now has imperial fatigue.[33]

Growing sentiment in the United States argues that paying the costs for this global role allows economic competitors to become free riders, benefiting from U.S. military spending but rarely meeting the full costs. In Empire 1.0 there was a one-to-one correspondence between maintaining the global order and U.S. domestic economic interests. U.S. corporations made things in the United States, thus ensuring access to global markets, enriched U.S. corporations, and provided jobs for U.S. workers. Empire 3.0 occurs at a time when the notion of what constitutes a U.S. corporation is more flexible and spectral as companies offshore more jobs. A corporation's profitability is more often based on how many jobs it can send overseas than how many jobs it can generate inside the United States. Maintaining order in this more globalized economy allows for a global shift in manufacturing and created the preconditions for a strong Japan, a resurgent China, and a growing India. Unlike previous empires, there is now a less clear connection between national and material interests. In contrast, Belgium held what was once called the Belgian Congo in a purely exploitative scheme to rape and pillage the territory resources and enslave its inhabitants.[34] It was an imperial mission whose only goal was national and in particular royal enrichment. In contrast, the United States in recent years has seen a divergence between geopolitical strategy and domestic economic interests.

The U.S. Empire was committed to maintaining and ensuring economic and political globalization. On the ground, this meant making sure that the oil flowed, the capital moved freely, the rule of law was adhered to, goods were sold, private markets operated, and profits were safe. The major concern of Empire was about extending and maintaining global economic connectivity. But this Empire is now uncoupling from domestic economic interest. Empire aids multinational companies to become global entities with long production chains that snake across national boundaries. The U.S. Empire extends the flattening space of economic globalization. To be sure, this aids the U.S. national economy by providing secure markets. But in an era of globalization, it also allows a frictionless space for China and a security cover for national economic competitors such as Japan and Germany. The Empire provided the means for a global shift in manufacturing and the rise of a middle class in Asia but also the decline of manufacturing in the United States and the squeezing of its middle class. The costs of Empire were twofold. They had to be paid from funds diverted from things such as domestic infrastructural improvement and the resultant globalization exacted a cost on many workers in the domestic economy.

THE UNITED STATES IN A NEW WORLD ORDER

There is profound criticism of the grand post–Cold War strategy, with its emphasis on spreading democracy, opening markets, and prizing stability with economic competitors rather than confrontation. While there were some successes, there were also mounting failures and sometimes the idea of democracy cloaked authoritarian regimes as long as they were anti-Communist and the promotion of free markets allowed immense concentration of wealth and growing inequality. The results, as many saw it, were failed wars, emboldened competitors, disgruntled allies, and debilitating engagements. It has been characterized as a series of small wars in obscure places that lacked strategic significance.[35]

A major part of an emerging new world order is the recalibration in the United States of the costs and benefits of Empire. The influential journal *Foreign Affairs* published a special issue in 2019 titled *Searching for A Strategy*. It took as granted the fact that "U.S. hard power is in relative decline; U.S. soft power has taken a huge hit" and "the managers of the empire need to wake up."[36] This is part of a long overdue assessment of U.S. priorities and the beginning of a shift in strategic thinking.

For decades, the United States sought to integrate powers such as China and Russia into an enlarging world order of international trading arrangements. The aim was to nullify the dangers of an isolated China and a bitter Russia. The United States ignored China's brazen theft of intellectual property, currency manipulation, statist protectionism, and the bullying of its neighbors in the South China Sea. A reset with Russia, announced in 2009, failed to stop the rise of Russian authoritarianism at home and adventurism overseas. Recent years have seen a shift in emphasis with policy makers becoming more aware of Russia's ambitious reach in Europe and the Middle East and China's rising power.

A new strategy was first hinted at in the 2017 *National Security Strategy*[37] and the 2018 *National Defense Strategy*,[38] which addressed the rise of great power competition and near-peer competitors. The strategy is still evolving in different parts of the U.S. state machinery at different times in different ways. Perhaps the nimblest is the Department of Defense, tasked to defend places such as Taiwan and the Baltic from possible Chinese and Russian aggression and now with a greater emphasis on fending off attacks at the beginning of hostilities with a mixture of long-range bombers, submarines, and artillery rather than just short-range fighter jets and amphibious vessels.[39] Alternative geopolitical strategies are also gaining credence, peeping out from universities and think tanks to greater official credibility and wider government discussion. Different geopolitical options are being mooted. In the *theory of offensive realism*, the system of great powers makes conflict inevitable.[40] One response is the *restrained realism* of offshore balancing, most associated with John Mearsheimer and Stephen Walt.[41] They argue that the United States should abandon its permanent global military posture and instead focus on maintaining U.S. dominance in the Western Hemisphere and resist, with strategic alliances, the rise of potential hegemons elsewhere. It is a form of hedging against rising hegemons without the need for a vast global permanent military presence. The United States should, so this argument goes, aim to block the rise of potential hegemons with the help of allies, only becoming involved if U.S. interests are directly involved and challenged. Offshore balancing is not a retreat from Empire but what its proponents consider a more effective means to maintain U.S. hegemony. The strategy entails balancing against the possibility of regional hegemons emerging that could threaten the United States.

A more radical *grand strategy of restraint* has been proposed.[42] The broad contours of the argument are that the United States faces limited threats because of its geographical position protected on two sides by wide oceans and sharing land borders with relatively much weaker countries, so international alliances are not needed and the military should be drastically downsized. In effect, it is a call for U.S. foreign policy unfettered from Empire. The proponents of restraint argue that extensive alliances come with real costs of entanglement and possibility of entrapment, that the pursuit of primacy is too costly and not all that effective in reducing arms proliferation or encouraging democracy. After almost two decades of futile wars, the idea of pursuing a strategy of restraint appeals to more people in the United States.

But it will take more than sophisticated, even correct, arguments to shift the grand strategy of the United States toward a strategy of restraint. Like a giant oil tanker plowing through the oceans, U.S. policy cannot change direction easily or quickly. There is too much momentum. And to shift metaphors: too many large and powerful appetites feeding at the trough of Empire. Yet a near-future shift is palpable. Decades of failed wars have moved public opinion toward a willingness to countenance a profound shift in U.S. geopolitical strategy, which since the 1950s, apart from the Vietnam War, has had a life of its own separated from popular public opinion, subject to debate only within the political elites. The new normal is that foreign policy, for now at least, is much more dependent on domestic opinion, perhaps creating a more pronounced cycle of involvement as compassion and anger are mobilized and the costs of involvement become ever more apparent.

The emergence of regional hegemons with global aspirations occurs at a time of a relative weakening of U.S. economic power. In the confused nature of a new world order, the postwar geopolitical consensus on engagements, alliances, and maintaining a global military posture is coming under greater scrutiny. The process is messy as traditional alliances are recalibrated along more transactional lines, debts are called in, and the balance of costs and benefits is more finely attuned to a narrowing range of interest.

The Greek historian Thucydides, writing around 2,500 years ago, made two observations that still have relevance for the contemporary United States. The first is the well-known *Thucydides Trap*, which states that when an existing power is threatened by rising power it has two options. If it does nothing, it risks the competitor becoming stronger, hastening a confrontation. If it confronts, it creates the conditions for war. Thucydides is now widely quoted when analysts model the possible trajectory of U.S.-China relations. While some see a negotiated settlement, many see conflict as the inevitable result.[43] But Thucydides also made another pertinent, though less well-known comment. "Your empire is now like a tyranny: it may have been wrong to take it; it is certainly dangerous to let it go."

China and the United States

As tensions increase between China and the United States, it is perhaps legitimate to ask, are we witnessing the start of a new Cold War? The last one pitted the United States and allies against the USSR and its allies and lasted for more than fifty years. Are we seeing the beginnings of a new conflict between China and the United States?[44]

On the one hand, there is a lot of shared interests and concerns that bind the two countries together, including extensive trading and economic links and the need to jointly address climate change and to reduce the risk of global pandemics. There is no obvious major ideological clash. The capitalism versus Communism of the last Cold War was a zero-sum game. You were either capitalist or Communist and one side's victory was a defeat for the other. Today, in contrast, both powers happily trade with each other and both are essentially capitalist countries. Despite the rhetoric they are remarkably similar economic entities. So, on the face of it, apart from the conflict engendered through jostling for influence and prestige, they could peacefully inhabit the same world. There is no inevitable logic that drives the countries apart.

On the other hand, there is the dangerous dynamic of a resurging and receding power. We should not underestimate the dangers posed to world order by an aggressive rising power and an anxious hegemon. One influential Chinese perspective, especially marked under Xi, is to see the United States as actively blocking the rise of resurgent China. A 2020 report from the Ministry of State Security to Xi and other top leaders predicted rising hostility from the United States.[45] China always looks for and is always able to find evidence that the United States is out to contain China's rise to world power status. The United States, in contrast, sees a resurgent China as a threat to the world order, undermining free trade, manipulating currency, abusing intellectual property rights, and unilaterally wielding its power in the South China Sea and exerting authoritarian control over Hong Kong. The growing tension feeds off itself as each power reacts to what it sees as either blockages to rightful rise (the Chinese perspective) or of a China undermining a stable and peaceful world order (the U.S. perspective).

In contrast to the Cold War, where the USSR and the United States had large and relatively stable alliances backing them, China and the United States do not have a similarly stable group of allies behind them in their conflict. China has cultivated too many important global economic connections for the United States to easily mobilize a consistently anti-China bloc. There are many national economies that rely on economic ties with China and so trim their foreign policies accordingly. The U.S. go-it-alone policy under Trump undermined the formation of a coherent and resilient anti-Chinese alliance. "Make America Great Again" did not generate the enthusiasm of allies repeatedly scolded about their military sending. It turned the conflict into an isolated conflict. So, we have two powers competing on the global stage with few natural allies, apart from those, such as Vietnam and Russia, whose policy may be more by "an enemy of my enemy is my friend" doctrine. Vietnam is always wary of China while Russia seeks to undermine U.S. global leadership. Tensions are high with narratives in both China and the United States, raising the rhetoric of confrontation. Trade disputes add hardcore material interests to the mounting tension. As the United States becomes more critical of China, then China feels even more threatened. It is difficult to see the future and gauge whether the current tension is merely a temporary downturn. But at the risk of getting it wrong, I think not. China under Xi is moving toward a more explicitly global role that seeks to change the existing world order to make it more Sinocentric, building up its economic and military power and already exercising it in East and Southeast Asia.

There are a number of possible outcomes. One, the United States retains global primary supremacy. This is unlikely; China's growth now looks almost inevitable and self-inflicted political damage further weakens the United States. Two, China replaces the United States as dominant global superpower. Maybe, but that would only be in the longer term. In the short to medium term, the United States already has enough economic and military power to maintain a strong position. Three, there is no obvious winner. In one variant, the two manage the difficult transition to a bipolar world of shared global governance. In another, while there is a relative shift with China becoming more powerful, there is a diminishing of both powers. Internal contradictions in both powers and their lack of allies may mean that we move into a more disordered world when the two largest powers wield less global influence. We can see some of this dynamic play out in the immediate responses to the coronavirus.[46] China's response revealed its authoritarian underbelly with scientists' warnings ignored and suppressed. The initial response in the United States was botched and disorganized, revealing its own problems of lack of social welfare, health care, and workers' rights. Neither country provided a model for the rest of the world. Trump then criticized China after initially praising it. His China-bashing became a way to mobilize his base, deflect criticisms from the fiasco of the federal response, and shift global blame to China. The United States eschewed any form of global leadership, instead launching a campaign against the World Health Organization. While the United States abandoned even any pretense of world leadership, China's claim to it rang hollow with the early suppression of vital information at a crucial time in the early evolution of the pandemic. While the United States abandoned global leadership, China's claim to it was treated with suspicion. So neither China nor the United States emerged as winners or leaders that anyone else would want to follow. Even if a Cold War breaks out between the United States and China there are few parallels with the first one. More and more of the world is disenchanted with both the models of governance and the political cultures presented by either country. Neither the American Dream nor the more recent Chinese Dream fills the world with much hope.[47] One has a capitalism without democracy while the other has a democracy that overwhelmingly benefits the wealthy.

GEOPOLITICAL HOTSPOTS: THE BORDERS OF THE UNITED STATES

Both the offshore balancers and the proponents of primacy refer to the unique geographical position of the United States, a continental power surrounded on two sides by vast oceans that give it an inherent advantage. The assumption is that its borders are settled and safe. While the borders may not have the explosive quality of, say, India and Pakistan or Ukraine and Russia facing off against each other, they have begun to rumble.

The Arctic

The northernmost U.S. frontier is quite literally warming. Rising temperatures are opening up the Arctic for shipping routes and resource exploitation. The Arctic is becoming less of an icy wilderness and more an economic opportunity. Trade routes from Europe to Asia would move goods more quickly and cheaply if container ships could move freely through Arctic waters. It is estimated that ninety billion barrels of oil and 1.6 trillion cubic feet of natural gas, more than 10 percent of the world's untapped reserves, lie beneath thinning ice and melting seas. Russia has a long presence in the Arctic region and is keen to exploit the possibilities. It has twenty-two state-owned icebreakers. The state-owned oil company Rosneft signed a deal with ExxonMobil to exploit the oil reserves in the Kara Sea, off the coast of Siberia. The U.S. Coast Guard, in contrast, only has one heavy-duty icebreaker, the *Polar Star*, that is effective in northern waters. While the U.S. Navy invests in very expensive aircraft carriers to fight on the open oceans, it is lacking in the ability to project power in a warming Arctic. In 2017 the U.S. Coast Guard announced that six icebreakers, three heavy and three medium-sized, were being developed with final delivery due in 2024. That same year the Coast Guard argued that more may be needed and that they may have to be equipped with more sophisticated weaponry.

The vast mineral reserves and the new sea routes open up economic opportunities. China's attempt to construct a *Polar Silk Road* and represent itself as a *near-Arctic state* and Russia's projection of military power and territorial extension in its Far North all pose challenges to the U.S. interests in the Arctic.[48]

Canada and the United States

The 5,525-mile border between Canada and the United States is the longest international border between two countries.[49] At the Treaty of Paris in 1783, a boundary line was drawn through the Connecticut River along the 45th parallel and through the St. Lawrence River and the Great Lakes. On the ground, the border was contested. The International Boundary Commission, created in 1796, provided a forum for disputes. From 1872 to 1876, it established the boundary line through the Rockies. In 1925, the commission was made a permanent organization responsible for maintaining boundary markers as well as a ten-foot deforested clearance on either side of the line. While the vast majority of the border is now agreed upon, there are still some small areas of disagreement, including Machias Sea Island (Maine/New Brunswick), Dixon Entrance (Alaska/ British Columbia), Beaufort Sea (Alaska/Yukon), and the Strait of Juan de Fuca (Washington/British Columbia).

Around three hundred thousand people cross the border every day. Until 9/11, the border was only lightly policed. Since then, security has tightened. In effect, the border has thickened due to increased border security.[50] The border impacts economic transactions. One Canadian study showed that the costs associated with border crossing have not significantly decreased as government spending on border security has markedly increased. After adding up the lowest values from the estimated ranges for all costs for trade, tourism/travel, and government programs, they estimated the border costs Canada C$19.1 billion each year, and nearly 1.5 percent of Canada's GDP.[51]

Mexico and the United States

The border between the United States and Mexico stretches 1,960 miles from the Pacific to the Gulf of Mexico. Up to a million people cross each day, close to three hundred fifty million each year along the forty-five official crossing points. The 1848 Treaty of Guadalupe Hidalgo, signed at the end of the Mexican-American War, defined the border. In the treaty, Mexico lost almost half of its landmass, including what are now the states of Arizona, California, Nevada, New Mexico, and Utah as well as parts of Colorado, Kansas, Oklahoma, and Wyoming. The United States gained almost a million square miles of "new" territory. Five years later the United States purchased a piece of land, the Gadsden Purchase, to ensure a railway right of way. The treaty and the purchase define today's border. There is effective control of the border along only seven hundred miles. For many years, the border was scarcely visible as people moved back and forth between the two national territories. It was never well fortified, policed, or managed. From 1942 to 1964, the U.S. government actively encouraged the immigration of seasonal agricultural workers from Mexico.

More than twelve million people now live in the border region, designated as 62.5 miles (100 kilometers) on each side of the international boundary (see map 4.3). Most reside in the fourteen sister-cities, such as San Diego–Tijuana and El Paso–Ciudad Juarez. Since 1965, the Mexican government has provided economic incentives for U.S. and international companies to establish assembly plants in the border region and in 1994 the implementation of the North American Free Trade Agreement (NAFTA) encouraged the clustering of *maquiladoras*— outsourced assembly plants—on the Mexican side of the border region.

The border between the two countries remains porous. Between 1.8 million refugees and eleven million undocumented workers already live in the United States. Not all came from across the border. But in the political imagination of many, the border with Mexico is a site of disorder, the entry point for the foreign other, a security risk, and an economic threat. The border played a pivotal role in the election victory of Trump because of his consistent refrains for a

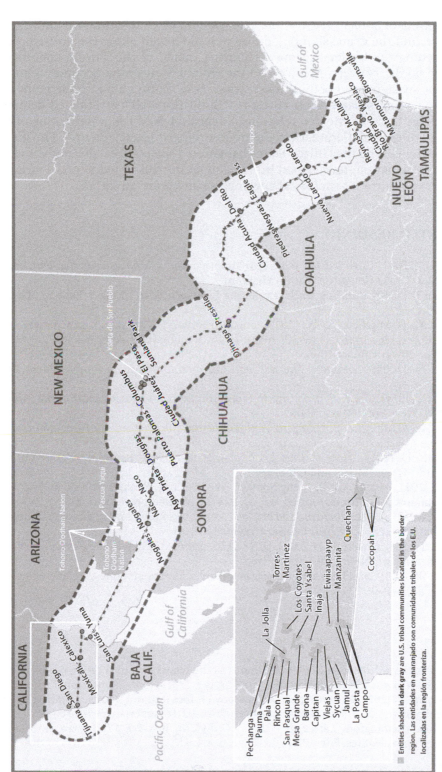

Map 4.3. The U.S.–Mexico border (Environmental Protection Agency)

CALIFORNIA

ARIZONA

NEW MEXICO

TEXAS

Pacific Ocean

Gulf of California

Gulf of Mexico

BAJA CALIF.

SONORA

CHIHUAHUA

COAHUILA

NUEVO LEÓN

TAMAULIPAS

Tohono O'odham Nation

Pascua Yaqui

Tohono O'odham Nation

Ysleta del Sur Pueblo

San Diego
Tijuana
Mexicali
Calexico
Yuma
San Luis

Nogales
Nogales
Naco
Naco
Agua Prieta
Douglas
Puerto Palomas
Columbus
Ciudad Juárez
El Paso
Sunland Park
Big Bend Park

Ojinaga
Presidio
Ciudad Acuña
Del Rio
Piedras Negras
Eagle Pass
Kickapoo
Nuevo Laredo
Laredo
Reynosa
McAllen
Ciudad Bravo
Río Bravo
Matamoros
Brownsville

Pechanga
Pauma
Pala
Rincon
San Pasqual
Mesa Grande
Barona
Capitan
Viejas
Sycuan
Jamul
La Posta
Campo

La Jolla

Torres-Martinez

Los Coyotes
Santa Ysabel
Inaja

Ewiiaapaayp
Manzanita

Quechan

Cocopah

☐ Entities shaded in dark gray are U.S. tribal communities located in the border region. Las entidades en anaranjado son comunidades tribales de los E.U. localizadas en la región fronteriza.

strengthening of border security, the construction of a seven-hundred-mile security fence, and the expression of a desire to build a wall along the entire border. Strengthening the border became a recurring theme of the Trump administration. The border between Mexico and the United States now occupies a hugely important space in the popular imagination. Now as much a rallying point as a line demarcating separate nation-states, "Build the wall" crystalized demands for a shift in U.S. and Mexico relations, a repeal of NAFTA, a tightening of immigration rules, and a dramatic reduction in refugee resettlement.[52] The border between Mexico and the United States has entered the political discourse and the populist imagination, reimagined from a simple territorial marker to a crowded discussion platform for rhetorical controversy and political fights.

SUGGESTED READINGS

Allison, G. (2017). *Destined for war: Can America and China escape the Thucydides Trap?* New York: Houghton Mifflin Harcourt.

Castaneda, E. (2019). *Building walls: Excluding Latin people in the U.S.* Lanham: Lexington Books.

Colby, E. A., & Mitchell, A. W. (2020, January-February). The age of great power competition. *Foreign Affairs*, 118–30. https://www.foreignaffairs.com/articles/2019-12-10/age-great-power-competition.

Ferguson, N. (2004). *Colossus: The rise and fall of the American empire.* New York: Penguin.

Grandin, G. (2019). *The end of the myth: From frontier to the border wall in the mind of America.* New York: Macmillan.

Hopkins, A. (2018). *American empire: A global history.* Princeton, NJ: Princeton University Press.

Immerwahr, D. (2019). *How to hide an empire: A history of the greater United States.* New York: Farrar, Straus and Giroux.

Kagan, R. (2021, March/April). A superpower, like it or not. *Foreign Affairs*. https://www.foreignaffairs.com/articles/united-states/2021-02-16/superpower-it-or-not.

Nicol, H. N. (2015). *The fence and the bridge: Geopolitics and identity along the Canada–US border.* Waterloo: Wilfrid Laurier University Press.

Thrall, A. T., & Friedman, B. H. (eds.). (2018). *U.S. grand strategy in the 21st century: The case for restraint.* New York: Routledge.

Williams, W. A. (1955). The frontier thesis and American foreign policy. *Pacific Historical Review, 24,* 379–95.

NOTES

1. For a current defense of the United States as the leader of global order, see Ikenberry, G. J. (2018). Why the liberal world order will survive. *Ethics and International Affairs, 32,* 17–29; Kagan, R. (2021, March/April). A superpower, like it or not. *Foreign Affairs.* https://www.foreignaffairs.com/articles/united-states/2021-02-16/superpower-it-or-not.

2. George Washington, *Letter to William Crawford*, July 25, 1767. http://media.huntington.org/uploadedfiles/Files/PDFs/LHGWlesson4.pdf.

3. Short, J. R. (2001). *Representing the republic: Mapping the U.S. 1600-1900.* London: Reaktion, 124–43.

4. Weinberg, A. K. (1976). *Manifest destiny: A study of nationalist expansionism in American history.* New York: AMS Press.

5. Williams, W. A. (1955). The frontier thesis and American foreign policy. *Pacific Historical Review, 24,* 379–95.

6. Johnson, C. (2010). *Dismantling the empire: America's last best hope.* New York: Henry Holt; Grandin, G. (2019). *The end of the myth: From frontier to the border wall in the mind of America.* New York: Macmillan.

7. Timeline: January 1899: Senate debate over ratification of the Treaty of Paris. https://www.pbs.org/crucible/tl17.html.

8. Tomkins, E. B. (1970). *Anti-imperialism in the United States: The great debate.* Philadelphia: University of Pennsylvania Press, 294.

9. Drabelle, D. (2017). Tough questions the nation faced after the Spanish-American War. https://www.washingtonpost.com/opinions/tough-questions-the-nation-faced-after-the-spanish-american-war/2017/01/27/0b630ac4-b66a-11e6-a677-b608fbb3aaf6_story.html.

10. Kinzer, S. (2017). *The true flag: Roosevelt, Mark Twain and the birth of American empire.* New York: Henry Holt.

11. Immerwahr, D. (2019). *How to hide an empire: A history of the greater United States.* New York: Farrar, Straus and Giroux.

12. Butler, S. (1935). America's armed forces: 2. "In Time of Peace." *Common Sense, 4,* 8–12. https://msuweb.montclair.edu/~furrg/Vietnam/butler.pdf.

13. Yergin, D. (1977). *Shattered peace: The origins of the Cold War and national security state.* Boston: Houghton Mifflin, 220.

14. Ibid., 245.

15. Cumings, B. (2010). *The Korean War: A history.* New York: Modern Library, 210.

16. I draw heavily on chapter 2 in my previous book: Short, J. R. (2013). *Stress testing the USA.* New York: Palgrave Macmillan.

17. Hobsbawm, E. (2008). *On Empire: America, war and global supremacy.* New York: Pantheon.

18. Vine, D. (2015). *Base nation: How U.S. military bases abroad harm America and the world.* New York: Metropolitan Books.

19. Eisenhower, D. D. (1953, April 16). "The chance for peace." Washington, DC. http://www.edchange.org/multicultural/speeches/ike_chance_for_peace.html.

20. Ibid.

21. Ibid.

22. See https://www.sipri.org/databases.

23. Quoted in *Washington Post,* November 2006, A1 and A10.

24. Hopkins, A. (2018). *American empire: A global history.* Princeton, NJ: Princeton University Press.

25. Priest, D. (2011). *Top secret America: The rise of the new American security state.* New York: Little, Brown.

26. Maghroori, R. (2019). *Globalism versus realism: International relations' third debate.* London: Routledge.

27. Ferguson, N. (2004). *Colossus: The rise and fall of the American empire.* New York: Penguin.

28. For the example of U.S. power in Afghanistan and Iraq respectively, see Chandrasekaran, R. (2012). *Little America: The war within the war for Afghanistan.* New York: Knopf; Chandrasekaran, R. (2006). *Imperial life in the emerald city.* New York: Knopf.

29. Maddow, R. (2012, March 28). Reaching the limit in Afghanistan. *Washington Post*, A19.

30. Bacevitch. A. J., et al. (2018, June). Combat high: America's addiction to war. *Harpers*. https://harpers.org/archive/2018/06/combat-high/; Fallows, J. (2015, January–February). The tragedy of the American military. *The Atlantic*. https://www.theatlantic.com/magazine/archive/2015/01/the-tragedy-of-the-american-military/383516/.

31. Will, G. (2011, May 3). The war that wasn't. *Washington Post*, A21.

32. See https://www.whitehouse.gov/briefings-statements/remarks-president-trump-2020-united-states-military-academy-west-point-graduation-ceremony/. However, in the very same speech he also defended the global role of the U.S. military to secure "The survival of America and the endurance of civilization."

33. Rose, G. (2019, May/June). Searching for a strategy: Four experts stage an intervention to rescue U.S. grand strategy. *Foreign Affairs*. https://www.foreignaffairs.com/articles/2019-04-16/searching-strategy.

34. Hochschild, A. (1999). *King Leopold's ghost: A story of greed, terror, and heroism in colonial Africa*. New York: Houghton Mifflin Harcourt.

35. Packer, G. (2019, May). The end of the American century: What the life of Richard Holbrooke tells us about the decay of Pax Americana. *The Atlantic*. https://www.theatlantic.com/magazine/archive/2019/05/george-packer-pax-americana-richard-holbrooke/586042/.

36. Rose, G. (2019, May/June). Searching for a strategy: Four experts stage an intervention to rescue U.S. grand strategy. *Foreign Affairs*. https://www.foreignaffairs.com/issue-packages/2019-04-16/searching-strategy.

37. Trump, D. J. (2017). *National Security Strategy of the United States of America*. Executive Office of the President. Washington, DC. https://ge.usembassy.gov/2017-national-security-strategy-united-states-america-president/.

38. Mattis, J. (2018). *Summary of the 2018 national defense strategy of the United States of America*. Washington, DC: Department of Defense.

39. Colby, E. A., & Mitchell, A. W. (2020, January-February). The age of great power competition. *Foreign Affairs*, 118–30. https://www.foreignaffairs.com/articles/2019-12-10/age-great-power-competition.

40. Mearsheimer, J. (2014). *The tragedy of great power politics*. New York: Norton.

41. Mearsheimer, J., & Walt, S. M. (2016). The case for offshore balancing. *Foreign Affairs*, 95, 70–84.

42. Thrall, A. T., & Friedman, B. H. (eds.). (2018). *U.S. grand strategy in the 21st century: The case for restraint*. New York: Routledge.

43. Allison, G. (2017). *Destined for war: Can America and China escape the Thucydides Trap?* New York: Houghton Mifflin Harcourt.

44. Stromseth, J. (ed.). (2021). *Rivalry and response: Assessing great power dynamics in Southeast Asia*. Washington, DC: Brookings; Tharoor, I. (2020). Is a U.S.-China cold war already under way? *Washington Post*. https://www.washingtonpost.com/world/2020/05/15/is-us-china-cold-war-already-under-way/.

45. Reuters. (2020, May 4). Exclusive: Internal Chinese report warns Beijing faces Tiananmen-like global backlash over virus. https://www.reuters.com/article/us-health-coronavirus-china-sentiment-ex/exclusive-internal-chinese-report-warns-beijing-faces-tiananmen-like-global-backlash-over-virus-idUSKBN22G19C.

46. Campbell, K. M., & Doshi, R. (2020, March/April). The coronavirus could reshape global order. *Foreign Affairs*. https://www.foreignaffairs.com/articles/china/2020-03-18/coronavirus-could-reshape-global-order?utm_campaign=Foreign%20Policy&utm_content=85046008&utm_medium=email&utm_source=hs_email.

47. Gill, B. (2019). Xi Jinping's grip on power is absolute, but there are new threats to his "Chinese Dream." *The Conversation.* https://theconversation.com/xi-jinpings-grip-on-power-is-absolute-but-there-are-new-threats-to-his-chinese-dream-118921.

48. Cohen, A. (2011). *Russia in the Arctic: Challenges to US Energy and Geopolitics in the high north.* U.S. Army War College: Strategic Studies Institute. https://www.jstor.org/stable/pdf/resrep12068.5.pdf; Woon, C. Y. (2020). Framing the "Polar Silk Road" (冰上丝绸之路): Critical geopolitics, Chinese scholars and the (Re) Positionings of China's Arctic interests. *Political Geography, 78,* 102141.

49. Grey, C. G. P. (2013, June 5). Canada and the U.S. (Bizarre Borders Part 2). *YouTube.* http://www.youtube.com/watch?v=qMkYllA7mgw.

50. Nicol, H. N. (2015). *The fence and the bridge: Geopolitics and identity along the Canada–US border.* Waterloo: Wilfrid Laurier University Press.

51. Moens, A., & Gabler, N. (2012). Measuring the costs of the Canada-U.S. border. *Fraser Institute Studies in Canada-U.S. Relations.* http://citeseerx.ist.psu.edu/viewdoc/download?doi=10.1.1.357.9042&rep=rep1&type=pdf; McCallum, J. (1995). National borders matter: Canada-U.S. regional trade patterns. *American Economic Review, 85,* 615–24.

52. Andreas, P. (2012). *Border games: Policing the U.S.-Mexico divide.* Ithaca, NY and London: Cornell University Press; Castaneda, E. (2019). *Building walls: Excluding Latin people in the U.S.* Lanham: Lexington Books; Koyama, J., & Gonzalez-Doğan, S. (2019). Displacement, replacement, and fragmentation in order making: Enacting sovereignty in a U.S.-Mexican border state. *Ethnography.* https://journals.sagepub.com/doi/full/10.1177/1466138119845395.

5

China and Its Neighbors

GEOPOLITICAL CONTEXT

The standard regional divisions of the world often make a distinction between Southeast Asia and East Asia. China's rise across the entire region renders this division problematic (see map 5.1). Therefore, this chapter combines these conventionally defined regions and is titled "China and Its Neighbors" as a nod to the geopolitical realities of an ascendant China across both East and Southeast Asia.

There are a number of significant geopolitical processes at work in this region. We can identify at least four. First, there are the consequences and fallout from the rise and fall of various empires. The region was long dominated by China as the center of a tributary system that extended across the region. China's decline in the nineteenth century and early twentieth century was in part due to the rise of Western powers and of Japan both looking to penetrate the Chinese markets, annex territory, and ensure monopoly trade routes and unfettered resource exploitation. China's long decline has been halted and reversed. The single most significant global geopolitical event of the past thirty years is the rise of China as a major world power. Today, China is now an entrenched global economic power, a major player in the global polity, and a rising military force. China is inaugurating a new world order as it pursues a *grand strategy* of securing supplies of raw material, markets for its goods, and opportunities for its foreign investments.[1]

This region was also impacted by imperial ventures internal and external. There was the rise of a militaristic and expansionist Japan seeking to emulate the United States and European countries in terms of economic growth and territorial acquisitions. The colonial history between Japan and Korea continues to be a factor in their interactions—a theme that we discussed in some detail in chapter 4. In Southeast Asia, Britain, France, and the Netherlands created formal empires that lasted until the end of World War II. The colonial legacy of France in Vietnam was the backdrop to the Vietnam War, referred to as the American War in Vietnam, where a struggle against colonialism was interpreted in Washington through the narrow lens of the Cold War. The break of European colonies was the context for newly independent countries such as Cambodia, Indonesia, Laos,

Map 5.1. China and its neighbors (International Mapping)

Malaysia, Myanmar, and Vietnam. Thailand is the only country in Southeast Asia not formally annexed by a European power.

Second, there are the geopolitics of postcolonial countries navigating a changing world order. Looking at just the relations with the United States: some are maintaining their connections with the United States, such as Japan and South Korea, others are engaging more such as Vietnam, others are reevaluating such as the Philippines under Duterte, while others such as Laos and Cambodia are being pulled more fully into China's orbit.

Third, there are the connections between this region and the global economy. This region saw the rise of the *development state* in its purest form. Japan, South Korea, and Singapore emerged as *Asian tigers*—so called because of their rapid and aggressive economic growth based on global export markets. Latterly, China has emerged as a powerful global economic force in the region and across the world. This region of the world is one of the fastest-growing economic centers of the global economy, shifting the balance of economic power and influence from the West to the Asian East.

Finally, there are international relations within the region. In general, there are few large-scale territorial conflicts between countries. The political conflicts tend to occur within *nation-states*, especially where there are states with more than one nation, such as China, Indonesia, and Myanmar. The conflict in the South China Sea, however, is a geopolitical issue with not only regional but also global significance as a rising China clashes with the rules-based order for maritime demarcations headed by the United States. The power struggle in the South China Sea is for control of a strategic maritime corridor vital to global trade. The South China Sea is the salty stage for the dangerous drama of growing conflict between a rising superpower and an existing superpower.

GEOPOLITICAL HISTORY

The geopolitical history of this region is dominated by the rise and fall of China, neocolonial interventions up to the Vietnam War, the rise and fall of imperial Japan, and a Cold War clash. Let's look at each in turn.

The Rise and Fall of China

China is one of the world's centers of early civilization, exerting a substantial influence and extending its language and culture throughout the wider region. Japan's script is still based on Chinese characters. China's expansion waxed and waned under different dynasties. Under the Tang Dynasty (618–907 CE), for example, there was territorial expansion into Mongolia and Central Asia. Under the Sung Dynasty (660–1126 CE), in contrast, there was a retreat from the conquest of frontier lands. The present-day borders of China first emerged in the early Qing Dynasty (1644–1912 CE).[2] Emperor Kangxi, who ruled for sixty-one years from 1661 to 1722, expanded the empire into Manchuria and Mongolia, taking control of Taiwan and Tibet, and was overlord to Burma, Korea, Thailand, and Nepal. The Qing Dynasty expanded China's influence by settling ethnic Chinese, usually referred to as "Han Chinese," along the frontier zones, a policy still in use today in Xingang and Tibet.

By the middle of the nineteenth century, however, China's power was in decline, and by 1912, the Qing Empire had collapsed. Sun Yat-sen characterized postimperial China as a "loose sheet of sand."[3] Competing and brutal warlords fighting for control and the bitter civil war between Nationalists and Communists weakened the state and undermined a sense of national spirit. Japan annexed Manchuria and then invaded China. It was only in 1949 that some form of territorial integrity was achieved when the Peoples' Republic of China (PRC) was established. After a shaky start and decades of economic dislocation and political turmoil, a resurgent China emerged only after the economic reforms of the 1980s.

For outsiders, it is crucial to remember that, after a century of turmoil and weakness, China's political leaders see national stability, national integration, and international standing as very important issues. After a century of being on the wrong side of asymmetrical relations with foreign powers and subject to dismemberment and annexations, China seeks to reclaim its former position as a preeminent world center of power and influence.

Colonial Interventions

Ever since the Italian merchant Marco Polo (1271–1292) wrote about his travels to China, this region held a special fascination for European traders. Stories of exotic luxury items such as silk, porcelain, and jade attracted Spanish, Portuguese, and Dutch traders. The Portuguese were the first Europeans to sail around the Cape of Good Hope in search of trading opportunities. In 1511, they sailed into Malacca, and a year later, they landed in Indonesia eager to establish contact with the fabled Spice Islands. The spice trade was so valuable that the region was the scene of intense rivalry. The Portuguese and Dutch and later the English/British fought for commercial mastery along the spice trade routes of Southeast Asia. By the beginning of the twentieth century, the region, with the exception of Thailand, was divided up among four major powers. The Dutch controlled Indonesia; the French held Indochina, consisting of Cambodia, Laos, and Vietnam; and the British held sway over Malaysia, Myanmar, and Singapore. The Philippines was a Spanish colony until the Spanish-American War in 1898 when it became a U.S. colony.

Initially, all the Western powers were defeated thoroughly in Southeast Asia in World War II, and their colonies came under Japanese occupation. The Europeans sought to reestablish colonial control after World War II, but independence movements proved too strong. In some cases, success was relatively easy and quick, as in the case of Myanmar, while elsewhere—such as in Malaysia and Indonesia—only after insurgency movements. A tragic case was in French Indochina. The French tendency to see the colonies as part of France meant it was difficult to countenance their independence. This commitment to retaining colonies also was an attempt to reestablish France as a legitimate world power after the abysmal showing of official and military France in World War II. The Germans easily defeated the French at the start of the war, and collaboration with the Nazi regime was rampant throughout the war. Indochina gave an opportunity to reburnish their reputation as a legitimate world power after an appalling performance against the Axis powers.

Vietnamese resistance fighters at Dien Bien Phu defeated the French in 1954, which should have marked the beginning of Vietnamese independence from colonial rule, in line with what was happening in Indonesia and Myanmar. But at this crucial juncture, the United States saw the world in Cold War terms and interpreted a Vietnamese resistance movement as a "Communist plot," part of a global strategy to achieve world domination. An independence movement was perceived, mistakenly by the United States, as part of a Cold War struggle. While other countries in the region achieved independence, the path for Vietnam, Cambodia, and Laos was littered with millions of dead and wounded. In Vietnam, it is referred to as the American War.

In East Asia, in contrast, foreign entry was very limited until the nineteenth century. The entry of the Western powers led to what the Chinese refer to as a century of "national humiliation," signaled by the Opium Wars with Britain. The Chinese wanted to restrict the import of the drug because of its debilitating effects on the population, but the British wanted the profits from the trade. With their defeat in the first Opium War of 1839–1842, China was forced to "open" up its ports to European traders. China lost control over its national space as treaty ports were placed under effective European domination rather than Chinese sovereign control. Hong Kong was ceded to the British and Macao to Portugal. A second Opium War (1856–1860) had similar results. More Chinese ports were opened up to foreigners. China had to pay vast indemnities and the European powers nibbled at China's territory. British surveyors in India extended Britain's imperial boundaries into China, and Russia annexed part of outer Manchuria to allow them access to the Pacific Ocean and to build Vladivostok.

The Legacy of Imperial Japan

In 1853 two ships under the command of U.S. naval officer Matthew Perry sailed into Tokyo Bay. This marked the opening up of Japan to foreign influence and the end of a regime that had promoted two centuries of seclusion. The new regime, known as the Meiji Restoration, embarked on a path of rapid modernization, industrialization, and militarization. Shipyards and factories were constructed, iron and steel industries were quickly established, and a national railroad system was soon built. The industrial military economy relied on imports of raw materials. Japanese elites imagined a new East Asian order of Japanese expansionism that would provide land, food, and resources for their rapidly growing nation.[4]

The first victim of this new order was the Ryukyu Kingdom, now known as Okinawa. It had been an independent state for more than 450 years and made regular tributes to China as a vassal yet sovereign state. Such suzerain states were the building blocks of a Sino-dominated Asian order in which China controlled the foreign policy of tributary states while allowing great autonomy. With Japanese expansionism, Ryukyu came under the joint management of China and Japan for a brief period. Then, as one local official noted, in a poignant geopolitical moment,

> In 1875, the first year of Guangxu and the eighth year of Meiji, we were ordered to immediately stop paying tribute to Qing and receiving throne appointment from Qing, to use Meiji as our era name, and to reform our system of public institutions based on Japanese laws. Our country sent envoys several times to lodge complaints, but Japan has never accepted our pleas.[5]

By 1879, Ryukyu was fully annexed into Japanese control and renamed Okinawa Prefecture. This was the beginning of a new Japanese imperial reordering of the region. Japan moved quickly to assert a wider role in the region, fighting against China and Russia, annexing Korea and Taiwan. After its defeat in the Sino-Japanese War of 1894–1895, China had to cede control to Japanese control not only in Taiwan but also in the Pescadores Islands and Liadong Peninsula in Manchuria. The treaty that ended the war also forced China to open up four new treaty ports and to pay substantial reparations to Japan. Korea also came under the influence of Japan, a prelude to its more formal colonial annexation from 1910 to 1945.

In 1931, Japan annexed Manchuria, setting up a puppet regime and invading China in 1937. In 1941, it launched an attack on the United States at Pearl Harbor and undertook an invasion of Southeast Asia. Japan's heavy reliance of its industrial growth on raw material imported for industrial and military growth was a major reason for Japan's expansionist policies and entry into World War II. Japan considered overseas expansion as a way to avoid economic stagnation, compete with the other major powers, and assert its role in a wider world. Main targets were other countries in the region. In its war with China, as just one example, the Japanese military killed over ten million Chinese. Approximately three hundred thousand were executed in one city over a six-week period in what is known as the Rape of Nanking.[6]

Japan's colonial legacy endures in the dispute with China over the Diaoyu/Senkaku Islands or in the naming controversies with Korea that we discussed in chapter 3. Without an understanding of Korean resentment against Japan's colonial record in Korea, it is impossible to understand the East Sea/Sea of Japan controversy between South Korea and Japan where South Korea claims that the *Sea of Japan* should also be known as the *East Sea*. It is equally difficult to explain China's reaction over the Diaoyu/Senkaku Islands without reference to the collective memories of Japan's brutal war and atrocities against China. These memories often are stoked by state-sponsored nationalism. In 2014, a new holiday, "Victory Day of the Chinese People's War of Resistance Against Japanese Aggression," was promoted and celebrated officially in China.

The Korean War

At the end of World War II, the Korean peninsula, under the domination of Japan from 1910 until 1945, was divided up by the USSR and United States into separate zones of occupation—the Soviet zone north of the 38th Parallel and the U.S. zone to the south. The initial plan was to place the entire country under the trusteeship of the United Nations. However, competing interests eager to grab their chance resulted in the country's partition. In 1948, the Republic of Korea (ROK, henceforth South Korea) was established in the south under the leadership of Syngman Rhee while Kim Il Sung established the Democratic People's Republic of Korea (DPRK, henceforth North Korea). Neither regime was democratic.

On June 25, 1950, at Ongjin, northwest of Seoul, fighting broke out when North Korean forces crossed the border. Events soon spiraled into the Korean War. North Korean forces quickly overran much of the peninsula as South Korean forces scattered and ran. By mid-September 1950, the North Korean army had pushed all the way to Pusan in the far south of the peninsula. The United States sent troops, persuaded the United Nations (UN) to become involved, and quickly pushed the North Koreans all the way back north up to the border with China on the Yalu River. The Chinese Army then entered the conflict on October 19, 1950, and launched a counteroffensive that pushed the U.S.-UN forces back to the 38th Parallel. Rapid advances and retreats on both sides stalled by June 1951, and the war became a static trench war. The divide between North and South, created after the cease-fire in 1953, became a front line between the Communist and Capitalist blocs of the Cold War.[7]

The Korean War was a bloody encounter. From hostilities breaking out in 1950 to the armistice in 1953, military and civilian casualties and deaths are estimated at between 5.2 million and 5.7 million. No formal peace treaty was signed. The 1953 armistice was an agreement among military commanders of the UN, North Korean, and Chinese forces to cease hostilities, to exchange prisoners of war, and to establish a demarcation line with a demilitarized zone stretching two kilometers in either direction from this line. The military cease-fire froze relations into a permanent war footing. A formal peace treaty that could provide some form of political resolution to the conflict remains a tantalizing possibility, and the continuing uncertain and unresolved arrangement constitutes a danger-ous situation.

The "temporary" armistice line has become a fixed element in the Korean landscape. A narrow but deep scar divides the South—an affluent democracy—from the North, a totalitarian dynastic state that crushes its people. A major legacy of the war is the continuing presence of U.S. forces in Japan and South Korea and China's continued support for North Korea.

THE RECENT RISE OF CHINA

China was once the largest and richest empire in the world. After almost two centuries of relative and absolute decline, it has reemerged as a great power. To what extent it threatens the hegemony of the United States is an important issue that captures the attention of Chinese and U.S. military and political leaders.[8]

China was devastated by decades of war and civil unrest before the Commu-nist Party took power in 1949. Poverty was widespread throughout a largely rural population. The Communist Party drew its support from the countryside and viewed the cities, especially the more cosmopolitan trading cities such as Shang-hai, with a wary eye. The early decades of the PRC were rough: it was involved in a costly war in Korea. In 1950, it sent three million troops to push back against South Korean, U.S., and UN troops. The entry of the Chinese military pushed the U.S. and UN forces back, but at the cost of roughly four hundred thousand Chinese troops killed and five hundred thousand more wounded.

In the early years of Communist control, China was a junior partner to the USSR in an alliance against the West. China became even more isolated in world politics, after the Sino-Soviet split of 1963. As relations between the USSR and United States began to warm periodically from their icy fastness, China was left the "odd man out," with few friends in either the Capitalist or Socialist worlds. There were also internal difficulties. China experienced a Mao-manufactured famine from 1959 to 1962 that killed almost thirty-five million people, then suffered through the dislocation of the Cultural Revolution from 1966 to 1976, when schools and universities were closed. Senior party officials, the educated and intellectuals, were sent to the countryside. It was only with the death of Mao in 1976 that China began to experience a measure of internal calm.

Geopolitical Consequences of Economic Growth

In 1978, the ruling Communist Party announced a new policy. It was known as Open Door, and it represented a dramatic shift. The previous commitment to a centrally planned economy, self-sufficiency, and national isolation was replaced by an encouragement of private markets and promotion of global trade to achieve rapid rates of growth. This policy was tested in a select range of coastal cities, then spread across the entire country.[9]

The speed and scale of China's subsequent economic rise is remarkable. It marked a dramatic shift from an emphasis on the politics of revolution to the prioritization of the economics of development. Before the economic liberalizations, China was a poor country and a bystander in the everyday operation of global society. China's rise since then is marked by a spectacular economic growth that has lifted close to four hundred million people out of poverty.[10]

The economic reforms saw the reemergence of a market economy. State firms still play important roles in heavy industry sectors, and the Communist Party still retains absolute political control. But the reforms did involve the promotion of private enterprise, the privatization of some state assets, and the personal accumulation of wealth. It is officially known as Socialism with Chinese Characteristics, although it is probably more accurate to describe it as Capitalism with Chinese Characteristics.[11]

The recent economic rise of China is spectacular on a scale and pace not seen in world history. Since 1978 China's GDP has grown at an annual average rate of 10 percent. In 1989, its GDP per capita was only $403 and only one hundred thousand people owned a car. By 2018 the GDP per capita had risen to $10,200 and 172 million people owned a car. China is now the world's second largest economy.

China's huge budget surplus and its vast foreign exchange, currently valued at a staggering $4 trillion, gives the country a fiscal heft that generates a massive sovereign wealth fund, with the ability to make foreign investments and to afford an expensive and ambitious military buildup. The imposing buildings of Chinese banks along the Bund in Shanghai, many originally built as the headquarters of foreign banks, are appropriate symbols for China's financial power (see photo 5.1). Economic growth has powered China into a globally significant geopolitical and geoeconomic position.

There are internal consequences of the rapid growth. The Communist Party's legitimacy now lies in large part on its ability to maintain China's growth so that living standards are maintained if not improved. The lifestyles of conspicuous consumption, only recently and in some cases precariously established, need to be maintained. But the more China is tightly linked to a global system, the more it is subject to the gyrations of the world economy with sometimes negative consequences. The global financial crisis of 2008–2009 caused a fall in demand from North American and European markets that rippled along the global supply chains and was eventually felt by Chinese factories. There was mounting labor

Photo 5.1.   Banks along the Bund in Shanghai (John Rennie Short)

unrest as thousands of workers went on strike in the city of Dongguan where 450 factories were suddenly closed. Since China neither has an extensive social safety net nor a free public health system, economic layoffs are punishing. During economic crises it tends to be the more market-oriented, small- and medium-sized businesses that go under, while the less efficient state-owned enterprises survive due to political support that assures them easier access to cheap credit. China's steel industry is a classic example of overproduction that is subsidized by the state. This cheap steel is dumped onto world markets. The more China is enmeshed in the gyrations of boom and slump in the global economy, the more the private sector is subject to crisis, while the politically connected but economically inefficient industries may survive. This leads to a less efficient national economy over the long term. Moreover, the growing inequality in the country is not as much of a problem when everyone's income is increasing, but it becomes more problematic during downturns. When incomes are falling, the social safety net is full of holes. There are also rising issues due to the close connection between the ruling party elite and wealth accumulation.

A rise in living standards has created a new set of expectations. For many young people in China, the only experience they have is that of increasing income and growing wealth. Any significant and lasting break in that trajectory raises issues of legitimacy. The increasingly authoritarian rule of the Chinese leader Xi Jinping, who came to power in 2013, can be seen in one sense as a response to the fear that global economic downturns will have such a negative impact on

China that social dislocation could undermine the legitimacy of the Communist Party. There are other mounting problems for China. The population is aging, other countries are considering tariffs and sanctions against China, and there are new centers of cheap production. The increasing use of authoritarian power is less a sign of strength than a sense that the leadership worries about future social unrest and wants to head it off with a more authoritarian police state. The more muscular foreign policy of Xi is one way to shore up support. The displays of Chinese power resonate, creating powerful populist sentiments. Although they are carefully managed and sometimes orchestrated by the party, they do entail some risk.[12] Too much support for particularly risky endeavors, however, such as a more aggressive posture in the South China Sea, can box in the options for a Chinese leadership unwilling to be perceived as weak. Just like yoking popular expectations to increasing living standards, so harnessing populist sentiment to more obvious displays of power runs the risk of backlash if things falter or fail.

Three things compromise long-term stability in China: corruption, an aging population—the country will "lose" 150 million workers in the next twenty years—and whether the party is able to meet popular expectations. In such a centralized society, economic performance is intimately tied to the government. China needs to create approximately ten million jobs a year to keep pace with the number of young people entering the job market. Economic growth is a sign of government competence and legitimacy while economic slowdown prompts criticism of government and the possibility of a legitimacy crisis. The present Chinese leadership is acutely aware of the fall of the Soviet Union and sensitive to the notion that it might be a harbinger if Chinese growth either falters or stalls.

The rapid economic rise of China was built on the basis of importing raw materials and exporting manufactured goods. From the 1980s to the 2000s, it was often assumed in the West that linking China to the global economy in this way would usher in social changes, perhaps even democratization. In fact, there is no proof that democracy comes in the wake of marketization. As China continued to pursue an economic capitalism with an authoritarian government, more repressive since 2013, the link between market and democracy is now seen for what it was—a chimera—only touted by those who want cover for doing business with China.

China's spectacular growth has caused some resentment and undercut the popular commitment to global free trade, especially in countries in Europe and North America, where there was a hollowing of manufacturing employment. It has proved difficult for foreign companies to gain access to the Chinese market, intellectual property theft is rampant, and for decades, China's currency was seriously undervalued in order to cheapen exports and make imports that much more expensive. In other words, China was able to gain enormously from the existing global trade model. But while China has benefited from free trade, it has rarely practiced it. A growing backlash was crystalized by the Trump administration's efforts to renegotiate trading arrangements and to address China's huge trade surplus with the United States. The growth of China is not the only reason but is a significant one in the mounting resentment against existing global trade arrangements. Recent examples include the U.S. abandonment of the Trans-

Pacific Partnership (TPP) in 2017. Paradoxically, this move aided China in the region more than the United States, because the TPP was specifically set up to exclude China.

China faces major issues as it seeks to move up the value-added chain to produce ever-more-sophisticated products. It needs a more efficient use of capital, more skilled workers, and a stronger culture of innovation. Yet intense international competition makes the earlier success based on relatively simple manufacturing less possible than ever. Countries and companies learned their lesson and are less willing to allow China to pirate technology, disrupt domestic markets, and game the global trading system.

Not only governments, but also some companies have rethought their response to China. Initially, China was seen as a huge market opportunity for foreign companies, but the uneven playing field for foreign firms has weakened corporate community support for improving relations. For many companies, Beijing's efforts to compel them to accept China's positions on sensitive issues such as Hong Kong and Taiwan have caused a reassessment of investing in China. However, China is such a huge market that many companies—Yahoo is just one example—tend to elide their corporate interests with those of the Chinese state. So, rather than a democratization of China we have witnessed a "Sinification" of corporate capitalism.

Open Door inaugurated a truly spectacular economic boom as China became the major manufacturing center of the global economy, sucking in imports worldwide as well as exporting goods across the globe. In 1978, foreign trade was less than 10 percent of GDP. By 2020, it was almost 40 percent. In 1978, China constituted only between 1 and 3 percent of the global GDP. It is now estimated at between 17 to 20 percent.[13] China is an important link in the global economy. It is the largest export destination for thirty-three countries and the largest importer for sixty-five countries. This prime position means that the Chinese state is actively involved with national economies around the world. China's booming economy requires a very active foreign policy to secure raw material and ensure access to markets, and this is where geopolitics and geoeconomics merge. One of the important elements of China's grand strategy is to maintain and expand its control over raw material supplies. And this involves signing deals and making trading arrangements with a range of countries, especially primary producers. China's capacity to maintain its economic position requires a carefully choreographed foreign policy of trade deals and arrangements with many nations across the globe. Where there is asymmetry between China and its trading partners, which is invariably the case except for the world's largest economies, China has the upper hand.

Significant foreign investment into China began around 1990 and has grown. China remains the second biggest recipient of foreign investment, but its economic success has resulted in a huge trade-and-budget surplus that is invested around the world. The Chinese government now holds 20 percent of all U.S. debt held overseas and around 7 percent of the U.S. total debt load.[14] Chinese private foreign investment has grown dramatically to over $200 billion. Perhaps the most visible sign of the deployment of the budget surplus for geoeconomics and geopolitical reasons is the Belt and Road Initiative (BRI).

Belt and Road

The Belt and Road Initiative (BRI) was announced in 2013. It was hailed as a major infrastructural project funded by the Chinese government, state-owned enterprises, and private companies. It was aimed at linking China with the rest of the world in a series of networks. It is a Chinese-oriented trading system that aims to link with 152 countries at a total cost of $1 to $5 trillion. By the end of 2019, $5.6 billion had already been invested in 138 ventures. BRI partner countries now number 138, with 43 in Asia, 40 in Africa, 26 in Europe, 19 in the Americas, and 10 in Oceania (see map 5.2). The Chinese government has injected huge amounts of money into import-export banks that can lend cheaply to Chinese state-owned enterprises and private companies that can then outbid foreign competitors. In 2015, for example, Chinese companies beat out Japanese bids to build a high-speed rail network in Indonesia.[15]

One of the maritime networks, for example, links the ports of Colombo in Sri Lanka ($300 million invested), Gwadar in Pakistan ($1 billion), Djibouti ($185 million), and Piraeus in Greece ($300 million). These investments were made by state-run shipping companies, including the Cosco Group, China Overseas Holding Co., and Chinese Merchant Holdings.

The BRI expands China's export market, reduces trade frictions, and also helps Chinese companies with overcapacity and too much savings. It merges geoeconomics and geopolitics as it makes some countries more dependent on China and extends China's global reach and economic dominance. China is now a major investor in sub-Saharan Africa. Chinese-funded projects, often involving large amounts of Chinese labor, are evident across the continent. In Kenya, for example, Chinese companies built the Mombasa to Nairobi railway at a cost of $3.2 billion, the largest infrastructure project in the country since it gained independence.

Chinese investment is particularly evident across South and Southeast Asia. In some cases, the investment was a debt trap. China gave loans for enlarging the port of Colombo in Sri Lanka, but when the port's activities racked up losses and were unable to service the debt and defaulted on the Chinese loans, the Sri Lankan government was forced to give Beijing control of its major seaport for ninety-nine years. Some countries have balked at the ancillary costs of projects and the dangers of a debt trap. The former prime minister of Malaysia, Mahathir Mohamad, expressed a concern about "a new version of colonialism" and canceled Chinese projects worth almost $23 billion, in order to avoid the same fate of Sri Lanka. In 2018, the new president of the Maldives scrapped a trade deal with China, claiming that it was a one-way treaty.

Myanmar has reversed course from its prior enthusiasm.[16] In 2011, the government of Myanmar halted construction of the Myitsone dam—one of China's largest investment projects in the country—due to concerns over growing Chinese influence and potential environmental damage. The project remains in limbo, but China still remains the largest investor in Myanmar, with more than $15 billion in business projects in 2018.

While Chinese investment improves accessibility and upgrades infrastructure, it also comes with costs. One report listed the many drawbacks: an erosion

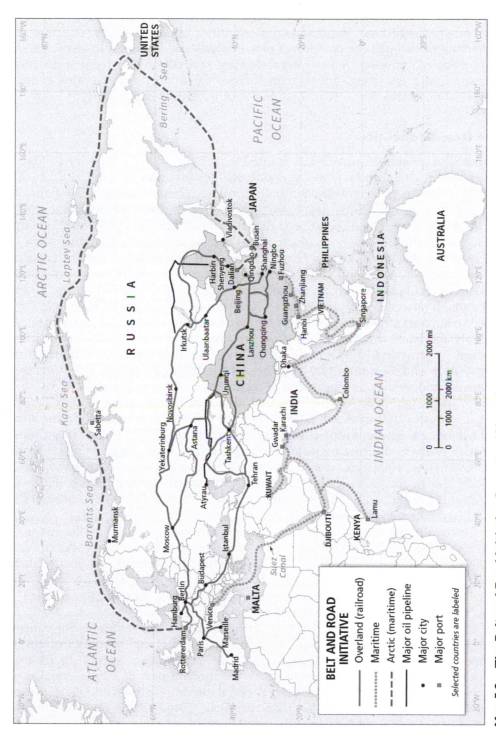

Map 5.2. The Belt and Road Initiative (International Mapping)

of national sovereignty for recipients, lack of transparency, large and possibly unsustainable financial burdens, and negative environmental impacts.[17] A positive spin on the BRI sees improved infrastructure and the possibility of economic development through the creation of new markets and increases in employment and technology transfer. A more negative view sees it as a new form of *neocolonialism*. The huge foreign investment increases China's power through control over vital networks not only in East and Southeast Asia but globally.[18]

The New Geopolitics

Spectacular economic growth has granted China the power necessary to play a larger role in global and regional geopolitics. This involves the centering of Chinese interests in global governance and international institutions.[19] Compared to just thirty years ago, China now has a greater engagement in organizations such as the World Trade Organization and the United Nations. It is now the third largest funder of the UN and is involved in global institutions of governance such as Interpol and the World Health Organization. It is actively involved in creating global standards, rules, and norms for a variety of practices from internet security and intellectual property rights to trade and banking. When denied access, it now has enough power to establish parallel institutions. When the U.S. Congress refused to support an increased role for China in the International Monetary Fund, China established the Asian Infrastructure Investment Bank (AIIB) in 2016 and pledged to provide $40 billion worth of funds for infrastructure improvement across Asia and Oceania. By 2020, the AIIB numbered seventy-eight member countries and twenty-four prospective members, and had committed $13.45 billion to sixty-eight approved projects, including a municipal water supply project in Bangladesh ($100 million), a fiber optic network in Cambodia ($75 million), and a flood management project in Manila, Philippines ($207 million). For China, the AIIB is a way of utilizing its vast foreign exchange and signposting its growing international prestige. It signals China's emergence as an active and major stakeholder in the global economic order. China is also using its soft power in the establishment of Confucius Institutes in schools and universities around the world to create a more favorable image of China to the external world.

China also wields its economic power to influence global public opinion. When the Chinese human rights activist, Liu Xiaobo, won the Nobel Peace Prize in 2010, the Chinese government not only complained bitterly but also wielded its economic muscle, banning salmon exports from Norway. The trade was worth more than $1 billion and was only restored in 2017, the same year that Liu Xiaobo died after almost ten years as a political prisoner.

China is now a major player competing with the United States for control and dominance over international organizations and global practices of governance. Some take a sanguine view, seeing it as natural outgrowth of the reemergence of China's great power as a recent yet integral part of a long-established international order. Others see an existential threat. Unlike the USSR, which was always economically weaker than the West, China cannot be economically contained so easily. Others see the emergence of a bipolar world: the United

States still a global power but competing with a China that will dominate in East and Southeast Asia.[20] Some even take a more Sinocentric view. In an influential book, Martin Jacques asks the question, what happens when China rules the world? His answer: a new world order with at its center "a Communist regime, a highly sophisticated statecraft, and an authoritarian Confucian rather than democratic polity."[21] He sees a future of China's growing global hegemony.

A resurgent China is also embodied in growing military power. Part of the increase in military spending is due to the increase in the size of the economy. Even if military spending remains a fixed proportion of GDP, the massive increase in GDP means more absolute spending on the military. Using traditional accounting methods, it appears that China devotes 1.9 percent of GDP to military expenditure compared to the U.S. 3.2 percent of GDP. In this standard accounting method, China has only the equivalent of 40 percent of U.S. military spending. But using purchasing parity, which considers differences in labor and operational costs, China's spending is closer to $455 billion or 75 percent to what the United States spends.[22] Nevertheless, it is an enormous amount to be used in support of China's emerging geopolitical goals.

A central part of Chinese geopolitical thinking is the *First Island Strategy*.[23] This strategy encompasses the maritime areas delimited by an arc of islands and peninsulas that stretch from Japan southward to the South China Sea. A more ambitious Second Island Chain extends northward as far as the Sea of Okhotsk to the Kamchatka peninsula and includes the Philippines and much of Indonesia (see map 5.3). The aim of the First Island Strategy is to seal off these seas around China to minimize vulnerability to attack, especially from the United States. Behind this island chain, also sometimes known as "string of pearls," China is seeking to secure itself from U.S. power. China's prior weakness in the region was exposed in 1996. In the run-up to Taiwan's presidential election, China conducted missile tests and military maneuvers to dissuade the Taiwanese from moving toward a formal declaration of independence. President Clinton sent two aircraft carrier groups, the *Independence* and the *Nimitz*, to the Taiwan Strait. The demonstration of overwhelming U.S. power cowed the Chinese in the short term. But in the long term, China responded with a buildup of military power, including ships, fighters, and submarines, and thus began their goal of annexing effectively the South China Sea and of threatening the Japanese over the contested islands of Diaoyu/Senkaku. It is building up a sophisticated force system, including ballistic, cruise, and hypersonic glide missiles and deploying a fleet of submarines armed with nuclear ballistic missiles. The overall aim is to generate a credible response to U.S. aircraft carriers and air bases in the Asia-Pacific region to deny the U.S. ability to threaten China.

The United States has significant military assets in the region, including important bases in South Korea and Japan and a powerful aircraft carrier force. During the COVID-19 pandemic in 2020, the USS *Theodore Roosevelt* was marooned in Guam, showing that even the world's premier carrier fleet is subject to unexpected setbacks. The Chinese military buildup is so large that it now provides a much more credible deterrence to U.S. power; it also assures that China could more easily invade Taiwan. Holding onto Taiwan would be another matter

Map 5.3.   Island chains

altogether. The U.S. response to China's buildup in the region was the *pivot to Asia*, an announcement in 2011 that heralded a shifting in the emphasis of U.S. naval deployment from the Atlantic to the Pacific.[24]

China continues to build up its military forces with the aim of achieving dominance in the Indo-Pacific region and of being a credible global competitor to the United States by 2049.[25] China is projecting military power across the region. The most obvious case is in the South China Sea, the subject of the Geopolitical Hotspot section in this chapter.

China released a report on June 24, 2019 about its future military strategy.[26] It stated that China would be willing to use force to assert its claims over the South China Sea and Taiwan and to resist the U.S. claim to be the hegemon on the region. The national policy was for a "New Era," commonly taken to mean a "new world order," with China playing a more important role. Military policy is now more braided with overall Chinese geopolitical thinking as Xi is now commander in chief and maintains absolute control after years of purges against those seen as disloyal.

CHINESE GEOPOLITICS UNDER XI

China has a long tradition of geopolitical writing and thought. Let's consider only one of the more recent writers. Wei Yuan (1794–1857) was a civil servant at a time of Chinese imperial decline when the Qing dynasty, after two centuries of growth and expansion, was hard-pressed by foreign powers, including Japan, Russia, the UK, and the United States. China's self-perception as the center of the world was coming to an end. In his 1826 text, *An Anthology of Statecraft*, Yuan sought out ways to strengthen the empire. After the Opium War of 1839–1842 when China was humiliated, he argued for repeating the early success of the Qing with stronger armed forces and expansion at the empire's periphery. He promoted Han emigration to Xinjiang. In order for China to return to greatness, he called for borrowing knowledge from foreigners. His *Illustrated Treatise on Sea Power*, written in 1844 at a time of British maritime dominance, called for improved Chinese sea defenses and enhanced sea power by building more warships. Wei Yuan wrote from a place of weakness at a time when China had to adapt to more powerful adversaries. He wrote about the ambiguities of China in a world when China was decentering from global power. His call for extension of empire and stronger armed forces in order to recenter the world on China was counterbalanced by the need to be careful and to learn from other stronger powers.

His ideas are interesting because they are echoed in the present era of official Chinese geopolitical thinking about reentering and recentering the global polity. The ambiguities and geopolitical hesitations noted by Yuan evidence contemporary Communist Party rule. One of China's paramount leaders, Deng Xiaoping, is reported to have said in 1990 "hide your strength and bide your time." He was counseling China to build up its power gradually without drawing too much attention to itself. Play the long game. No need for drawing attention until the time is absolutely right. Subsequent leaders followed Deng's advice until President Xi Jinping (1953–present) came to power in 2012 after the enigmatic Hu Jintao. Xi's father was an early member of the Communist Party who rose to the position of vice premier but was purged in the Cultural Revolution and sent to the countryside for reeducation. The experience did not dim Xi's chances of success. As a princeling—a child of revolutionary heroes—he found it relatively easy to move up the party hierarchy after the Cultural Revolution fizzled out and its architect, Chairman Mao, was criticized. Xi became a provincial governor before becoming general secretary of China's Communist Party in 2012. Previous incumbents had come and gone in ritual, stage-managed succession. Xi had other plans. He solidified his position by concentrating his power over the military and the direction of social reforms. He established a shadow cabinet made up of old school friends and brought corruption charges against his political enemies. In 2014 alone, one hundred thousand officials were charged with corruption. He was instrumental in abolishing term limits for presidency and, like Mao before him, his thoughts were published and became part of the state constitution. Xi centralized power by purging competing factions, often under the guise of rooting out corruption.[27]

Xi Jinping is different from all the other previous leaders since Mao. He has centralized power around the cult of his personality, more reminiscent of Mao than of Deng. He has pursued policies of greater social control through mass surveillance and internet censorship, a more assertive foreign policy, a larger military, and an increased global profile. In 2017 he gave an address to a congress of senior Communist Party officials.[28] He noted that now was the time for China to take center stage in the world, becoming the dominant power in the East Asia region and a major power throughout the rest of the world. He mapped out a global geopolitics centered on Beijing. He stressed the aim to have a world-class military by 2025. The emphasis was to be on a fighting force rather than a deterrence force. They were not empty words. China now has the biggest and fastest shipbuilding program. It has the largest navy (though it is short on aircraft carriers compared to the United States), coast guard, and maritime militia, and the largest conventional ballistic- and cruise-missile force in the world. China is now a power determined to shape the world and challenge the United States.[29]

Whereas Deng had promoted economic growth over military buildup, Xi's rule marks a new era, marked by a tighter authoritarian control over Chinese society, a vast military buildup, and a more muscular foreign policy. It has its detractors inside China who have argued that Deng's advice should still be followed. Too obvious a demonstration of Chinese power and global ambitions only provokes the United States and its allies. Why not wait, is the advice of some. But the more Xi has concentrated power, stifled opposition within the Party, and taken greater control over the military, the less these alternative opinions are voiced.

China's growing assertiveness is obvious. In 2020, during the middle of the COVID-19 pandemic, for example, the military made incursions into Indian territory high in the Himalayas, Chinese vessels continued their increasing harassment in the South China Sea confronting Malaysian and Vietnamese boats and sailed an aircraft carrier through the Taiwan Strait, twice, just to make the point more forcefully and to rattle the Taiwanese government. The Chinese government also cracked down on protestors in Hong Kong and by the end of summer 2020 had effectively dismantled the relative autonomy of the former British colony.[30]

A popular Chinese description of recent history is that China stood up under Mao, got rich under Deng Xiaoping, and got powerful under Xi Jinping. The pithy remark combines the trajectory of the establishment of an independent China, then the emphasis on economic growth, and the more recent commitment to China as a major world power eager to assert its influence.

The Territorial Integration of China

October 1 is celebrated as National Day in China. The year 2019 had special significance because it marked seventy years since the establishment of Communist rule in 1949. Beijing put on a huge parade. In Tiananmen Square, more than 15,000 troops and 100,000 civilians marched past, 600 vehicles drove past, and 180 aircraft flew overhead. The thousand-strong army band was joined by a 2,100-adult choir and a 400-children choir. Yet at the very same time as this tightly choreographed flag-waving, singing, and marching suggested a fully integrated and carefully controlled society, demonstrators in Hong Kong were taking to the streets, Taiwan was still independent from China, a million Uighurs were effectively imprisoned, and many Tibetans were still not comfortable with Han Chinese taking over their lands. Behind the grand celebration of national unity in Beijing, there were significant cracks in the territorial integrity of the vast country.

Han Chinese constitute more than 91 percent of China's vast population of 1.3 billion. "Han" is not unchanging ethnic reality but a nineteenth-century invention to describe what was in fact an amalgam of races to contrast with the Qing rulers, who were Manchus, and with the foreign Westerners. Han Chinese have spread across into the furthest reaches of China. In the past twenty-five years, millions of Han Chinese have settled throughout greater China, diluting the local influence and affecting the language and culture of the non-Han. Distinct ethnic minorities persist in Tibet and Xinjiang despite the central authority's attempt to Sinicize them.

Tibet and Xinjiang

Long isolated from the rest of the world by inaccessible mountain ranges and a hermitic society, Tibet developed as a feudal Buddhist theocracy. It came under Chinese control under the Qing dynasty, but it was always on the edge of effective Chinese power. Troops of imperial China invaded in 1792, incited by fears of a Britain expanding from its base in India, and declared Tibet a protectorate. Tibet managed to break away in 1912 and become a sovereign state. In October 1950, more than forty thousand China troops invaded Tibet. It proved an easy and lucrative annexation. It was a weak and vulnerable state on China's border with few powerful allies and important resources such as minerals (uranium and lithium) and water. The Dalai Lama, both the spiritual and political leader of the country, was forced to flee the country after a failed uprising against Chinese control in 1959. The Chinese embarked on a policy of secularization as more than six thousand monasteries were destroyed, and a modernization program with new roads and railways. The in-migration of Han Chinese was encouraged. Tibet's resources were exploited for China's "growth machine." Water resources, for example, were exploited. Glacier run-off is an important source of water in the region, allowing the construction of many dams. Major environmental impacts of this massive dam building included deforestation.[31] This damming also has major consequences downriver for 750 million people in India, Bangladesh, Burma, Cambodia, and Laos. The control over this vital water supply gives China tremendous leverage in the wider region.

Protests against China's rule have erupted sporadically. While there is still a Tibetan diaspora and Tibet government in exile in India, there is declining support for an independent Tibet. Too many governments and businesses are too leery of upsetting China. An independent Tibet remains a dwindling object of concern in the global political community.

Xinjiang is home to an ethnic Muslim minority called the Uighurs, a Turkish-speaking Muslim people. They constitute around 43 percent of the total population of twenty-two million in the region that came under PRC rule in 1949. With a distinctive ethnicity and religion, located far from central government, the Uighur region presents a possible threat to China's territorial integrity. Many

Uighurs fear that the invasion of Han Chinese is destroying their culture. They have long chafed at Chinese rule and the immigration of Han peoples into the region and separatist sentiment lingered. In 1997 there were mass arrests and executions by Chinese forces in the city of Ghulam. Clashes in 2009 caused more than two hundred deaths and a hundred more in 2013. A terrorist attack in Beijing, which in 2013 killed five people when a jeep veered into a crowd in Tiananmen Square, prompted a crackdown. There is now a vicious cycle as Chinese authorities clamp down with more surveillance and more overt policing that tends to provoke ever more Uighur resentment. The independence struggle is sometimes clothed in the rhetoric of a more conservative Islam. The rumblings on China's western border will continue. More than a million Uighurs in far western China are being held in camps that the Chinese government describes as "reeducation centers," and most foreign press describes as "prisons."[32]

Hong Kong

After China's defeat in the Opium War (1839–1842), Britain laid claim to the island of Hong Kong and then annexed part of the mainland, known as Kowloon. In 1898, they signed a ninety-nine-year lease for the territory with China. The city grew as a trading port, and people flooded in from the mainland. From the 1950s to the 1970s, the city was an important manufacturing center and then emerged as an important banking center. In the 1960s, British plans for direct elections were quashed by China, which wanted the colonial status upheld prior to the handover. Hong Kong was returned to China in 1997, when it was established as a special administrative region under the slogan of "one country, two systems." The slogan was meant to indicate that the PRC would respect the distinct character of Hong Kong as a private, market-based economy at least until 2047, when it was set to return to full Chinese control. The Chinese authorities promised to grant universal suffrage by 2017. Today, only half of the legislative seats are directly elected. Most power resides with the chief executive, who is always carefully vetted by the PRC. The island's economy, especially the lucrative property market, is dominated by a small number of tycoons.

Hong Kong accounted for 16 percent of China's GDP in 1997 but only 3 percent in 2019. Other Chinese cities, especially Shanghai, are now key financial hubs linking the region to the rest of the world. As a result, Hong Kong's economic primacy was under threat and so, too, was its relative political autonomy. Yet Hong Kong remained important. There were no capital controls, so it was a good place for Chinese companies to raise capital from overseas. Thousands of foreign companies were attracted by the English legal system and rule of law. Things began to change, however, when in 2003 the first chief executive, Tung Chee-hwa, a shipping tycoon from Shanghai, tried to push through an extension of police powers, especially for treason and sedition. Half a million people filled the streets to protest. In 2012, students again took to the streets to protest the introduction of "patriotic education" as extolled by the Chinese Communist Party (CCP). In 2014, as part of the worldwide Occupy Movement, young protestors demanded political reform and took to the streets to demand free and open elections. The Chinese authorities cracked down heavily: it was clear that the

Chinese authorities interpreted the two-system designation as allowing Hong Kong to be a separate economic entity but not a separate political entity. Popular protests began again in the summer 2019 against a plan by the non-elected, pro-Chinese chief executive, Carrie Lam, to allow for the extradition of people to mainland China. Many saw this as yet one more element of tightening PRC control. For several months, there was escalating confrontation as police used tear gas to move demonstrators. The airport was shut down, businesses closed, and in a spiral of violence, there were more arrests and injuries. The people's voice was loudly heard in local elections held in late 2019 when anti-Chinese and pro-democracy candidates won sweeping victories. In April 2020, Beijing orchestrated the arrests of pro-democracy activists and, a month later, announced anti-sedition laws that allow for the operation of national security agencies inside the city. The full incorporation of Hong Kong signaled the death knell of a quasi-autonomous Hong Kong. The two-systems system—at least as initially interpreted by the Hong Kong public and the international community—is over. Xi is less interested in maintaining the two systems than he is in asserting Chinese authority. The protests gave Xi an opportunity to deflect discontent at home with an orchestrated portrayal of "foreign interference" in Hong Kong. In response, the United States and other nations are reconsidering their economic relations with a Hong Kong that for all intents and purposes is now fully incorporated into the PRC.

Taiwan

Taiwan was annexed in 1683 by the Qing dynasty during its expansionary period. It came under Dutch colonial rule (1624–1662) when millions of Han Chinese were encouraged to settle on the island. Taiwan was then enmeshed by aggressive Japanese expansion and became part of the Japanese Empire in 1895. When the CCP took control over mainland China in 1949, their defeated enemies, the Nationalists, set up a government in Taiwan. Two million mainland Chinese moved to Taiwan, where six million people already lived. The mainland Chinese soon established themselves as the political and economic elite. Taiwan, officially the Republic of China, was given a seat at the United Nations. It received and continues to receive U.S. military support. However, after 1971, when the PRC was accepted into the United Nations, Taiwan lost international legitimacy.

China claims Taiwan as one of its twenty-three provinces, and all official Chinese maps display Taiwan as a province of the PRC. For years, both states existed in a state of guarded and slightly uncertain political relations. Although the official CCP position is that Taiwan was a part of China, the CCP seemed content to play the long game and wait for reunification without forcing the issue in the short to medium term. The policy was known as "mutual nondenial." But under a more confrontational Xi, the delicate balance of the older order is upset. China has stepped up its goal of isolating Taiwan from the global community, such as banning it from aviation and global health forums. China seeks to isolate the island and has drawn up plans for an invasion, although there are competing voices within Chinese leadership with the military most likely behind a more muscular response and the political leadership promoting a policy of coercion without violence.[33]

There is a backlash in Taiwan against the flexing of China's muscles. Tsai-Ing-wen was first elected Taiwan president in 2016. Although she was not especially popular, she won a resounding victory in January 2020, amassing more than eight million votes and securing 57 percent of the total vote compared to her pro-PRC rival with 39 percent. Her campaign drew heavily on media coverage of the 2019 protests and police crackdown in Hong Kong. In response, Xi has doubled down with even more explicit talk of a military response.[34]

NEW GEOPOLITICS IN THE REGION

The rise of China has created a new power source in East and Southeast Asia. The shifting balance of power between the U.S. and China axis is the primary force field for new geopolitical relations in the region.[35]

For the previous fifty years, the United States was the dominant geopolitical and military force in the region. After the post–World War II fall of the colonial powers, the United States was the major power able to exert its influence, although not always for the good, waging an ill-conceived war in Vietnam, carpet-bombing large parts of Laos and Cambodia, encouraging bloody purges in Indonesia, and propping up a corrupt regime in the Philippines. The United States created strong military alliances with Japan, Philippines, and South Korea. Some of these alliances have remained *despite* the rise of China; others remain *because of* the rise of China. New geopolitical configurations are being forged in the furnace of U.S.-China rivalry. Let us look at some of the more important ones.

Korea, China, and the United States

South Korea has strong ties with the United States and hosts large U.S. military bases. The United States has air force bases in Kunsan and Osan; a navy base in Busan, and eleven army bases, including Yongsan, Daegu, and Seongnam. Almost twenty-five thousand U.S. military personnel are stationed in South Korea. Until very recently, U.S. and South Korean armed forces regularly participated in large-scale military war games. The ties between South Korea and the United States form an alliance against China and North Korea.[36]

North Korea is the more unpredictable threat.[37] Since the ending of the Korean War in 1953, South Korea and North Korea have drifted far apart in terms of democratization and economic development, though still tied by animosity and distrust. With no formal peace treaty, their relationship is tense and potentially very dangerous with massed militaries on either side of their shared border. South Korea tends to follow a cyclical pattern of administrations seeking reconciliation then replaced with less conciliatory administrations when little progress is made. North Korea remains more resolutely and stubbornly antagonistic with official rhetoric bordering on war mongering. South Korea has democratized, becoming richer and more inserted into the global polity. In contrast, North Korea remains an isolated country with the majority of its population impoverished and vulnerable to food insecurity: it is less a state and more a family dynasty, a personality cult with an appalling human rights record. North Korea does have important mineral resources, and China is its major trading partner, but it can barely afford to feed its own people in part because it must support a large military, an expensive missile program, and a nuclear arsenal. North Korea has one of the largest armies in the world—close to one million—and nuclear weapons, launching its first nuclear test in 2006. It is one of the few *nuclear states* in the world, which gives the North Korean leadership important leverage, providing deterrence against the forcible overthrow of its corrupt and brutal regime. This leadership uses its nuclear arsenal as an insurance against any external and existential threat to its rule.

China and North Korea share an 880-mile border. This northern border is North Korea's lifeline to the world. North Korea's dynastic dictatorship carries a thin, almost threadbare, justificatory mantle of socialism. It is not socialist brotherhood that ties China to the rogue state, however. There are important trading links. China is North Korea's largest trading partner, but more important is the geopolitical relationship. Although North Korea remains a threat to world peace and global order, the Chinese leadership is worried that the collapse of their immediate neighbor would unleash millions of refugees overrunning adjacent Chinese provinces and pave the way for a pro-Western state on its immediate border. The Chinese fear is that the fall of North Korea would extend South Korea, with its strong U.S. alliance, all the way to the Yalu River on China's border. Under a 1961 treaty, China is obligated to defend North Korea against unprovoked aggression. But rather than China protecting North Korea, we can also interpret the situation as North Korea having captured China's support. The Chinese leadership seems unwilling to unsettle the North Korean regime and so is left with an unpredictable ally that in turn uses China's guaranteed support and nuclear capability to pursue its own saber-rattling rhetoric. A series of six party talks that include North and South Korea, China, Japan, Russia, and the United States—the first in 2003—have so far failed to rein in the nuclear expansion in North Korea. Nuclear weaponry is too big a bargaining chip for the regime and one that they will not negotiate away. It allows them, through what we described in chapter 2 as *asymmetric escalation*, to intimidate their neighbors and play an outsized role on the world stage.

Japan, China, and the United States

The relationship between Japan and China is complex. China and Japan are two legs of a three-legged stool. The other leg is the United States. All three have tried to leverage power at the expense of the other.[38]

As we have already noted, Japan was an important geopolitical force in the region since 1895 when it defeated China and gained Formosa (present-day Taiwan). It turned Korea into a colony in 1910, annexed Manchuria in 1931, and invaded China in 1937. In 1941, it led a preemptive strike, before declaring war, on the U.S. naval base at Pearl Harbor. The incident brought the United States into World War II and initiated a major war in the Pacific, that by 1945 forced Japan's unconditional surrender. From 1945 to 1952, Japan was under U.S. occupation.

In the immediate aftermath of the war there was a range of opinions—many of them critical of the old regime—about the war, its strategy, tactics, and indeed the basic orientation of Japanese society. But the United States allowed the Japanese to forget their war crimes. Japan was soon considered an important ally in the Cold War and so escaped a full reckoning of its wartime atrocities or of an overhaul of political elites. Countries such as China, Indonesia, and Philippines never got their day in court about wartime atrocities committed by the Japanese Army, and so Japan could create a sense of victimization rather than victimizer. And they had a strong basis for this argument, with three million dead and the horrors of U.S. Air Force bombing campaigns of Japanese cities. The nuclear bombing of Nagasaki and Hiroshima undercut any U.S. moral superiority. Thus, Japan was allowed to have amnesia over its war crimes while the United States bolstered much of traditional society revolving around the emperor. There was no massive social revolution, or an upending of the old order as occurred in Russia in 1917 or in Germany after 1945. The emperor was kept in power, and only a few old men were tried as war criminals. Much of the economic and political elite survived. The heavy concentration of capital in war-mobilized companies, such as Mitsubishi for example, became the basis for Japan's rapid postwar economic growth. Structural legacies of both prewar and wartime Japan guaranteed job security, a tight corporate subcontracting of a small number of banks, a large bureaucracy, and a tendency to authoritarianism carried over into the postwar era. Japan's military was severely curtailed, but that meant more energy and capital was devoted to building a very successful export-led manufacturing sector. Japan grew to the second-largest economy in the world, at least for a while, exporting ever-more-sophisticated manufacturing goods. Japan became an important U.S. ally: the colonial experience of Korea or of the wartime atrocities in the Philippines and China were erased, forgotten, or marginalized. Japan did democratize and grew into a global economic powerhouse. But behind this major economic transformation was a national narrative that reinforced the sense of distinctiveness and superiority.

In the San Francisco Treaty of 1951, Japan became allied to the United States and became a linchpin of the Pax Americana of the postwar period. Japan was an important platform for U.S. military forces along with South Korea. Close to the Chinese coast, Okinawa is still an especially important base for U.S. military strategy in East Asia. Having such a U.S. military base on its national soil but still conveniently far from Tokyo was a vital form of security insurance, especially for a Japan with such severe limitations on its defense capabilities. For decades, the Chinese could look around the region and only see the explicit projection of U.S. power. With bases in South Korea, Japan, and Philippines and with the constant rotation of supercarriers, this large U.S. military presence was considered a threat by the Chinese.

Since the 1990s and especially the 2000s, however, events in the East now unfurl against a background of an overstretched United States, a declining Japan, and a resurgent China. The increased presence of China has also shaped U.S.-Indian relations.[39] There is an unraveling of the old postwar order, one in which the United States was dominant and a weaker China having to defer its external ambitions. Today China is strengthening its military by shoring up its defense perimeter against U.S. naval attack, resulting in an increased ability to annex Taiwan.

China's actions are not all conflict-generating. There is a strong, growing economic cooperation between China, Japan, and South Korea. The former Cold War enemies are integrated in a global economic system that could be more of a win-win than a zero-sum game of confrontation and conflict. Japan has sought to recalibrate its relationship with China and South Korea, but this has proven difficult because of lingering resentments and the ongoing issue of contested islands.

Colonial-era resentments have resurfaced in the region. South Korea has a campaign to hold Japan more accountable for its colonial crimes. The relationship between the two countries now zigzags between economic collaboration and conflict over long-running issues. The conflicts include the dispute over ownership of Dokdo Island; the renaming of the East Sea as the Sea of Japan—an issue discussed in chapter 3—and reparations for Korean "comfort women," women press-ganged into prostitution for the Japanese Army during World War II.

Tension between China and Japan crystalizes in the conflict over a group of uninhabited islands between China and Okinawa.[40] They are known as Diaoyu Islands in China and Senkaku by the Japanese. They came under Japanese colonial control from 1895 until Japan's defeat in World War II. They then came under U.S. control from 1945 until 1972, when they were returned to Japan. In 2012, the issue was nationalized when the islands were purchased by the Japanese government. The islands have limited intrinsic value, consisting only of five tiny, uninhabited islands and three barren rocks, but they have symbolic and increasingly geopolitical significance, as the basis for claims to fishing, oil, and gas reserves. Since 2016, the Chinese have strengthened activity with Chinese fishing boats and coast guard and naval vessels regularly encircling the islands. Both Japan and China use the islands to mobilize popular support against the other.

Shifting Alliances

The region is the scene of shifting alliances as different countries recalibrate their position between a distant United States and a nearby, resurging China.

The Philippines has a long history with the United States. It was a U.S. colony from 1898 until 1945. The United States supported the corrupt Marcos regime from 1965 to 1985, ignoring its obvious human rights abuses. U.S. support for leaders like Marcos recurred throughout the Cold War as authoritarian regimes were propped up and legitimate popular resistances characterized as Communist insurgency. The voraciously venal leader Marco eventually ran out of both popular legitimacy and guarantees of U.S. support. After the effective overthrow of Marcos in 1985, the large U.S. military bases were closed, Clark Air Base in 1991 and Subic Bay in 1992. Another major rupture occurred with the election of Rodrigo Duterte in 2016. He articulated a new foreign policy with emphasis on good relations with China and Russia. In 2016, he terminated the joint U.S.-Filipina naval patrols in the South China Sea and showed greater willingness to establish bilateral talks with China over maritime claims. In 2020, he ordered his government to terminate the Visiting Forces Agreement with the United States that involved hundreds of "engagement and military exercises between the countries." But in a reminder of the changing nature of relation in the region, after well-publicized cases of Chinese maritime aggression in the South China Sea, the Filipino government rescinded the termination decision only several months after it was first announced.

Vietnam, in contrast, is moving in a different direction. Vietnam is a front-line state with a land border with China, a long contentious history of invasion and resistance, and a contested maritime domain. Vietnam is an unlikely candidate for closer ties to the United States. Between 1955 and 1975 more than 2 million civilians, 1.1 million North Vietnamese and Viet Cong troops, and around 250,000 South Vietnamese troops died in what the Vietnamese refer to as the American War. However, Vietnam is now more concerned with its huge neighbor. China is seen as a permanent threat to Vietnam. The longer history of Vietnam is one of constant Chinese invasions and Vietnamese resistance. French colonialism and the American War are mere blips in long-sustained China-Vietnam tension. Even as recently as 1979, China invaded Vietnam. The brief but bloody war reinforced Vietnam's sense of vulnerability to its giant neighbor. Vietnam now sees its main threat as a powerful China, able to exercise its will even in the face of international condemnation. An ever-stronger China worries Vietnam as it makes huge claims to Vietnam's maritime waters and poses a threat to the Vietnamese fishing industry as well as to its oil and gas fields in the South China Sea. While Vietnam is unlikely to allow U.S. military bases in its country, it is now looking for more bilateral military and economic relations and stronger trading links with the United States. Vietnam is keen to create a stronger Association of Southeast Asian Nations (ASEAN) more independent from China.

Other countries in the region are also having to reconsider their position. Some, such as Laos and Cambodia, are too poor and too geographically close to China to resist becoming enmeshed in China's orbit. Laos, for example, is now an important hydroelectric power source for China. China is less concerned than the United States with corruption, human rights, or environmental protection and therefore can invest in large dams that negatively impact local communities. The United States remains Cambodia's largest trading partner, but China is its greatest donor and most important source of foreign investment (see photo 5.2). After funding dams, China was awarded a ninety-thousand-acre concession to build a trade and ecotourism center on the coast of Cambodia.

Others, such as Malaysia and Indonesia, are large enough, rich enough, and/or far enough away to have more room for maneuverability. Malaysia, for example, has substantial oil and gas reserves in its territorial waters, though that makes it vulnerable to Chinese incursions in the South China Sea (see photo 5.3). There are also the traditional U.S. allies at the edge of the region. Australia and New Zealand, along with Canada, the UK, and the United States are members of the Five Eyes Club, who share most intelligence and pledge not to practice their (spying) craft on each other. In terms of shared history, cultural affinities, and geopolitical perspectives, Australia and New Zealand are much closer to the United States than to China. However, China's huge economy draws in goods and raw materials. China buys $87 billion of Australia exports, more than 36

Photo 5.2. Chinese aid in Sihanoukville, Cambodia (John Rennie Short)

percent of total annual exports. Australia managed to escape the ravage of the 2008 global recession experienced by other mature economies because China's continued importation of raw material, especially coal, iron ore, and other minerals, avoided an economic downturn in Australia. The ties between Australia and China extend beyond the export of raw materials. In 2019 fee-paying Chinese students pumped $12 billion into the Australian economy. The revenues are so large that the government was able to reduce direct funding of public universities, but this makes Australian universities even more dependent on Chinese students and ultimately the goodwill of the Chinese government. China's influence is reinforced by the *soft power* of Chinese-friendly Confucius Institutes and through the funding of public relations campaigns. The growth of Chinese influence in Australia is so rapid and large that it has prompted a local backlash.[41] The Australia intelligence service warned recently against unprecedented foreign intervention from China.[42]

Australia and New Zealand remain part of what used to be called a Western alliance, but their economies are drifting inexorably into China's orbit. Even at the farther edges of the region, they can still feel China's economic, military, and soft power.

China is seeking to become the dominant power in the region with a buildup of military power, aggressive policies against Japan and Vietnam, and effective annexation of the South China Sea. Its ultimate goal is to push the United States out of East Asia.[43] The problem for the United States is how to respond. Do nothing and risk the establishment of Chinese world order, first in East and Southeast Asia, and then possibly and ultimately across the world? Or do something and risk a conflict?

Photo 5.3   Malaysian exploitation of gas reserves in the South China Sea (John Rennie Short)

TRADITIONAL GEOPOLITICAL ISSUES

The changing U.S.-China relationship is not the only geopolitical dynamic in the region. There are the traditional ones of border disputes, internal conflicts. and territorial integrity.[44] Let's look at some examples.

Border Issues

There are relatively few remaining terrestrial border issues in this region. From 1990 onward, China has settled its border issues with fourteen neighbors. Conflict between China and Russia, for example, over the two islands at the confluence of the river border between the two countries, was finally settled in 2004. After eighty years of occupation and forty years of negotiations, Russia returned to China 174 square kilometers consisting of all of Yinlong Island and half of Heixiazi Island. This was part of a growing engagement between Russia and China.[45] In December 1999, China and Vietnam signed a land border treaty that resolved all existing disputes and allowed both countries to move military forces away from the border. Hundreds of thousands of troops were stationed at the border after their brief war in 1979 and the subsequent sporadic border conflicts from 1979 to 1985, peaking in 1984–1985. In November 2009, China and Vietnam finally signed an agreement confirming the exact boundary demarcation and cooperation programs for land border management.

But the decline of border disputes does not mean a lack of activity along the borderlands. Chinese troops are now more obvious along its central Asian border in countries such as Tajikistan. China is eager to buttress its western border and effectively seal off any diffusion of radical Islam in Xianjing. Some disputes remain unsettled, such as the China-India border, discussed in chapter 10.

Most of the boundaries of the states in Southeast Asia are compromise agreements formed in the wake of decolonization. Despite this opportunity for disagreements, most territorial disputes have been resolved. In 1985, Vietnam and Cambodia settled their dispute over an island in the Gulf of Thailand, and in 1990 the Laos-Vietnam border dispute was settled. Some remain outstanding such as between Vietnam and Cambodia. Although minor clashes over territory may arise occasionally, they do not provide the basis for sustained conflict. In a few cases, however, tensions remain. The French drew up the boundary between Thailand and Cambodia in 1907. An area around Preah Vihear was allocated to Cambodia. In 2011, there were military skirmishes across the border, and the area remains in dispute. The International Court of Justice has confirmed Cambodian sovereignty, but Thailand still controls the area on the ground.

Territorial Integrity

In many postcolonial regions of the world, national territorial integrity remains an issue. Parts of the region are marked by state stability and cohesion. Japan and South Korea, for example, provide examples of ethnic homogeneity and resultant state cohesion, and while Okinawans always feel ignored by Tokyo, and those in South Korea living outside Seoul often feel ignored, there are no real separatist movements in either Japan or South Korea.

Elsewhere in the region, religion and ethnicity can play a role in causing cracks in national cohesion. Ethnic Chinese are encountered throughout Southeast Asia, often initially settling in towns and forming trading communities. As a successful mercantile class, they frequently face discrimination. Malaysia, Indonesia, and Vietnam all have had outbreaks of anti-Chinese sentiment. In Malaysia, the main division in the country is between the Islamic Malay majority and a Chinese minority. Ethnic Chinese are concentrated in the cities and in the business sectors. Malaysians are given preferential treatment in government employment and services. A standard refrain in Kuala Lumpur is that the Chinese do all the work and Malays get all the government jobs.

The Chinese form the backbone of the urban commercial economies in Vietnam and Indonesia. Occasionally, anti-Chinese sentiment is provoked by political entrepreneurs, leading to social unrest. China's war with Vietnam in 1979 had numerous causes, but one of them was the expulsion in 1978 of thousands of ethnic Chinese. In Indonesia in 1998, more than one thousand people were killed when anti-Chinese rioting occurred in the cities of Medan and Jakarta.

The rise of a militant Islam also has created a network of non-state actors that look to challenge the existing nation-states, and some even propose a form of Islamic caliphate. Groups in Thailand, Indonesia, and the Philippines—some with links to international networks, others more homegrown, and some simply fronts for gangster activity—are destabilizing forces to national unity. The southern province of Thailand, the region around Mindanao in the Philippines, and Aceh in Indonesia are all fertile grounds for these militant groups.

Groups such as the Jemaah Islamiyah (Islamic congregation) are active in Indonesia, Singapore, Malaysia, and Philippines. They were responsible for the bombing of a nightclub in Bali in 2002 that killed 202 people and injured 201.

In the Philippines only 5 percent of the population of one hundred million are Muslim, but they are concentrated in the south, mainly in Mindanao, which was traditionally the home of Muslim sultanates until the Spanish arrived in the sixteenth century. The Moro Islamic Liberation Front has long pushed for greater autonomy for the mainly Muslim region, but is now eclipsed by Aby Sayyaf, which has strong links with the Islamic State of Iraq (ISIS) and to al Qaeda. Aby Sayyaf finances its operations through kidnap, ransom, and extortion. In the three southern provinces of Thailand with a significant Muslim population, there are at least five different groups that work for a separate Muslim state.

Islam in Southeast Asia is traditionally more tolerant than the Saudi version and is fused with older indigenous beliefs. However, when more conservative Muslims fear a secular state or experience a distant government, then militants can turn their disquiet into support for anti-state actions. Terrorist attacks are often organized by local groups such as Darul Islam with transnational groups such as al Qaeda or the Islamic State of Iraq and the Levant (ISIL) providing money and other assistance.

Indonesia has issues with territorial integrity on its eastern rim. Indonesia became independent from the Netherlands in 1945. It laid claim to all the territory of the Dutch East Indies that then included the western half of the island of Papua. But the Dutch held onto the territory of Papua, keeping control of the huge mineral resources of the region until 1962, when it came under the control of Indonesia. This easternmost province is very different from the rest of Indonesia. The local people are animists and ethnically Melanesian. A Free Papua Movement has long conducted low-level insurgency against mining projects and government officers. Thousands have died in a conflict that shows little sign of dissipating.[46]

Timor Leste consists of the eastern part of the island of Timor and adjoining small islands. It was a Portuguese colony until 1975, when it became independent after anticolonial struggles. Nine days after Timor Leste declared independence, Indonesian military forces invaded. Subsequent Indonesian rule was marked by violence as the military sought to extract as much revenue as possible from the local economy. An independence movement continued to fight, and a brutal war ensued. Indonesia eventually relinquished and Timor Leste became a sovereign state in 2002.

GEOPOLITICAL HOTSPOT: THE SOUTH CHINA SEA

Beneath the waters of the South China Sea lie rich reserves of oil and gas (see photo 5.3). In 2016 the Permanent Court of Arbitration in the Hague ruled against China's claim to a vast area of the South China Sea. The case brought by the Philippine government argued that China had no legal basis to this claim, that it was constructing man-made islands to bolster these invalid claims, and that it was violating Philippine sovereignty. Despite the ruling, China continues to weaponize contested islands and pursue ever-more-aggressive behavior.[47]

The South China Sea is where today's global rivalries are being played out.[48] It is a hotspot where the geopolitical relationship between the United States and its near-peer competitor, China, evolves up close and in real time. Questions about what a bipolar world of U.S.-China might look like, or arguments about how the United States should manage a resurgent China, often have a "sometime-in-the-near-future," placeless, and theoretical character. In the South China Sea, they take on a particularly pressing reality because the basic geography of a *nearby China* and a *more distant United States* creates a sharper and more immediate edge. The South China Sea provides an early look at what a more muscular China really looks like. What should the United States do about China's effective control and overt militarization of the South China Sea? What *can* it do? And what are the costs and benefits of the two main options of what I will call "Abandoning the Region to a Chinese World Order" or "Maintaining a Rules-Based Order."

The Background

The legal framework that guides international maritime claims is the United Nations Convention of the Law of the Sea (UNCLOS), which came into operation in 1982. UNCLOS was a *constitution of the oceans*: it introduced Exclusive Economic Zones (EEZs), by which states can claim exclusionary rights over marine resources, including fish, oil, and gas, and also can construct artificial islands and build installations. EEZs reach out two hundred nautical miles (370 km) across the sea from the coastal baseline. Where EEZs overlap, it is up to the states to delineate the maritime border. UNCLOS has no conflict resolution procedures to ensure equity or adjudicate competing claims, and the Permanent Court of Arbitration has no enforcement mechanisms.

Six countries, by virtue of their geography, have claims in the South China Sea: Brunei, China, Malaysia, Philippines, Taiwan, and Vietnam (see map 5.4). In a perfect world, using the UNCLOS framework could result in an equitable, easily constructed division of the sea. In our imperfect world, in contrast, China makes claim to a vast swath of the sea, impinging on the EEZs of the other countries, especially Vietnam, in a naked assertion of *great power politics*. Their "nine-dash line," also called "the cow's tongue" because of its distinctive shape, projects China's claim deep into the other countries' EEZs right up to the coastlines of Brunei, Malaysia, Philippines, and Vietnam.

There is no legitimate legal or historical basis for China's maritime claims that can stand any form of serious scrutiny.[49] For centuries, the sea was contested, shared, and ungoverned. The twentieth-century history is a confusing one with colonial-power involvements, Japanese advances and retreats, and differing interpretations of international treaties. China's current historical justification is a prime example of the *invention of tradition* to justify dominance in the region. Nurtured by Chinese political leadership is the idea of the South China Sea as China's "natural" right. This idea is now so entrenched in domestic public opinion that it boxes in the leadership with limited ability to change tack without risking a legitimation crisis.

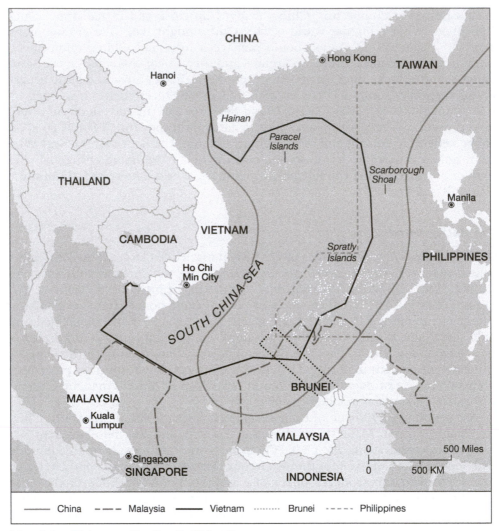

Map 5.4. Claims on the South China Sea

Since the 2016 Ruling

The 2016 decision did little to halt China: it simply ignored the ruling and pursued bilateral negotiations. Things were made easier for them in the Philippines after Rodrigo Duterte replaced the Aquino government in the 2016 election. Duterte quickly pivoted toward China and away from the United States, signing deals with Xi Jinping in 2018 for joint oil and gas exploration. Brunei and Malaysia have remained quiet. Vietnam tries to resist China's encroachment into its EEZ but has failed to mobilize much global or even regional support. The ten-country ASEAN has proved ineffective due to its member nations' divergent and often-conflicting interests, especially with regard to China.[50] The 2018 Code of Conduct for the South China Seas, signed by the foreign ministers of ASEAN and China, was a weak and compromised document that did not challenge Beijing's claims.

The Chinese continue to militarize the disputed islands. In the Spratly Islands, for example, they built on existing rock outcrops and reefs. Sand was pumped up from the sea floor and spread across islands, even across the live coral of submerged reefs. Mischief Reef and Subi Reef were once submerged and are now permanent islands with docks for ships and runways for planes. In the Paracel Islands, the Chinese established a surface-to-air missile defense system on Woody Island and recently built a helicopter base on Duncan Island. In the Scarborough Shoal, they installed equipment on seven islands to allow them to monitor U.S. naval vessels. Many of the disputed islands in the South China Sea are now, in effect, permanent Chinese military bases.

China is also very active in the *gray zone* between war and peace that avoids U.S. blowback yet reaps the benefits of military actions while affording a degree of official deniability. China's gray zone warriors in the South China Sea are the Chinese Coast Guard (CCG) and their commercial fishing fleet. They form an effective maritime militia that harasses the fishing fleets, naval ships, and commercial traffic of other nations. Hundreds of Chinese fishing vessels regularly surround islands administered by other nations to disrupt supplies. Supply ships to Vietnam's oil rigs are regularly harassed by CCG and Chinese fishing vessels. In December 2019, a small fleet of Chinese fishing and coast guard vessels operated without permission in the EEZs of Brunei, Indonesia, and Malaysia. The CCG vessels, sailing in November from the new harbor at Subi Reef, included a 5,000-ton patrol ship and a 2,700-ton ship with a 76-mm cannon.

There is also the rhetorical attack. The Chinese deploy a consistent diplomatic message that the disagreements should be handled not through international organizations and institutions but only through bilateral talks. The power inequality with its Southeast Asian neighbors ensures that this bilateral format always favors China. China easily outmuscles individual ASEAN countries.

China also seeks to marginalize the United States by describing it as the "extra regional power." In other words, this is a Southeast Asian issue, and outside nations must be sidelined. The narrative constructed by Chinese think tanks and government agencies is that *freedom of navigation*, a bedrock of global trade, is merely a cover for U.S. military deployment. These government-sponsored think tanks also promote the *rights of coastal states*. That of course would include China and further marginalize the United States. It was also uncomfortably familiar to hear—as I did at an international conference in 2019 in Vietnam on the South China Sea—Chinese scholars respond to documented cases of Chinese gray zone activity as "fake news" and the idea of freedom of navigation as "political correctness."

China has overruled an international rules-based order in favor of a Chinese world order that would look very familiar to the Ming and early Qing dynasties.

China's Goals

The South China Sea is now a Chinese lake. China has gained effective control over its southern maritime border, a globally significant sea territory with huge reserves of oil and natural gas, vast fisheries, and some of the world's busiest sea lanes. It has succeeded in extending its southern maritime border, fulfilling part of its long-held strategic aim of a "First Island Chain," stretching from the Kuril Islands in the North to Borneo in the South, to ensure a more effective Chinese defense against the United States. It also gives strategic advantage should China ever decide to invade Taiwan. Most war-game scenarios now assume that China has the capability to invade and hold the island. At some cost, to be sure, but only twenty years ago this was not thought possible. This new strategic advantage will shape China's attitude to Taiwan for years to come.

The South China Sea is where President Xi's muscular nationalism has fully displaced Deng Xiaoping's 1990 advice of "hide our capacities and bide our time." The Xi doctrine seems to be "show your power now and challenge the hegemon where you can." The South China Sea is the active testbed for this geopolitical strategy.

The U.S. Response

For the United States, the South China Sea is the kind of wicked problem embodied in the Thucydides Trap. If the dominant power does not respond to a rising power, it risks being displaced. If it does respond it risks a confrontation. Currently, U.S. policy is an odd combination of facilitating the abandonment of the region to a Chinese world order while also running the risk of escalation.

This may be an acceptable outcome for those who counsel a U.S. grand strategy of greater restraint. What does the United States really lose if a regional hegemon dominates, as long as the container ships of global trade sail unhindered? The geopolitical reality of a *near China* and a *faraway United States*, some realists would argue, almost ensures Chinese hegemony over the region. The downside: China gains control of a vital chokehold of global trade, continues to intimidate its neighbors, and poses an existential threat to Taiwan.

The U.S. Navy regularly sails through the disputed waters to reinforce the principle of freedom of navigation, conducting at least twenty freedom-of-navigation (FON) exercises over the past three years. In August and September of 2019, for example, the 9,200-ton guided missile destroyer, USS *Wayne E. Meyer*, left Pearl Harbor to sail around Mischief Reef and Fiery Cross Reef in the Spratly Islands before participating in a five-day U.S.-ASEAN joint exercise. These exercises make a point, but they come with some risk. An overanxious CCG vessel and a U.S. Navy ship may get entangled in an encounter that could escalate. Large tragedies can spool out from such small incidents.

A major shift in U.S. policy was announced by Secretary of State Pompeo in a speech in July 2020, when he noted, "Beijing's claims to offshore resources across most of the South China Sea are completely unlawful, as is its campaign of bullying to control them."[51] To date, it was the most vigorous, high-level official response to China's activities in the South China Sea that signals to the rest of the world the U.S. commitment to upholding a rules-based order rather than its acquiescence to a Chinese order. It is too early to say whether the marked change in tone and strategy will also signal a change in tactics. FON exercises will probably continue and there is also the possibility of sanctioning commercial organizations involved in illegal activity. How effective or wide-ranging such sanctions could be is very debatable. What is not questionable is that the South China Sea is one of the hottest geopolitical hotspots because it frames a U.S.-China clash where a rules-based global order competes with a Sinocentric world order.

SUGGESTED READINGS

Bolt, P. J., & Cross, S. N. (2018). *China, Russia, and twenty-first century global geopolitics*. Oxford: Oxford University Press.

Cha, V. (2018). *The impossible state: North Korea, past and present*. New York: Harper-Collins.

Flint, C., & Zhu, C. (2019). The geopolitics of connectivity, cooperation, and hegemonic competition: The Belt and Road Initiative. *Geoforum, 99*, 95–101.

Goldstein, A. (2020). China's grand strategy under Xi Jinping: Reassurance, reform, and resistance. *International Security, 45*, 164–201.

Hayton, B. (2014). *The South China Sea: The struggle for power in Asia*. New Haven: Yale University Press.

Hayton, B. (2020). *The invention of China*. New Haven: Yale University Press.

Jacques, M. (2012, 2nd ed.). *When China rules the world*. New York: Penguin.

McGregor, R. (2017). *Asia reckoning: China, Japan, and the fate of U.S. power in the Pacific century*. New York: Penguin.

Westad, O. A. (2012). *Restless Empire: China and the new world since 1750*. New York: Basic.

Yoshihara, T., & Holmes, J. R. (2018). *Red star over the Pacific, revised edition: China's rise and the challenge to U.S. maritime strategy*. Annapolis: Naval Institute Press.

NOTES

1. For a range of interpretations on Chinese geopolitics and grand strategy, see Friedberg, A. L. (2018). Globalization and Chinese grand strategy. *Survival, 60*, 7–40; Goldstein, A. (2020). China's grand strategy under Xi Jinping: Reassurance, reform, and resistance. *International Security, 45*, 164–201; Khan, S. W. (2018). *Haunted by chaos: China's grand strategy from Mao Zedong to Xi Jinping*. Cambridge, MA: Harvard University Press; Lind, J. (2017). Asia's other revisionist Power: Why U.S. grand strategy unnerves China. *Foreign Affairs, 96*, 74–82.

Woon, C. Y. (2018). China's contingencies: Critical geopolitics, Chinese exceptionalism and the uses of history. *Geopolitics, 23*, 67–95.

2. Westad, O. A. (2012). *Restless Empire: China and the new world since 1750*. New York: Basic.

3. Sun Yat-sen. (1924). The three principles of the people. *World History Commons*. https://worldhistorycommons.org/sun-yat%E2%80%93sen-three-principles-people.

4. For a discussion of Japanese geopolitical thinking at the time, see Watanabe, A. (2018). Greater East Asia: Geopolitics and its geopolitical imagination of a borderless world: A neglected tradition? *Political Geography, 67*, 23–31.

5. Park, Sam-Heon. (2019). The Ryukyu Kingdom, the first victim of changes in the East Asian order. *Northeast Asian History Foundation Newsletter*. https://www.nahf.or.kr/eng/webzine/view.do?cid=60155.

6. Chang, I. (2014). *The rape of Nanking: The forgotten holocaust of World War II*. New York: Basic.

7. Pembroke, M. (2018). *Korea: Where the American century began*. London: Hardie Grant.

8. Dreyer, J. T. (2015). The rise of China and the geopolitics of East Asia. *Orbis, 59*, 518–29.

9. Vogel, E. F. (2013). *Deng Xiaoping and the transformation of China*. Cambridge, MA: Harvard University Press.

10. Schnell, O., & Delury, J. (2013). *Wealth and power: China's long march to the twenty-first century*. New York: Random House.

11. Huang, Y. (2008). *Capitalism with Chinese characteristics*. Cambridge: Cambridge University Press.

12. Weiss, J. C. (2014). *Powerful patriots: Nationalist protest in China's foreign relations*. Oxford: Oxford University Press.

13. The Global Economy. (2020). China: Percent World GDP. *The Global Economy.* https://www.theglobaleconomy.com/China/gdp_share/. Precise estimates vary due to different estimates of purchasing parity. Other estimates put the change from 1978 to 2018 from 2 percent to 23 percent.

14. Amadeo, K. (2020, April 11). The U.S. debt and how it got so big: Five reasons why America is in debt. *The Balance.* https://www.thebalance.com/the-u-s-debt-and-how-it -got-so-big-3305778.

15. For discussions of the geopolitical consequences and implications of BRI, see Flint, C., & Zhu, C. (2019). The geopolitics of connectivity, cooperation, and hegemonic competition: The Belt and Road Initiative. *Geoforum, 99*, 95–101; Jones, L., and Zeng, J. (2019). Understanding China's "Belt and Road Initiative": Beyond "grand strategy" to a state transformation analysis. *Third World Quarterly, 40*, 1415–39; Bingbing, W. (2017). The New Silk Road and China's evolving grand strategy. *China Journal, 77*, 110–32.

16. Liu, D., Yamaguchi, K., & Yoshikawa, H. (2017). Understanding the motivations behind the Myanmar-China energy pipeline: Multiple streams and energy politics in China. *Energy Policy, 107*, 403–12.

17. Kliman, D., Doshi, R., Lee, K., & Cooper, Z. (2019). Grading China's Belt and Road. *Center for a New American Security.* https://www.forum2000.cz/files/report-what-to -know-as-europe-travels-china-s-belt-and-road-compressed.pdf.

18. O'Dea, C. R. (2019). Ships of state? *Naval War College Review, 72*, 62–95.

19. Hart, M., & Johnson, B. (2019, February 28). Mapping China's global governance ambitions: Democracies still have leverage to shape Beijing's reform agenda. *Center for American Progress.* https://www.americanprogress.org/issues/security/reports /2019/02/28/466768/mapping-chinas-global-governance-ambitions/.

20. Zakaria, F. (2020, January–February). The new China scare. *Foreign Affairs*, 52–69.

21. Jacques, M. (2012, 2nd ed.). *When China rules the world*. New York: Penguin, 535.

22. Robertson, P. (2019, October 1). China's military might is much closer to the U.S. than you probably think. *The Conversation.* https://theconversation.com/chinas-military -might-is-much-closer-to-the-U.S.-than-you-probably-think-124487.

23. Yoshihara, T., & Holmes, J. R. (2018). *Red star over the Pacific, revised edition: China's rise and the challenge to U.S. maritime strategy*. Annapolis: Naval Institute Press.

24. Anderson, N. D., & Cha, V. D. (2017). The case of the pivot to Asia: System effects and the origins of strategy. *Political Science Quarterly, 132*, 595–618; Silove, N. (2016). The pivot before the pivot: US strategy to preserve the power balance in Asia. *International Security, 40*, 45–88.

25. Office of the Secretary of Defense. (2019). *Annual report to Congress: Military and security developments involving the People's Republic of China 2019*. Washington, DC: U.S. Department of Defense. https://media.defense.gov/2019/May/02/2002127082

/-1/-1/1/2019_CHINA_MILITARY_POWER_REPORT.pdf; Defense Intelligence Agency (2019). China Military Power: Modernizing a force to fight and win. *Defense Intelligence Agency.* https://www.dia.mil/Portals/27/Documents/News/Military%20Power%20Pub lications/China_Military_Power_FINAL_5MB_20190103.pdf.

26. The State Council Information Office of the People's Republic of China. (2019). *China's national defense in the new era.* Beijing: Foreign Languages Press Co. Ltd. http://www.xinhuanet.com/english/download/whitepaperonnationaldefenseinnewera.doc. For a U.S. perspective on this Chinese document, see Center for Strategic and International Studies. (2019). *China's new 2019 defense white paper: An open strategic challenge to the United States, but one which does not have to lead to conflict.* https://www.csis.org/analysis/chinas-new-2019-defense-white-paper.

27. McGregor, R. (2019, September–October). Party man: Xi Jinping's quest to dominate China. *Foreign Affairs.* https://www.foreignaffairs.com/articles/china/2019-08-14/party-man.

28. Phillips, T. (2017, October 18). Xi Jinping heralds "new era" of Chinese power at Communist party congress. *The Guardian.* https://www.theguardian.com/world/2017/oct/18/xi-jinping-speech-new-era-chinese-power-party-congress.

29. For a range of recent writings see Dyer. G. (2014). *The contest of the century.* New York: Knopf; Ward, J. (2019). *China's vision of victory.* Washington, DC: Atlas; Zakaria, F. (2020, January–February). The new China Scare. *Foreign Affairs,* 52–69.

30. Fifield, A., & Slater, J. (2020). Far from being weakened by coronavirus, China pursues sovereignty with claims on all fronts. *Washington Post.* https://www.washingtonpost.com/world/asia_pacific/china-india-border-clashes-coronavirus/2020/05/27/a51545f6-9f14-11ea-be06-af5514ee0385_story.html.

31. Buckley, M. (2014). *Meltdown in Tibet: China's reckless destruction of ecosystems from the highlands of Tibet to the deltas of Asia.* New York: Palgrave Macmillan; Chellaney, B. (2011). *Water: Asia's new battleground.* New York: HarperCollins.

32. BBC Staff Writer. (2019, November 24). Data leak reveals how China "brainwashes" Uighurs in prison camps. *BBC News.* https://www.bbc.com/news/world-asia-china-50511063; Zenz, A. (2019). Brainwashing, police guards and coercive internment: Evidence from Chinese government documents about the nature and extent of Xinjiang's "Vocational Training Internment Camps." *Journal of Political Risk.* http://www.jpolrisk.com/brainwashing-police-guards-and-coercive-internment-evidence-from-chinese-government-documents-about-the-nature-and-extent-of-xinjiangs-vocational-training-internment-camps/.

33. Peck, M. (2019, October 5). Invasion: China is more ready that ever to take back Taiwan by force: Can America stop them? *The National Interest.* https://nationalinterest.org/blog/buzz/invasion-china-more-ready-ever-take-back-taiwan-force-85501.

34. Blanchard, B., & Lee, Y. (2020, January 13). China could flex military muscles to pressure Taiwan post-election. *Reuters.* https://uk.reuters.com/article/uk-taiwan-election-analysis/china-could-flex-military-muscles-to-pressure-taiwan-post-election-idUKKBN1ZC0LJ.

35. Lee, H. (2017). Power politics behind the transforming geopolitics in East Asia. *East Asia: An International Quarterly, 34,* 307–20.

36. Kim, A., & Kim, J. (2018). China's aggressive "periphery diplomacy" and South Korean perspectives. *Pacific Review, 31,* 267–77; Pembroke, M. (2018). *Korea: Where the American century began.* New York: Simon and Schuster.

Swenson-Wright, J., & Frank, R. (eds.). (2013). *Korea and East Asia: The stony road to collective security.* Leiden: Brill.

37. Cha, V. (2018). *The impossible state: North Korea, past and present.* New York: HarperCollins.

38. McGregor, R. (2017). *Asia reckoning: China, Japan, and the fate of U.S. power in the Pacific century*. New York: Penguin.

39. Madan, T. (2020). *Fateful triangle: How China shaped U.S.-India relations during the Cold War*. Washington, DC: Brookings.

40. Chapman, B. (2017). Geopolitical implications of the Sino-Japanese East China Sea dispute for the U.S. *Geopolitics, History, and International Relations, 9*, 15–54; Manicom, J. (2014). *Bridging troubled waters: China, Japan, and maritime order in the East China Sea*. Washington, DC: Georgetown University Press.

41. Cave, D. (2019, May 20). Australia's China challenge. *New York Times*. https://www.nytimes.com/2019/05/20/world/australia/australia-china.html.

42. SBS News Staff Writer. (2018, May 25). Foreign interference unprecedented: ASIO chief Duncan Lewis warns foreign actors are attempting to influence and shape the views of Australians. *SBS News*. https://www.sbs.com.au/news/foreign-interference-unprecedented-asio.

43. Mearsheimer, J. J. (2010). The gathering storm: China's challenge to U.S. power in Asia. *Chinese Journal of International Politics, 3*, 381–96.

44. DeRouen, K. R., & Bercovitch, J. (eds.). (2011). *Unraveling internal conflicts in East Asia and the Pacific: Incidence, consequences, and resolution*. Lanham: Lexington Books.

45. Bolt, P. J., & Cross, S. N. (2018). *China, Russia, and twenty-first century global geopolitics*. Oxford: Oxford University Press.

46. Human Rights Watch. (2007). Indonesia, protest and punishment: Political prisoners in Papua. *Human Rights Watch*. https://www.hrw.org/sites/default/files/reports/papua0207webwcover.pdf.

47. Lee, W. (2017). Introduction: The South China Sea dispute and the 2016 arbitration decision. *Journal of Chinese Political Science, 22*, 179–85; Zhao, S. (2018). China and the South China Sea arbitration: Geopolitics versus international law. *Journal of Contemporary China, 27*, 1–15.

48. Schreer, B. (2019). Towards contested "spheres of influence" in the Western Pacific: Rising China, classical geopolitics, and Asia-Pacific stability. *Geopolitics, 24*, 503–22; Turner, O. (2016). China, India and the US rebalance to the Asia Pacific: The geopolitics of rising identities. *Geopolitics, 21*, 922–44.

49. Hayton, B. (2014). *The South China Sea: The struggle for power in Asia*. New Haven: Yale University Press.

50. Emmers, R. (2018). Unpacking ASEAN neutrality: The quest for autonomy and impartiality in Southeast Asia. *Contemporary Southeast Asia: A Journal of International & Strategic Affairs, 40*, 349–70.

51. U.S. Department of State Press Statement. (2020, July 13). *U.S. Position on maritime claims in the South China Sea*. https://www.state.gov/u-s-position-on-maritime-claims-in-the-south-china-sea/.

6

Russia and Its Neighbors

GEOPOLITICAL CONTEXT

Geography is as much burden as opportunity. Russia's geopolitical position in the center of the Eurasian landmass has made for the conflict-laden possibilities of an expansionist ideology and border insecurity. Compare Russia's geopolitical position in map 6.1 with the greater strategic security afforded to the United States as shown in map 4.1. This geography alone does not explain the recurring Russian sense of feeling under threat, but it does give it a context.

The geopolitics of this region can only be understood from the perspective of *Empire*, the rise and fall of the Russian and then the Soviet Empire. The imperial fortunes of these two polities over the past five hundred years dictated much of the political life across much of Eurasia. Imperial Russia and then the Soviet Union also played a major role in wider world history. Russia was an important player in the *great power politics* of the nineteenth century. It was involved in the global struggle between empires in a shifting set of alliances. For example, it was at times in conflict with the British in India and Afghanistan but at other times in war alliances against France during the Napoleonic War. The British, for their part, both feared Russian expansionism into the territories of the Ottoman and their own Indian Empire but also allied with Russia to balance forces against other European powers. Later, in the twentieth century, the Soviet Union became part of a *bipolar world*. During the *Cold War* period from 1945 to 1990, the world was divided into the two main camps headed by the United States and USSR.

Across the region, the shifting state boundaries were forged by the creation and also the dissolution of the Russian/Soviet empires. Imperial rise and decline were thus the driving forces behind the annexation of states and then their reemergence. Since 1989–1990, while some of the newly independent states remain within the Russian orbit, others have sought greater integration with the countries of Western Europe. The distinction between the two groups reflects the length of their previous political independence, their sense of nationhood, political history, cultural affinities, closeness in both distance and economy, integration to present-day Russia, and sometimes the size of their Russian-speaking

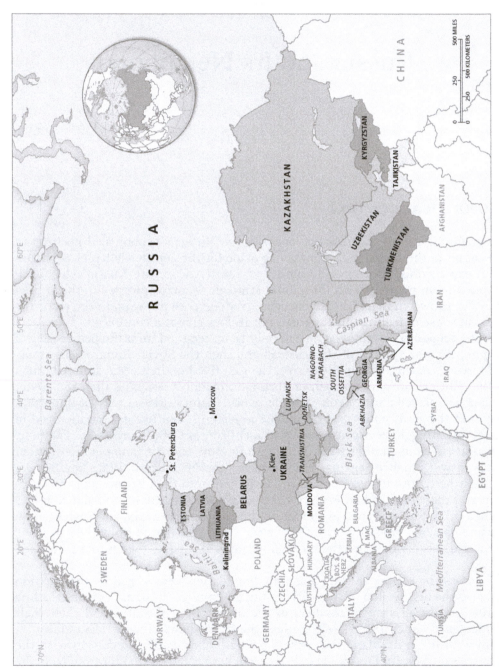

Map 6.1. Russia and its neighbors (International Mapping)

population. Former Soviet allies in Europe have tended to reorient westward toward an integrating Europe. The Baltic republics, despite their large Russian-speaking populations, are resolutely in the Western camp. In a more liminal zone, Belarus remains, at least for now at the time of writing, within the Russian orbit while Ukraine is making efforts to achieve escape velocity.

On the contemporary world stage, Russia's influence is less than that of the former Society Union but still significant. It has nuclear weaponry, foreign bases, and alliances with a number of countries. Despite the economic weakness of a narrow reliance on primary commodities and hence being subject to fluctuating world commodity prices, especially for oil and gas, it retains and seeks to expand its geopolitical heft. Russia's relation with its former existential enemy of the Cold War remains difficult. The United States, in what seems like a recurring variation on the theme of containment first announced by George Kennan in the *Long Telegram* of 1946 that we discussed in chapter 1, seeks to engage with Russia but also to contain what it sees as malign activity. Russia, on the other hand, constantly feels under threat, both real and imagined, from the West, especially along its borders. Any change in political regime along the rim of former Soviet republics is carefully watched for Western interference. A great power mentality still motivates much of Russia's geopolitical thinking—a need to be in the forefront on the world stage. In some cases, it is achieved as shown in the success of the Sputnik COVID-19 vaccine, the very name an echo of a previous technological success in the early space race. A great power mentality also conjures up threats and slights. Putin's worst fear for Russia is geopolitical irrelevancy and loss of great power status. It is a mindset that requires a constant threat, a position that the United States often fulfills. Domestic critics of the existing order are always portrayed as working for foreign powers (i.e., the United States). Russia does punch above its weight in the *gray zone* of cyberwarfare. And while it may be a fading great power measured on many traditional metrics, it is emerging as a legitimate cyber superpower.

As a continental power, Russia must contend with the three major geopolitical spaces of Eurasia, Euro-Atlantic, and Asia-Pacific.[1] The strategies and tactics adopted in each of these spaces is explored in this chapter.

THE RUSSIAN EMPIRE

In his annual address to the Federal Assembly in Moscow in 2005, President Putin described the fall of the Soviet Union as "the biggest geopolitical catastrophe of the century."[2] In a century of mass killings, two world wars, the Holocaust, and truly horrendous bouts of ethnic cleansing around the world, this is a bold claim. The dissolution of the USSR, an empire that lasted from 1922 to 1991, did put an end to a unique political system founded on Marxist-Leninist principles. The Soviet Union was unable to keep pace with a more dynamic, capitalist West and was suffering from "internal contradictions," to use its own Leninist terminology. The Soviet system, like the last ponderous dinosaur on a cooling planet, was unable to survive in a new era. Few, outside of Russia, agreed with Putin's assessment. Across the newly liberated Eastern Europe, in deep contrast, there was positive joy at the system's demise. So, we can only understand Putin's plaintive remark from a Russian perspective. In many ways, the Soviet Union was a continuation of the Russian Empire. Putin was grieving not so much for the loss of a political system as for the loss of empire.

The Russian Empire first emerged from a relatively small area centered on Moscow. By the fifteenth century, after decades of civil war and resistance against Mongol suzerainty, Moscow emerged as an important independent center. When in 1462 Ivan III ("the Great," the first to be called "Tsar") began his reign, he controlled fifteen thousand square miles. When his grandson Ivan IV ("the Terrible") came to the throne in 1547 he ruled over one million square miles.

Geography is a significant factor in the expansion. Moscow is situated on a vast plain and thus is vulnerable to attack. Therefore, one way to defend the region requires extending the borders as far from the center as possible. This expansionary imperative is reinforced by its northern latitude. The very short growing season meant that agricultural surplus and sustained food supplies required control over more arable lands. Add in the existence of surrounding enemy forces, and you have the recipe for an almost existential requirement for territorial expansion.

The early extensions are sometimes referred to as the "gathering" of Russian lands. Expansion continued past the land of the Russians. In the second half of the sixteenth century, this expansion pushed into Lithuania and Crimea. In the seventeenth century, Siberia was conquered, and Russian power extended through forts built along the river systems all the way to the Pacific. In the eighteenth century, expansion continued east to Mongolia and south and west into Ukraine, the Baltic states, and parts of Poland. By the end of the century, Russia extended its reach into Alaska. In the nineteenth century, Kazakhstan, the Caucasus, Finland, Moldova, and the rest of Poland came under Russian control. By 1914, the empire extended across 6.2 million square miles of the Eurasian landmass (see map 6.1). Russia controlled much of what Mackinder had dubbed *the world island*.

Ideology

All expansionist empires have justifying ideologies. In the Russian case, there was a similar mix of ideas about religious mission, exceptionalism, and torch-bearers of a unique civilization. The Kremlin sits in the middle of Moscow and at the heart of the Kremlin is a cluster of old churches in Cathedral Square. It is a sacred space. The creation of a Moscow patriarchate in 1589 marked the beginning of a Russian Orthodox religion separate from the Byzantine/Greek Orthodox Church. Moscow was envisioned as the "Third Rome"—after Jerusalem and Constantinople—and Russians imagined as a "chosen people," charged with the promulgation and protection of the Russian Orthodox Church as their sacred duty. The ruling family embodied the relationships between God and Russia. The long-lasting Romanov dynasty (1613–1917) gave a sense of stability, an absolutist rule that reassuringly enacted the rituals and practice of Empire.

It is instructive to note that the justifying ideology, with a few tweaks, was easily transferred from the Russian to the Soviet era with Marxism-Leninism an easy substitute for Orthodox religion. They were both global missions undertaken by a chosen people. Mother Russia easily changed into the protector of the proletariat; Russian Orthodoxy was easily replaced by world Communism; Moscow was no longer the capital of the Romanovs but now the center of the worldwide workers movement, the home of the party leaders.[3]

State-building and empire-making were one and the same. Building the Russian Empire was unlike, say, the British in North America or Australia, something separate from the metropole. Indeed, making the state and building an empire were the same thing, providing a certain ease of transition from the Russian to the Soviet Empire. While the political system experienced a radical disjuncture, from absolutist monarchy to dictatorship of the proletariat, an imperial project remained remarkably similar.

There was always a rhetorical clash between East and West. Some, such as Sergei Soloviev (1820–1879) worried that an eastward expansion drew population from settled areas and obstructed economic development, a fear that moving east involved loss of contact with a "civilized west."[4] There was a struggle over the "true" character of Russia: was it to be Eurasian or European? "Eurasian" implied Russian Orthodoxy, a uniquely Russian civilization, a special and distinct space. If it was European, then it shared the discourses of Enlightenment, of liberalism, and of rationality. The European view was epitomized by Peter the Great (r. 1682–1725). Anxious to modernize his empire, he changed the name from "Tsardom" to "Empire," and himself from "Tsar" to "Emperor" in order to align more closely with European-style titles. He proposed a beard tax, for example, to encourage a more modern, clean-shaven look among his subjects. He built a new city on the Baltic because he wanted a window on Europe as well as to shift the capital from Moscow: it was part of a plan of modernization and imperial expansions to pivot Russia toward the West. St. Petersburg was built on piles driven into a marsh. This construction project was a huge endeavor: it took more than five years, and almost twenty-five thousand workers died under the brutal conditions. From their bones arose a beautiful Enlightenment city laid out in a grid of grand avenues. A fortress, navy yards, and palaces were constructed. In 1712, merchants and nobles were forced to move from Moscow: it became the capital of the Russian Empire. Tsarina Elizabeth and Catherine the Great expanded the city, and the city became a center of science, culture, and art as well as the official residence of the Royal Family and the court. By 1800, the city had a population of close to 220,000 and was the capital as well as the main intellectual center of the Russian Empire.

Throughout the nineteenth century, the city grew as an industrial city, and the 1861 emancipation of the serfs increased rural migration to the city. The city was the major industrial city of the empire with 250,000 workers mostly in large factories: the ideal setting for a political radicalization and the setting for some of the novels of the great Russian writers, including Dostoyevsky, Gogol, and Pushkin. In Dostoyevsky's novel *Crime and Punishment* (1866), the story of the murder of an old woman by the student Raskolnikov, the city is depicted as a place of great poverty, and the disorder and the noise of the city is meant to reflect Raskolnikov's tortured mental state. The city was a setting of social conflict and political uprisings. In 1905, a strike brought out 150,000 workers.

It is referred to as the "First Russian Revolution" to imply its importance as a forerunner to the more well-known and more transformative revolution of 1917.

In 1918, the capital was moved to Moscow. It is perhaps too simplistic to equate Moscow with Eurasia and St. Petersburg with Europe, yet the two cities do embody significant differences. Moscow is landlocked, with onion-domed churches, the Kremlin, a part of deep Russia. St. Petersburg is open to the sea, very European with its Neoclassical buildings, its Enlightenment town-plan, and its design as the "Venice of the North" with its architectural grandeur along its many canals—not only a window to Europe but also an homage to Europe (see photo 6.1).

Photo 6.1.   Neoclassical St. Petersburg (John Rennie Short)

The two national narratives of European and Eurasian persist in their interaction rather than their separation, in the merging and mingling of the two strands, creating a tight braid of Russian identity. They exist in the same city. As another metaphor, consider that Alexander II (r. 1855–1881) was initially a reforming Tsar. The emancipation of serfs occurred during his early reign in 1861. To counter rising protests, he proposed parliamentary reforms. Despite his attempts at liberalizations, he was assassinated by nihilists in St. Petersburg in 1881. His son quickly reversed direction and embarked on a policy of repression, squashing civil rights, which marked a return to absolutism, a crucial feature of the Eurasian model. He ordered a church to be constructed on the site of his father's death, the Church of the Savior on Blood. Built between 1883 and 1907 in the style of medieval Russian architecture, it sits alongside a canal in St. Petersburg (see photo 6.2). The church built by a reactionary son at the death of his more liberal father was a Eurasian reaction, Holy Russia now evident in the heart of the city of the rational Enlightenment. The struggle over Russian identity between the European and Eurasian imaginaries continues to inform contemporary national narratives.

Photo 6.2.   Eurasian St. Petersburg (John Rennie Short)

The Costs and Benefits of Empire

The Russian empire generated both benefits and costs. The benefits came in the form of the resource utilization of an expansive territory. The early conquest of Siberia, for example, allowed control of the valuable fur trade, a trade that promoted the Russian move all the way into the Pacific Northwest of North America. The conquests of Ukraine and the Volga river valley, in contrast, gave access to fertile agricultural lands. These vast territories provided economic opportunity for Russians to migrate to the lands under the control of the tsar.

Development was relatively basic, mainly resource extraction, with industrialization only occurring in the late nineteenth century around Moscow, St. Petersburg, and in the Ukraine. The empire, it seemed, could mobilize wealth only for the opulence and conspicuous consumption of a tiny elite. The vast disparities sowed the seeds of popular discontent. Yet, the expansive territory and large population meant that no matter how rudimentarily developed, Russia was a major power with vast reserves of military personnel.

Empire had its costs: it had to be managed and controlled. Not an easy proposition in a vast territory with a huge range of peoples of different religions, languages, ethnicities, and primary loyalties. During the nineteenth century, these differences often became centrifugal forces working against the coherence of the empire beyond the Russian core. The unruly edges of the empire, such as the Caucasus and Poland, were given special attention with periodic bouts of repression and active Russification.

A major cost of a vast, enduring empire was the geopolitical reality of coping with a heterogeneous population inside the borders while dealing with an ever-changing variety of other empires and states. Because of its geography, Tsarist Russia shared borders and contested spheres of influence with the British Empire, the Chinese Empire, the Ottoman Empire, the Austro-Hungarian Empire, and, more latterly, with the German and Japanese empires. Tsarist Russia was dragged as well as leaped into the churning geopolitical turmoil of rising/declining empires and the constant creation/dissolution of myriad states. This constant geopolitical shuffling and reshuffling necessitated military interventions that bled the economic resources of the empire and stunted its economic development. The Russian Empire, unlike the case of the British, was the corollary of economic backwardness.

Russia was often up against more powerful, better organized empires and thus needed allies to hold its own.[5] Alliances shifted and changed. Consider solely the case of Russia's relation with the British. Russia fought with the British against Napoleon (1805–1815) and then against the British, French, and Turks in the Crimean War (1853–1856), all the while playing the *Great Game* by jostling with the British Empire from approximately 1813 to 1907 for control and influence of Afghanistan, India, and Persia.[6] Later, Russia joined the alliance of Britain and France against Germany in World War I.

The beginning of the end of Tsarist Russia started with a war in the Far East against a Japan with imperial ambitions. The Russo-Japanese War (1904–1905) was a conflict between a declining and an ascending empire for control over southern Manchuria. Russia's defeat fomented the First Russian Revolution of 1905. Although not successful in overthrowing the ruling regime, it was a foretaste of things to come in the next decade. Defeats and huge Russian losses in WW1 were the initial catalysts for the better-known Russian Revolution of 1917.[7] In order to get Russia out of the war, German agents helped Lenin travel from his exile in Zurich, Switzerland to St. Petersburg.[8]

The benefits of Empire also came with enormous and ultimately destructive costs.

THE SOVIET EMPIRE

In its earliest years, the new state was especially vulnerable. Britain, France, and the United States sent military forces to help the White Army of anti-Bolsheviks in the Russian Civil War (1917–1923), almost snuffing out the new state at birth. The Allied interventions reinforced the long-standing Russian sense of vulnerability to foreign attack, a historical experience from the time of Napoleon's march on Moscow to the German invasion of World War II. The new regime was only established officially as the USSR in 1922.

The turmoil of the early years after the 1917 revolution provided an opportunity for some parts of the collapsed Tsarist empire to secede. Some took it: Lithuania became an independent state in 1919, and a year later Poland, the Baltic States, and Finland successfully declared themselves independent states. Some tried: there were breakaway movements on the southern rim. In 1917, Chechnya, Dagestan, and Ingushetia proclaimed independence, but by 1921, the Red Army had brought them to heel. A similar fate befell Georgia, which briefly attained independence in 1917, but was then brought back under Soviet control after a Soviet troop invasion in 1921.

By 1921, the USSR was very similar to the old Tsarist Empire minus Poland, Finland, and the Baltic states. The territory was then divided into Socialist Soviet Republics (SSRs) that had varying degrees of limited autonomy: they were organized along nationalities, such as Kazakhstan, Turkmenistan, and Uzbekistan. In the earlier years, there was a policy of *koreizatsiia* (indigenization) that gave preference to the dominant—sometimes referred to as the *titled* or *titular nation*—nationality in each SSR. The policy of the 1920s and early 1930s of promoting non-Russian culture was then replaced by a more pronounced Russification, Russian becoming the more universal language. By the end of the Soviet era there were fifteen SSRs. While some SSRs had a measure of historical reality, many (especially in Central Asia) were Soviet inventions of arbitrary boundary lines drawn across the steppe with little regard to local and complex realities. Despite their recent invention and arbitrary demarcation, many SSRs became the organizing territorial space after the break for the USSR.

The Bolshevik Revolution inaugurated a new form of government and a new economic system. Compared to the rudimentary development of the Tsarist empire, the Soviets promoted collectivization of agriculture and rapid industrialization. The economic potential of the SSRs was realized through economic planning that stressed their contribution to the wider Soviet economy. To feed the resource needs of the wider Soviet system, parts of Central Asia became a monoculture of cotton production; oil was exploited in Azerbaijan; and coal was mined in eastern Ukraine. The Soviet system—despite the straitjacket of a lumbering, slow-to-innovate central planning system—did lead to marked economic growth compared to the Tsarist regime, turning the USSR into a major industrial power. There were some similarities between the old and new regimes: absolutist party rule replaced absolutist monarchy, leaving no space for the evolution of civil society. The Bolsheviks also inherited the awkward landmass of the Tsarist regime.

World War II had an enormous impact on the Soviet Empire, extending its range and changing its character, beginning with the German-Soviet Nonaggression Pact—also known as the Molotov-Ribbentrop Pact—signed on August 23, 1939. The two countries agreed to carve up Eastern Europe between themselves. Soviet troops invaded Poland and Finland, and the USSR annexed eastern Poland, the Baltics, and parts of Romania. The Finns resisted and remained independent. The Allies—Britain and France—pledged to respond if the Nazis attacked Poland. World War II started with a German troop crossing into Poland on September 1, 1939 and by Britain's and France's declaration of war on Germany two days later.

The German-Soviet pact did not last long. On June 22, 1941—less than two years later—Adolf Hitler sent three million troops to attack the Soviets. It was the military enactment of the *lebensraum* ideology enunciated decades earlier by German geopoliticians. The extension and creation of the German Empire into the eastern lands, along with the annihilation of the Jews, were two central components of Hitler's ideology. The German advance into Russia proved costly. The greatest losses—military and civilian—occurred on the Russian front.[9] The Soviet Union's loss of death was 26 million, or 13.7 percent of its entire 1940 population. In contrast, the UK death toll was 451,00, or 3.2 percent of its 1939 total population. The United States suffered a loss of 419,400 or 0.9 percent of its 1939 population.[10] Most UK and U.S. losses in World War II were due to military engagements. In contrast, a majority of Soviet losses were borne by civilians, killed and starved. In one winter alone, more than one hundred thousand people died of starvation in the Ukrainian town of Kharkov while under German occupation. This total of civilian deaths in just one town in just one winter was higher than the entire civilian death toll in the entire war for the United States and UK combined. Death was especially common in what Timothy Snyder describes as the "Bloodlands" along the Soviet-German front in Eastern Europe.[11] The data backs up the description. The percentage of the population that died in Belarus was 16.3 percent and a staggering 26.3 percent in Ukraine.

The invasion of Russia—involving troops from Finland, Romania, Hungary, Italy, Slovakia, and Croatia fighting alongside Germans—was very successful. In the beginning. By September of 1941, German armies reached the outskirts of Leningrad and three months later the edge of Moscow. By September 1942, they reached the city of Stalingrad. This was to be the Germans' furthest reach into the USSR. Map 1.1 records the sweep of German power across Eastern Europe and into western Russia. The tide then turned with the Soviet victory in Stalingrad in early 1943. From then on, it was a steady Soviet pushback. Germany's counteroffensive at Kursk in the summer of 1943 was their last serious resistance. By the summer of 1944, the Red Army had liberated most of Eastern Europe from Nazi rule, and by January 1945 had crossed the Oder River into Germany. But at great cost. Photo 6.3 is

Photo 6.3. Soviet war cemetery in Weimar, Germany (John Rennie Short)

a cemetery for Soviet war dead in Weimar, Germany. Berlin surrendered to Soviet forces on May 2, 1946.

There were important geopolitical impacts of World War II on the Soviet Empire. The huge losses were stamped indelibly into the collective memory of Russians, reconfirming Russia's vulnerability to attack from across its western borderlands. There was also the Soviet annexation of the Baltic states that had experienced a brief period of independence since 1919. The Soviet Empire of the USSR was now looking more like the old Tsarist Empire. The Red Army's advance extended Soviet power westward into the heart of Germany. The troops not only defeated Hitler and Nazism but undergirded the Soviet control of what became an Eastern Europe of one-party Communist states. The ruling Communist parties in these one-party states owed their allegiance and their continued hold on power to the USSR. As a vital part of the winning coalition, the Soviets earned a place at the table of great power leaders drawing up the shape and character of a world after the defeat of Japan and Germany. The USSR was now a world power and recognized as such: it became a key player in the postwar world.

Postwar, the Soviet Empire had three distinct parts: an internal empire of SSRs, which after the annexation of the Baltic states looked much like the old Tsarist empire's territorial reach; an external empire in Eastern Europe of states enmeshed by the Red Army where the Communist Party eventually came to power, often illegally; and an informal empire of an archipelago of pro-Soviet states around the world.

The Eastern European bloc initially comprised Albania, Bulgaria, Czechoslovakia, East Germany, Hungary, Poland, and Romania. Because Yugoslavia was "liberated" by partisans under Tito rather than the Red Army, it could more easily escape the iron grip of Soviet rule. After 1948, Yugoslavia saw itself as a leader in the non-aligned group during the Cold War. In 1968, Albania pulled out of military and economic relations with the USSR and became a Stalinist oddity in a cell-like insularity. The remainder of the bloc came under the shadow of one-party rule, of joint economic relations under COMECON (founded in 1949), of a mutual defense arrangement known as the Warsaw Pact (founded in 1955) and of the 1968 *Brezhnev Doctrine* that stated that any threat to Communist party rule in the Eastern bloc would be seen as threat to all. It was the Soviet equivalent to the *Truman Doctrine* of 1947 and to the *Reagan Doctrine* of 1985. The doctrine was used to justify Soviet intervention. It was a threat that hung over the countries in the bloc. Even before its formalization, the doctrine was applied to deploy Soviet forces in 1956 against the uprising in Hungary, in 1968 against Czechoslovakia to undermine what is known as the Prague Spring, and to justify the Soviet invasion of Afghanistan. Soviet rule restricted political freedoms and dampened nationalist cultural expressions in the countries of what had become known as Eastern Europe. Yet many of them had been sovereign states with varying degrees of civil society and cultural legacies that predated Communist ideology. Roman Catholicism in Poland was an important part of national identity and of anti-Soviet resistance.

There also was the wider external empire of a changing set of client states around the world, including at various times Afghanistan, Angola, Benin, China, Cuba, Ethiopia, Laos, Mongolia, Somalia, South Yemen, and North Vietnam. The

USSR had less formal control over these client states than over the states in Eastern Europe. Nevertheless, the Soviets could wield considerable power over these clients through favorable economic relations and military ties. The USSR purchased most of Cuba's sugar crop, for example, as a way to support Castro. In the Cold War, the USSR and the United States sought to establish friendly regimes and to support political allies around the world, especially in the fertile context of decolonializations and of revolutionary ruptures, beginning in the 1960s. U.S. client states included the military alliances of the North Atlantic Treaty Organization (NATO), the Central Treaty Organization (CENTO), and the Southeast Asia Treaty Organization (SETO), effectively encircling the Soviet Union. The United States and its allies became reconciled to the Soviet control of Eastern Europe, doing little to seriously challenge the invasions of Hungary and Czechoslovakia. During the Cold War, separate spheres of influence were recognized, accepted, and solidified across Europe. It was different in the competition for the wider global theater of client states: here, the Cold War was played out for real.

The Fall of the Soviet Union

Empires built over decades and centuries can fall very quickly. The fall of the Soviet Empire was rapid after years of weakening by a slow economy, a political system lacking legitimacy, and crippling Cold War expenditures. There also were more specific events that in retrospect look like harbingers of collapse. Two stand out. One is the doomed invasion of a client state, Afghanistan, which led to an almost decade-long brutal and unsuccessful campaign that lasted from 1979 to 1989. It was the very epitome of *imperial overstretch*. The disastrous war led to a split between the Communist Party and the military, undermined the image of a powerful Soviet military, and weakened the power of the party. The second, in 1986, was the explosion of a nuclear reactor at Chernobyl in the Ukraine SSR. The plume of radioactive debris was easily and quickly monitored by the West and so forced the government to become more transparent. In the face of the declining legitimacy of his regime, a failed war, and a horrible, avoidable nuclear contamination that revealed the deep crises at the heart of a failing and flailing system, President Gorbachev introduced *glasnost*, a policy of greater transparency that weakened party rule and created more space for critics of the regime.

The end came quickly in Eastern Europe. There was little genuine popular support for Communist parties now filled with apparatchiks and opportunist hacks running cynically corrupt regimes. In 1989 the independent political party, *Solidarity*, won the election in Poland. Hungarians set a date for free elections, the Berlin Wall fell, Bulgaria's slavishly pro-Soviet leadership was overthrown. The Communist Party leadership in Czechoslovakia was forced to resign and the East German leader was placed under house arrest. In Romania, the Communist dictator Ceausescu was toppled and later killed after a brief "trial." The leader of the USSR aided the breakup. Gorbachev refused to send in troops when requested in 1989 by the East German leader. Gorbachev played a major if unwitting role in the fall of the Soviet Empire.[12] Inside the USSR, the power of the Communist Party was weakening. The Baltic SSRs were the first to press for independence. On Christmas Day 1991, the Soviet hammer and sickle was lowered from the Kremlin, replaced by a new Russian tricolor. The Soviet Empire was officially at an end.

THE CREATION OF NEW STATES: PROBLEMS AND OPPORTUNITIES

The most obvious impact of the Empire's fall was the creation of new states. All the former SSRs quickly obtained independence. Some, most notably the Baltics, had a prior history of national identity and of state formation. Others had to fashion a national identity and state government practices around territory demarcated by arbitrary lines informed by the imprecise ideas of the then dominant "national" and "ethnic" identity. In the post-Soviet world, the ethnic diversity of many of these new states created problems of state cohesion, problems partially "solved" with the overt promotion of *ethno-states*. There are also remnants of *frozen conflict* (see map 6.1 and table 6.1) where breakaway regions continue to exist in a liminal position.[13]

Table 6.1. Post-Soviet Frozen Conflict Zones

Zone	Established	De Jure State
Transnistria	1990	Moldova
Nagorno-Karabakh	1991	Azerbaijan
South Ossetia and Abkhazia	1991	Georgia
Crimea	2014	Ukraine
Donetsk Republic	2014	Ukraine
Luhansk Republic	2014	Ukraine

The Baltic Republics Return to Europe

The Baltic republics of Estonia, Latvia, and Lithuania made a quick and determined breakaway from the USSR, having long chafed under what many experienced as a Soviet occupation. Their national identity predated Communist ideology. They had different religious traditions from Russian Orthodoxy—Lutheranism in the case of Estonia and Latvia, and Roman Catholicism in Lithuania. They were more European than Eurasian with a recent experience, albeit brief, of independence during the interwar era. They also had experience with commercial agriculture and of market systems driven by price signals rather than plans from a distant committee. They had an identity, a level of economic development, and a socioeconomic legacy that made the transition to democracies and private markets that much easier than for the Central Asia republics. Estonia, for example, quickly pivoted away from Russia. The Soviet history was erased and in its place the story of Estonian nationalism was established. One example: a public space in the capital Tallinn was remade to celebrate the 1918–1920 war of independence. For non-Estonian speakers, the quote etched on the wall in photo 6.4 exhorts Estonians "to lift the national flag as the wind of independence is sweeping across, it is time to swear an oath to resist the yoke of other nations."

All three Baltic countries quickly reoriented to Western Europe. All three are now members of the EU and NATO. Estonia, to take just one example, became a member of the European Union (2004), NATO (2004), the Schengen Area (2007), and the Eurozone (2011), and sent troops to Iraq and Afghanistan. All three countries have fostered economic and cultural ties with Nordic countries. The capital

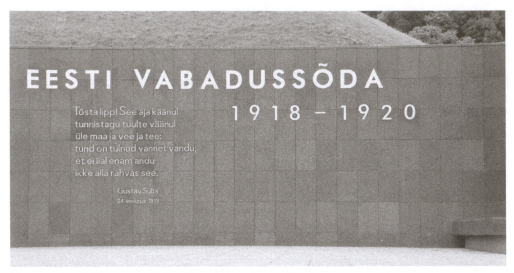

Photo 6.4.   Public space in Tallinn, Estonia (John Rennie Short)

of Estonia, Tallinn, is only two hours by ferry from Helsinki in Finland, and there are plans to build a tunnel to connect the two capital cities. The Baltic republics are reinvigorating old trade links with their Finnish and Nordic neighbors.

As part of extended U.S. and Western European military and economic unions, these countries are positioned uncomfortably close to a Russia that is pushing back against what it sees as the extension of NATO power right up against its border. Russian cyberattacks against Estonia and occasional airspace incursion are now part of a recurring pattern of Soviet probing of western defenses in the Baltic. While Baltic countries distance themselves politically from Russia, proximity encourages economic ties and cross-border trade. However, such nearness also comes with potential risks. Their NATO membership provides security against direct attack somewhat, but there is still room for gray zone activity by an emboldened Russian state.

There is also the issue of ethnic Russians residing in these Western-looking republics. Around 25 percent of the population of Estonia and Latvia are ethnic Russians. Russia continues to claim the poor treatment of ethnic Russians, especially in Estonia and Latvia. As the years pass, and ethnic Russians return to Russia, there is likely to be a gradual assimilation.

A New Eastern Europe?

There is a group of countries, including Belarus, Moldova, and Ukraine, that may be considered a border area between Russian and European spheres of influence. In Ukraine, the European/Russian divides the country. We will discuss Ukraine as a geopolitical hotspot later in the chapter. The question mark used in the subtitle of this section is suggestive of such liminal space.

Belarus is the country in this group closest to Russia, with a similar language and a shared religious history of Russian Orthodoxy. It is tightly bound economically with ties to its eastern neighbor. Reminiscent of the Soviet era, Belarus retains the centralized power of an authoritarian leader, Alexander Lukashenko, who has been in power since 1994 and is regularly described as "Europe's last dictator." I would dispute only the implied claim in the quote that he is European. He acts more like a Eurasian despot. The majority of the population are Belarusian, very similar to Russian—so similar in fact that there was no real appetite for an independent state after the fall of the USSR. In a referendum held in 1991, a majority stated that they wanted to stay with Russia. Belarus emerged not as the result of clamor of separatist sentiments, but as a decision made by Russian leaders. Statehood was shoved on them. With no tradition of civil society, Communist apparatchiks quickly emerged as undemocratic leaders. Lukashenko was a typical party hack, a director of a collective farm during the Soviet era. The country remained closely tied to Russia. Its dictator periodically encouraged Western trade and investment, more as a way to strengthen his hand in negotiations with Russia than as a radical reorientation.

Lukashenko had rigged elections for years through the suppression of opposition leaders and blatant vote manipulation. The security forces limit public expression of discontent. The election of August 2020 initially proved no different, with opposition leaders gagged, deported, or imprisoned and Lukashenko claiming victory. The official results again showed Lukashenko as the clear winner. This time, however, the public refused to accept the official results. Public protests mounted and drew in factory workers. Lukashenko may be able to hold onto power in the short term, but this is unlikely in the longer term. The question is what Russia will do. Supporting Lukashenko may have limited traction; he has run out of legitimacy. Yet Russia is unlikely to allow a Western-oriented regime to take power. Russia will try to keep Belarus firmly within the Russian sphere of influence.

Moldova, with a current population of 2.6 million (excluding Transnistria), was ceded in 1812 to the Tsarist Empire by the Ottomans. Its transfer was part of the expansion of the Russian Empire and the weakening of the Ottoman Empire. It briefly broke away in 1917 and became part of Romania. Under the Molotov-Ribbentrop Pact of 1939, Moldova was reassigned to the Soviet Union and subsequently became the Moldovan SSR. After World War II, Soviet planners drew the boundaries so that it remained landlocked—its sea outlet was allocated to Ukraine—and hence less likely to secede. Moldova became an independent state in 1991. Transnistria, part of the Soviet Union since 1924, to the east of the River Dniester, with a population of around 469,000, rejected the decision. The mainly Russian speakers of this region resisted the imposition of the Moldovan (Romanian) language. Cossack forces, militia, and elements of the Russian Army fought a war with pro-Moldova troops who had support from Romania. More than a thousand military personnel and around five hundred civilians were killed in the conflict. Eventually a cease-fire was declared in 1992. The territory of Transnistria remains unrecognized but has tacit Russian support: it is part of the *frozen conflict zones*, shown in map 6.1 and noted in table 6.1, that are a legacy of the awkward breakup of the USSR. With part of its official territory a breakaway republic and unable to make a full leap into the European Union, Moldova is one of those post-Soviet states awkwardly balancing between the pull of Europe and the shadow of Russia.

The Caucasus: Independence and Turmoil

Three former SSRs in the Caucasus became independent states in 1991: Armenia, Azerbaijan, and Georgia. Their post-Soviet history in this region is marked by tension between Georgia and Russia, close connections between Armenia and Russia, and simmering conflict between Armenia and Azerbaijan. It is a region of geopolitical projections by not only Russia, but also Iran and Turkey.[14]

Georgia represents a very different experience from, say, Belarus: it is more distinct from Russia than Belarus. Georgian is a distinct Caucasian language, and there are also Persian-speaking Ossetians. There are a few ethnic Russians in the country concentrated along the borderlands with Russia. Georgia tried to break away from the Tsarist Empire during the revolution upheavals but was forcibly brought back under Soviet control in 1921. In 1956 Soviet troops crushed a budding secessionist movement. No surprise then that a majority of the population opted for independence in 1991. In 1993, separatists in Abkhazia evicted Georgian troops from the region, which became an unrecognized state supported by Russia. By recognizing and supporting the breakaway state of Abkhazia, which had key port facilities along its coastline, Russia secured access to the Black Sea. Later, in 2008, Russian troops invaded Georgia to support separatists in South Ossetia and reinforce the "independence" of Abkhazia. The rest of Georgia remains more pro-Western, and the country currently seeks entry into the EU and NATO. In 2004, the election of a more Western-oriented leader by a democratic movement known as the "Rose Revolution" signaled the country was moving Westward rather than Eastward. The sensitive geopolitical situation and the rampant corruption has kept away significant Western investment and interest. When presidential candidate John McCain announced in August 2008, with reference to the Russian invasion of Georgia, that "Today, we are all Georgians," the statement failed to catch the attention of the U.S. electorate.[15] So soon after the failed war in Iraq and the never-ending conflict in Afghanistan, the U.S. public was suffering *imperial fatigue* and could muster little enthusiasm for direct U.S. involvement in a distant land. Georgia was too far away, too corrupt, and too close to Russia. The Russians, in contrast, were motivated more, believing that the United States was acting behind the scenes to encourage a Georgian orientation to the West. Russia sees Georgia's attempts to join both NATO and the EU as a threat.[16]

Armenia and Azerbaijan are very close neighbors with very different identities. Armenia is a predominantly Christian country. Azerbaijan, comprising chiefly Turkic people, is a predominantly Shia Muslim country. Post-Soviet independence released old tensions, especially over the complex social geography of Armenian and Azerbaijani communities spread throughout the two countries. Azerbaijan has four *exclaves* (political fragments of a state not connected physically to that state and surrounded by the territory of other states) in Armenia, the largest being the Nakhchivan Autonomous Republic that covers 580 square miles and comprises a population of 410,000. In the 1920s, the Soviets allocated the Armenian-populated area of Nagorno-Karabakh to the Azerbaijan SSR. When the two countries became independent in 1991, they soon came to war over the disputed area. This war, fought between 1990 and 1994, resulted in massive population displacement as 230,000 Armenians left Azerbaijan and 800,000 Azeris left Armenia. Subsequently, although Nagorno-Karabakh, with around 140,000 living in 1,700 square miles, was legally part of Azerbaijan, in practice it had a predominantly Armenian population and was effectively part of Armenia whereas most Azerbaijanis have left or been forced out. In 1993, Turkey closed the border with landlocked Armenia in support of Azerbaijan. In 2016, conflict between the two neighbors again erupted with shelling and border incursions. In the six-week Nagorno-Karabakh War in 2020, Azerbaijan troops, supported by Turkey, gained control of southern Nagorno-Karabakh. Thousands were killed in the conflict, with Turkish drones used by the Azerbaijan forces proving especially lethal. The result was a victory for Azerbaijan and a humiliating defeat for Armenia. Azerbaijan kept control of its territorial gains in Nagorno-Karabakh; all Armenia controlled territory surrounding Nagorno-Karabakh was returned to Azerbaijan, which also gained guaranteed access to its exclave of Nakhichevan. The final agreement led to protests in the cities across Armenia. Two outside powers increased their influence: Turkey, which tipped the balance in Azerbaijan favor, and Russia, which now has two thousand of its troops stationed between Armenia and Nagorno-Karabakh and deployed as a peace-keeping force until 2025.

Armenia considers Russia an ally in this conflict with Azerbaijan and Turkey. There is a Russian military base in Armenia. Russia supplies Armenia with cheap gas guaranteed until 2043 and is the main supplier of arms and military equipment. There are also significant economic ties. More than a fifth of Armenia's national income originates from Armenians living and working in Russia. Because Armenia is a member of the Eurasian Economic Union, Armenians find it relatively easy to work in Russia: they dominate construction and asphalt-laying in Moscow. Their remittances are an important source of national income.

Azerbaijan is more fortunate in that it has substantial gas and oil reserves. Pipelines link the country's oil fields to Europe and the rest of the world. With private oligarchs replacing Soviet commissars, the centralization of the old Soviet system persists. Azerbaijan is wealthy because of its rich natural resources, but there is a marked inequality within the country and a limited exercise of democratic rights. As a rich oil state—though suffering from the typical problems of a resource curse—it can maintain some distance from Russia, a distancing reinforced by the alliance of Russia and Armenia on the one hand and its increasingly strong alliance with Turkey on the other.

Central Asian Republics

The post-Soviet collapse meant independence for the former SSRs of Central Asia. They include Kazakhstan, Kyrgyzstan, Tajikistan, Turkmenistan, and Uzbekistan.[17] Their boundaries were drawn by Soviet planners using arbitrary demarcations of dominant—if rather hazily understood—ethnicities. Since ultimate power was centralized in Moscow, the actual boundaries of these SSRs merited neither much attention nor any real concern at their inception. Things changed after independence; internal politics became marked by state encouragement of dominant ethnic groups despite their arbitrary boundaries and multiethnic character. Arbitrary and hazy distinction became codified and solidified in citizenship and political rights, drawn up rather haphazardly as ethnic units. These units are becoming *ethno-states* as ethnic Russians leave, and policies are promoted that advance the culture of the dominant ethnicity. The geopolitics of these new ethno-states is shaped by three factors; relations with Russia, external relations with each other, and internal tensions.

Relations with Russia

The geopolitical economic realities of being in the middle of the Eurasian land-mass so close to Russia informs—if not always determines—the foreign relations of these Soviet-designed SSRs turned into independent states. They all remain in the shadow of Russia. On a continuum from closer to further we can locate Kazakhstan and Kyrgyzstan at one end and Turkmenistan at the other, with Uzbekistan and Tajikistan in between.

Kazakhstan and Kyrgyzstan are closer to Russia: they have significant ethnic Russian minorities, 23 percent in the case of Kazakhstan (down from 43 percent in 1960) and 12 percent in Kyrgyzstan. Underneath the vast steppe, the traditional home of Kazak and Kyrgyz nomads, lie vast reserves of oil and gas that now supply markets in Russia, Europe, and China. Vital pipelines must cross Russia to connect with the huge markets of Europe. The two countries are also more formally linked to Russia as part of the Russian-dominated economic pact, the Eurasian Economic Union (EEU). More than 40 percent of Kyrgyzstan's GDP is in the form of remittances from people working in Russia. With their important mineral reserves and their strategic position at the heart of Eurasia sharing borders with China, Russia keeps these two states as close as possible. The two countries' authoritarian leadership is a continuation of the role of the commissars, providing little room for democratic expression.

Tajikistan is not a member of the EEU, but of the more than one million Tajikistan migrants working abroad, most are in Russia, and their remittances are a major source of national income. Uzbekistan is a Turkic-speaking country with a predominantly Sunni Muslim population that was an SSR from 1924 to 1991. It was a place where Soviet authorities "dumped" Chechens and Tatars. Uzbekistan became significant in the Soviet economy as a cotton-growing region as well as an exporter of natural gas, minerals, and tobacco. The shift from a command to a market economy is slight with the state retaining important controls as an authoritarian regime that squats over its citizenry. Foreign investment is small. In 2001, when Russia had a less confrontational stance against the West, Uzbekistan allowed the United States to use its air bases for action in Afghanistan. Later, Russian pressure rescinded those privileges. Under the giant shadow of Russia, Uzbekistan remains poor and doubly landlocked, surrounded by landlocked nations. In 1991 at the creation of the new states, a half-million Uzbeks ended up in Kyrgyzstan and Tajikistan.

Turkmenistan is the most homogeneous of the "stans," with a population of ethnic Turks constituting 85 percent of the population. Turkmenistan has huge reserves of natural gas, which give it a degree of economic independence from Russia, especially after a pipeline was built to China in 2009.

External Relations

The densely populated, fertile agricultural region of the Fergana Valley is a flash-point between Kyrgyzstan, Tajikistan, and Uzbekistan. Kazakhstan, Kyrgyzstan, and Tajikistan inherited border disputes of the old USSR with China, although these were settled by 1999. By 2014, most of the disputes were reconciled, and most countries, apart from Uzbekistan, now have demilitarized borders.

This region has a long Islamic heritage. Religious beliefs, as well as goods and ideas, traveled along the Silk Roads that linked China and central Asia with the Middle East and Europe. Traders diffused the new religion along the route so that all the "stans" except Tajikistan became Sunni Muslim. Tajikistan was more under the influence of Persia, resulting today in a majority Shia Muslim population. Islam is more moderate in Tajikistan than Afghanistan, Pakistan, or Saudi Arabia, and so there is less purchase for firebrand fundamentalism.

There are some non-state actors. The Islamic Movement of Uzbekistan, affiliated at various times to both al Qaeda and ISIS, was especially active from 1998 to 2015. Initially an ethnic Uzbek movement, it has tried to extend its membership to Afghan's Tajiks, Turkmens, and Uighurs, with promises of a central Asian caliphate. This has limited appeal. There are incursions by militants from nearby Afghanistan, but the governments have worked to limit their appeal and the force of their attacks. There was some religious dimension to some recent conflicts. In Tajikistan, the brutal civil war pitted democrat and modern Shia against ex-Communists, but it was primarily a proxy conflict between Russia and Iran. Al Qaeda and ISIS do not have a natural base of support in Tajikistan.

The "stans" occupy a pivotal position between Afghanistan, Pakistan, and China.[18] The porous border with Afghanistan, in particular, provides an opportunity for drug smuggling. The insecure borders, a huge global demand for opiates, and a ready supply in Afghanistan are the basis for insidious drug smuggling that reflects a corrupt system and corrupts politics even further. Afghanistan is one of the largest producers of raw opium and heroin in the world. Kyrgyzstan and Tajikistan now act as transits in the movement of Afghan opiates to Russia and Europe. The illegal activity is so lucrative, as in the case of Central America, that it leads to a criminalization of state apparatus, including police, judiciary, and political officeholders. Leaders of criminal trafficking groups have at various times occupied important government positions. Both countries have been defined as *narco-states*.[19]

Internal Tensions

When the fluid borders of the SSRs became the more solid borders of the new states, many new ethnic minorities were created. In 1991, a half-million Uzbeks ended up in Kyrgyzstan and Tajikistan and millions of ethnic Russians found themselves in these new states—almost two million in an independent Kazakhstan. State policies hardened ethnicity as the former SSRs became *ethno-states*. This tendency was reinforced when ethnic enclaves were created, an attempt to solve the tension by containing minorities in specially designated exclaves of their "homeland." Paradoxically, this can heighten the tensions reinforcing the idea that minorities are so different, so "other," that they cannot occupy the same national space and must be corralled into a separate, different space.

In the past twenty years, Kyrgyzstan has become more dominated by Kyrgyz as other ethnic groups have left in large numbers, responding to the political uncertainty, growing ethnic tensions, and poor economic performance. The country has four Uzbek and two Tajikistan enclaves, and ethnic unrest between Uzbeks and Kyrgyz continues. Kyrgyzstan has an exclave in Uzbekistan.

After it became an independent country in 1991, Tajikistan was wracked by a civil war between Russian- and Iranian-backed groups. More than 100,000 people were killed and 1.2 million were made refugees in a country with a population of eight million. There was a famine in 2001, and food security remains an issue in this poorest of the "stans." Tajikistan has two exclaves in Kyrgyzstan and one in Uzbekistan.

Uzbekistan is a Turkic-speaking country with a predominantly Sunni Muslim population. A policy of Uzbekistanization further marginalizes the minority of Tajik speakers. Bukhara and Samarqand, long-established centers of Tajik culture and learning, are now part of Uzbekistan. Uzbekistan has four exclaves in Kyrgyzstan. One of them, Sokh, has a population of seventy thousand and to add to the complexity, most of them are Tajiks. Uzbeks also constitute the second-largest ethnic group in Tajikistan, Kyrgyzstan, and Turkmenistan.

The transformation of multiethnic SSRs into independent, singular ethno-states, patchworked with exclaves and enclaves, has created tensions. Some of the tension is released with migrations—often tantamount to removal—of ethnic minorities into their home countries and the creation of exclaves, which gives some measure of security to minority groups. Apart from the brutal war in Tajikistan, there have been few outbreaks of outright war. Yet there are mounting challenges. Water conflicts between Tajikistan and Uzbekistan, for example, have increased. Uzbekistan's water needs for its cotton-growing is constrained by Tajikistan control of the headwaters. The ethnic tensions that lie simmering in this dispute are exacerbated by state nationalist agendas and are always more visible during economic downturns.

A POST-SOVIET RUSSIA

Russia has certainly moved on since 1991. The Communist Party no longer wields power, a capitalist economy has emerged, and a new generation of Russians—aged under thirty—only have an acquaintance with a post-Communist Russia and have no direct experience of life in the Soviet Union. And yet, modern Russia has numerous characteristics that stem directly from the Soviet past.

Continuities

The first is the territorial extent. While the former SSRs achieved independence and the USSR was diminished, that still left a huge Russian "rump state" that contained elements of both the Soviet and indeed Tsarist empires. Russia is still one of the largest countries in the world, constituting 13 percent of the earth's surface, down from 17 percent in 1913, and extending over eleven time zones, as it stretches from the Baltic to the Pacific. Surrounded as it is by such a wide range of countries, this new Russian state faces the same geopolitical issues as previous regimes. And ethnic Russians living beyond its borders gives Russia an active interest in neighboring countries where they may live. There are now some twenty-five million Russians living outside of Russia in substantial, absolute, and relative numbers in Latvia (26.2 percent of total national population), Estonia (24.8 percent), Kazakhstan (23.7 percent), Ukraine (17.3 percent), and Kyrgyzstan (12.5).

To understand the range of geopolitical consideration resulting from its size, we can consider its westernmost and easternmost territories. Russian national territory reaches beyond its contiguity into the heart of Europe. Kaliningrad is an exclave of Russia, situated far to the west of the main Russian territory and surrounded by the Baltic, Lithuania, and Poland (see map 6.1). This exclave has a population of almost 450,000. For centuries, Kaliningrad was part of East Prussia, with a strong German influence. After World War II, the region came under Soviet control; Germans were evicted, the main city of Konigsberg was renamed Kaliningrad, and it was made the home port of the Soviet Baltic fleet. Because of the strategic importance of the region, three air bases and a naval base are still sited there. It remains a part of Russia surrounded by NATO and EU countries. Kaliningrad provides Russia with proximate military access to the Baltic and to the heart of Europe.

Russia is also part of East Asia, sharing a 2,615-mile land border with China and a much smaller one with North Korea. The border with North Korea is only eleven miles long, the shortest of Russia's international borders. It means, however, that Russia is part of the six-party talks that involve North Korea, South Korea, Japan, the United States, and China. Russia also has a maritime border with Japan. Imperial Russia used to have a land border with Japan through Sakhalin Island. In 1875, Japan ceded its claim in exchange for the Kuril Islands, a long chain of eleven islands that runs from the Kamchatka peninsula of Russia to the Japanese island of Hokkaido. In 1945, during the dying days of World War II, the Soviets secured the entire island chain in amphibious landings. Japan was forced to renounce its claims but did not recognize the four southernmost islands as part of the chain. There was just enough confusion to create a long-standing dispute. Map 6.2 depicts the main towns on Sakhalin—Okha, Poronaysk, and Yuzhno-Sakhalinsk (and their Japanese names)—and the four disputed Kuril Islands. In 2011 and 2013, Russia offered to give up the two smaller southernmost islands, but Japan refused. Both countries fight their cases because there are important fishing areas plus offshore gas and oil reserves. There are also strategic implications. Russia wants a Pacific presence and currently maintains a military base on the island of Kunashir. Control over the islands allows it to maintain a foothold in the Pacific and a base to launch military, especially airplane sorties in various geopolitical scenarios of the Pacific theater. Japan, on the other hand, does not want Russia so close to its national territory or to appear weak in its territorial claims, especially as it has conflicts with China over the disputed Senkaku/Diaoyu Islands.

Map 6.2. Sakhalin and Kuril Islands (Wikimedia / OpenStreet-Map contributors. Modifications by Eddal.)

In the breakup of the USSR, Russia lost control over many resources and especially over the lucrative, vast oil and gas reserves in Azerbaijan, Kazakhstan, Kyrgyzstan, and Turkmenistan. Yet, the territory of Russia still has the good fortune of being endowed with a rich resource base. Oil and gas in Siberia and the Arctic region allow Russia to be a major carbon-based power still. Much of Russia's export is oil and gas, to the extent that the very recent history of Soviet/ Russia is tied to their fluctuating price. The dramatic fall in the price of oil was a background factor in the fall of the USSR, while the resurgence of Russia and Putin's domestic popularity in the first fifteen years of the twentieth-first century was linked to rising world prices. Oil and gas exports to China and Europe provide the bulk of Russia's foreign earnings. Changing world prices of these commodities may enrich or impoverish state coffers.

The new Russian state, as its previous empires, is multiethnic. There are at least 180 officially recognized ethnic groups that include the Russians, by far the largest group at 77 percent of the 142.5 million population, and numerous ethnic and language groups that range from the more than five million Tatars to the thousands of Uyghurs in Central Asia, close to the border with China. There are also indigenous peoples, who are listed as titular nations to autonomous areas, such as the Chechens, Karelians, Komi, and Yakuts. Russia is considered the "title" nation; Russians are the dominant ethnic and language group.

The Russian state faces problems from its imperial legacy of territorial annexation. There is the Islamic southern rim. Chechens are a mountain people living in the Caucasus. They resisted domination in alliance with the Avars in neighboring Dagestan in the long Russo-Caucasian war from 1816–1864. Chechnya, along with Ingushetia and Dagestan, proclaimed independence from Russia in 1917. Soviet troops crushed the breakaway movement in 1921. During World War II, the entire Chechen population was rounded up on orders from Stalin and shipped to Kazakhstan, accused of collaboration with the Germans. They were allowed to return only in 1956. In 1990, Chechen separatists declared independence and got their hands-on Soviet weaponry. The Russian argument against their independence was that Chechnya, unlike Estonia or Georgia, was not an independent entity in the USSR. Independence for non-SSRs would provoke other groups to claim independence, and the region was too important to the Russian oil economy and to broader geopolitical strategy. In 1994, Russia reclaimed the territory by armed force. Russian forces regained control of the main city, Grozny, but at some costs. After Chechen rebels seized 1,600 hostages at a hospital in Russia, a truce was signed in 1996 and a brief period of a shadowy independence followed. Fearful of Islamic-inspired terrorism sweeping into other provinces in the region as well as response to attacks in Russian cities, Russian troops entered the region again in 1999. Most troops were pulled out ten years later in 2009, but an ongoing threat of insurgency and terrorist attacks remains. The Chechen separatist movement has morphed over the years. In the immediate breakup of the Soviet Union, the movement was mainly secular and nationalist. From 1999, the movement was motivated by Islamic fundamentalism, and since 2009, it has aligned with other groups in the area with the aim of establishing a Caucasus Emirate. The capital city of Grozny is the site of frequent terrorist attacks.

The new Russia also bears the hallmark of the two previous regimes. The Soviet era iconography on a bridge in contemporary St. Petersburg is a physical legacy (see photo 6.5). There are also enduring social legacies. Under the Tsarist and Soviet imperium, there was little development of *civil society*, all those civic organizations that generally form the seedbed of an inclusive and active citizenry. Subjects of absolutism became citizens of a totalitarian state and then of an authoritarian state. Russia has little experience with democracy and with few traditions of community organizing, civic engagement, and democratic government, it was that much easier for a Russia led by an ex-KGB officer to become an authoritarian state. What is surprising is not the lack of democracy but the extent to which democracy tries to flourish, given its lack of historical depth in Russian history and political experience. The tough environment of an increasingly authoritarian state is a major obstacle as well.

The Geopolitics of a Eurasian Russia

The Russian state was in a weakened position in the immediate aftermath of the fall of the USSR: it had lost assets, wealth, territory, prestige, and most importantly, power. The early years were chaotic as a brutal form of neoliberalism forced the sale of state enterprises. A tiny minority of well-placed insiders, often ex-Communist Party members, essentially looted the nation's wealth for their own enrichment. It was a time when the terms "Russian" and "oligarch" were used together in a common combination.

Russia's geopolitical position was weakened as it lost its hold in Eastern Europe, and the West flaunted its power. Many Russians believe that Gorbachev agreed to the reunification of Germany on the condition that NATO would not extend its reach. Yet in 2004, NATO added Bulgaria, Estonia, Latvia, Lithuania, Romania, Slovakia, and Slovenia to its list of member states. NATO's reach

Photo 6.5.   Soviet-era bridge post in St. Petersburg (John Rennie Short)

expanded to the very edges of Russia's border, heightening Russian fears and sense of vulnerabilities.

The leadership of Boris Yeltsin, in office from 1991 to 1999, marked a nadir in Russian power and influence. By the end of his presidency, a bankrupt and reeling Russia appeared set to join the ranks of faded, shrunken empires. It looked like the geopolitical catastrophe that Putin noted in his famous 2005 remark. The new century, however, marked the beginnings of a reconfigured Russia. Vladimir Putin was elected to the presidency in 2000 and has ruled in one form or another since with a leadership style more reminiscent of the tsars than the commissars.

Putin pursued a number of geopolitical goals. The first was the creation of a strong state. Oligarchs who wanted to influence politics were intimidated, threatened, and ultimately jailed. The state would be the repository of political power, not the rich or the civic organizations that were often promoted by the West. Political power was centralized under the authoritarian control of Putin. In the last years of his presidency, Yeltsin looked both drunk and weak; Putin reversed the imagery to reinforce the change. The strong state idea was embodied in the conscious display of his own virility in numerous staged and photographed events. The Russian public was given images of Putin bare-chested, of Putin riding a horse, of Putin hunting. The choreographed images of a vital muscularity, in rich contrast to the last years of a doddering Yeltsin, were meant to invoke a new Russia, manly and strong. The images proved popular to a population still smarting from Western triumphalism and the loss of Russian power-prestige. He was fortunate in one regard. With an increase in the global demand for oil and gas in his first presidency, the Russian treasury had more money to spend. Putin could thus allocate more on social welfare and military buildup. In the first decade of the twenty-first century, the lot of many ordinary Russians improved. With growing incomes and lessened restrictions on personal liberties if not political liberties, Putin became a very popular leader. His leadership does not neatly parallel the commodity prices, given the time-lags and intervening factors, but it does track closely. The strong state, now flush with cash, enabled a military expansion after years of neglect, which included a buildup of military hardware, an increase of combat readiness, and a greater deployment of gray zone operations. When world prices are high, the state can spend more, but when prices drop and with so few export alternatives, the resource curse kicks in, and there is less wealth to spread around.

A second goal was to secure Russia's *near abroad*. This involved procuring Russian power in some places as the Caucasus and Ukraine.[20] I will look in detail at Ukraine as an example of a geopolitical hotspot in the liminal space of Russian borderland.[21]

A third goal was to push back more generally against the West. Western triumphalism now met Russian resentment. In his early years in power, Putin sounded like a Europeanist. In 2000, he spoke about the very real possibility of Russia joining NATO. The subsequent shift in Russian policy makes that now sound inconceivable. A *Russia in the West* was made to feel second- or even third-rate with the choice of either folding into the West or of utter marginalization.[22] Hallowed Western terms seemed false promises to Russia. In a play on words that marked a sense of anger, the term "democracy" was known often in Russia as "dermokratiya," which can be translated as "shitocracy."[23] No surprise then that a Eurasian perspective, always there in the background, emerged from the shadows to take a more prominent position. A "Russia against the West" replaced the notion of "Russia in the West." The reestablishment of a global role for a Eurasian-defined Russia was mapped out by geopoliticians such as Alexander Dugin. His *Foundations of Geopolitics* was published in Russian in 1997.[24] He described Russia as a unique Eurasian civilization, as a vital bulwark against American hegemony.

In views that parallel Mackinder, he conceptualized a world conflict between conservative land powers and more liberal maritime powers. In his version of Manifest Destiny, Russia is imagined as a pivot to a more conservative order based on Russian exceptionalism.[25] A Russia of Moscow rather than a Russia of St. Petersburg is invoked, a Eurasian balance to Western decadence. Russia imagined as the center of a Eurasian empire facing off against an American-led West.

Dugin is the extreme end of the Eurasian perspective. He argued vehemently for the Russian annexation of the whole of Ukraine. After he made incendiary calls for violence against Ukrainians in 2014, more than ten thousand people signed a petition demanding he be fired from his post at Moscow State University. He subsequently left the university. Although he may be at the more extreme end of the Eurasian perspective, combining as he does a deep Orthodox religiosity, an outright fascism, and demands to invade Ukraine with calls to take on the evil Atlanticists, Dugin's basic views do reflect a shift in how Russia sees itself. In contemporary Russian geopolitics, Mackinder's idea has been resuscitated as "a positive vision of the Russian-Eurasian heartland in the form of a consolidated, self-contained and self-sufficient civilization."[26]

The Eurasian perspective may also be part of what the historian Timothy Snyder delineates as the *politics of eternity* that witnesses an endless cycle of repetition with a nation at the center of victimhood in a constant struggle for survival. In the case of Russia, it is a politics of resentment against liberalism, cosmopolitanism, and ultimately, democracy.[27] Snyder contrasts this view with the *politics of inevitability* and the attempt to uncover truth by process of experimentation and with ideas subject to criticism, abandonment, transformation, and the need for tolerance above all. Snyder sees the politics of eternity, not only in Russia but also in illiberal democracies such as Hungary and in its leader's criticisms of a rootless cosmopolitanism—an old trope for anti-Semitism—and of liberalism as a misguided cosmopolitan venture.

Putin has reimagined Russia as a Eurasian power in permanent conflict with the West. Older Soviet geopolitical allies have fallen by the wayside, heralding tough times for former client states such as Cuba with no obvious strategic interest to a Eurasian Russia. Cuba's economy was devastated when Russia no longer purchased its sugar crop. The more pressing goal for this newly reimagined Russia is to build up its military and push back against the tide of Western European influence across the former SSRs and to advance its interests in strategic locations. It is extending its military and political reach in the Middle East and Mediterranean. Russian airstrikes in Syria in 2015 effectively kept Assad in power and guaranteed Russian naval and military bases in the country. In Libya, Russia backed the rebel commander of the eastern-based forces, sending military jets in 2020 to support his attack on Tripoli. The aim is to access oil reserves on Libya's coast, secure military bases in the Mediterranean, and ensure billions of dollars of contracts that were lost when NATO forces overthrew Gaddafi in 2011. Russia's struggle with the West also brings into play a rich and exotic mix of temporary allies. In Syria, it is allied with Iranian-backed forces, in Libya its allies include United Arab Emirates (UAE), Saudi Arabia, and France. So rather than a fixed and uncompromising ideological confrontation as there was in the Cold War, the new engagements are flexible, with alliances cobbled together to meet specific goals seen as vital to Russia's military and economic interests.[28]

One of Russia's broader goals is to weaken what it sees as a U.S.-led world order. As part of this agenda, it seeks greater economic and military ties with China as a way to undermine U.S. hegemony by allying two near U.S. peer competitors.[29] Russian state policy, which seeks also to undermine the cohesion of the West, has taken the form of encouragement of anti-EU movements. These movements include Brexit in the UK and populist national parties in countries such as France and Italy. Russia also seeks to undermine the political stability of the United States. Russia's relations with the United States and the West in general can be understood as a complex arena of shared interests over such issues as arms control and climate change but also as an inherent conflict as the United States seeks to maintain its global dominance and a weaker Russia seeks to exploit its asymmetric advantages.[30]

Russia wants to be at best a challenger to leadership of the world order and at worst to be in the forefront in the shaping of world order. The worst fear of the current political leadership is global irrelevancy and geopolitical impotence. Russia is considerably weaker than the United States and less wealthy than Western Europe but manages to punch above its military and economic weight through gray zone activity. This takes a variety of forms, including the annexation of eastern Ukraine and Crimea through paramilitary troops and Russian weaponry. There is also the attempted weakening of its enemies through cyberwarfare. The Russian military's self-assessment of their performance during the 2008 invasion of Georgia concluded that Russia lost the information war. The conclusion was that cyber operations must be a vital part of the Russian military transformation.[31] In 2013, the Russian military leadership proposed a greater "nonmilitary" emphasis, which would include concealed military efforts using special operation troops as well as cyberspace activities. It became known as the *Gerasimov Doctrine*, named after the general of the army. In the 2013 report, Gerasimov outlined a new strategy with greater emphasis on nonmilitary means (such as political and economic actions) supported by gray zone activity, noting, "The role of nonmilitary means of achieving political and strategic goals has grown, and, in many cases, they have exceeded the power of force of weapons in their effectiveness."[32] While there is a vigorous debate about the meaning and force of the doctrine, it is indisputable that Russia now uses cyberwarfare very effectively.[33]

Much of Russian cyber surveillance and cyberwarfare began with the monitoring of internal dissidents. A common method of this appraisal was to look through emails of "subversive" organizations for compromising personal details that were then made public to embarrass officials in the organization. Attention also turned overseas, searching for military and industrial secrets as well as advancing broader goals of undermining competitors.

Cyberwarfare now is used extensively to undermine the democratic institutions of the West. In the United States alone, hackers working for the Russian government have hacked the White House, State Department, Defense Department, the electric grid, and most famously the National Committee of the Democratic Party.[34] The security apparatus of the United States has affirmed that Putin was actively involved in the 2016 election in order to harm the candidacy of Hilary Clinton.[35] It is perhaps doubtful whether the operatives thought they could elect Trump; most people considered that highly unlikely. These agents merely sought to promote Trump enough to wound Clinton enough that her presidency would get off to a bad start. The aim was to weaken the United States by undermining its political system and its political leadership.

In the past ten years, cyberactivity organized by Russian military intelligence (GRU) in Moscow and the Internet Research Agency in St. Petersburg have generated copious amounts of disinformation on social media. This activity is intended to undermine existing institutions such as the European Union and the legitimacy of elections in the United States and to promote the causes of disruptive political groups such as right-wing nationalist candidates in Europe. One such manufactured story was about a young girl raped in Berlin by an illegal immigrant. The propaganda used anti-immigrant racist tropes to incite right-wing national sentiment.[36]

In perhaps their most successful campaign to date, Russian intelligence agencies effectively compromised and perhaps even undermined the U.S. presidential election in 2016. They tarnished the image of Hilary Clinton and promoted the candidacy of Donald Trump. A series of U.S. Senate reports found clear evidence of Russian meddling in the U.S. political process from 2014 to 2017.[37] To get some idea, consider one popular but fake Twitter account, claiming to come from Texas, but actually coming from a Russian operative in St. Petersburg, Russia. The account owner's biography described him as "Business owner, proud father, Christian, patriot, gun rights, politically incorrect. Love my country and my family . . . #WakeUpAmerica."[38] You get the idea. There were also fake accounts, ostensibly from minorities, that promoted racial discord.

The Russian campaign did not create political polarization, racial discord, and extreme partisanship in the United States; it simply exacerbated existing divisions. The goal of undermining the U.S. political system was spectacularly successful. All states pursue strategic and tactical goals through cybercampaigns. The Russians just happen to be more successful in this. It remains a matter of some debate whether this success is primarily due to the sophistication of their efforts or to the easy targets provided by the deep division in the societies of their strategic competitors.

GEOPOLITICAL HOTSPOT: UKRAINE

Where is the eastern edge of Europe? After recent events we now know. It runs right through Ukraine. The country straddles the border zone between, on the one hand, a Western Europe seeking to extend a coherent Europe and, on the other, a resurgent Russia looking to maintain influence on its border with the West and to resist the expansion of NATO. In the west, Russia has a fear of NATO's expansion into its own sphere of influence.[39] Ukraine is not only a setting for strategic considerations, but also the stage for gray zone tactics, annexation, and ongoing unresolved conflict. As befits its straddling location, it is a geopolitical hotspot for both Europe and Russia.[40]

Ukraine has a complex history. A brief synopsis would draw a distinction between eastern and western Ukraine. In the east, Ukraine was long under Russian influence even before the USSR. Ethnic Russians have long moved to this area, attracted by the rich agricultural lands and more recently as part of the Soviet policies of the rapid industrialization in the coal mining areas of the Donbas. The western region, more rural, more distinctly Ukrainian and less Russian, was contested between different empires. Take the city of Lviv in the west of the country. In 1900 it was a city in the Austro-Hungarian Empire, then very briefly part of the short-lived Western Ukrainian Republic before being swallowed up in Poland. When the USSR invaded Poland in 1939, the city became part of the USSR. For centuries it had a vibrant Jewish culture and large Jewish population, one-third of the city's population. In 1941 it came under the authority of the Nazi-German government of Poland. Before the Holocaust, the city's Jewish population was one hundred thousand. Fewer than eight hundred survived. After World War II, there was a literal shifting of borders as Russia gained territory from Poland. Lviv rejoined the USSR as part of the Ukraine SSR.

Ukraine has a population of forty-two million, around 80 percent ethnic Ukrainian and 20 percent ethnic Russian. It became an independent country in 1991. More than 90 percent voted for independence, including 80 percent in the eastern region but only 54 percent in Crimea, a region, it should be noted, that was only handed over to Ukraine in 1954 by way of a gift from Khrushchev. In Moscow, Ukraine was seen as within a Russian sphere of influence. The geopolitician Alexander Dugin called for the annexation of the whole of Ukraine, a country that he defined as New Russia. In 2004, a Russian-backed Ukrainian politician, Viktor Yanukovych, won a rigged election. The other candidate, Viktor Yushchenko, who drew support from the west of the country, was poisoned. This was and still remains a favored technique of Russian security services in dealing with opponents of the regime. He survived, though his face was badly and permanently scarred. After mass protests, known as the Orange Revolution, Yushchenko was installed as president. In 2010, Yanukovych reentered the political scene, this time winning the presidential election with around 48 percent of the vote. Social unrest exploded in 2013–2014 when Yanukovych decided against further integration into the EU orbit and instead signed a deal with Russia that included $15 billion in a stimulus package and a one-third reduction in the cost of Russian natural gas. It signaled an end of attempts at integration into Europe. There were popular protests, especially in the western part of the country. Protest was centered on Maidan Square (Independence Square) in the capital city of Kyiv. Protestors chanted, "Ukraine is part of Europe." More unrest erupted when riot police killed protestors, and eventually Yanukovych fled the country.[41] A pro-Western government was installed. This raised the fears of those Russian speakers in the east of the country and in Crimea. Russia saw an opportunity to resist the growing Western influence. Putin believed that the 2004 and the 2014 protests were funded and organized by the West in general and the United States in particular. The U.S. secretary of state at the time, Hilary Clinton, was perceived as the architect of the plan to undermine the existing order, install a pro-Western government, and further contain and constrain Russia. One reason behind Putin's intervention in the 2016 U.S. election was to get back at Clinton. Pro-Russian military forces, including Russian troops without official insignia—one of the most well-known examples of gray zone activities—moved into Crimea and the eastern part of Ukraine where two new "independent" zones were established in Donetsk and Luhansk (see map 6.1 and table 6.1).[42] After a referendum, Crimea became a part of Russia. Russia continues to arm and support separatists in the eastern part of Ukraine. The Donetsk and Luhansk polities exist in a netherworld state of frozen conflict after a cease-fire was announced in 2015.[43] The conflict is officially ended but tensions remain high.[44] There is also a mounting economic crisis. Luhansk and Donetsk rely overwhelmingly on coal exports. To fund their operations, the separatists rely on the export of anthracite coal through Russia to avoid sanctions. However, a downturn in global demand has meant fewer coal-filled railcars heading to Russia, to make a surreptitious way onto world markets. Falling revenues are leading to social unrest as miners are thrown out of work and social welfare is limited.[45]

Russia's annexation of Crimea and its support for separatists in eastern Ukraine generated sanctions from the West. Despite the economic penalties, Russia shows no signs of handing back Crimea or in deserting its offshoot in Luhansk and Donetsk. Europe, it appears, ends in the middle of the Ukraine, where Europe's furthest eastern edge comes up against the strategic interests of a nearby Russia.

SUGGESTED READINGS

Boterbloem, K. (2020). *Russia as empire: Past and present*. London: Reaktion.

Clark, J. R. (2019). Russia's indirect grand strategy. *Orbis, 63*, 225–39.

Coyle, J. J. (2017). *Russia's border wars and frozen conflicts*. Cham: Springer.

Davies, N. (2006). *No simple victory: World War II in Europe, 1939–1946*. New York: Viking.

Schlogel, K. (2018). *Ukraine: A nation on the borderland*. London: Reaktion.

Snyder, T. (2018). *The road to unfreedom: Russia, Europe, America*. New York: Tim Duggan Books.

Toal, G. (2017). *Near abroad: Putin, the West and the contest over Ukraine and the Caucasus*. Oxford: Oxford University Press.

Tsygankov, A. P. (2018). The sources of Russia's fear of NATO. *Communist and Post-Communist Studies, 51*, 101–11.

Tsygankov, A. P. (2019). *Russia and America: The asymmetric rivalry*. Cambridge: Polity.

Van Herpen, M. H. (2015). *Putin's wars: The rise of Russia's new imperialism*. Lanham: Rowman & Littlefield.

NOTES

1. Svarin, D. (2016). The construction of "geopolitical spaces" in Russian foreign policy discourse before and after the Ukraine crisis. *Journal of Eurasian Studies, 7*, 129–40. See also Clark, J. R. (2019). Russia's indirect grand strategy. *Orbis, 63*, 225–39.

2. AP Staff Writer. (2005). Putin: Soviet collapse a "genuine tragedy." http://www.nbc news.com/id/7632057/ns/world_news/t/putin-soviet-collapse-genuine-tragedy/#.Xs0V5y-ZMjc.

3. Boterbloem, K. (2020). *Russia as empire: Past and present*. London: Reaktion.

4. Bassin, M. (1999). *Imperial visions: Nationalist imagination and geographical expansion in the Russian far east, 1840–1865*. Cambridge: Cambridge University Press.

5. Lieven, D. C. (2002). *Empire: The Russian empire and its rivals*. New Haven and London: Yale University Press; Boterbloem, K. (2018, 2nd ed.). *A history of Russia and its empire*. Lanham: Rowman & Littlefield.

6. Hopkins, P. (1990). *The great game*. London: John Murray; Meyer, K. E., & Brysac, S. B. (2009). *Tournament of shadows: The great game and the race for empire in Central Asia*. London: Hachette.

7. Lieven, D. (2016) *The end of tsarist Russia: The march to World War I and revolution*. New York: Penguin.

8. "The most grisly of weapons . . . like a plague bacillus" in Churchill's oft-repeated remark. Churchill, W. (1923–1931). *The world crisis* (vol. 6). London: Butterworths, 73.

9. Davies, N. (2006). *No simple victory: World War II in Europe, 1939–1946*. New York: Viking.

10. World War II casualties: https://en.wikipedia.org/wiki/World_War_II_casualties.

11. Snyder, T. (2011). *Bloodlands: Europe between Hitler and Stalin*. New York: Random House.

12. As one astute historian wrote, "No other empire in recorded history ever abandoned its dominions so rapidly, with such good grace and so little bloodshed. Gorbachev cannot take direct credit for what happened in 1989—he did not plan it and only hazily grasped its long-term import. But he was the permissive and precipitating cause. It was Mr. Gorbachev's revolution."
Judt, T. (2005). *Postwar: A history of Europe since 1946*. New York: Penguin, 633.

13. Coyle, J. J. (2017). *Russia's border wars and frozen conflicts*. Cham: Springer; Tudoroiu, T. (2016). Unfreezing failed frozen conflicts: A post-Soviet case study. *Journal of Contemporary European Studies, 24*, 375–96.

14. Hunter, S. T. (ed.). (2017). *The new geopolitics of the South Caucasus: Prospects for regional cooperation and conflict resolution*. New York: Lexington; Kamrava, M. (ed.). (2017). *The great game in west Asia*. Oxford: Oxford University Press; Torosyan, T., & Vardanyan, A. (2015). The South Caucasus conflicts in the context of struggle for the Eurasian heartland. *Geopolitics, 20*, 559–82.

15. CBS News. (2008, August 12). McCain: "Today, we are all Georgians." https://www.cbsnews.com/news/mccain-today-we-are-all-georgians/.

16. Toal, G. (2017). *Near abroad: Putin, the West and the contest over Ukraine and the Caucasus*. Oxford: Oxford University Press.

17. Liu, M. Y. (2011). Central Asia in the post-Cold War world. *Annual Review of Anthropology, 40*, 115–31.

18. Collins, K. (2014). The limits of cooperation: Central Asia, Afghanistan and the new silk road. *Asia Policy, 17*, 18–26.

19. Kupatadze, A. (2014) Kyrgyzstan–A virtual narco-state? *International Journal of Drug Policy, 25*, 1178–86; Paoli, L., Rabkov, I., Greenfield, V. A., & Reuter, P. (2007). Tajikistan: The rise of a narco-state. *Journal of Drug Issues, 37*, 951–79.

20. Gachechiladze, R. (2010). Geopolitics in the South Caucasus: Local and external players. *Geopolitics, 7*, 113–38; Toal, *Near abroad*.

21. Schlogel, K. (2018). *Ukraine: A nation on the borderland*. London: Reaktion.

22. Browing, C. S. (2003). The region-building approach revisited: The continued othering of Russia in discourses of region-building in the European North. *Geopolitics, 8*, 45–71.

23. Remnick. D. (2014, August 11 & 18). Watching the eclipse. *The New Yorker*, 52–66.

24. Dugin, A. (1997). *Osnovy geopolitiki*. Moscow: Arktogeia.

25. Clover, C. (2016). The unlikely origins of Russia's manifest destiny. *Foreign Affairs*. https://foreignpolicy.com/2016/07/27/geopolitics-russia-mackinder-eurasia-heartland-dugin-ukraine-eurasianism-manifest-destiny-putin/.

26. Bassin, M., & Aksenov, K. E. (2006). Mackinder and the heartland theory in post-Soviet geopolitical discourse. *Geopolitics, 11*, 99–118; 106. See also Clover, C. (1999). Dreams of the Eurasian heartland: The reemergence of geopolitics. *Foreign Affairs, 78*, 9–13; Kerr, D. (1995). The new Eurasianism: The rise of geopolitics on Russia's foreign policy. *Europe-Asia Studies, 6*, 977–88. And for other contributions to Russian geopoliti-

cal theory, see Tsygankov, A. P. (2017). In the shadow of Nikolai Danilevskii: Universalism, particularism, and Russian geopolitical theory. *Europe-Asia Studies, 69*, 571–93.

27. Snyder contrasts the *politics of inevitability* as the attempt to uncover truth by process of experimentation, with ideas subject to criticism and above all, tolerance with its opposite what he terms the *politics of eternity*. He sees this form of politics not only in Russia but also in illiberal democracies. Snyder, T. (2018). *The road to unfreedom: Russia, Europe, America*. New York: Tim Duggan Books.

28. Van Herpen, M. H. (2015). *Putin's wars: The rise of Russia's new imperialism*. Lanham: Rowman & Littlefield.

29. Wilhelmsen, J., & Flikke, G. (2011). Chinese-Russian convergence in central Asia. *Geopolitics, 16*, 865–901.

30. Tsygankov, A. P. (2019). *Russia and America: The asymmetric rivalry*. Cambridge: Polity.

31. Giles, K. (2011). "Information Troops": A Russian cyber command? http://conflict studies.org.uk/files/Russian_Cyber_Command.pdf.

Van Herpen, M. H. (2015). *Putin's propaganda machine: Soft power and Russian foreign policy*. Lanham: Rowman & Littlefield.

32. Galeotti, M. (2014, June 6). The "Gerasimov Doctrine" and Russian non-linear war. *Moscow's Shadows*. https://inmoscowsshadows.wordpress.com/2014/07/06/the-gerasimov-doctrine-and- russian-non-linear-war/.

33. Fridman, O. (2019). On "Gerasimov Doctrine": Why the West fails to beat Russia to the punch. *Prism, 8*, 101–12; Galeotti, M. (2018). The mythical "Gerasimov Doctrine" and the language of threat. *Critical Studies on Security*. https://doi.org/10.1080/2162488 7.2018.1441623.

34. Office of The Director of National Intelligence. (2019). *World wide threat assessment from the Director of National Intelligence.* https://www.dni.gov/files/ODNI /documents/2019-ATA-SFR---SSCI.pdf.

35. Office of The Director of National Intelligence. (2017). *Background to "Assessing Russian activities and intentions in recent U.S. elections": The analytic process and cyber incident attribution.* https://www.dni.gov/files/documents/ICA_2017_01.pdf.

36. Cilluffo, F. J., & Cardash, S. L. (2016). Russia's aggressive power is resurgent online and off. *The Conversation.* https://theconversation.com/russias-aggressive-power-is-resurgent-online-and-off-64336.

37. U.S. Senate Select Committee on Intelligence. (2018–2020). *Russian active measures, campaigns and interests in the 2016 U.S. Election.* https://www.intelligence.senate .gov/sites/default/files/documents/Report_Volume1.pdf; https://www.intelligence.sen ate.gov/sites/default/files/documents/Report_Volume2.pdf; https://www.intelligence .senate.gov/sites/default/files/documents/Report_Volume3.pdf; https://www.intelli gence.senate.gov/sites/default/files/documents/Report_Volume4.pdf; https://www.intel ligence.senate.gov/sites/default/files/documents/report_volume6.pdf.

38. Rid, T. (2020). *Active measure: The secret history of disinformation and political warfare*. New York: Farrar, Straus and Giroux.

39. For a Russian perspective, see Tsygankov, A. P. (2018). The sources of Russia's fear of NATO. *Communist and Post-Communist Studies, 51*, 101–11.

40. Dickinson, P. (2018, November 1). Russia understands Ukraine's geopolitical importance but does the West? *Atlantic Council.* https://www.atlanticcouncil.org/blogs /ukrainealert/russia-understands-ukraine-s-geopolitical-importance-but-does-the-west on 28 May 2019; Kuzio, T. (2017). Ukraine between a constrained EU and assertive Russia. *Journal of Common Market Studies, 55*, 103–20.

41. An excellent source is the 2015 documentary *Winter on fire: Ukraine's fight for freedom*, directed by Evgeny Afineevsky and available on Netflix.

42. Ragozin, L. (2019, March 16). Annexation of Crimea: A masterclass in political manipulation. *Aljazeera.* https://www.aljazeera.com/indepth/opinion/annexation-crimea-masterclass-political-manipulation-190315174459207.html.

43. Davies, L. (2016). Russia's "governance" approach: Intervention and the conflict in the Donbas. *Europe-Asia Studies, 68,* 726–49.

44. Giuliano, E. (2019, March 18). Is the risk of ethnic conflict growing in Ukraine? New laws could create dangerous divisions. *Foreign Affairs.* https://www.foreignaffairs.com/articles/ukraine/2019-03-18/risk-ethnic-conflict-growing-ukraine.

45. Warrick, J., & Mufson, S. (2020, June 12). Dirty fuel. *Washington Post.* https://www.washingtonpost.com/national-security/2020/06/12/dirty-fuel-ukrainian-separatists-sell-pilfered-coal-keep-war-economy-rolling/?arc404=true.

III

REGIONAL REALMS

Europe

GEOPOLITICAL CONTEXT

Europe has global geopolitical significance and not only because of its current importance as a tight cluster of very rich and powerful countries. The imperial and colonial history of these countries also left their mark across the world. Nevertheless, many countries in Europe no longer possess the same economic and political power. As individual countries, their previous geopolitical grandeur is diminished, and they are now facing, in some cases, separatist challenges to the integrity of their territorial cohesion.

For decades, the dominant geopolitical project in Europe focused upon greater European economic, political, and military interconnection. There are now significant challenges to such European cohesion, especially from *populist nationalisms*. Some states, such as the UK, have withdrawn from the project, while others such as Poland and Hungary question the long-standing European commitment to liberal values. Meanwhile, some EU members in the east borderlands are wary of an emboldened Russia. An integrated Europe faces the dual challenges of a resurgent Russia and perhaps a diminishing U.S. interest in securing European security.

THE GLOBAL SIGNIFICANCE OF EUROPE

The dominance of the English language in North America, the prevalence of Roman Catholicism in Central and South America, and the existence of French pastry shops in Hanoi are just some of the many consequences, large and small, of the European conquest and annexation of the wider world. This began with Portugal, a small state on the edge of Europe but with access to the Atlantic Ocean and to a wider world. While the merchants of Venice and of the Hanseatic League were at the very apex of their power, in the limited, closed-sea economies of the Baltic and Mediterranean, Portuguese ships sailed down the coast of Africa, reaching the coasts of Ghana in 1471 and of the Cape of Good Hope in 1488. In 1500, they made landfall in Brazil. By the 1520s, Portuguese traders were active in India and along the Straits of Malacca. Lasting more than five hundred years, Portugal can claim to be Europe's longest-lived global empire. This imperial presence only ended in 1999 with the transfer of Macao from Portugal to China. Other European countries also took part in overseas expansion early on. Spain became a global empire with territories that encircled the world from the New World to the Philippines. Denmark, England, France, the Netherlands, and Germany took part in colonial subordination later. In 1884, even the king of Belgium laid claim to a vast area in central Africa that was seventy-six times larger than his kingdom. Active colonialism by European powers lasted well into the twentieth century. In 1935, Italy invaded Ethiopia, building on its earlier annexation of Eritrea in 1890 and of Tripoli in 1914. The fact that the great powers of the day largely acceded to Italy's twentieth-century annexations is testament to the very recent acceptance of European subordination of other people and their territories.

European colonialism changed the world. The enduring consequences are linguistic, cultural, political, and economic. English and Spanish, for example, are the first languages in many countries around the world beyond the UK and Spain. Much of the world was understood, represented, and narrated from a narrow range of countries in Europe. Systems of knowledge justified and legitimized colonial rule with racist ideologies. There is even a contemporary embodiment in the "national treasures" of museums in London, Paris, and Copenhagen that contain the cultural artifacts of exploited peoples and annexed territories. There are wide-ranging political consequences, which include the creation of *collaborative elites* and of systems of indirect rule that favored some groups over others. Tribalism in sub-Saharan Africa, for example, was in large part a colonial invention built on precolonial realities. Progressive ideas that first crystalized in Europe, such as individual rights, democracy, and rule of law, were also exported abroad, sometimes wholesale, other times tweaked and modified. Anticolonial agitators often employed the words and ideas of Europeans to protest the colonial rule of European others. Thus, the imperial legacy continued into the postcolonial. Decolonization often followed in imperial tracks, forming countries with little national cohesion beyond their colonial boundaries. New trading patterns were established as the global economy was transformed. The slave trade, for example, arose from the need for labor for the plantations and mines of European colonies in the New World.

At its heart, colonialism was a commercial enterprise. The aim was to enhance national wealth by exploiting the labor of people and of their treasures in the colonies. There was a transfer of wealth from the colonial periphery to the metropolitan core. The Baroque churches of Spain, the splendid palaces of France, or the Victorian buildings of Britain owe much to the labor and resources of colonial subjects. The wealth of present-day Europe is in large measure built on the exploitation of the rest of the world.

"Empire" was also a fantasy, an imagining, a creative rendering of possibilities where European states could construct narratives of grandeur and greatness, geopolitical significance, and historical meaning. "Empire" was a drama with numerous characters. There were apologists of Empire who argued for the civilizing mission of bringing enlightenment to "savage" peoples. There were also the missionaries and doctors genuinely trying to provide either spiritual salvation or medical assistance. There were the hard-nosed merchants, the eager investors, the overseers, and the adventurers looking to replace the confines of home with the intriguing possibilities of the colonies. There were the hardworking administrators, the local elites working to get rich in the process, metropolitan critics, and anticolonial agitators. There were the vast range of fantasies, characters, and practices, but at its beating heart, European colonialism was about transferring wealth from the periphery to the core. And it was successful: European powers and their colonies remade the global economy to their benefit.

There were always costs to Empire. Territorial acquisitions had to be defended, administered, and funded. Too little spending could result in weakly defended colonies liable to be taken over by someone else or to be saddled with territories with too little infrastructural investment to generate wealth. Too much spending risked generating more costs than benefits. This was the fiscal side of *imperial overstretch*. There were also longer-term costs. The British Empire, for example, provided sheltered markets for domestic production but at the cost of being internationally uncompetitive in the longer run. Britain's endemic post–World War II lack of productivity was a legacy of imperially protected industries. Empire could provide benefits, but it also entailed costs.

The more indirect the rule, the less costs and the greater the possible benefits. The great success story of British commercial success was not the *formal empire* but the *informal empire* in Latin America, in such countries as Argentina and Uruguay, where investments in land and railways provided rich returns without having to shoulder the costs of direct colonial rule.

Empire could also grow in a haphazard and expensive fashion, less as result of hard-nosed economic calculations and more from the dynamics of colonial enlargement as either local administrators forced the issue or countries sought to head off the machination of competitors. For example, even though British Colonial Secretary, Lord Stanley, regarded colonial annexation as "a regrettable source of unnecessary expense and needless conflict," he reluctantly annexed Natal in Africa in 1842 due to wider strategic considerations and local pressure.[1] Proconsuls on the ground often had enough space and time to dictate the actions of the metropolitan centers. Imperial annexation was often more the result of decisions by local actors than leaders in the imperial capitals. Imperial ventures were also part of broader geopolitical strategies. Britain's involvement in Afghanistan at huge costs had little direct commercial value; it was part of a geopolitical struggle with Russia.

Although Europe's colonial involvements are complex, we must not forget that even if the benefits to Europe may be difficult to assess exactly, they came at a huge price for the colonies. In the Congo, for example, more than twenty million people were enslaved in the harvesting of ivory and rubber for their Belgian overseers. It is estimated that ten million people died through starvation and violence. Even decolonization racked up the body count. The Algerian war of independence lasted from 1954 to 1962, costing the lives of 150,000 freedom fighters and 25,600 French troops. One million Europeans fled and two million Algerians were displaced. The unwillingness of France to withdraw from its colonies in Southeast Asia led to the Vietnam War. In a brilliant analysis of late imperial Kenya, Caroline Elkins describes how the British colonial administrators responded to an independence movement by detaining almost 1.5 million people in a vast system of detention camps with a death toll estimated at around one hundred thousand.[2]

SHIFTING STATES

Portugal stands out not only as the one of the first colonial powers but also because it is one of the few countries that has retained its territorial integrity over the centuries. The stability of national borders varies across the rest of Europe. There was somewhat greater stability along the Atlantic and North Sea littoral. The UK, France, Spain, Portugal, Netherlands, Belgium, and the Nordic bloc were relatively stable territorial units, and by 1900, Germany and Italy had solidified into large states. Elsewhere, the rise and fall of empires created a constant reconfiguration of national borders, especially in Central and Eastern Europe, a *shatter zone* of contested national identities, competing empires, and imperial collapse. Nineteenth-century independence movements and the Ottoman defeat in World War I led to the new states of Bosnia, Serbia, Romania, Montenegro, Bulgaria, and Greece. The collapse of the Austro-Hungarian Empire after World War I led to the establishment of Austria, Hungary, Czechoslovakia, and Yugoslavia. The fall of Tsarist Russia led to the independence of Finland and to the brief emergence of Baltic Republics before the imposition of rule by USSR. After World War II, the USSR claimed territory that had formerly been part of Romania and Poland. Poland successfully claimed German territory. After 1945, the German cities of Breslau and Danzig became the Polish cities of Wroclaw and Gdansk.[3]

In the aftermath of World War II, there was not only a significant shifting of borders but also a substantial movement of people. Formerly multiethnic, multicultural cities, regions, and countries became more homogeneous. In 1946, Bulgaria transferred 160,000 Turks to Turkey. More than a half-million Germans and Italians left northern Yugoslavia. Nearly three million Germans were expelled from Czechoslovakia, and in total more than thirteen million Germans were moved or were expelled to Germany from countries in Eastern and Central Europe. In the process, Poland became more "Polish" and Czechoslovakia became more "Czech" and "Slovak." And the vibrant Jewish communities of Warsaw, Berlin, Budapest, and Vilnius were no more. The Jewish population of Central and Eastern Europe was subject to the horrors of the Holocaust. More than two-thirds of Europe's prewar population, six million in all, was systematically murdered by the German Reich and its allies.[4] Take one city: in 1938 almost 40 percent of the population of Vilnius in Lithuania was Jewish. The city was home to such a dazzling concentration of treasures, libraries, theaters, synagogues, and yeshivas that it was referred to as the "Jerusalem of the North." Today, there are fewer than three thousand Jews in a country that used to be home to 265,000, and the splendors of Jewish Vilnius are long destroyed.

The borders then took on a permanency as the Cold War froze the postwar state boundaries. The states became fixed containers for projects of national identity and cohesion. Throughout the states of Central and Eastern Europe, the population became more homogeneous, less diverse.

The end of the Cold War and the collapse of the Iron Curtain meant major changes, three relatively peaceful and the other tragically brutal. The first was the reunification of East and West Germany in 1990.[5] The reunification joined two different states, both German speaking, but with different recent histories, one a liberal, capitalist democracy and the other a Stalinist state. The new unified Germany immediately took on a "Western European" feel as it retained membership in NATO and the European Union. In effect, East Germany became part of West Germany. There were enormous disparities. East Germany had a dilapidated and underfunded infrastructure and an inefficient economy that could not survive in a globally competitive market. A solidarity tax was levied on all citizens to bring the East up to the standards of the West. The costs of reunification are estimated at one hundred billion euros a year for twenty years, with the bulk of it spent on the economic reconstruction and infrastructure upgrading of East Germany. Differences still remain. Unemployment is still twice as high in the East as in the West. The legacy of disparity in investment is evident in the newer roofs in the villages and towns of the old West compared to the old East with its abandoned factories and depopulating towns. Even after twenty years, the integration between East and West is still an unfolding process rather than a destination and incomes still remain lower and unemployment higher in the East compared to the West. There is still a need for an "inner reunification" to fully integrate the parts of the country. But there are also signs of a smoothing out. Despite the economic jarring, especially to the former East, the reunification was a peaceful process.[6]

Second, as with the reunified Germany, the countries of the former Soviet bloc pivoted west to Europe and away from Russia. They joined or tried to join NATO and the European Union. To be part of Europe was the goal of progressive reformers across Eastern Europe. When Ukrainians first began demonstrating against the pro-Soviet policies of their government in Maidan Square, Kyiv in 2013–2014, they chanted "Ukraine is part of Europe, Ukraine is part of Europe." Countries emerging from the Soviet grip wanted to reposition themselves as inside Europe, not as on the edge of Russia. I remember visiting Prague in 1993 and arriving at a city busy promoting itself as "a city in the heart of Central Europe." To be in Eastern Europe was to be connected with a tarnished past. To be in Europe was to move forward into the future.

Third, there was the dissolution in January 1993 of Czechoslovakia into two separate countries of Czechia and Slovakia in what is known as the Velvet Divorce. The name echoes the peaceful end of the Communist regime, described as the "Velvet Revolution." Czechoslovakia comprised two main language groups, Czech and Slovak. The Czech part of the country was always more economically successful; therefore, a language divide was overlain with economic disparities.[7] Not everyone wanted the dissolution. Opinion polls were evenly split in each part of the country. There was no popular referendum; it was a top-down decision.[8] But, since both countries soon joined NATO and the EU, their split was offset by their integration into a wider Europe. Few territorial breakups were as easy as Czechoslovakia's.

The fourth example brings the Czech and Slovak case into relief because of its darkness. At the same time as Czechoslovakia was experiencing a "velvet divorce," the former Yugoslavia was collapsing into genocide.[9]

Yugoslavia was one of those never-ending jigsaw puzzles of Europe, continually being assembled and reassembled. In the Balkan Wars of 1912–1913, Montenegro and Serbia—along with Bulgaria and Greece—achieved independence from the Ottoman Empire. At the end of World War I, the defeated Austro-Hungarian Empire was broken up, and Bosnia and Croatia now joined with Montenegro, Slovenia, and Serbia in forming the Kingdom of Yugoslavia. Yugoslavia became a republic in 1945 and in the following year a Communist state under the control of the wartime partisan leader, Josip Broz. It was organized as six constituent republics, Bosnia and Herzegovina, Croatia, Macedonia, Montenegro, Serbia, and Slovenia. The names of the republics belied their often-complex population geography. There were, for example, Serbs in Croatia and both Serbian Christians and Bosnian Muslims in Bosnia. In World War II, Croatia was a client state of Nazi Germany and persecuted Serbs, Jews, and Roma, further complicating this problematic history. Serbia, in contrast, was invaded by the Axis powers and dismembered. Both states had both pro- and anti-Nazi supporters. Yugoslavia was a composite state with different histories, ethnicities, religions, and national affiliations and a bloody history with deep wounds and enduring enmities. There were three national languages, Macedonian, Slovene, and Serbo-Croat. There are major dialectal differences in Serbo-Croat. It is considered a pluricentric language with four mutually intelligible varieties of Bosnian, Croatian, Montenegrin, and Serbian. The national language, just as the country, embodied major differences behind a guise of national unity. Tito's rule held the divergent state together. However, the tensions increased after his death in 1980. With the end of the Cold War, the state began to fracture. During the ten-year Yugoslav War from 1991 to 2001—sometimes referred to as the "Third Balkan War"—various republics sought independence. It is a fitting reminder that this has been a zone of conflict for more than one hundred years.[10] Republics fought against each other; various groups within each republic fought each other. The breakup revealed old rivalries, renewed old hostilities, and unleashed chaos and bloodshed. Sometimes mere prose is not enough to carry the full weight of tragedy. The Irish poet W. B. Yeats wrote these words in 1921:

> Things fall apart; the centre cannot hold;
> Mere anarchy is loosed upon the world,
> The blood-dimmed tide is loosed, and everywhere
> The ceremony of innocence is drowned;
> The best lack all conviction, while the worst
> Are full of passionate intensity.[11]

Some republics broke away without much bloodshed. Macedonia gained independence more easily than most in 1991. However, the country is home to two main groups. Macedonians constitute the majority; around a quarter are Albanians. Around 360,000 Albanian refugees from Kosovo entered the country in 1999, further destabilizing relations. There was a brief Albanian insurgency in

2001 and an outbreak of inter-ethnic violence in 2012. Albania's efforts to join the EU were blocked by Greece, which disputes its name and worries that its existence promotes separatism among its own Macedonian population. In February 2019, the country was renamed North Macedonia.

Montenegro—with a majority Slav population—remained with Serbia after the initial breakup of Yugoslavia. Montenegrin troops and police joined with Serbian forces fighting in Croatia and Bosnia. In a 2006 referendum, a majority of voters opted for independence from Serbia, which—although a fellow Slav nation—was now a toxic liability viewed suspiciously by the international community.

The third Balkan War was in fact a series of wars.[12] Slovenia seceded from the federation in 1991. In a brief, ten-day war, there were skirmishes when the Yugoslav People's Army (JNA), its officer class dominated by Serbians and Montenegrins, fought to secure border crossings. Then there was a Croatian war of independence from 1991 to 1995. Forces representing Croatian nationalists on one side and Croatian Serbs and the approximately seventy thousand JNA troops on the other were involved in numerous clashes. Photo 7.1 depicts a wall plaque in the Croatian city of Zadar. The internecine nature of the conflict is suggested by the reference to the "rebellious Serbian population." The city of Dubrovnik was bombed and prisoners of war massacred.

Historical nucleus plan of the city of Zadar with marked damages made by the Serbian, Montenegrian and Yugoslav army aggression of Zadar assisted by the rebellious Serbian population in Croatia, in Zadar from 1991 to 1995.

Mjesto udara raketnih i topničkih projektila /
Place hit by rocket and artillery shelling

Photo 7.1.   Plaque in Zadar, Croatia (John Rennie Short)

The Bosnian War of 1992–1995 certainly ranks as one the most brutal wars of recent years in Europe.[13] In 1992, Bosnia and Herzegovina declared independence. A war erupted between the Bosnian Muslims, known as Bosniaks, and Bosnian Serbs, who were aided by Serbia and at times Croatia. Bosnian Croats were initially allies of the Bosniaks, until they too started fighting against each other. This war became infamous for the ethnic cleansing as armed personnel killed and displaced targeted ethnic groups. In 2005, approximately eight thousand Bosniaks, boys and men, were massacred in Srebrenica by Bosnian Serb militia, who then systematically raped Bosniak women and girls. This was the worst crime on European soil since the horrors of World War II.[14]

The Kosovo War of 1998–1999 pitched Serbian forces against Kosovar Albanians in Kosovo, a region inside the borders of Serbia with sites of historical significance to Serbian identity but populated mainly by Albanian-speaking Kosovars. A NATO bombing campaign against Serbian forces swung the balance. In 1999, Kosovo came under transitional UN control. In 2008, the country declared independence from Serbia. While some countries recognized this declaration, others did not, seeing it as a provocation to Serbia. Such provocation generated yet another source of animosity and instability in a region not noted for its comity or stability. Russia in particular used its power at the UN to block the membership of Kosovo, which was seen widely as a corrupt state.

The breakup of Yugoslavia was not a "velvet divorce" but a genocidal dissolution awash in blood. It resulted in the savagery of ethnic cleansing, massacres, and mass rape. Thousands were killed and millions were displaced and traumatized. The Balkans remains a separate part of Europe. Only Croatia and Slovenia are part of both NATO and the EU. The EU candidacy of Montenegro has been delayed from consideration until 2022. EU officials are worried about the role of corruption in the economy. Montenegro is perceived widely as a hub of criminal cartels, operating cigarette smuggling, narcotics, and gun running. Bosnia and Herzegovina, Montenegro, Serbia, Kosovo, and North Macedonia are members of neither the EU nor of NATO. They are in Europe but currently not of Europe, still a very different Europe.

Internal Colonialism

It is a common trope to compare the instability of the Balkans with the stability of countries in Western Europe. On closer inspection, and with a longer historical perspective, this distinction becomes less apparent. State stability in many of the states in Western Europe was built on annexation, incorporation, and the consequent peripheralization of regions. The older states of Europe and especially those with long-established borders suggest a sense of stability that in some cases masks what has been termed *internal colonialism*.[15] This is the process whereby parts of a state are exploited for the benefit of a core region. The seemingly stable states of Western Europe often hide a long history in which peripheral regions were incorporated into the core, much as in the overseas colonies. Internal colonialism needs some refinement because for some peripheral regions, economic benefit may accrue, at least for a while. In the case of Spain, for example, the Basque region and Catalonia were controlled by a Castilian Spain centered in

Madrid, yet they were more industrialized and wealthier. The deeming of internal colonialism is just as often as much due to perceptions of cultural and political marginalization as to economic exploitation. A resistance to the perception of internal colonialism continues to fuel some of the separatist movements in contemporary Europe to this day.

Consider the UK, a country whose very name implies a coherent integrated state. An introduction to its different names. England refers only to England, a fact that many in the United States seem to forget. Great Britain refers to England, Wales, and Scotland. The UK refers to those three plus Northern Ireland (see map 7.1).

England's overseas colonialism is well known. Yet also there is an internal colonialism in which English power centered in London gradually incorporated other parts of the islands. The Kingdom of England emerged in 927. Wales became an English colony after being conquered by the English king in 1282. English kings called their immediate successor the prince of Wales to reinforce their control over the territory. Wales became integrated more fully only three hundred years later when English laws and customs were extended to cover the principality.

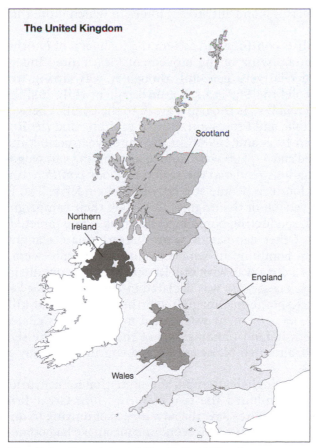

Map 7.1.   Countries of the United Kingdom

Ireland is England's first overseas colony: it came under the domination of England after the Tudor conquest (1529–1603). English law, language, and religion were imposed on a Gaelic Catholic Ireland. English-speaking, Protestant colonists from Scotland and England were encouraged to colonize Ulster, a province in the north of the island, from land forfeited by Gaelic chiefs. In the south, a "Protestant Ascendancy" of landowners, clergy, and professional groups dominated economic and political life.

The Catholic Irish were marginalized from economic and political power. Irish nationalism grew in the nineteenth and twentieth centuries. The Irish famine (1845–1849) hardened sentiment against the Protestant landowners and British rule. During April 24–29, 1916, around 1,200 men seized important sites in the city of Dublin, an event known as the Easter Rising. The British government sent in troops and police, eventually regaining control. One hundred and forty-three British troops and police were killed; more than two thousand civilians were wounded; sixty-six rebels were killed and sixteen rebels were executed. Although British forces regained control, they had lost the population. In 1919 an Irish Republic was declared, and the Irish Republican Army (IRA) launched a guerrilla war. Under an agreement signed in 1921, Ireland gained independence, but Northern Ireland remained part of the UK. There was a brief civil war in 1922–1923 between pro- and anti-treaty forces in which more than two thousand people died.[16]

Irish nationalists continued to call for the inclusion of Northern Ireland. The IRA was the military wing of the movement for a united independent Ireland. Things remained relatively peaceful, though it was jarring to visit Northern Ireland (as I first did in 1969) to see armed police while mainland police were unarmed. "The Troubles" is the name given to the conflict between paramilitary forces, both Catholic and Protestant, British military, and the Royal Ulster Constabulary between 1968 and 1998.[17] In the thirty-year period, more than 35,000 people were killed and 47, 500 were injured as bombing campaigns and sectarian-violence assassinations rendered the region a bloody *conflict zone*. In 1972, British troops killed fourteen people at a rally in Londonderry. The Provisional IRA, a more militant version of the original IRA, took their campaign of terror to the British mainland, conducting bombing campaigns, some targeted at military and political leaders. Other campaigns were indiscriminate slaughter such as the 1974 Birmingham bombing, in which twenty-one people were killed and 182 injured. This was a dirty war with cruelty and brutality on all sides. After a year of more atrocities, a cease-fire was declared in 1994. It did not last. A breakaway IRA group planted a bomb in Omagh in Northern Ireland that killed twenty-nine civilians. Finally, an agreement was signed in 1998 that signaled an end to the violence. Northern Ireland remains part of the UK, and the sectarian violence largely has ended, although Northern Ireland continues to play an outsized role in British politics.

Scotland resisted English attempts at domination for centuries until the 1707 Act of Union that combined the two countries into Great Britain. Scotland's economic and political elites saw the advantages of uniting to an imperial power with access to global markets. The economic incentive had come to the fore after the abject failure of a scheme to create a Scottish colony on the Panama isthmus. The Darien Scheme attracted investments and savings across Scotland.[18] It ended badly with settlers killed off by malaria and tropical diseases and was finally abandoned in 1700. A formal alliance with England offered a way out of this national economic debacle. There was some provision for maintaining a Scottish identity by upholding the separate education system, banks, and the centrality of the Scottish Presbyterian Church. Scotland gained some economic advantages. Industries in Lowland Scotland now had access to growing imperial markets, and Scots represented a significant element in the running of the Empire. However, the Highlands of Scotland were subject to more brutal forms of internal colonialism, complete with language discrimination, forced displacements, and evictions.[19] When the economic advantages began to wither as the imperial power evaporated and emphasis was placed on financial services in London, there was enough of a separate identity to provide a platform for separatism sentiments. More of this later in the chapter in the geopolitical hotspot section.

What is clear from this very brief description of the United Kingdom is that the "stable" states of western Europe often were constructed from specific regions at the expense of others. Italy and Germany emerged only recently from an amalgam of petty kingdoms with some more powerful and influential than others. In Italy, for example, the division between north and south remains a persistent feature of both the economic geography and the political geography of the country. Even the longer-established states such as France and Spain were all built on the basis of annexation and the creation of political peripheries. Many Catalans and the Basques have long resisted state power centered in Madrid, and many would consider themselves Catalan and Basque as much as Spanish. Most residents of Madrid, in contrast, see themselves as Spanish. A political history similar to that briefly outlined for the UK could be constructed for France and Spain with eerie parallels. A good example of such parallelism is the ETA (a militant Basque separatist group active from 1959 to 2010) seeking independence for the Basque region of northern Spain and southwestern France. The ETA's violent campaigns resulted in more than eight hundred people killed and thousands injured. Such peripheral resistances have lost their violent edge but continue in a variety of forms. France, for example, is a state built from the center of Paris. Its rebellious regions have long remained on the periphery. The "yellow vest protests"—so-called because participants wore the yellow vest all drivers are required to keep in their vehicles in the event of an emergency—were organized in 2018 against increasing fuel costs.[20] These demonstrations started in the rural provinces of France. It was not just that the people in the provinces have to drive more than people in Paris and are thus more impacted by rising fuel costs; they also tend to have lower incomes. France is still dominated by Paris, the home to the economic and political elites who have done especially well from globalization. The fuel-cost increases seemed to many in France's regions outside of Paris as just one more imposition by an uncaring center. This hardworking yet ignored perimeter already had been nursing perceptions and feelings of marginalization and peripheralization for quite some time.

THE DEEPENING AND WIDENING OF EUROPE

The twentieth century marks a pivot point in global geopolitics. At the beginning of the century, global power, while starting to shift to the United States, was still centered in Europe. Traditional colonial powers such as France, Netherlands, and the UK laid claim to vast colonies that both enriched and ensnared them. Belgium, Germany, and Italy were more recent claimants to territory in Africa, and Germany also laid claim to portions of the South Pacific. The UK was the dominant sea power. Global geopolitics was dominated by these world powers' interaction and competition, especially by a Germany eager to expand its role in the world, creating a world order that ultimately led to two world wars. These wars became global in part because of the colonial holdings. In World War II, the UK had to fight an expansionist Germany at home while resisting an expansionist Japan threatening British Asian colonies.

At the end of World War II, most of Europe was in ruins, shattered and/or bankrupt. The former colonial powers had trouble reasserting their control in their colonies, especially in Asia where the Japanese victories had undermined any remaining ideas of Western superiority or "right to rule." The major European powers were either defeated, in the case of Germany and Italy, or much weakened, as in the case of France and Britain. The war devastated large swaths of urban industrial fabric on the continent, left millions homeless and stateless, and bankrupted national treasuries. Europe was then sliced in half with a new demarcation of Eastern and Western Europe. Global geopolitical power in the West shifted to the United States, which ended World War II as the only great power whose industrial base was strengthened and not destroyed. In the East, a Soviet Empire was enlarged by its grip on Eastern European countries.

In his celebrated novel *1984*, George Orwell imagines three great powers, "Eurasia," "Eastasia," and "Oceania," assumed to be based upon Russia, China, and the United States, respectively. Writing in 1948 with access to the currency of ideas regarding Europe's reemergence, Orwell nevertheless could not imagine a separate Europe that was part of neither Eurasia nor Oceania. To imagine anything else was impossible in the midst of a fractured, demoralized, and bankrupt postwar Europe. Although still a contested and challenged process, such European reconceptualization is much more possible, seventy years on.

By the end of the twentieth century, Europe had been rebuilt and reformed as democratic, wealthy societies rebuilt by strong economies with generous social welfare programs. Europe shifted to improving the lot of its citizenry more than building up its military. Europe emerged as the shining example of a mixed economy that ensured social peace. At the very beginning of the twenty-first century, the future of Europe looked bright. A continuation of the European project in a further deepening and widening of Europe seemed inevitable. Until it didn't.

The European Union

The move toward greater European integration began with the Treaty of Rome, signed in 1957 by Belgium, France, Italy, Luxembourg, Netherlands, and what was then known as West Germany. The treaty created the European Economic

Community (EEC), an attempt to preclude further conflicts in the region with the creation of shared economic interests of a common market. In 1968, all internal tariffs were removed among the six countries. As postwar Europe began to recover and flourish, the EEC's economic success attracted wider interest. In 1961, the UK applied to join, but the bid was vetoed by France because of the UK's close ties with the United States. The French were worried that the UK would become a platform for U.S. domination of the new European bloc. European integration increased as other economies joined and supranational regulatory regimes were established, then tightened, across national borders. In 1973, Denmark, Ireland, and the UK joined. Greece was admitted in 1981 and Portugal in 1986. In 1993, the European Union (EU) became a single market with a free movement of goods, people, capital, and common policies for agriculture, transport, and trade. As the EU got bigger, membership was proving more attractive. In 1995, Austria, Finland, and Sweden joined and later, with the fall of the Iron Curtain, former Eastern bloc countries newly independent from Soviet control were admitted (see map 7.2). There are some events so significant that they are known by their numerical date. If "9/11" remains a significant date as the attack on the World Trade Center in New York City and the beginning of the Long War on Terror, then its numerical reversal, "11/9," celebrates the fall of the Iron Curtain. While 9/11 evokes a tragedy, 11/9 signifies the creation of a new, more coherent Europe.

By 2014, the EU covered all of Europe except Switzerland, Norway, the UK, and the Balkan groups of countries, including Albania, Serbia, Bosnia, Montenegro, North Macedonia, and Kosovo (see map 7.2). The EU now consists of twenty-seven countries with a combined population of 447 million and constituting almost a quarter of global GDP. The EU extends as far east as Cyprus and Bulgaria and as far west as Ireland and Portugal, stretching north to south from Finland to Malta.

In many ways, the EU is spectacularly successful, enabling the rapid postwar success of many countries whose improvement since 1945 is a truly remarkable achievement. The wealthiest countries created generous welfare systems that both improved living standards and secured social peace. Countries that had wreaked imperial havoc across the world and caused two world wars were now bastions of peace and stability (at least if we exclude the Balkans); this is an achievement that is not inconsiderable. However, problems remain. First, as an economic project, there remain marked regional differences in economic development.[21] The EU has a threefold category of "more developed regions," "transitional regions," and "less developed regions." There is a wealthy core oriented around an axis that runs from London to Paris, through industrial Germany and into northern Italy. It is an area of high productivity, high incomes, and higher levels of public services. Away from this core region, disparities become more marked, and when they are overlain with political and ethnic differences, the problems of integration remain. The less developed regions constitute many of the former Eastern bloc countries and many of the more peripheral areas of western Europe. One consequence is the economic migration from the periphery to the more central regions. The number of Poles working in London, for example, increased dramatically. By 2016, there were just over one million Poles working

Map 7.2.   Europe (International Mapping)

in the UK. And this created a backlash especially during economic downturns, when fellow EU citizens became "foreigners taking our jobs."

Second, as a political project the EU has widened to an extent that it now contains a variety of civil societies. There is a world of difference between the *liberal democracies* of France and Germany and the *illiberal democracies* of Poland and Hungary and the *flawed democracies* of Bulgaria and Romania. The EU is not a smooth space of political affiliation but a deeply pockmarked political landscape of vertiginous differences in the level of civil society, of adherence to the rule of law, and of commitment to democracy. It was assumed that the post-Communist society of Eastern Europe, freed from the Communist yoke and led by anti-Communists, would develop along democratic lines. To be anti-Communist or post-Communist, it was assumed, was to be pro-liberal, pro-democratic. But anti-Communists also include those without much belief in democracy. They were against Communism because of its attacks on national identity and on organized religion. Anti- and post-Communists can be religious, nationalist conservatives. Hungary under Orban and Poland under Duda are illiberal democracies that stress religious observance, social intolerance, and a narrow nationalism more than the exercise of democratic rights. And then there are countries such as Bulgaria, where Communist hacks and members of organized crime easily slid into post-Communist government positions simply as a way to enrich themselves.

Third, the fiscal project of the EU—the Economic Monetary Union (EMU)—has had mixed results. The EMU was formed in 1992 with a common currency, the Euro, issued by the European Central Bank. The EMU comprised nineteen of the twenty-seven EU members. I, for one, was sorry to see the beautifully colored currency of the Netherlands supplanted by a rather dull currency, though one that appealed to my cartographic sensibilities. Notice that the map depicted on the ten-Euro note in figure 7.1 shows a Europe without national borders. The European Central Bank is primarily charged with keeping prices low; it was cumbersomely slow in dealing with the fiscal impacts of the global financial crisis of 2008–2009. Compared to the Federal Reserve Bank of the United States, it lacks the ability to quickly coordinate and respond to crises. At times it seems to lack the authority and willingness to coordinate rapidly needed policies such as stimulating failing economies. There is often a schism between the more frugal members, such as the Netherlands, Finland, and Germany, who do not want to bail out what they perceive as their more extravagant fellow members such as Italy, Greece, and Spain. The difficulty of coordinating very different national economies using the same currency was revealed during the 2008 fiscal crisis faced by Portugal, Italy, Ireland, Greece, and Spain when they were unable to refinance government debt or bail out their overextended banks. Previously, they were able to take on debt in large part because they were on the same currency as much stronger economies such as Germany. The crisis exposed the difficulties of maintaining fiscal discipline in a group of countries sharing the same currency but with different economic growth rates and public spending levels.

Fourth, there is a rising crisis of legitimacy. There was a backlash to growing integration even before the economic crisis of 2008–2009. Yet after the crisis, there was increasing backlash to the free movement of labor. Power in the EU is concentrated in Brussels and Strasbourg. Brussels is the home to the bureaucracy while Strasbourg houses the European Parliamentary. As growth faltered and immigration increased, there was a widening between popular sentiments and EU policymakers and their policies. There was growing distaste of the centralization of power and of the perceived shift in power away from the people toward what is often seen as a distant, faceless bureaucracy and as an insulated political elite. There was a sense that the centralization took too much power from both popular and democratic accountability at both the local and regional level. A declining legitimacy, reinforced by failing economies and rising populist rhetoric against the foreign "other," fueled the falling public support for the EU and aided the rise of nationalist and populist political parties.

Figure 7.1.   The Euro (detail; photo by John Rennie Short)

Fifth, while it was successful as an economic unit and moderately successful as a political and monetary unit, the EU remains less successful in translating its combined economic power into geopolitical power. There are a number of reasons. As the dominant economic power, Germany has long resisted being too obvious a force in geopolitics because of its wartime activities. There was also popular resistance against a military buildup. Most EU members oversaw a steady decline in military spending from 1990 to 2016. Not only were there fewer soldiers but also there was no willingness to use them and even less willingness to commit to an EU military force. The EU's economic power is not matched by a matching coherent military force. Europe's military forces are nationalized effectively still, and when they do join up, it is either in the form of joint UN or NATO missions.[22] There is no particularly noteworthy and effective European defense force that is credible. While many national militaries are involved in NATO and UN peacekeeping missions, and individual countries sometimes conduct police action—such as France in Mali—the EU has no military equivalent. If the U.S./NATO relationship becomes more problematic, then European security, especially in the face of Russian aggression, may face problems. The EU is a coherent economic market, a successful but at times struggling political project that lacks geopolitical coherence as well as combined and integrated military power. The Europe that has become a continent of more peaceful, more equitable societies—no mean achievement—has yet to be translated into a Europe as a world power. There are considerable barriers to becoming a coherent geopolitical force, including but not restricted to an unwillingness of a majority of public opinion to become a coherent geopolitical force.

The Schengen Area

Although it's often considered the same thing as the EU, the Schengen Agreement is slightly different. All EU countries are members except Ireland and those awaiting membership such as Bulgaria, Croatia, Cyprus, and Romania. Members of Schengen, but not in the EU, include Iceland, Norway, Switzerland, and Liechtenstein. The Schengen Agreement allows for the passport-free movement of people within Europe. It first came into effect in 1985 when five members signed an agreement in the Belgian village of Schengen. By 2020, the agreement allowed passport-free movement across the common borders of twenty-six European countries, including twenty-two EU member states.

The agreement also allows third country visitors to travel freely once they are admitted into the Schengen Area. Some countries use their privileged position to leverage mobile capital. In Latvia, for example, anyone who buys property worth at least 50,000 Lats (US$96,000) in provincial cities and 100,000 Lats (US$192,000) in Riga, receives a five-year residency permit that allows them access to other countries in the Schengen Area. The program, introduced to prop up the property market, allows easy access for wealthy people, especially from China, Russia, and Kazakhstan. Greece, Spain, and Hungary also have programs that provide visas in exchange for money. Since 2012, Portugal has had a "golden visa," guaranteeing a two-year residence in return for a 500,000-euro investment in real estate investment or a one-million-euro investment that creates thirty jobs. Most visas were issued to Chinese applicants. Many of the applicants are reported to remain in China, but the program allows them the ability to access educational opportunities as well as the possibility of European residency for their children—a very important insurance against economic and political upheaval in China. In 2013, Spain and Greece adopted similar programs for real estate investments of 500,000 euros and 250,000 euros respectively. The same year, Hungary gave a residence permit in return for an investment of 250,000 euros and a payment to "partners" of the government for at least 40,000 euros. Cash-strapped nations in the Schengen Area can use their entry opportunity as a way to attract mobile capital in return for residency and for fast-track citizenship that provides even wider European mobility. Malta proposed an Individual Investor Program that offered citizenship for a straight fee of 650,000 euros. There were neither any investment nor residency requirements. After heavy criticism both domestically and from European partners that the Malta program was "selling" European citizenship, the program was placed on hold and then in November 2013, a revised program offered citizenship in return for 1,150,000 euros.

The Malta case highlights the problem of a unified system of territorial integrity with differing national rules for entry. One way to plug a fiscal gap, generate revenue, and fill the national coffers, especially for smaller, poorer countries and especially for those undergoing property collapses, fiscal problems, and economic uncertainties is to effectively sell access to Europe and EU citizenship to the wealthy. And the competition, especially for the wealthy Chinese investor class, is driving down the entry barriers. In 2012, Portugal offered 500,000 euros for residency; the next year Greece asked for only 250,000 euros. There is a backlash. The initial Malta proposals were condemned roundly at home and overseas. As citizenship for sale became a more political issue, it raises wider issues about differential access to citizenship.

NATO

The North Atlantic Treaty Organization (NATO) is a military alliance among European countries, Canada, and the United States (see map 7.3). The agreement was signed on April 4, 1949, at the height of the Cold War. It was organized as a collective defense group with the member states agreeing to mutual defense in response to an attack on any member. NATO guaranteed the collective security of a Western Europe then facing the military power of the Soviet Union and the Warsaw Pact. Later, in 1952, Turkey joined along with Greece, extending NATO's reach and allowing the close monitoring of Soviet Navy ships sailing from the Black Sea to the Mediterranean. During the Cold War, NATO undergirded European defense with U.S. involvement, U.S. troops, and the U.S. nuclear umbrella. NATO represented the U.S. commitment to Europe. The United States still accounts for 75 percent of NATO defense spending. One positive view of

Map 7.3.   NATO (Wikimedia / Addicted04)

NATO sees it as stopping European wars for global supremacy, institutionalizing the U.S. commitment to Europe, and securing the peaceful termination of the Cold War.[23] No mean achievement.

NATO as a cohesive force for European integration always was undercut by its partial list of members. Austria, Ireland, Sweden, and Finland have never been members. France has dropped out on occasion and still will not commit its nuclear-armed submarines to the alliance. With the collapse of the Warsaw Pact at the end of the Cold War, there was less need for NATO, yet its membership expanded. Table 7.1 highlights the expansion into what was formerly Eastern Europe. With the fall of the Soviet Union, NATO looked like an anachronism. There was no Soviet threat and the Warsaw Pact was no more. The countries that joined in 1999 and 2004 were more about pressing a claim to a European identity than seeking a security partnership. NATO pivoted to international engagements in Kuwait, Bosnia, Kosovo, Afghanistan, and Libya. In Libya, for example, NATO planes flew 9,500 strike sorties against pro-Gaddafi forces.

Table 7.1. NATO Members

Date of Joining	
1949	Belgium, Canada, Denmark, France, Iceland, Italy, Luxembourg, Netherlands, Norway, Portugal, United Kingdom, United States
1952	Greece, Turkey
1955	Germany
1982	Spain
1999	Czech Republic, Hungary, Poland
2004	Bulgaria, Estonia, Latvia, Lithuania, Romania, Slovakia, Slovenia
2009	Albania, Croatia
2017	Montenegro
2020	North Macedonia

NATO expansion concerned Russian strategists, who worried that they were being encircled by unfriendly states. Russia effectively annexed eastern Ukraine and Crimea to resist such Western influence on its western border. NATO also repivoted to Europe again with the rise of a more belligerent Russia. The annexation of Crimea focused the attention of NATO members on the Russian threat to the international order. Russian *gray zone* military activity increased in the waters and airspace of NATO countries, especially of those bordering Russia, such as Norway and Estonia, reigniting NATO's initial mission as bulwark against an expansionist Russia.

The single most important member of NATO is the United States; it provides the bulk of the finances and has an extensive system of bases throughout some of the member states in Europe. However, the U.S. commitment is not a given. The United States is now demanding more publicly that other members pay a larger share. Few countries manage the agreed requirement of 2 percent of GDP. With a declining European fiscal commitment to NATO, it was only a matter of time before some in the United States began to question member imbalance in fiscal commitments. At the same time, a U.S. pivot to Asia means a

U.S. repositioning away from Europe to Asia. To meet the challenge of a rising China seen as the main threat, more U.S. resources and strategic thinking will become focused on East Asia than on Europe. European countries are now having to imagine the difficult future of a NATO with less U.S. support, the enormous difficulties of creating a European-only force at the same time seeking to meet the challenge of a more forceful Russia.[24]

THE BACKLASH

Europe as a coherent unit was organized around NATO and the EU (see maps 7.2 and 7.3). In the past two decades, cracks in the integrity of the European project are becoming more visible. They take a variety of forms.

There is backlash to the widening of the EU. There is growing popular resistance in many EU countries to the extension of the EU further into Eastern Europe and Turkey. The enlargement of Europe in the early years of the EU looked like a good thing: it was seen as an enlargement of similarly democratic societies with roughly similar levels of civil society and political transparency. In the immediate wake of the end of the Cold War, there was tremendous optimism about including the countries of the former Eastern bloc into an extended Europe. More recent extensions, especially to countries such as Poland, Hungary, Bulgaria, and Romania, mean that the EU now consists of a widening range of societies with unequal commitments to democratic accountability. Political cohesion is more difficult with different commitments to democracy, to the rule of law, and to an independent judiciary.

As the difference between the core and peripheral countries increases, with resultant migration as people follow the jobs and pursue better economic opportunities, there is growing suspicion of the "European other." There is also a backlash against the deepening of EU integration with a perceived sense of national democracies being undermined by supra-nationalist entities in Brussels and Strasbourg. Just as there is resistance across the United States to the centered gravity of power in Washington, a similar resentment is apparent in the EU. Except, unlike the United States, European integrity does not have a two hundred-year-old shared history and political coherence to dissipate that anger.

The past three decades have seen the development of breakaway movements and political parties, which have gained followers and been so successful that they have shifted the terms of the narrative from integration to growing caution and to outright rejection. It was the British Conservative Party that successfully campaigned to get the UK into Europe. More recently, facing dissension from their English nationalist wing and worried by the rise of English populist parties, they allowed the referendum that voted for a formal departure from the EU.

Populist parties proclaim the sovereignty of their nation-states and rebel against what they see as imposition of bureaucratic control from Brussels or political mandates from Strasbourg. These populist movements have taken on a new urgency and have achieved greater power and prominence in the wake of the global financial crisis that undermined peoples' sense of economic security and in the wake of increased immigration that created national anxiety about the "foreign other." Economic uncertainty and cultural anxiety have created fertile conditions for those seeking to stop, resist, and turn back European integration. The nation-state as an independent unit continues to have a life of its own in large parts of Europe.

There is also the backlash against NATO. For much of the Cold War, NATO was seen as a vital defense against the threat of the Warsaw Pact. With the ending of the Cold War, the immediate significance of NATO disappeared. Moreover, there was a shift in attitudes about military spending. European countries tend to spend less on military and more on social welfare than the United States. Voters in Europe, and especially in the richer countries further away from the Russian border, have little interest in boosting military expenditures. Most European countries, in contrast with the United States, do not have such a strong and well-funded lobby prompting military spending or a national rhetoric that enshrines military might. European voters seem more concerned with social and economic issues than in keeping their militaries strong.

Just as the commitment of the United States and some Western European members—but not Eastern European members—to NATO may be lessening, the threat from Russia seems to be mounting. As the United States begins a drawdown from the long wars of imperial overstretch, including its commitment to NATO, a resurgent Russia is trying to undermine European coherence and the military ties that connect Europe with the United States. A product of the intense period of the Cold War, NATO may be an anachronism. Even a resurgent Russia is less of a military threat than a cyberthreat, which NATO is ill-equipped to handle. However, as long as Russia probes the weaknesses and defenses of the West, NATO's demise may be delayed for decades to come.

There is also mounting distrust of the United States by its more democratic allies. The Trump administration represented a worrying demonstration that all was not right with the republic. That another Trump-like figure could emerge is scary. That a sitting president could lambast democracies while lauding autocracies and dictatorships was disturbing. That an international order built around the United States was reduced to a series of cynical transactions was a disheartening lesson. But it was a lesson learned. The United States will find it difficult to mount international initiatives in the future; allies will be reluctant to sign up with a superpower of wavering commitments, uncertain strategies, and cynical alliances. The U.S. position in the world is permanently weakened because its allies have lost trust in its ability to be a consistent superpower.

One consequence of the narrowing nationalism of the United States and its pivot to Asia is a shift away from Europe. While Europe held a key position in the Cold War for the United States—with U.S. troops and bases throughout the region—in the post–Cold War world, Europe has less significance. Are we at the beginning of the end of a postwar order enshrined by a strong U.S. commitment to Europe and NATO?

GEOPOLITICAL HOTSPOT: THE BREAKUP OF THE UK

By "breakup," I refer to both the possible division of the United Kingdom and to its disconnection from the EU. It is terminology that engages a number of familiar themes throughout Europe, including the rise of separatist groups and a souring on the European project. The UK is a more extreme version of these EU-wide trends.[25] The UK is the canary in the EU coalmine that is dying.

The Case of Scotland

Scotland joined the UK relatively late, compared to, say, Wales, and retained a semblance of nationhood through its separate education system, its dominant religion different from England's, and a sense of Scottishness that encompasses language, sports, and many of the accoutrements of nation-states. The French theorist Louis Althusser identified an *ideological state apparatus* of public education that acts as a form of indoctrination into adherence to capitalism and the state.[26] However, he assumed—naturally enough for a Frenchman—that public education fulfilled that role in easy transmission of clear-cut messages. The fact that Scotland retained a separate education system meant that it was creating a British sensibility only partially; it also was creating a Scottish national identity. The Italian theorist Antonio Gramsci argued that *ideological hegemony* was a form of domination, maintained not simply by brute force but by social institutions that transmitted a view of the world that legitimized the existing order with highly vaunted "common sense."[27] In the case of Scotland, however, such order was mixed-messaged; social institutions such as education and religion and (Scottish) mass media presented the commonsense idea of a distinct Scotland. This ideological sense of Scottishness, a form of *banal nationalism*, provided a platform for subsequent nationalist movements.

The early connection to the UK proved economically advantageous, at least to Lowland Scotland. The industrial base grew with the imperial connection, though it tied Scotland's economy to heavy industry that by the 1960s was proving disastrous. The decline of coal mining, the collapse of heavy industry, and massive deindustrialization meant a steady economic decline. People had to move to find employment. From 1931 to 2001 Scotland's population remained much the same, around five million, despite a relatively high birth rate. A steady hemorrhage of talent left the country in search of jobs.

There was little demand for independence until the late twentieth century. The discovery of oil in the North Sea stimulated debate about the financial viability of an independent Scotland. Margaret Thatcher's reign of power from 1979 to 1990 proved disastrous for Scotland; her policies negatively impacted Scotland's working class and its industrial base. She was deeply unpopular in Scotland. A political system that kept a more left-wing Scotland under the control of English Conservative governments fueled the independence movement.

In order to head off the independence movement, British politicians of the two major parties sought to calm the waters with legislative offerings that in retrospect helped to solidify a separate and distinct Scottish political identity. A Labour Party election promise led to a referendum in 1997 to gauge support for a Scottish Parliament. More than 75 percent of the voters cast their votes in favor. The new Scottish Parliament opened in Edinburgh in 2004 (see photo 7.2). Scotland now had one of the essential trappings of an independent state. The cultural nation was transforming into a nation-state. Scottish nationalism moved from the fringe to the center of British politics as the Scottish Nationalist Party (SNP) continued to gain support, and by 2007 had a majority of seats in the Scottish Parliament, winning an overall majority in 2011. The power of the SNP forced the Conservative Government to hold a referendum on Scottish independence in 2014. A majority 55 percent voted against independence. What was interesting, however, was the significant size of the vote for independence. Support was strong especially among the youth, leading to the obvious conclusion that independence will come, one funeral at a time. The referendum result signaled an end to the calls for independence, at least for the foreseeable future. The future is arriving earlier than expected because of another referendum result.

Photo 7.2.   Scottish Parliament Building (John Rennie Short)

Leaving the EU

The UK is an island nation geographically closer to Europe than to the United States. The English Channel is only twenty-one miles wide, while the north Atlantic is around three thousand miles wide. However, many in the UK imagine a special relationship that links the two countries despite the geographic distance.

The special relationship was one way for a declining power to assuage its loss of grandeur by attaching itself closely to yet dominant power. Harold Macmillan, the British prime minister from 1957 to 1963, described the UK throughout his career as being like the ancient Greeks to the Roman Empire, providing sage guidance to the brash new imperial power.[28] The close ties with the United States made it difficult for the UK to enter the EEC. The special relationship continues. The UK government, under both Conservative and Labour party control, has been stalwart in support of U.S. overseas incursions—except when the Prime Minister Harold Wilson refused to send British troops to support the American war in Vietnam. The UK provided support, troops, and legitimation for the U.S. invasion of Iraq and the war in Afghanistan.

The UK entry into Europe came after a previous bid in 1961 was rejected essentially because France worried that it was a Trojan horse for U.S. influence in Europe. The UK entry in 1973 was promoted by a Conservative Government eager to make Britain a more modern, postimperial country. A referendum held in 1975 regarding continued membership received 67.2 percent of voting support. The "yes" vote was strongest in England and weakest in Scotland and Northern Ireland. Then something strange happened. There was a reversal of support. The Conservative Party is a coalition between pro- and anti-EU forces, embodied in forward-looking financiers eager to connect to a global economy and backward-looking wannabe patricians, eager to return to an Edwardian England. As the European project lost legitimacy while immigration and economic insecurity increased, the anti-EU wing increased its influence over the party. Meanwhile, the Labour party became more pro-EU as the European project seemed like a good way to ensure public investments and maintain social welfare programs. Regions of the country such as Scotland, which voted against initial EU membership, were now keen supporters, seeing the EU as a defense against an English neoliberalism.

With the rise of populist nationalist English parties such as the UK Independence Party nibbling at the Conservative voter base, the prime minister made an election pledge to hold a referendum on continued EU membership. The vote was held on June 23, 2016. Fifty-one percent voted to leave and 48.1 voted to remain.[29] As can be seen in map 7.4, there is an interesting geography to the results.

A major area of support for remaining in the EU was centered on London. London has emerged a global financial center, attracting expertise and investment from across the globe and around Europe. London is hard-wired into the financial circuits of the EU and global economy. As the UK became a more unequal and divided society, the cleavage between London and the South East and the rest of the country is becoming more marked. The rest of the country in England and Wales, and especially the lower-income groups in those regions, was bypassed by the emphasis on the London money machine. Class conflict was often spatialized into the South East versus the rest of the country, although in reality the divisions were as much social as spatial. But discontent in the England outside of the London region could not be expressed in demands for political separation as it could in Scotland. There was no constitutional basis, and thus the rest of England seethed at the rising inequality and neglect. There was also some evidence that the pro-Brexit vote was higher in areas of England and Wales that had experience of government austerity measures.[30] The exit vote was a vote against govern-

Map 7.4.   The Brexit vote (Wikimedia / Mirrorme22)

ment indifference and against the dominance of London and the political establishment. The exit vote managed to capture popular resentment against the status quo, just as the votes for Trump and Sanders did in the United States in 2015.

All districts in Scotland voted to remain in the EU. This is a complete reversal to the 1975 referendum when Scotland voted against joining the EU as much of the rest of the country embraced the European project. "What happened?" The EU provided benefits to Scotland that the London-biased UK government did not. Scotland's political culture, it turns out, is closer to the EU than to that of London-based Tories. And years of punishing Thatcher rule soured many in Scotland against a reliance on the UK political system. The EU softened the neoliberalism of English Tory rule. The Brexit vote raised demands for another referendum on Scottish independence. The result could be different from the one in 2014 when 55 percent voted to stay in. The Brexit vote may herald the breakup of a union first created in 1707.

Northern Ireland, as a whole, voted to remain in the EU. Northern Ireland is in a similar economic position to Scotland but in a very different political context. The province is split between those who want to join up with Eire and those who want to stay in the UK. Sinn Féin, the party that seeks union with Ireland, proposed a vote on all Ireland unification after the referendum results were announced. Northern Ireland is the only part of the UK that will share a land border with the EU. If this 310-mile border between the UK and Ireland becomes a *hard border*, then it could have huge economic and political impacts that would threaten cross-border trade and the political peace that was so hard won in the 1998 peace agreements. This border issue was central to the UK breakup negotiations with the EU.[31]

The Brexit vote revealed and embodied the deep divide in the UK between the different regions of England and Wales and especially between the affluent London and the South East. This division is unlikely to heal soon. The different voting patterns between Scotland and England may yet herald the breakup of the UK. The Brexit vote is likely to exacerbate the breakup of Britain.

SUGGESTED READINGS

Browning, C. S. (2018). Geostrategies, geopolitics and ontological security in the Eastern neighborhood: The European Union and the "new Cold War." *Political Geography, 62*, 106–15.

Clarke, H. D., Goodwin, M. J., Goodwin, M., & Whiteley, P. (2017). *Brexit*. Cambridge: Cambridge University Press

Foxall, A. (2019). From Evropa to Gayropa: A critical geopolitics of the European Union as seen from Russia. *Geopolitics, 24*, 174–93.

Gehler, M. (2020, 2nd ed.). *Three Germanies: From partition to unification and beyond*. London: Reaktion.

Grygiel, J. (2015). The geopolitics of Europe: Europe's illusions and delusions. *Orbis, 59*, 505–17.

Mojzes, P. (2016). *Yugoslavian inferno: Ethnoreligious warfare in the Balkans*. London: Bloomsbury.

Sokolsky, R. D. (2017). *The New NATO-Russia military balance: Implications for European security*. New York: Carnegie Endowment for International Peace

Szulecki, K. (2015). Heretical geopolitics of Central Europe: Dissidents, intellectuals and an alternative European order. *Geoforum, 65*, 25–36.

Widuto, A. (2019). *Regional inequalities in the EU*. European Parliamentary Research Service.

Wigell, M., & Vihma, A. (2016). Geopolitics versus geoeconomics: The case of Russia's geostrategy and its effects on the EU. *International Affairs, 92*, 605–27.

NOTES

1. Cannadine, D. (2017). *Victorious century: The United Kingdom, 1800–1906*. London: Allen Lane, 229.

2. Elkins, C. (2005). *Imperial reckoning: The untold story of Britain's gulag in Kenya*. London: Macmillan.

3. Davies, N., & Moorhouse, R. (2002). *Microcosm: Portrait of a Central European city*. London: Jonathan Cape.

4. Gilbert, M. (1985). *The Holocaust: A history of the Jews of Europe during the Second World War*. New York: Henry Holt; Snyder, T. (2015). *Black earth: The Holocaust as history and warning*. New York: Tim Duggan Books.

5. Gehler, M. (2020, 2nd ed.). *Three Germanies: From partition to unification and beyond*. London: Reakion.

6. Hancock, M. D. (2019). *German unification: Process and outcomes*. London: Routledge; Shingleton, A. B. (ed.). (2019). *Dimensions of German unification: Economic, social, and legal analyses*. London: Routledge.

7. Pavlinek, P. (1995). Regional development and the disintegration of Czechoslovakia. *Geoforum, 26*, 351–72.

8. Innes, A. (1997). The breakup of Czechoslovakia: The impact of party development on the separation of the state. *East European Politics and Societies, 11*, 393–435.

9. Bookman, M. Z. (1994). War and peace: The divergent breakups of Yugoslavia and Czechoslovakia. *Journal of Peace Research, 31*(2), 175–87.

10. Glenny, M. (1996). *The fall of Yugoslavia: The Third Balkan War*. New York: Penguin.

11. Yeats, W. B. (1921). The Second Coming. https://www.poetryfoundation.org/poems/43290/the-second-coming.

12. Ramet, S. P. (2018). *Balkan babel: The disintegration of Yugoslavia from the death of Tito to the fall of Milosevic*. London: Routledge; Mojzes, P. (2016). *Yugoslavian inferno: Ethnoreligious warfare in the Balkans*. London: Bloomsbury.

13. Toal, G., & Dahlman, C. T. (2011). *Bosnia remade: Ethnic cleansing and its reversal*. Oxford: Oxford University Press.

14. Mockaitis, T. (2020, July 8). Srebrenica, 25 years later. *The Conversation.* https://theconversation.com/srebrenica-25-years-later-lessons-from-the-massacre-that-ended-the-bosnian-conflict-and-unmasked-a-genocide-141177.

15. Hechter, M. (1977). *Internal colonialism: The Celtic Fringe in British national development, 1536–1966*. Berkeley and Los Angeles: University of California Press.

16. Townshend, C. (2013). *The republic: The fight for Irish independence, 1918–1923*. London: Penguin.

17. Dixon, P. (2008). *Northern Ireland: The politics of war and peace*. London: Macmillan International Higher Education; McKittrick, D., & McVea, D. (2002). *Making sense of The Troubles: The story of the conflict in Northern Ireland*. New York: New Amsterdam Books.

18. Devine, T. (2003). *Scotland's empire 1600–1815*. London: Allen Lane.

19. Mackinnon, I. (2017). Colonialism and the Highland clearances. *Northern Scotland, 8*, 22–48.

20. Cigainero, J. (2018). Who are France's yellow vest protestors, and what do they want? NPR. https://www.npr.org/2018/12/03/672862353/who-are-frances-yellow-vest-protesters-and-what-do-they-want.

21. Widuto, A. (2019). *Regional inequalities in the EU*. European Parliamentary Research Service. https://www.europarl.europa.eu/RegData/etudes/BRIE/2019/637951/EPRS_BRI(2019)637951_EN.pdf.

22. Howorth, J. (2017). EU–NATO cooperation: The key to Europe's security future. *European Security, 26*, 454–59.

23. Brzezinski, Z. (2009). An agenda for NATO: Toward a global security web. *Foreign Affairs, 88*, 2–20.

24. Sokolsky, R. D. (2017). *The New NATO-Russia military balance: Implications for European security*. New York: Carnegie Endowment for International Peace; O'Hanlon, M. (2017). *Beyond NATO: A new security architecture for Eastern Europe*. Washington, DC: Brookings.

25. Hobolt, S. B. (2016). The Brexit vote: A divided nation, a divided continent. *Journal of European Public Policy, 23*, 1259–77.

26. Althusser, L. (1984). *Essays on ideology*. London: Verso.

27. Gramsci. A. (1971). Selections from *The Prison Notebooks*. London: Lawrence and Wishart. http://abahlali.org/files/gramsci.pdf.

28. Thorpe, D. D. (2010). *Supermac: The life of Harold Macmillan*. New York: Random House.

29. Clarke, H. D., Goodwin, M. J., Goodwin, M., & Whiteley, P. (2017). *Brexit*. Cambridge: Cambridge University Press; Bachmann, V., and Sidaway, J. D. (2016). Brexit geopolitics. *Geoforum, 77*, 47–50.

30. Fetzer, T. (2019). Did austerity cause Brexit? *American Economic Review, 109*, 3849–86.

31. Gormley-Heenan, C., & Aughey, A. (2017). Northern Ireland and Brexit: Three effects on "the border in the mind." *British Journal of Politics and International Relations, 19*, 497–511.

8

The Middle East

GEOPOLITICAL CONTEXT

Let us begin with the problematic notion of the title of this chapter. The Middle East is not a geographic given. Like many of the other world regions used in geopolitics, it "is not a naturally existing place waiting to be defined, labeled, and described but a discursive construct that is enmeshed in a variety of power relationships."[1] In this chapter we explore some of the complex *power relations* that helped to shape the idea of the Middle East. The Middle East is one of the most contentious areas of the world. It provides examples of state fragility, unsettling demographic transformations, international conflicts, great power machinations, powerful non-state actors, and both intra- and interfaith rivalries. It is important to give some historical dimension to these complex assemblages because the past casts such a giant shadow across the region.

THE SHADOW OF THE PAST

This region was home to some of the world's earliest empires. One of the first, the city-state of Uruk, for example, began its expansion almost six thousand years ago. We will concentrate, however, on just three of the more recent, the Persian, Arab, and Ottoman empires. Each left a significant mark on the contemporary geopolitical landscape.

Persian Empires

There is no singular Persian Empire, rather a series of dynasties that lasted on and off for more than a thousand years. The first, the Achaemenid Empire (550 BCE–330 BCE) was established by Cyrus the Great in 550 BCE.[2] It is best known in the West as the empire that fought against the Greek city-states, most notably in the battles of Marathon and Thermopylae. For many Western commentators, the Achaemenid Empire is an embodiment of an authoritarian East as a counterpoint to the plucky proto-West democrats of Athens. It is a fanciful but persistent myth. Then there was the Sassanid Empire (224 CE–651 CE) which competed with the Roman-Byzantium Empire for territory and influence.[3] The language of modern-day Iran is Persian, not Arabic, and is a continuation of the official language of the Sassanid Dynasty, which drew on even older versions of Persian. The epic poem *Shahnameh*, a chronicle of Persian rulers, is still accessible to Persian speakers a thousand years after it was written. Later, the Safavid Dynasty (1501–1736) created much of the character of today's Iran. The Safavid Dynasty's potent power, conferred by an early adoption of newly invented military technology earned it the designation of *gunpowder empire*. The other *gunpowder empires*, the Ottoman and Mughal, also shaped the early modern period across the entire region.

At its greatest extent, Persian power spread across the Middle East from India to the Mediterranean and from the Caspian Sea in the north to the Arabian Sea in the south. Persian and its variants are still the official languages of Tajikistan (known as Tajik) and Afghanistan (known as Dari) and are still spoken in parts of present-day Azerbaijan, Iraq, Russia, and Uzbekistan. The word *stan*, which is part of the names of many countries in Central Asia, is a Persian word meaning "country," "land," or "nation" and reflects Persian imperial reach. The Persian ruler was known as Shananshan, "king of kings," in order to denote the territorial annexation of other (lesser) kingdoms. Persian arts and culture influenced the courts of the Mughal and Ottoman empires.

The abiding geopolitical legacy of the Persian empires is a strong state in the center of the region with a distinct sense of national identity, Persian, not Arab and Shia, not Sunni.

The Arab Empire

When the merchant Muhammad (570 CE–632 CE) founded the new religion of Islam in the seventh century, it marked the beginning of a new and powerful geopolitical force. Islam was a religious doctrine that encompassed ideas about the ordering of society. After being forced to flee Mecca in 622 (the year marks the beginning of Muslim calendric time), Muhammad established a polity in Medina comprising warring desert tribes built around a set of rules and obligation constructed around interpretations of the *Quran*. This text is believed by Muslims to be the words of God first revealed to Muhammad in 610. Society was to be shaped by this human understanding of God's will. Islam can be translated into English as "submission to God" or "commitment to God." Muhammad and the new religion quickly gained converts from pagan tribes. In 630, with thousands of Muslim converts, he returned triumphantly to take Mecca and soon afterward established total control over most of the Arabian peninsula. After his death, the religious-political leaders known as "Caliphs" quickly extended an empire dominated by Arabs with Islam as its spiritual heart. The Muslim armies gained impressive victories against the Byzantine and Sasanian empires, both weakened by devastating epidemics and their constant war between each other.[4] By 634, Arab armies had gained control of Damascus, Alexandria by 641, reaching the easternmost border of the Persian empire by 651. It was self-evident to its adherents that God must be on their side when empires crumbled before their onslaught. The

Sasanian Empire collapsed, while Byzantium was much reduced in size. The empire diffused Islam across the region as pagans, Jews, Christians, Hindus, and Zoroastrians converted to the ruling religion. By 750, Islam controlled most of the Middle East, as far east as India and as far west as Spain and Portugal. Islam was diffused even wider by Arab and Muslim traders along the overland trade routes that linked the Middle East with Africa and Asia and along the maritime trading routes to the coastal ports of East Africa and Southeast Asia. The calling of the faithful by the muezzin to prayer was heard from Samarkand to Aceh and from Mombasa to Mindanao. Later, the Mughals spread Islam into the heart of India.

The Arab Empire was an Islamic state ruled by a caliph. Three distinct Arab caliphates have been identified. The Rashidun Caliphate followed on from Muhammad's death and comprised only four rulers. In a very short time, this caliphate extended Arab conquests. The Byzantines were defeated at a major battle in 636, ending their rule in North Africa, Egypt, Palestine, and Syria. A Persian army was defeated in 637, and the Sasanian Empire quickly collapsed. The fourth caliph, Ali, ruled from 655 until he was assassinated by rival claimants in 661. This is the source of the Shia-Sunni split. The Shia believe Ali is the most important figure after Muhammad, the only legitimate political heir to the Prophet. Seen as apostates by the majority Sunni, the Shia still have a profound sense of martyrdom and a distinctive sense of communal pain.

The Umayyad Caliphate lasted from 661 to 750 and was centered in Damascus. The Umayyad extended Arab-Muslim dominance. Their rule is best described as a *conquest polity*, a military regime that needed constant territorial annexation to maintain status and revenues. The wealth from conquered lands was used to pay troops and fund government services. Conquest and expansion continued for more than a century. In 711, the Umayyad invaded Spain and undertook two sieges of Constantinople in 674 and again in 716–717. At the height of their territorial expansion, the Umayyad fought a battle with the Franks at Tours in France in 732. The Frankish victory marked the limit of Umayyad extension into Western Europe.

The Umayyad "Arabized" much of the Middle East with the adoption of Arabic as the official language and as the dominant common language. They created a linguistically unified territory, a functioning bureaucracy, and a standardization of Islamic practices that provided a strong foundation for the next caliphate.

The capital of the Abbasid Caliphate (750–1517) was Baghdad, which became a global center of science, philosophy, and invention.[5] The cultivation of science and arts, medicine and literature made Baghdad an important transmission point, keeping alive Greek science and literature while adding new Arab scientific works, thus providing the essential basis for the European Renaissance. Linguistic legacies of the Arab contribution remain in our continued use of Arabic words in science such as *algebra* and *algorithm*. The Abbasids had a well-functioning bureaucracy and a cosmopolitan culture. Power was centralized and run by an efficient bureaucracy. The sophisticated polity came to an end in 1258 after the Mongols sacked the city. The caliphate moved to Cairo but gradually lost its connection to a territorial empire and limped along until 1571 with religious but not much geopolitical power, much reduced from the heyday of Arab-Muslim expansion.

Part of the territorial drive was material. Conquered lands provided workers, money, and material. But expanding the realm of Islam was also a religious duty to extend the Dar al-Islam (House of Islam) into the rest of the world, defined as the Dar al-harb (House of War): it was God's will. This religious-geopolitical idea undergirds the notion that Islam should be extended into the wider world. The geopolitical legacy of the Arab Empire was that the Middle East and North Africa became more Arab and more Muslim.[6] Not entirely, of course; Christians, Jews, and others continued to practice their faith. The Muslim divide between Shia and Sunni sects remains a seismic fault line, quiet for years when hidden from view but at other times actively exposed.

The Ottoman Empire

A fourth Caliphate came under the control of the Ottomans, who claimed this primary spiritual role from 1517 until 1924. Their claim rested on the power and influence of the Ottoman Empire. This vast enterprise grew from small beginnings.[7] A Turkish tribal leader, Osman, is considered the founder. During his reign from 1299 to 1326, he extended his tiny territory at the expense of the neighboring Byzantine Empire. The Ottomans then expanded into Anatolia and into the Balkans. The fall of Constantinople in 1453 marked the end of the Byzantine Empire and the beginning of the spectacular territorial gains by the Ottomans. Between 1453 and 1566 the empire expanded into Europe, Asia, and Africa. Under Suleiman the Magnificent (r. 1520–1566), Ottomans captured Belgrade in 1521, extended their rule into Hungary, took Baghdad from the Persians, and pushed all the way into central Europe. They were only just stopped from taking Vienna in 1529–1532. The Ottomans also built a considerable naval force, competing with the Venetians and Genoese for lucrative Mediterranean and Black Sea trade routes.

After such rapid and massive territorial annexation, it was only a matter of time before imperial overstretch became apparent. The Ottomans were repulsed in their attempt to capture Malta in 1563 and defeated by a combined force of Spanish and Venetian ships in the naval battle of Lepanto in 1571. This marked the beginning of the long end. The extent of the Ottoman Empire in 1683 is shown in map 8.1. From 1683 onward, there were recurring defeats and territorial withdrawals, culminating in Napoleon's invasion of Egypt in 1798. By the early nineteenth century, a variety of separatist and independent movements revealed the costs of imperial overstretch. From Serbia to Arabia, Ottoman rule was questioned and contested. By the middle of the nineteenth century, a common metaphor employed by the great powers of Europe was of the Ottoman Empire as the "sick man of Europe." The question was how to manage its decline to achieve some form of peace and secure the geopolitical aims of the major powers. Britain wanted the Ottoman Empire sustained to act as a bulwark against Russian expansion. The Ottoman, French, and British were allies in the Crimean war (1853–1856) against the Russians. At the Berlin Congress of 1878, the Ottoman Empire in the Balkans was dismembered to create Serbia, Romania, Bulgaria, and Greece. Britain took control of Egypt in 1882.

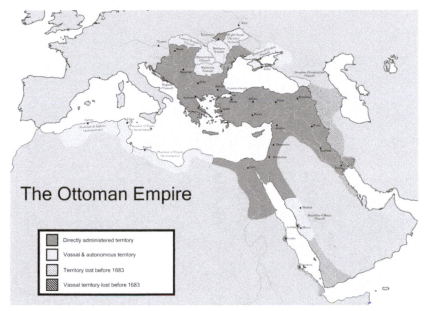

Map 8.1.   The Ottoman Empire in 1683 CE (Wikimedia / Chamboz)

By the beginning of the twentieth century, the empire was weakened but still extended across North Africa and the Middle East. Its increasing weakness and wide territorial spread ensured that the conflicts heightened and the wars accelerated. The Ottomans fought to defend their border in Libya against the Italians (1911–1912), against a Balkan coalition of Greece, Bulgaria, and Serbia (1912–1913), against the Russians in the Caucasus (1915–1917), against Australian, British, and French forces in Gallipoli (1915) and against British-backed Arab rebels in Palestine and Arabia (1916–1918). When the Ottomans made the fateful decision to ally with Germany at the start of WWI, the subsequent Allied victory tolled the death knell of the Ottoman Empire; the British and French then set about carving up the remaining Ottoman lands and establishing a new geopolitical order. The breakup of the Ottoman Empire created the geopolitical landscape of the contemporary Middle East.[8] Under the secret Sykes-Picot deal struck in 1916, the Ottoman territories were divvied up by Britain and France. Egypt became a British protectorate, Transjordan (Jordan and Israel) and Iraq became British mandates, while Syria and Lebanon came under a French mandate. These mandates were ruled by the respective countries ostensibly on behalf of the League of Nations with the intention that they would achieve independence eventually. For Britain and France, the Ottoman defeat provided the opportunity to extend their sphere of influence into the Middle East and ultimately gain tighter control of the resources of the region.[9] This Franco-British division of the Ottoman territory was the template for a number of postcolonial states. The resultant nation-states shown in map 8.2 were a complex patchwork of sheikdoms, nations without states, and states with more than one nation.[10]

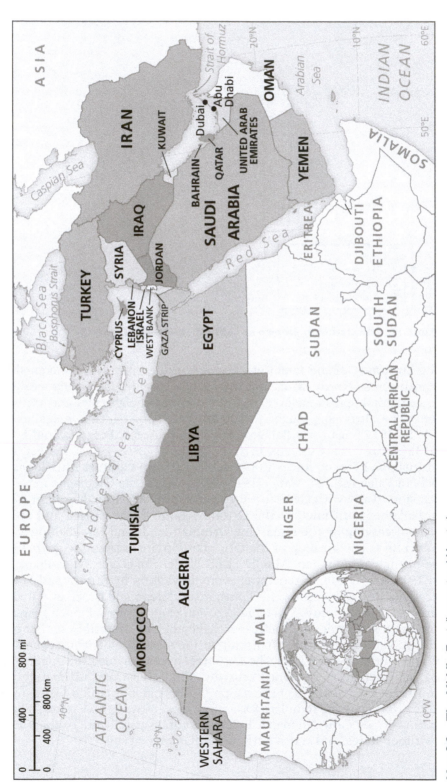

Map 8.2. The Middle East (International Mapping)

THE OUTSIZED POWER OF THE SHEIKDOMS

There are a variety of states in the region that retain the traditional power structure of a ruling family. The oil sheikdoms and kingdoms range from small enclaves to the large territory of Saudi Arabia. They play an outsized role in world affairs because they have some of the largest and most easily accessible—and hence cheapest—oil and gas reserves in the world. The combination of large revenues and small populations results in great national wealth. Yet, there is also the "resource curse" of too heavy a reliance on a narrow range of exported commodities. The sheikdoms are vulnerable to commodity price fluctuation, especially as ever more companies and national economies try to minimize their carbon footprints. Then there is the corruption and inefficiencies that come with most oil-based economies. The carbon trade revenues allow the leaders to spend on generous welfare benefits, but they also undermine other forms of more sustainable economic growth. Most of the work in the oil sheikdoms is done by foreigners on short-term contacts. There are two streams of economic migrants: the well-paid, professional groups and an underclass of laborers from South Asia who build the gleaming towers and sweep the immaculate streetscapes. The oil and gas reserves will not last forever, and all the states are looking to create post-carbon economies with varying degrees of success. Dubai presents the longest and most sustained effort to reposition the city with deeper connections to the wider world through tourism, airlines, and encouraging inward investment flows.

There is a complex network of alliances and allegiances in the region.[11] Most of the rulers are Sunni and so are drawn into the orbit of Saudi Arabia in the Saudi-Iran geopolitical split. That is the big, but not the whole, picture, however; some of the states try to maintain a distance, especially from the more aggressive foreign policies of the Saudi crown prince, Mohammed bin Salman (MBS). Despite U.S. support for Israel, most of the sheikhdoms are pro-United States. There is a symbiosis based on oil. The sheiks were kept in power by the presence of U.S. military forces in the region. The United States built up strong ties initially in order to ensure oil supplies and more latterly for their support in the war on terror. At times, this support skated over the most obvious fact that Saudi Arabia had long supported the Taliban in Afghanistan and was home to the majority of terrorists directly involved in the 9/11 attacks on the U.S. homeland. The sheikhdoms, in return, try to use the United States as a shield and battering ram against their traditional enemy, Iran. The Gulf War and the invasion of Iraq led to U.S. military forces permanently stationed in the region. The United States now has significant military forces in the region and especially in the sheikdoms of the Persian Gulf.

The small sheikdoms owe their existence to the indirect rule-politics of the British. The British wanted to maintain control over the area to protect its vital sea routes to India. The small Arab sheikhdoms strung out along the Persian Gulf were vital and strategic holdings for the British Empire. Prior to 1971, the "Trucial Sheikdoms" of Abu Dhabi, Dubai, Sharja, Ajman, Umm al-Qaiwain, Fujairah, and Ras al-Khaim were under British protectorate. In 1971, they became independent and formed the United Arab Emirates (UAE). Their vast wealth, generated almost entirely from oil and gas, has been turned into enough military hardware to make them a *middle-range power*.

There are differences between them. Abu Dhabi has much larger oil reserves than Dubai, which perhaps explains Dubai's rush to become more than just an oil exporter. The transformation of Dubai to global hub of Emirates Air, as host of global events from golf competitions to film festivals, and the self-conscious marketing of the city as a cosmopolitan, more tolerant place, is in part driven by the brute fact that oil will run out in less than twenty years. The spectacular urbanism that characterizes Dubai is a complex message that says it is a city in the Arab world (see photo 8.1) but also a city of the future, a city that transcends the Middle East, Islam, or even oil urbanism (see photo 8.2). In contrast to Dubai, the other more oil-rich emirates can maintain their more austere religious norms, but even they are faced with the need to diversify economies precariously dependent on carbon fuels.

In the major divide in the region between Iran and Saudi Arabia, the UAE supports the Saudis and tends to see Iran as an enemy stirring up trouble in the region. The UAE joined with Saudi Arabia in the war in Yemen against the Iran-

Photo 8.1.   Burj al Arab (John Rennie Short)

Photo 8.2.   Dubai skyline (John Rennie Short)

backed Houthis, although for a while they backed different anti-Houthi forces. The UAE is also actively involved in the Libyan civil war. In 2020, at least five thousand U.S. military personnel were stationed in the emirates.

Kuwait became a British protectorate in 1896. This status lasted until 1961, when it became an independent country. Its oil reserves were developed after the end of World War II. It supported Iraq in the Iran-Iraq war (1980–1988) but refused to forgive Iraq's $65 billion debt. Tensions between the two countries of Iraq and Kuwait also increased over a disputed oil field and Kuwait's decision to increase oil production when Iraq wanted a reduction in output. The Iraqi invasion of Kuwait in August 1990 initiated the Gulf War when a U.S.-led alliance retook the country the following year and defeated Saddam Hussein's forces. Kuwait became an important platform for the U.S. invasion of Iraq in 2003. In 2020, at least thirteen thousand U.S. military personnel were stationed in Kuwait.

Bahrain became a British protectorate in 1892 until it became independent in 1971, but was always claimed by Iran. Oil companies were active in the region from the 1920s. It has a Sunni sheik ruling over a predominantly Shia population. With a failed coup in 1981, unrest from 1994 to 1999, and protests as part of the Arab Spring in 2011–2013, Bahrain is one of the more contested states in the Gulf. In 2020, at least seven thousand U.S. military personnel were stationed in Bahrain.

Qatar was a British protectorate from 1916 to 1971. Oil was discovered in 1938 but not developed until after World War II. Since 2017, its relations with other sheikdoms have deteriorated, ostensibly because of possible terrorist connections, but in reality because of its unwillingness to go along with Saudi dominance. Qatar was an ally to the United States during 1991 and 2003 military involvements and is home to at least thirteen thousand U.S. military personnel.

Saudi Arabia

Under the Ottoman Empire, Saudi Arabia was led by local sheiks. Arab resistance to Ottoman rule was supported by the British. Abdulaziz Ibn Saud, the patriarch of the ruling house of Saud, led various revolts against the Ottomans as well as competing tribes. He declared the Saudi state in 1932. Intially, Saud had the support of Ikhwan, a tribal army inspired by Wahhabism that had grown quickly after its foundation in 1912. Later, at a battle in 1929, Saud's forces defeated the Ikhwan, although the influence of Wahhabism's austere and fundamentalist form of Islam remained and still remains a significant feature of Saudi society. Oil was discovered in 1938. In the early years of oil and gas exploration, most of the assets were owned and operated by foreign companies, but over the decades the Saudis gained ever more control over production and profits. Most of the revenues that previously went to the oil companies now comprise the national wealth of oil-rich states. When oil prices were jacked up in 1973, they inaugurated a huge shift in global wealth. The sheikdoms and other oil producers became the *nouveau riche* of the global economy. The increased oil and gas revenues enlarged the fiscal capacities of the sheikdoms very quickly, enabling both social welfare and military procurements. The oil-rich nations of the Middle East are a significant force not only in the region but also in the global economy. There are few as rich or as powerful as Saudi Arabia.

The country is controlled by the Saud family dynasty. Members of the Saud family control all the levers of power. Only sons and grandsons of the nation's founder Ibn Saud have been kings. The year 1979 was pivotal for Saudi Arabia. After the Iranian revolution of 1979, Iran's clerics became persistent critics of Saudi family wealth. Also, that same year, the Grand Mosque in Mecca was seized briefly by insurgents who rejected the Saudi monarchy as corrupt and wanted to establish a theocracy. Shaken by the uprising and by Iranian rhetoric, Saudi Arabia became more conservative, giving conservative religious forces more power and influence. The Saudi ruling elite saw the answer to the mounting crisis of legitimation as more religion. Cinemas were closed, gender segregation reinforced, and religious police became more active in monitoring public space.

Saudi Arabia has long been pro-United States. U.S. support for the country has ensured long-term supplies of cheap oil, but at a political price for the United States. Throughout the Middle East, reformers could argue that U.S. support for such a theocratic and undemocratic state undermined any notion that the United States was a force for democratization in the region. The religious conservatives in the region also saw U.S. support for a regime they considered too corrupt and too secular. In other words, the United States lost the support of both the more liberal reformers in the region and the religious conservatives.

The relationship between the United States and Saudi Arabia has taken a new twist. Fracking has allowed the United States cheaper access to more domestic sources of energy, reducing reliance on Saudi Arabia. Political power has shifted inside the kingdom with the rise of Crown Prince Mohammed bin Salman, popularly known as MBS.[12] He was appointed crown prince in 2017 at the young age of thirty-one by his father, King Salman. On the one hand, he is a reformer. He has pursued ambitious policies of economic and cultural liberalization. He has sought to move to a post-carbon economy and to a more open society free from the religious strictures that had sealed the country off from modernity. But on the other hand, he has centralized power, ruthlessly suppressed any criticism of his rule, and adopted brutal tactics of intimidation. He was responsible for the hideous murder of the journalist Jamal Khashoggi in 2018 in the Saudi consulate in Istanbul. He has humbled and pursued those who disagree with his rule. He has embarked on a more military role for Saudi Arabia in the region. The Saudi-UAE military coalition injected lethal airstrikes into the civil war in Yemen. Saudi foreign policy has become more militaristic, more far-reaching, and more destabilizing under a young crown prince eager to make his mark. The relations between MBS and the United States were especially close and warm during the Trump administration but post-Trump they may become more distant and cooler, especially after the release of a U.S. National Intelligence Report that stated that MBS was responsible for the operation that killed Khashoggi.[13]

NEW STATES

The Middle East is composed of relatively new states. They arose from imperial boundary-making, colonial carve-ups, and hasty state formation. There are states with more than one nation and nations without states.

The Mediterranean Littoral

Along the Mediterranean coastline, Algeria, Morocco, Tunisia, Libya, and Egypt emerged as independent states after the ending of World War II. Much of the territory was previously under Ottoman control (see map 8.1). Located in the Mediterranean basin, these territories attracted the interest of European powers such as the UK, France, Spain, and Italy. Morocco was carved up by France and Spain in 1912 and only achieved independence in 1956. Spanish troops only left the Western Sahara in 1976, where an independence movement of the Sahrawi people, the Polisario Front, long waged a campaign for independence. Although a cease-fire was signed in 1991 between Morocco and the Front, Western Sahara remains a contested region.

Algeria was part of France's colonial empire, first annexed in 1830. More than a million people from France immigrated into the country and became a majority of the population living in the cities of Algiers and Oran. The local population—mainly Arab-Amazigh Sunni Muslims—resisted French domination. France's defeat in World War II encouraged an independence movement but pro-independence demonstrations in 1945 were brutally suppressed. From 1954, when the National Liberation Front was established, to 1962, a bitter struggle was waged. Casualties vary in estimates from four hundred thousand to one million. The war was given dramatic representation in the film *Battle of Algiers*.[14] The film depicts the changing tactics of the French colonial power and the local resistance movement. It is such a detailed and realistic account of an urban insurgency that it became required viewing for U.S. military intelligence officers planning the invasion of Iraq. After the bitter struggle, Algeria gained independence in 1962. The oil industry was nationalized, and industrialization was pursued. The economy is still based on the export of oil and natural gas. In the first free elections, held in 1990, the Islamic Salvation Front (FIS) had a sweeping victory, but the army intervened so that they could not take power. An insurgency campaign against the authorities resulted in one hundred thousand deaths with the unrest only diminishing by 2000; since then the government has pursued a policy of national reconciliation. However, protests in the streets during the Arab Spring prompted some reform but there was still resentment against the entrenched power of the economic and political elites. When plummeting energy prices impacted the economy, social discontent increased. In 2019 street protests led to the resignation of the increasingly unpopular president, who has been in power since 1999. It was a delayed Arab Spring.

Tunisia was under Ottoman control from 1534, though the control did not extend much beyond the Mediterranean coast, until the French Army invaded in 1881. It was then a colony of France until it became independent 1956, but there is still a marked division between the more liberal urbanized cities of the coastal area and the more conservative rural interior. It was the birthplace of the Arab Spring.

Libya was also part of the Ottoman Empire from 1551 to 1911, until it was invaded by Italy. Italy ruled the country from 1911 to 1943 and encouraged more than half a million Italians to emigrate. The country became independent in 1951. Gaddafi took over in 1969 and was able to use the vast oil revenues to fund his geopolitical ambitions.[15] He was overthrown in 2011 and the country unraveled between competing Eastern and Western power centers; it is not only a *failed state* but also an *incoherent state*.

Egypt was a province of the Ottoman Empire. The completion of the Suez Canal in 1869 attracted the attention of the world's superpower of the day, the UK, which saw it as a vital link between metropole and its imperial holdings in India and Southeast Asia. Against a background of rising nationalism, the UK invaded Egypt in 1882. The international partition of Africa was in part prompted by these British actions. The UK retained effective control even when the province was a kingdom from 1922 to 1953. It finally became independent from the British with the establishment of a republic in 1953. Soon after, in response to the proposed nationalization of the canal, the British again tried to assert their will, this time in an ill-fated invasion by the combined forces of the UK, France, and Israel in 1956. The United States stepped in and forced the armed forces of the three powers to withdraw. The Suez Crisis, as it was known in Britain, marked a new world order. It signaled the end of the UK and France as great powers able to act independently from the United States in vital strategic matters. It strengthened anticolonial struggles against the UK and France. It confirmed the United States as the dominant Western power. It also heightened the appeal of the Egyptian leader, Nasser, in the Arab world, giving him a key place in the pan-Arabism project.[16] Soviet support for Nasser became an important element in the growing Soviet influence in the region.

Nations without a State: The Case of the Kurds

The post–World War I political architecture of the region was largely designed by the French and British eager to secure spheres of influence and to control the valuable commodities in the region.[17] The new postcolonial boundaries often led to states with warring nations and even to nations without a state. The most obvious, but not the only, example of a nation without a state is the Kurdish nation. It consists of forty million Kurds spread across the national boundaries of Armenia, Georgia, Turkey, Syria, Iran, and Iraq. After World War I, the French and British carved up the Ottoman territory. Early on, it looked as if a "Kurdistan" would emerge. However, the line that divided the French and British zones cut right through the Kurdish territory. In the Sykes-Picot agreement, the British wanted a big bloc to counter French claims in what is today Lebanon and Syria. A small Kurdish nation-state would not suffice. The allies also wanted the Kurds to balance the Shia in what was emerging as Iraq; this was the usual idea of rendering states relatively weak with internal divisions to make them that much easier to control. Another reason was the possibility of oil in Kurdish territory. The Kurds revolted in 1919 against these maneuverings that denied them their own state and tried to create an independent nation next to what was then Turkey.[18] But in 1920, Turkey occupied the area, and the French and British lost interest in the Kurds, who were then doomed to be a nation without a state. As the new national boundaries hardened and tightened, the Kurds were further ignored and abandoned by the outside world. In eastern Turkey and northern Iraq, the Kurds remain a strong presence, always warily eyed as actual or potential separatists by the central authorities of each country. Kurdish separatist forces remain strong in Turkey. In post–U.S.-invasion Iraq, a distinct and prosperous Kurdish region emerged in the north. Under Saddam Hussein, they were marginalized and oppressed but they achieved self-governing regional autonomy, initially under the protection of U.S. air power since 1992, and especially since 2003. The Kurdish region remained relatively peaceful and prosperous, capable of exporting a million barrels of oil a day. In recent years, they faced threats at the borders of their region from the Islamic State of Iraq (ISIS).

States with More than One Nation

Ever since the fall of the Ottoman Empire, the region has had a complicated political geography with national borders created by imperial cartographers in the West for the West, cutting across religious communities, tribal loyalties, and ethnic identities. The Anglo-French division of the central part of the Middle East created a number of new states that contained different nations. They include Iraq, Syria, Lebanon, and Turkey. Let us consider Iraq; it represents a pronounced example of the unravelling of a state with warring "nations" and the consequent civil disorder and geopolitical uncertainty.

The Unraveling of Iraq

After World War I, that territory of the Ottoman Territory that is now Iraq, Israel, and Jordan came under British control. Iraq became an independent country in 1932. Its national boundaries are a result of imperial cartography rather than national coherence. There was always an uneasy alliance between the Kurdish north, the Shiite south, and the Sunni center. Under Saddam Hussein, the Sunnis held political power while the Kurds and Shiites were kept on the margins. When Hussein invaded Kuwait in 1990–1991, he was quickly defeated by the U.S.-led coalition but remained in power. The Kurdish north was protected by U.S. air power, but the Shiites in the south paid a heavy price for their attempted insurrection.

In 2003, Iraq was invaded by a U.S.-led coalition falsely claiming the country had weapons of mass destruction. Tens of thousands of Iraqis died in the wake of the invasion and more than two million were displaced. The invasion toppled Hussein but led to the unraveling of the former country; the Kurds effectively broke away to the safety of their core region and Shia engaged in a bitter, bloody sectarian struggle with Sunnis. The country was devastated by the U.S. invasion and subsequent civil unrest: it has yet to fully reassemble.

The turmoil also impacted religious minorities. The number of Assyrian Christians in Iraq fell from 1.4 million in the late 1980s to around 400,000 by 2010. The Yazidi religion combines ancient Mesopotamian beliefs with elements of Sufi Islam and Christianity. They are concentrated in a region across Iraq, Syria, and Turkey. More than 650,000 live in northern Iraq. Since the 1990s, persistent persecution has forced more than 200,000 Yazidi to move to Europe. In 2014, ISIS targeted the Yazidi for extinction as an act of Islamic purification.

The U.S. invasion and the consequent insurgency also exacerbated religious tensions. Under Hussein, the Sunnis were in control and the Shiites were denied access to power. They were often used as cannon fodder in the bloody Iran-Iraq War of 1980–1988, pitting fellow Shiites against each other. After the fall of Saddam, the conflict between Sunnis and Shiites exploded. In 2006, Sunni extremists bombed the al-Askari mosque—a holy site for Shia Muslims—in Samarra, Iraq, destroying the magnificent golden dome. The bombs set off a spree of revenge killings and attacks on Sunni religious sites. A year later, another bomb destroyed the remaining minarets in Samarra. When a car bomb killed at least sixty-eight people close to the al-Abbas mosque in Karbala—another sacred Shiite site—the Shiite-Sunni conflict resumed. Death squads, murders, and forced displacements reinforced and solidified the animosity between the two communities. The conflict spiraled out from Iraq into Syria as a significant part of Iraq came under the control of Sunni-dominated ISIS.

The gradual, though not complete, departure of U.S. forces—there are still around six thousand U.S. personnel in the country—from Iraq has not brought peace to the country. The government is widely considered corrupt with spoils divided between the different religious, ethnic, and tribal groups. There is endemic animosity between the Sunni and Shis communities; ISIS poses a real threat in some of the Sunni-dominated areas outside of Baghdad; the country is a battleground for outside interests. The presence of U.S. troops, Iran-backed militias, and Saudi-funded fundamentalist groups all make the country an unstable incoherent state. Meanwhile, living standards are worse than before the U.S. invasion. The national government lacks legitimacy with the bulk of the population deeply distrustful of the government's ability and willingness to provide equity and justice. The U.S. invasion toppled a dictator but created chaos and confusion as the country collapsed into warring and antagonistic groups.

REGIONAL POWERHOUSES

By virtue of their size and power, there are five regional powers in the Middle East. They include Saudi Arabia, Iran, Turkey, Egypt, and Israel. We have already discussed Saudi Arabia.

Iran

Iran is one of the largest countries in the Middle East, situated at the heart of the region, bordering seven different countries. Its present borders constitute the core region of numerous Persian empires. Under different dynasties, Persia was one of the most powerful states in the region. However, by 1907, it was divided into separate spheres of influence: Russia in the north, the UK in the south, with an Iranian rump in the middle. Russia withdrew as it transformed into the USSR after 1917, leaving most of Iran under British control. The British established the Anglo-Persian Oil Company to exploit the vast oil reserves. In 1926, Reza Shah Pahlavi, formerly an officer in the Persian Cossack Brigade, elevated himself to Shah and embraced a form of authoritarian modernity. His son, Mohammed Reza Pahlavi, came to power in 1941 after his father was deposed. Power was centralized in this Shah, who ruled from 1941 until 1979.

There are three key moments in more recent history: First, in 1953 a coup organized by the United States and the UK overthrew the democratically elected Mohammed Mosaddegh. His crime? He wanted a more careful audit of the Anglo-Iranian Oil Company and more of the profits directed to the Iranian coffers. The CIA was actively involved.[19] It was part of a Cold War mentality, especially central to the worldview of the Dulles brothers. John Foster Dulles was the U.S. secretary of state from 1953 to 1959. Allen Dulles was deputy, then director of the Central Intelligence Agency from 1953 to 1961. Mossadegh's legitimate concerns were interpreted as part of a Communist conspiracy. The Dulles brothers never saw a national liberation movement that could not be explained as Soviet inspired. The overthrow of Mossadegh heightened the repressive rule of Shah Mohammed Reza Pahlavi, ultimately stimulating Muslim fundamentalism and a deepening anti-Americanism.

Second, the Shah launched the White Revolution in 1963. This was a massive program of modernization and a series of wide-ranging reforms, including allowing women to vote. The more liberal policies offended the conservative Shia clergy, who became an important source of resistance to his rule. The 1960s and 1970s were boom years as high oil prices allowed Iran to modernize and to build up its military arsenal with expensive equipment. The Shah relied on U.S.

support, who in turn saw him as a powerful ally at the heart of an unstable region. Iran's main geopolitical strategy was to maintain good relations with the United States. He presented himself as a bulwark against Communism—every right-wing dictator did in those days—and against radical Arab Muslim forces. For several years Iran was the biggest single purchaser of advanced military technology in the world. Iran did not participate in the 1973 oil embargo but did influence OPEC to raise prices almost 470 percent in little over a year. The bloated revenues allowed massive modernization projects, a vast military buildup, and a major source of rampant corruption in the country. Denied access to democratic institutions, critics were seen as enemies and a fearsome police state emerged that ruthlessly weeded out dissidents. Despite the liberal reforms that created more schools and universities and abolished old restrictions of women, the Shah's rule was ruthlessly authoritarian.

Third, 1979 marks a major turning point. The Shah and his family left the country after massive street demonstrations, strikes, and rioting against his rule. The Shia cleric, Ayatollah Khomeini, a persistent critic who had long railed against the liberalism, corruption, secularism, and pro-U.S. stance of the Shah, returned from Paris and became the supreme leader. Student activists held U.S. diplomats hostage, initiating the U.S.-Iran hostility that continues to this day. Iran became a clerical autocracy with a profoundly anti-Israel and anti-U.S. stance. Women were required to wear hijab, were formally segregated in public spaces, and were purged from the government and judiciary.[20]

Even in a theocracy, with a religious figure as the supreme leader of Iran, there are other and sometimes competing sources of power. Presidents are elected. There are more liberal figures such as Hassan Rouhani, who has held the presidency since 2013, succeeding the conservative populist figure, Mahmoud Ahmadinejad, who was president from 2005 to 2013. Ruling clerics and politicians also face popular resistance. There were mass protests in 2009 against the disputed victory of Ahmadinejad. It was one of the "color protest" movements, this one known as the Green Movement. Women played prominent roles as sources of resistance against the clerical regime and were also active again in the 2019–2020 protests against economic deterioration and the large increase in fuel and food prices.

Politics in Iran are more fluid than the description of it as a theocracy would suggest. There is a more liberal and young middle class in Tehran who complain about the restrictions on civil rights and even more Iranians complaining about falling living standards. There are changes in the regime itself. In some areas the clergy is losing authority over civil agencies. Iran is moving from clerical to military autocracy with the military taking more control, especially after the dismal official response to COVID-19.

There are multiple militaries operating under the flag of Iran. There are the regular forces charged to protect borders and maintain social order, and then there is the Islamic Revolutionary Guard Corps (IRGC), formed in 1979. They came to greater prominence in 2009 with the election of the populist conservative Ahmadinejad. They have approximately 125,000 personnel and play a key role in policing the Persian Gulf. They have control over large sections of the economy—auto, oil and gas, and even an airline—and they use the proceeds to fund Shia militias in Lebanon, Syria, and Yemen. When their finances are impacted by falling oil prices and COVID-19, they turn more to smuggling. The IRGC has two other units, one internal, the other external. The Basij, nominally under the control of the IRGC, is a ninety-thousand-volunteer paramilitary group that acts as shock troops to quell social discontent inside the country. Iran's supreme leader uses the IRGC and Basij to disburse money and aid to needy Iranians—no surprise then that their base of support is the poor and lower-income classes.

The foreign operations force is called the Quds. It numbers only between two thousand and five thousand and aids Iran's Shia allies in Syria, Iraq, and Lebanon, and possibly Bahrain and Yemen. The Quds is the vehicle for Iran to project power beyond its border through the effective use of surrogates across the region. Iranian proxies have expanded Iranian influence across the region. In 2020, Iran-backed Hezbollah gained control of the Lebanese government for a period. There is pushback. Popular demonstrations in Iraq in 2019–2020 were targeted at the influence of foreign interests, including Iran.

The IRGC is virulently anti-Western and anti-Israel and tends toward the more confrontational, so incidents in the Persian Gulf may be less the result of Iranian government policy deliberations than the result of local IRGC commanders flexing their muscles.

There are three important features of Iranian geopolitics. The first is a strident anti-U.S. position, reinforced by Iranian conflict with two key U.S. allies in the region: Israel and Saudi Arabia. The United States is often caught in its attitudes toward Iran between the more confrontational approach proposed by Israel and the more conciliatory preferences of European allies. Under the Trump administration it adopted a more aggressive posture, including a punishing system of sanctions that weakened the Iranian economy and led to real economic stress for Iranians. Israel tends to see Iran as one of its biggest existential threats and seeks to guide U.S. policy toward an even more aggressive posture against Iran. Whether economic sanctions will force a change in the regime or stiffen anti-U.S. sentiment is a moot point. It will probably vary across the Iranian population, making the lower-income groups more supportive of the regime and higher-income groups more critical of the regime.

The second, and very much related to the first, is the Iran-Saudi conflict. The two countries embody the major divide in Islam with Saudi Arabia the main Sunni power and Iran as the major Shia power. Iran seeks to aid Shia populations throughout the region in Iraq, Lebanon, Syria, Bahrain, and Yemen. The Saudi-Iran split helps to fuel numerous conflicts in the region from protest movements in Bahrain to the collapse of Syria to tensions inside Iraq (where the two enemies support rival groups). With a more aggressive MBS-controlled Saudi Arabia, Saudi-Iran relations may even worsen over the years. Iran sits at the center of what had been termed the *Axis of Resistance* to both U.S. and Saudi-Sunni power in the region. Unable to compete against its stronger and better-armed opponents with traditional military responses, Iran has engaged in mobilizing the Shiite minority in the region with gray zone activities and what some military theorists term fourth-generation warfare (4GW) that allows weaker states and non-state actors to pursue their aims against stronger, better-armed opponents.

4GW allows the creation of military alliances through proxy warfare. In Syria, Lebanon, Yemen, and Iraq, Iran has advanced Shia-led resistance to Saudi and U.S. hegemony in order to create client states in what one analyst described as a *proxy empire*.[21]

Finally, there is the basic geography of Iran. It sits at the center of the region and is thus involved through shared borders and human movement with a variety of countries. Iran is also positioned in a strategic location for the global oil trade. In 2020 a major deal between China and Iran was made public. China seeks to make Iran a major hub in the Belt and Road Initiative (BRI), investing up to $400 billion in return for discounted oil. The Strait of Hormuz is a *strategic maritime chokehold* where 90 percent of global trade by weight and 20 percent of global crude oil flows across through the twenty-one-mile-wide narrows (see map 8.3) To maintain freedom of navigation, the United States has considerable naval presence in the gulf. So, we have U.S. naval ships, a sometimes unpredictable IRGC, rising geopolitical tensions, and a vital commodity passing through a very narrow chokehold. What could go wrong?

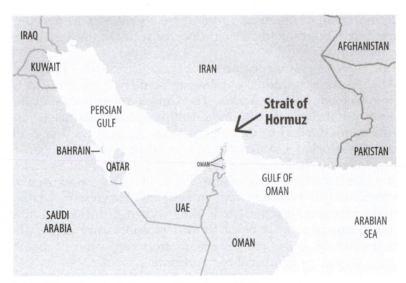

Map 8.3.   Strait of Hormuz (State Dept./D. Thompson)

Turkey

Turkey is the remnant of the once-vast Ottoman Empire that stretched across Europe, Africa, and the Middle East. Turkey's defeat in World War I marked the end of its centuries-old empire. Its present-day boundaries were established at its founding in 1923 as a modern secular state. Western clothing was encouraged, the fez was banned, and the Gregorian calendar and the Roman alphabet were adopted. Turkey embraced a Western-influenced modernity as a national defining character and a secular state emerged.

For those with an interest in political terminologies, Turkey was also the first country described in the 1970s as having a *deep state*, defined as a constellation of anti-democratic forces embedded in a state's administrative, military, and judiciary apparatus. It was also used in the 1990s to refer to the collusion between the Turkish military and criminal elements to fight a dirty war against Kurdish nationalists.[22] The state, both deep and narrow, is now confronted by the recent rise of more religious-based political parties and social movements. The Islamic revival is expressed in the Justice and Development Party that came to power in 2002 as a more overtly and explicitly religious political movement.

Turkey stands at the crossroads of Asia and Europe, with territory on either side of the traditional continental division of the Bosporus Straits. During the Cold War, it was a strategic ally against the Soviet bloc because of its effective control over the narrow passage of the Bosporus Straits through which Soviet ships and submarines had to pass in order to reach the Mediterranean from their bases in the Black Sea.

The contemporary geopolitics of Turkey are shaped by four forces. First there is the concern with Kurdish nationalism. There is a significant Kurdish population: of the population of 81.6 million, more than fourteen million are Kurds. Their traditional region is in the east and southeast of the country even though more than half now live outside of this region in towns and cities throughout Turkey. From 1984 to 2000, the Kurdish Workers Party (KPP) escalated the struggle for cultural recognition into a bloody campaign. Much of the traditional Kurdish region came under repressive military rule and was closed to foreign travelers. More than forty thousand people died in the war between Turkish forces and the KPP. Since 2000, the violence and repression has lessened with occasional flare-ups. There is an ongoing military campaign by the Turkish state in the east of the country where most Kurds live. The rise of a strong, semi-autonomous Kurdish region in northern Iraq and Syria worries the Turkish government, who fear the emergence of a greater Kurdistan that could lay claim to parts of Turkey. The Turkish government is always on the lookout to see the events outside its immediate border as possibilities for aiding a Kurdish territorial breakaway.

Second, there is the deep historical context to contemporary Turkish geopolitics. After World War I, the 1920 Treaty of Sevres imposed tough conditions on Turkey. It had to renounce all its claims to lands in North Africa and the Middle East. Much of its former empire was divvied up between Britain and France while Italy and Greece gained control over numerous Aegean islands. For Turks, the Treaty of Sevres was the imposition of Western dominance over Turkey that "still stalks the Turkish political imagination."[23]

Third, there is its geographical position close to the unraveling states of Syria and Iraq with their waves of displaced refugees. Turkey houses more than 3.7 million refugees from the conflict in Syria. Towns in southern Turkey along the border with Syria are now sites of refugee camps, aid missions, and political intrigue. The unstable state also gives an opportunity for Kurdish groups to create and expand a Kurdish region. Ankara worries that outbreaks of Kurdish autonomy both inside and along its borders threaten their territorial integrity. The Turkish military is involved in Syria in order to protect their borders and to weaken Kurdish breakaway movements. They are less concerned with overthrowing the Assad regime.

Fourth, there is the regional geopolitical situation. Turkey is truly at a geographic crossroads: it shares borders with an unraveling Iraq, a collapsing Syria, the regional powerhouse of Iran, the ex-Soviet republics of Georgia and Armenia, and the European countries of Bulgaria and Greece. Each one of these neighbors requires a careful response. Some are marked by centuries-old enmities. Armenians have a long-troubled history with Turkey.[24] Not surprising then that some Armenian analysts see evidence of what they describe as Turkish micro-imperialism of aggressive and expansionist policy emerging especially strong after the failed attempted coup in Turkey in 2016. They argue that after the coup, the Erdogan government became less constrained as it weakened links with Europe and the United States and recognized opportunities for distinctly Turkish objectives across the region.[25]

Relations between Greece and Turkey have long been tense. Ever since Greece won independence from the Ottomans in 1830, they have eyed each other with apprehension. They fought four wars in 1897, 1912–1913, 1914–1918, and 1919–1922, which led to an exchange of populations. They have fought over the island of Cyprus, which contains both Turks and Greeks, although Greeks are the vast majority. It became independent from Britain in 1960. In 1974, after a Greek military coup d'état sought to annex the island to Greece, Turkish troops invaded. After thousands were displaced on both sides, the island was portioned into a Turkish-controlled north, and an independent Republic of Cyprus in the south, separated by a UN buffer zone. The relations between Turkey and Greece continue to be unsettled by recurring irritants of airspace violations, fishing claims, and nationalist rhetoric. Maritime claims are an increasing source of tension. The idea of an expansive *Blue Homeland* has been gaining currency in the Turkish government since formulated in 2006 by the naval officer Cem Gurdeniz. It asserts rights to a large body of water that includes Greece's current Exclusive Economic Zone (EEZ). The boundary of Greece's EEZ runs well to the east of almost all the islands off the west coast of Turkey shown in map 8.4. Turkey's Blue Homeland is a nationalist territorial claim that implicitly argues that the islands given to Greece in the Treaty of Sevres undercut Turkish maritime sovereignty. It also has major economic implications; the offshore waters of the Mediterranean are being surveyed for oil and gas reserves.[26]

Turkey is also involved in wider regional issues beyond its immediate borders.[27] It is an active participant in the Libyan civil war and provides military support to the UN-backed Government of National Accord (GNA), based in Tripoli against the Libyan National Army (LNA) based in Tobruk and led by Khalifa Haftar. The UAE and Egypt, along with Russia, openly support the Haftar forces. Turkey's involvement, which includes drones, mercenaries, and military trainers, has been key to recent victories for the GNA and its repulsion of an LNA attack against Tripoli. Turkey's involvement is part of a strategy to confront what it sees as two anti-Turkish power constellations, UAE-Egypt-Saudi Arabia and Greece-Cyprus. Turkey feels hemmed in by these opposing power forces. The Turkish backing for the GNA is closely linked to agreements that grant access to Mediterranean gas fields. Hafter's backers are seen by Turkish leaders as competitors trying to contain Turkey's influence in the region and to limit its access to vital oil and gas reserves.[28]

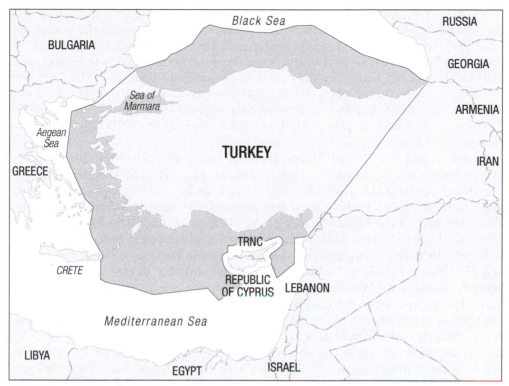

Map 8.4. Turkey's Blue Homeland (Everybody Wiki / Cihat Yaycı)

For decades, Turkey was a reliable member of NATO. It has long sought closer relations with Europe and applied to join the European Union and its forerunner the European Economic Community. Currently, its membership is blocked. Greece and Cyprus are perennial naysayers while Western European states worry that Turkish membership would result in an influx into their cities of millions of conservative Muslim peasants from Anatolia. Officially, the EU argues that Turkey, while a strategic copartner on migration and counterterrorism, does not guarantee the rule of law and fundamental rights. In 2018, the negotiations broke down completely. Turkey holds an important bargaining chip in its relations with Western Europe. It is the transit point for millions of refugees from the Middle East trying to make their way to Europe. Turkey houses close to 4.1 million refugees—3.7 million from Syria alone—and has bargained hard with the EU for aid. The risk of unleashing these refugees into European countries is real.

In 2015–2016, more than one million refugees crossed from Turkey into Greece and then fanned out across Europe. In March 2016, the EU signed an agreement with Turkey. In return for $6.7 billion from the EU, Turkey would prevent migrants from crossing into Europe. In February 2020, the Turkish government announced it would no longer hinder migrants.[29] The threat was minimized by the travel restrictions across the EU in the wake of the COVID-19 crisis, but it remains a threat that is real and very worrying for Greece and Western European countries.

Turkey's relations with the United States are also evolving. Turkey was committed to the Western Alliance against the Soviets, but with the end of the Cold War, relations are now more complex.[30] The United States closed eight of its twelve bases in 1991—part of the peace dividend of the Cold War ending—but Turkey allowed the United States use of its airspace and airbases in the Gulf War in 1991. In more recent years, relations have soured, specially under the more conservative-nationalist and more explicitly religious government of Recep Erdogan, who has been in power, first as prime minister from 2003 to 2014, and then as president.

Turkey and the United States are now going through what looks like a rather messy public divorce.[31] Turkey did not support U.S. sanctions against Iran, fought against U.S. Kurdish allies in Syria, and bought a Russian air defense system in 2018. The Turkish president continues to mouth conspiracy theories about the role of the United States in the 2016 coup. And although the United States still has an airbase at Incirlik, it is shifting resources to bases in Qatar and Romania. In 2018, Trump ordered sanctions against Turkey—to force the release of a U.S. pastor held in a Turkish jail—and the currency devalued by almost 20 percent in one day.[32] Whether it's a tiff or a divorce is a question that hinges on many things, including the trajectory of Turkish domestic policies. Turkey and the United States are still allies with shared security interests and economic relations. Turkey is the fifth-largest U.S. export market. As it pivots away from its role as an important anchor of the Western Alliance in the Middle East, Turkey is taking more independent decisions, aligning more with Russia in regional geopolitical issues and emerging as one of the more distinctive geopolitical forces in the region involved in Syria, Libya, and the dispute between Armenia and Azerbaijan. Turkey's aim of becoming a regional energy hub involves contentious maritime claims and involvement in the energy geopolitics in Eurasia and the Mediterranean.[33]

Egypt

Egypt is the largest Arab country in population, with eighty-nine million people. One in three Arabs in the world are Egyptian. It was one of the first independent Arab countries when in 1922 it broke away from British control after centuries of Ottoman rule and became a center for pan-Arabism, both secular and religious.

Egypt is a key ally of the United States. When it signed a peace deal in 1979, it was the first Arab state to officially recognize the state of Israel. Egypt is also involved in the fight against Muslim fundamentalism and is fighting a long campaign against an insurgency in the Sinai region. It remains such an important U.S. ally in the fight against Islamic terrorism and as an anchor of Arab support for Israel that the United States has supported a series of authoritarian and military-backed regimes. Even after the Egyptian military grabbed power in a coup d'état in 2013, the United States soon rewarded them with $3 billion in military aid.

The military plays an outsized role in the political and economic life of the country. It has the twelfth-largest military in the world. The army has intervened regularly in political affairs: in 2013 it overthrew the elected although increasingly unpopular leader Muhammed Morsi, and installed an army general as leader. In the resultant social conflict two thousand to three thousand were killed and there are now more than forty-two thousand political prisoners. The army-backed government directly and indirectly owns 50 percent of the economy and the officer class forms an important economic and political elite.

Egypt's leadership role in the Arab world is waning. Many other countries in the region see it as too subservient to the United States and Israel. Its economic power has diminished due to a crumbling, inefficient, and deeply corrupt economy. Even its relationship with the United States has weakened. The United States did not support the ailing President Mubarak when he faced popular uprisings during the Arab Spring. In the subsequent election, Mohammed Morsi, who had strong links to the Muslim Brotherhood, came to power—only briefly. He was overthrown by the military coup led by General Abdel Fattah el-Sisi, who is the current president of Egypt and whose rule is marked by continuing corruption and an authoritarian crackdown on dissent. However, the United States still provides military and economic aid to the country. Compared to the pan-Arabism of Nasser and to the savvy geopolitical strategy of Sadat, the current leadership in Egypt seems enmeshed in domestic turmoil and economic decline.[34]

Israel

In the nineteenth century, the Zionist project was to establish a Jewish homeland. Palestine, then part of the Ottoman Empire, was only one of the possible areas considered. At the time, more than half a million Arabs, Bedouins, and Druze lived in the region. At the end of World War I, as part of the Anglo-French carve-up, Palestine came under British control. In the famous Balfour Declaration of 1917, Lord Balfour wrote in a letter to Lord Rothschild, "His Majesty's Government views with favor the establishment in Palestine of a national home for the Jewish people . . . it being clearly understood that nothing shall be done which may prejudice the civil and religious rights of existing non-Jewish communities in Palestine."[35]

Some Zionists, such as Theodor Herzl (1860–1904), imagined a Jewish homeland that was not exclusively Jewish.[36] Other Zionists, such as the German-born Arthur Ruppin (1876–1943), believed that the control of land, especially in concentrated blocks, was important for defense and to provide the basis for a Jewish state. He bought land on the coastal plains from absentee Arab landlords. Arab nationalism grew as the Arab peasants were displaced. There were Arab-Jewish confrontations that by 1947–1948 erupted into a full-scale civil war. The day after the state of Israel was founded, on May 14, 1948, the armies of Egypt, Jordan, Iraq, Syria, and Lebanon invaded. The Israeli Defense Forces (IDF) successfully repelled the attacks. In July of that same year the Arab town of Lydda was forcibly emptied of Arabs. The Palestinians refer to their displacement by Israeli forces as "Nakba," the Arabic word for "catastrophe."

Israel remained under constant threat. In 1967, the Egyptian army entered the Sinai, and, in a preemptive strike, Israel destroyed the air forces of four Arab states and within six days, captured the Sinai, East Jerusalem, the West Bank, and the Golan Heights. Israel now had "occupied" territory. The Israeli cabinet initially thought it could trade this land for peace. The trade never took place, and the land was opened for settlement, an especially attractive proposition for ultra-orthodox Jewish settlers who flooded in after 1967, especially from the United States, and who saw the Jewish claim to the territory as sanctioned and approved by their God. The large number of settlers' political parties and organizations plays a major role in domestic Israeli politics.

The Israeli victory had a number of consequences. It revealed Israel as a major power in the region. The stunning military victory also attracted U.S. interest, which now saw a strong ally in the region. U.S. support was important at the founding of the state. When President Harry Truman recognized the provisional Jewish authority as the legitimate government, he gave international legitimacy to the state's founding. But U.S. support was not total. In 1956, President Eisenhower did not support the Anglo-French Israeli invasion of Egypt and worked to get the invading troops removed. After 1967, however, U.S. support of Israel became almost total and unconditional. As international opinion shifted to a more critical attitude toward Israel occupation and military tactics, the United States remained a stalwart supporter. Even as politics in Israel became more influenced by Jewish fundamentalists and Zionist zealots, the United States remained a supporter and did little to halt the settlements in the occupied land.

Israel is always in the top five countries that receive U.S. aid. Some have argued that U.S. support needs to be reconsidered. The political scientists John Mearsheimer and Stephen Walt argue that unwavering support for Israel undermines U.S. foreign policy interests. The democratic nature of Israel does not impress these two commentators, who argue that the two countries have disparate interest in the region. Their argument, from a policy realism position, rather than the anti-Semitism their critics often charge them with, makes the point that Israel is important but no more important than other allies and certainly not worth the high collateral costs.[37]

For decades, the U.S. support for Israel enjoyed bipartisan approval. In the earlier years, Democrats were often more pro-Israel. American Jews were long a bedrock of Democratic support. The debate has shifted, especially under the Israeli leadership of Benjamin Netanyahu, who was prime minister from 1996 to 1999 and from 2009 to the time of writing in 2021. He has courted Evangelical and Republican support, even entering directly into U.S. presidential politics in his criticism of President Obama and his explicit support for President Trump. He has politicized what was once almost the only non-partisan issue in U.S. foreign policy. Then there is the mounting criticisms of Israeli occupation and treatment of Palestinians, though more muted in the United States compared to much of the rest of the world and especially compared to liberal newspapers in Israel such as *Haaretz*. Yet even within the Jewish community in the United States, there are now more dissenting views. The power of the pro-Israel, influential, and bellicose American Israel Public Affairs Committee is now only partly offset by organizations such as J Street, founded in 2007 as a pro-Israel, pro-peace liberal advocacy group that mentions Palestinian civil rights.[38]

Israel is now the recognized homeland for Jews. In 1897, only fifty thousand Jews lived in Palestine, and they accounted for less than 1 percent of 0.4 percent of world Jewry. By 1950, it was 10.6 percent and now with six million Jews in

Israel, it is 45 percent. By 2050, the majority of all Jews in the world will live in Israel. Israel is a Jewish homeland that has a substantial non-Jewish minority estimated at around two million people, or almost one-fifth of the population.

Israel is an exception. A Jewish state surrounded by Arabs, a democracy in a region that lacks it. Exceptionalism takes other forms. It increasingly sees itself as under threat yet is one of the largest military powers in the region with a nuclear capability. It emerged from the ashes of the Holocaust but is increasingly seen around the world as an occupying force, the last of the openly colonial powers. And as many nation-states reimagine themselves as multicultural and multiethnic, Israel defines itself ever more narrowly as an explicitly Jewish state, albeit with a significant non-Jewish minority. Israel sees itself as a beleaguered nation but has a powerful military and from 1967 up until now, with the unqualified and uncritical support of the global superpower.

To its supporters, Israel is one of the few states that is threatened with annihilation. To others it is also one of the few democratic states that is occupying territory to which it has no internationally recognized mandate. The Israeli author Ari Shavit asserts that those on the left address occupation and ignore intimidation while those on the right address intimidation and dismiss occupation. "Only a third approach," he argues, "that internalizes both intimidation and occupation can be realistic and moral and get the Israel story right."[39]

The geopolitics remains vexing. First, there is the issue of occupation. Israel has control over the West Bank, East Jerusalem, and the Golan Heights. These areas, especially East Jerusalem and the West Bank, contain considerable Arab populations. There are more than 2.5 million Arabs in the West Bank. Since 1967, there have been substantial Jewish settlements. There are now 390,000 Jewish settlers in the West Bank, including several illegal settlements. There is considerable friction between the two communities. Israel plans a twenty-five-foot, four-hundred-mile wall that follows the 1949 armistice line along the West Bank. Proponents of the wall see it as defense against terrorist attacks, while critics point to the dismemberment of the territory of a future Palestine. The occupation raises moral issues for a democratic country committed to personal freedoms.[40]

Second, there is the issue of governing the occupied territories and the "policing" of Palestinian territory, especially Gaza. The Gaza strip is a narrow coastal strip of land between Israel and Egypt under Palestinian authority, as is the West Bank, and houses 1.7 million people, almost all Muslims. There are now no Jewish settlers. Israel launched an attack against the region in order to remove Hamas. In 2014, after rockets were launched against Israel from Gaza, the IDF launched a major offensive, shelling the area. More than ten thousand homes were damaged or destroyed; 1,500 were killed, almost 70 percent of them innocent civilians. Israel lost sixty-five soldiers. More than one hundred thousand residents in Gaza were still displaced even a full year after the invasion. Many locals refer to Gaza as an "open-air prison," locked up between Israel and Egypt.

The West Bank is nominally under the authority of the Palestine Authority, but Israel controls the water and the finances as well as policing security zones in the territory in order to secure the safety of settlers. The occupation also involves a disparity in the treatment of Israelis and Palestinians.[41] There is a vigorous debate within Israel between settlers and their political representatives and more secular Jews worried about the costs—military and moral—of occupation.

The Middle East has two things that make it important to the United States: Israel and Arab allies. Juggling these competing interests is neither easy nor simple. A number of countries in the region—all Muslim-dominated countries—such as the Gulf States, Saudi Arabia, and Iraq have rich and easily accessible oil reserves that are vital to the smooth functioning of the global carbon-based economy. Protecting Israel and securing oil supply makes for a difficult dance as the United States secures Israel's defense yet also does not want to antagonize the oil states. One way out of the dilemma was the promotion of a two-state solution that guaranteed Israel's right to exist and a promised state for the Palestinians.[42]

It was a redo of much older plans. In 1937, the British proposed a division of Palestine with an Arab state, a Jewish state, and British control of Jerusalem.[43] The Jews accepted the plan, but the Arabs refused. A similar UN partition plan in 1947 also was agreed to by the Jews but rejected by the Arabs. The more recent variant of the idea emerged over the course of various meetings, conferences, and summits. In the Oslo accord, a two-state solution was signed between Israel and the Palestinian Liberation Organization in 1993 (Oslo I) and 1995 (Oslo II). Of course, the devil was always in the detail. Would displaced Palestinians have the right to return? Would the borders be the pre-1967, original borders of Israel? The process floundered as most Arab nations lost interest in the plight of the Palestinians and Israeli settlement in occupied territories accelerated and undermined the viability of future Palestinian state. In the West Bank 134 approved settlements and 100 unofficial settlements now house 400,000 Israeli citizens among 2.6 million Palestinians. The protection of these settlements by the IDF renders moot a Palestinian viable state. It was rendered even more moot when the United States announced in 2019 that Jewish settlements did not violate international law. The Netanyahu government believed a Palestinian state would compromise these settlements, and in 2019–2020 proposed an annexation of 30 percent of the territory of the West Bank to extend Israel sovereignty over most of these settlements. Under this scheme—hastily pursued in order to ensure the Trump administration was still in power—an enlarged Jewish state will emerge but not a Palestinian one. The annexation plan was put on hold. In 2020 the UAE signed a peace agreement with Israel, only the third Arab state to recognize Israel, if the annexation was halted.

The promotion of a "two-state solution" allowed the United States to protect Israel and appease Saudi Arabia without confronting the emerging and mounting problem of Israeli settlements in occupied territory. The U.S. support for Israel provides an easy and often-used rallying call for anti-U.S. sentiment in the region. The collaborative elites in the oil-producing countries are rarely either progressive or democratic, so U.S. support alienates many in the Arab world. It was not always thus. When President Kennedy was assassinated in 1963, there were scenes of genuine mass mourning in cities across the Arab world. But as the United States became an uncritical supporter of both Israel and Arab authoritarian elites, it also was spectacularly successful in creating an anti-U.S. attitude in populations across the Arab world. At its very worst, then, its unwavering support for Israel, even as illegal settlements multiplied, and its enduring alliance with authoritarian collaborative elites in the Arab world, even as they became even more authoritarian, make the United States an object of contempt for jihadists in the Middle East.[44]

THE LURE OF THE CALIPHATE

The Caliphate, a transnational authority guided by Islamic principles, is a long-held belief of Islamic fundamentalists. In reality, of course, the original caliphates were often more multicultural and progressive societies—certainly in comparison to most of their then state contemporaries in Europe—but the current ideas are based not on historical reality but on the creation of a Caliphate creatively reimagined as a response to modernity.

The imperial history of subjugation by foreign powers, and the long, relative economic decline of the Muslim world in the Middle East, fuels discontent. The economic record is dismal especially compared to rapid growth in East Asia. Some of the discontent has a specifically anti-modern, anti-globalization, anti-secular cast and is distinctly anti-United States. It has long roots. The Egyptian Sayyid Qutb (1906–1966), for example, saw the West as a source of immorality and materialism. A commitment to Islam and Sharia law, he argued, was the only way to pull Middle East countries from the morass. Local elites and the United States were barriers to the full realization of an Islamic utopia. Qutb was one of the leaders of the Muslim Brotherhood. His ideas persisted down through the years, given sustenance by continued economic stagnation and the presence of corrupt regimes seemingly unable to promote either the political or economic emancipation of their citizenry. The ideas also achieved popular resonance because many of the more locally based organizations provided charity and relief that poor and unresponsive states did not provide. The good works of pious charities often filled the huge social welfare gap left by uncaring states. Criticisms of modernity, materialism, and secularism were directed primarily against the United States because of its support for Israel and for the collaborative elites in the region.

Al Qaeda

Al Qaeda was formed sometime around 1988. It was linked ideologically to the Muslim Brotherhood, shaped in the experience of Afghanistan, and funded by Saudi money. Leading lights included Osama bin Laden, Ayman Zawahiri, and Khalid Sheikh Mohammed. Bin Laden was a member of a prominent and rich Saudi family, who spent some time in Afghanistan and funneled money to the insurgents fighting the Soviets. Zawahiri was an Egyptian who joined the Muslim Brotherhood when he was only fourteen. During the 1980s he also spent time in Afghanistan, where he met bin Laden. Khalid Sheik Mohammed was born in Kuwait to parents from Pakistan. All three men spent time in Afghanistan. They were heartened by the success against the Soviets and realized that acts of terrorism were effective. Their overall aim was to overthrow the collaborative elites in the Middle East countries, destroy the power of the United States, and inaugurate a medieval caliphate based on fundamentalist readings of the Quran. Zawahiri was the ideologue; bin Laden, the money; and Khalid Sheik Mohammed the operational guy.

In 1993, they organized for a truck bomb to detonate below the North Tower of the World Trade Center. The plan, worked out by Khalid Sheik Mohammed, was to topple the tower so that it crashed into the South Tower, with a combined fatality of 250,000. The failed attempt suggested incompetence; it was easily dismissed by the authorities and provoked no major response. Then there was the bombing of the Khobar Towers residential complex, housing U.S. service personnel, in Saudi Arabia on June 25, 1996. Twenty-three U.S. troops died in the truck bomb attack. The U.S. government blamed the attack on Hezbollah and the Iranians, although it is likely that al Qaeda was involved. On August 7, 1998, almost simultaneously, truck bombs exploded outside U.S. embassies in Nairobi and Dar es Salaam. It was the eighth anniversary of U.S. troops entering Saudi Arabia in Desert Storm. Two hundred twenty-nine people were killed and four thousand were wounded; the vast majority were local people, and twelve Americans were killed. On October 12, 2000, while in harbor in Aden in Yemen, the navy destroyer USS *Cole* was attacked by a suicide bomber. A small boat with more than one thousand pounds of explosives sailed straight into the hull of the ship. Seventeen sailors were killed and thirty-nine were injured. There were also failed attacks planned for the new millennium in 2000. Four sites in Jordan, visited by Israeli and U.S. tourists; the Los Angeles Airport; and the USS *The Sullivans* were all targeted. The plots were foiled, failed, or aborted.

A spectacular terrorist attack had been on al Qaeda's agenda for some time. Khalid Sheik Mohammed along with Ramzi Yousef hatched a plan to assassinate the pope in January 1995 during his visit to the Philippines and then to explode eleven airplanes simultaneously in mid-flight to various destinations in Asia to the United States. Almost four thousand people would have been killed in fiery mid-air explosions above the Pacific Ocean. After this plot was thwarted, a new plan was called for. An initial plan for one plane to crash into the headquarters of the CIA was dismissed by bin Laden as having too little impact. Khalid Sheik Mohammed came back with an elaborate plan to hijack ten planes in the United States and crash nine of them across the country. The tenth one would land, and Khalid Sheik Mohammed would step off and make a speech. When he "bought" the U.S. journalist Daniel Pearl in Karachi, rather than barter him for money or personnel swaps, he videotaped his beheading. His particular eye for the spectacular was more psychopathic than religious.

Terrorism was not so much a political philosophy as channeled anger. The objectives were not to evoke change through building a mass movement or forming resistance. Rather, the agenda was to undertake acts of spectacular terrorism to undermine political stability and to provoke confused reaction, particularly in cities, which were ideal sites for the spectacularization of terror. Terrorists aspired to high-profile acts for attention and to incite outrage and hostility. It was a bloody nihilism parading as Islamic redemption.

Al Qaeda is now a worldwide terror network—a global franchise with local affiliates: al Qaeda in Iraq, al Qaeda in the Islamic Maghreb, al Qaeda in the Arabian Peninsula, and al Shabaab in Somalia. They have varying degrees of impact and slightly different goals, some more local than the overthrow of the Great Satan. U.S. drone strikes and counterterrorism efforts have not eliminated the network entirely but have substantially weakened it. The ability to pull off spectacular attacks, that by necessity involve more easily tracked activities and transactions across national borders and cyberspace, is much degraded because of improved surveillance. Al Qaeda's franchise model allows a fading organization the illusion of vitality and relevance by being connected to ongoing efforts; it also allows local groups to claim legitimacy because of their link with a global network and grand strategies.

The Rise and Fall of ISIS

ISIS (Islamic State of Iraq), also known as Daesh, is a Sunni Muslim movement that emerged in post-invasion Iraq from Sunni terrorist groups affiliated with al Qaeda. It became a military force when it linked up with former Baathist military personnel. By 2013, it was a terrorist group motivated by Sunni Islamic fundamentalism—including violence against Shia Muslims and Christians—with a military staffed by former Iraq army personnel. ISIS became self-funded by capturing oil depots, taxing residents and businesses under its control, and through extortion and smuggling. In the failed states of Syria, undergoing civil war, and of Iraq, beset by religious tensions, ISIS flourished. By 2014, it had captured territory across Iraq and Syria. Map 8.5 depicts ISIS territorial control at its greatest extent in 2015. Over the subsequent years, troops from Iraq and Syria, Kurdish and Iranian forces, as well as Russian and Allied plane strikes combined to destroy the territorial hold of ISIS and its claim to a caliphate.[45]

ISIS (and al Qaeda) gains some measure of support from the alienated and bored Muslim youth who feel marginalized in Europe, North America, or Australia. Of its thirty-one thousand fighters in Iraq and Syria, almost twelve thousand are foreign nationals from eighty-one countries. Fundamentalism appeals to a youthful population without jobs, hope, or any sense of belonging. ISIS also employs sophisticated marketing, using social messaging and the internet. Its images of pornographic violence also attract the unglued, the unhinged, and the violent.[46]

ISIS has extended its reach beyond Syria and Iraq through the declaration of separate provinces in the Afghanistan-Pakistan border region, Libya, Egypt, Yemen, Saudi Arabia, Russia (North Caucasus), and Nigeria. In some cases, this involves encroaching on al Qaeda, as in the Afghanistan-Pakistan border area, Russia, and Yemen. Elsewhere, it involves the incorporation of existing insurgencies such as Boko Haram in West Africa and al Shabaab in East Africa.

THE ARAB SPRING

The twenty-six-year-old fruit and vegetable seller had had enough. On December 17, 2010, Mohamed Bouazizi did not have a permit to sell his produce in the market. When he refused to hand over his goods to police, he was slapped by a policewoman. Humiliated and exhausted, he walked to a government building

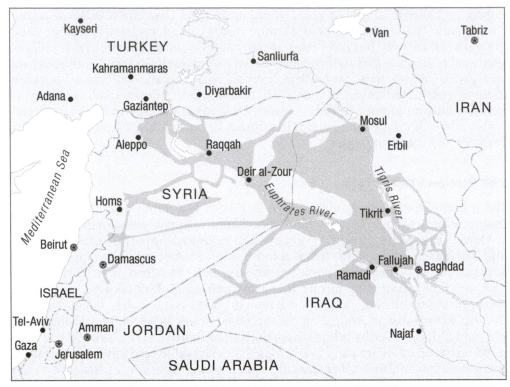

Map 8.5. ISIS-controlled territory, 2015 (Wikimedia / Sémhur, Flappiefh)

in Sidi Bouzid and set himself on fire. Protests in the town erupted the following day. They were captured on cellphones and quickly became a sensation across the Arab World. Bouazizi died of his burns on January 4, 2011. His death sparked the Arab Spring. Inside weeks, protests had sprung up all over the region, as people took to the streets to protest against rising prices, corrupt governments, and lack of economic opportunities. They also had had enough. The protests grew and led to the overthrow of regimes that had been in power for decades. On January 14, the government in Tunisia was overthrown. On January 26, protests centered on Tahir Square erupted in Cairo. By February 11, Mubarak stepped down as president after being in power since 1981 and just as he was poised to hand over the reins of power to one of his sons. In Yemen, anti-government protests began on February 15 against the rule of President Saleh and by August 23 the government was overthrown. In Libya, the forty-two-year rule of Muammar Gaddafi came to an end. Protests also took place in Algeria, Bahrain, Iraq, Jordan, Kuwait, Morocco, and Oman.

The Demographic Background

There are many ways to explain the Arab Spring. Let's look at just one of the factors, the demographic background.[47] Most of the countries are experiencing a *youth bulge*. This is when there is a rapid increase in the number of people, especially of those aged between fifteen and twenty-nine. This occurs after a rapid reduction in child mortality occurs and before a rapid falloff in fertility. When this bulge constitutes more than 20 percent of the population, it has been linked to an increase in political instability and the possibility of increased political violence. Table 8.1 shows for the percentage of the population aged under thirty for a range of countries in the Middle East and for the United States and UK as a comparison. There are many more young people in the Arab World and, for those of working age, finding employment is extremely difficult. Youth unemployment is roughly double that for those aged forty and above.

Mohamed Bouazizi lived with his mother and six siblings. His informal job in the market was the main source of income for the large family. In 2010, fully 51 percent of the population of Tunisia was under thirty. For those aged fifteen to twenty-four, the unemployment rate was 30.7 percent, double the rate for older adults.[48] Across the Middle East and North Africa, the fifteen–twenty-nine age cohort, which constitutes 21 percent of the total population and 34 percent of the working-age population, has a 26 percent unemployment rate.

Table 8.1.   The Demographic Bulge

Country	Under Thirty as Percentage of Total Population
Yemen	39.2
Palestinian Territories	38.2
Iraq	37.0
Libya	33.7
Egypt	33.6
Syria	33.5
United States	18.5
UK	17.6

Neither the private market nor the government in much of the Middle East is able to provide jobs for this bulging youth cohort. A number of studies have confirmed the connections between the youth bulge and political unrest.[49] Economic stagnation plays an important role in turning the bulge into a tinderbox of unmet expectations, frustrations, and anger. Younger people more easily take to the streets. They have less to lose. They also have the energy as well as the time and the motivation to protest. Many of them have access to cellphones and computers that allow them to see what is happening elsewhere and to organize street protests. The internet heightened the demonstration effect. Young people responded in sympathy to the images of protest and the messages of revolt. It is not simply the large number of youths in the Middle East that flamed the Arab Spring, but also that a large, organized, and digitally connected cohort responded to a very limited range of opportunity for active and meaningful participation in economic and political life.

The Arab Spring protests arose from a complex range of interlinked factors, including inflation, corruption, lack of freedom, greater use of cell phones, and, in some countries, higher levels of education.[50] It was not just the level of unemployed youth, but the large number of unemployed youth who had some education and access to the internet. The Arab Spring had many causes, but a disenfranchised youth bulge was certainly a significant factor.

The Consequences

The Arab Spring quickly swept through the Middle East. A decade on from the momentous events, we have an opportunity to see some of the longer-term consequences.[51] Let's consider them from best to worst. Tunisia, where the initial spark occurred, made one of the more successful transitions to democracy. There are still recurring issues of unemployment and corruption. Secularists worry about the rise of very conservative Islamists, but overall, there really was a "spring" after a decades-long "winter" of corrupt and sclerotic governance. Elsewhere, many existing rulers weathered the storm—in some cases, with some reform. In Morocco, for example, a new constitution was introduced with more parliamentary power, although final power still resides in the monarchy. In Algeria, the government was weakened and survived until street protests in 2019 finally led to the fall of the octogenarian president. Many of the kingdoms and sheikdoms survived without too much reform, including Bahrain, Jordan, and Kuwait. The Saudi military was employed to crack down on the mainly Shia protestors in Bahrain.

The Arab Spring sent shock waves through the existing power structures. Some reformed, some survived, and some cracked. In Egypt, the end of Mubarak was followed by the election of Morsi before a military coup and the installation of an authoritarian government. Some broke down completely. Libya, Yemen, and Syria all experienced the disintegration of the state and bloody civil wars.

Libya

The mercurial Colonel Gaddafi ruled the oil-rich country of Libya for forty-two years. In the 2011 Arab Spring, violent protest occurred in the east of the country. Gaddafi's main power was in the west, centered in Tripoli, and so it was not surprising when protest broke out in the east where residents of Benghazi and Tobruk had long chafed at the rule from Tripoli. Armed rebels with the support of a NATO bombing campaign overthrew Gaddafi. On October 20 he was dragged from the drainpipe where he was hiding, tortured, and killed.

There was anarchy in the aftermath of the collapse of the Gaddafi regime. A variety of armed groups ruled the streets and normal governance evaporated. The country descended into anarchy. The Islamic State held the city of Sirte until 2017 but is now restricted to the desert interior. It would take an entire book to enumerate the various interests of the different actors. Put simply, two main competing centers emerged, a Government of National Unity (GNA) under Fayez al-Sarraj based in Tripoli and a government in Tobruk with Khalifa Haftar as the military leader of the Libyan National Army. A full-scale civil war became internationalized as Turkey, Qatar, and Italy aided GNA, which was officially recognized by the UN and most Western countries (but not France). Russia, Egypt, UAE, and Saudi Arabia backed the Tripoli regime, with France and Jordan providing more moral than military support. In 2019 Haftar led an attack on Tripoli. The Russians supplied military jets to Haftar's forces, and the UAE backed Haftar's attack with 900 air strikes on Tripoli. In response, Turkey deployed drones and carried out 250 strikes against Haftar's forces as they moved on Tripoli. By 2020, the attack was defeated and Haftar's former allies started to look around for another local leader for the eastern forces.

The fatalities in Libya during the Arab Spring are estimated at between 2,500 and 25,000. Since then, almost a quarter of a million are now internally displaced and 1.3 million are in need of aid. The collapse of a recognizable government and resulting anarchy created the ungoverned space for Libya to become a transit point for migrants from sub-Saharan Africa and the Horn of Africa, hoping to find a route across the Mediterranean to Italy and to Greece and entry into the EU. It is estimated that almost 650,000 desperate people are in Libya waiting to escape to Europe.[52]

By 2020, the country was fractured into three distinct regions with ever-changing boundaries and levels of control. Military forces under the leadership of Haftar control all of the east and center and have waged a campaign to capture Tripoli, while the GNA under Fayez al-Sarraj controls and defends the area around Tripoli. Local forces, including Islamic State, operate in the southern border area.

Yemen

In 2011 in Yemen, a state that only came into being in 1990 with the federation of North and South Yemen, street protests forced the resignation of President Saleh. Houthis, a Shia sect in the north, gained control over much of the north and west, eventually capturing the capital city of Sanaa as the government of Saleh's successor, President Hadid, disintegrated. It was only the latest act of a long-running Houthi insurgency since 2004.[53] After the Houthis took control of Sanaa in 2015, a Saudi-UAE coalition, with the support of the United States, entered the conflict. The U.S.-Saudi-UAE coalition saw the Houthis as a proxy for Iran. The Saudi military, with prompting from the crown prince, MBS, pursued a deadly policy of indiscriminate bombing and food blockades. The city of Sanaa has been inhabited for more than two thousand years. It is an important urban site for the development of early Islam. More than six thousand houses exist from before the eleventh century. There are more than 103 mosques. Saana, a wonderful example of architectural homogeneity, the importance of religious architecture, and the organic nature of continuous urbanization, was shelled by jet fighters from Saudi Arabia and UAE, with logistical support from the United States.

There are multiple actors and different actors. Even the Saudi-UAE coalition fractured for a short period, when the UAE supported a southern regional breakaway group's bid to capture control of Aden. The UAE seek to counter what they see as the too-close links between the government of President Hadid and the Muslim Brotherhood. They also want to have access to the strategic port of Aden. In the east and throughout the country, al Qaeda and Islamic State are

active. Al Qaeda in the Arabian Peninsula is considered one of the most dangerous local affiliates of al Qaeda.

The tragic result is a humanitarian disaster. The civil war, fracturing into
splintered and rival groups, some aided by outside forces wreaking havoc with
indiscriminate bombing and the halting of food supplies, stressed an already
vulnerable people and drought-ridden land. In a country of twenty-four million,
between sixteen million and twenty million Yemenis suffer from hunger; ten
million are on the verge of starvation. More than 3.6 million have been displaced.
It is estimated that almost a quarter of a million Yemenis have died from the
fighting, starvation, and illness.[54]

GEOPOLITICAL HOTSPOT: THE TRAGEDY OF SYRIA

In 1916, Britain and France divided up the Middle East into separate spheres of
influence. After the end of World War I, Britain gained control of the territory
now consisting of Iraq, Jordan, and Palestine while France took Syria and Lebanon. Syria was a patchwork state carved out by the French. Although 90 percent
Arab, it contains various religious groups, including Sunni (70 percent), Shia (15
percent), and Christian (10 percent). It also has significant numbers of Druze
(seven hundred thousand) and Kurds (two million). Druze is a secretive religion
that first emerged in the eleventh century with a belief system that combines
elements of different religions. The believers are tightly concentrated in a region
now bisected by Syria, Israel, and Lebanon. Syria encompasses a distinct social
geography.

The Christian, Druze, and Shia communities are found along the mountain
and valley region of the coastline; the Kurds inhabit the northern area close to
Turkey; and the Sunnis dominate the interior and the desert region bordering
Iraq.

The French chose one particular Shia sect, the Alawites, as their partners to
rule the territory. The Alawites number between two and three million, roughly
15 percent of the total population. Under the French mandate, Alawites were allowed to enter the military and were preferred for the more lucrative military and
government jobs. Consequently, the Alawites became the military and political
elites when Syria achieved independence from France in 1946. Since 1970, the
country has been ruled by the Assad family who are Alawites.

The tragedy of Syria is that the threadbare national coherence was torn
apart by interfaith differences and external forces.[55] The country was struggling
before the Arab Spring. Syria does not have the rich oil and gas reserves of the
sheikdoms. There was mounting discontent leading up to the Arab Spring. Lack
of true democracy and deteriorating economic conditions had alienated much of
the people from the government. From 2007 to 2010, drought conditions pushed
people from the countryside into the cities, exacerbating poverty and unrest.
Preferential treatment for Alawites stoked communal resentments. In early
2011, as the Arab Spring swept across North Africa and the Middle East, there
were peaceful protests in the southern city of Deera as people took to the streets
in their thousands. Fifteen young boys were rounded up and tortured for writing

anti-government graffiti on a wall. One of them died. More protests ensued and the Assad regime responded by killing hundreds and imprisoning thousands. In July 2011 defectors from the Syrian Army formed the Free Syrian Army to overthrow the government. By 2012 the country slid into a bloody civil war. "Wars" is a more accurate term. Rather than one war there was a series of wars as different groups fought to advance their interests.[56]

The Syrian army stayed loyal to Assad, as did most of the Alawites, fearful of what would happen to them if Sunnis took over and they lost their privileged position. The Syrian armed forces fought a vicious campaign against rebel strongholds, bombing civilian sites indiscriminately. In the northeast, Kurdish forces now saw a chance to break away from the Syrian state. In the east, where the fields turn into desert, the Sunni-dominated ISIS became a more powerful force in the chaos and power vacuum, and for a brief period, created a caliphate in the territories of Syria and Iraq (see map 8.5).

External forces also piled in. The United States pursued an aerial bombing campaign to dislodge ISIS and to support Syrian Democratic Forces, an alliance of Kurdish and Arab militias. Until 2018, when they abandoned them, the United States sent almost two thousand troops to support the Kurdish forces.[57] Eager to support their ally Assad, the Russians entered the war in 2015. They also undertook bombing campaigns against ISIS and anti-Assad rebels. Iran and its proxy Hezbollah also supported Assad to secure a Shia-friendly state. Saudi Arabia and Turkey supported Sunni-led, anti-Assad forces. Turkey sent troops and planes to fight against ISIS and Kurdish groups near its border. Even Israel became involved carrying out air raids against Hezbollah and pro-Assad forces.

This was not a typical civil war with pro- and anti-government forces, but multiple forces with multiple agendas in multiple alliances, fighting multiple enemies. By 2015, the country had disintegrated with at least one thousand different militia and insurgency groups, warlords, and criminal gangs. A snapshot: Hezbollah supported Assad. In the war against ISIS it forged alliances with Shiite and Christian villages in Syria against the Sunni rebel forces. In 2015 ISIS attacked thirty-five of the farming villages of Assyrian Christians in the Khabur Valley region, desecrating churches and kidnapping women and children.

Syria's tragedy was that it became the deadly setting for wider conflicts: Saudi Arabia/Iran, Turkey/Kurds, Sunni/Shia, U.S./Russia and all these intersecting conflicts and agendas made a settlement harder to come by and prolonged the agony for the Syrian people. The result was human carnage and a humanitarian tragedy of biblical proportions. More than a quarter million people were killed in the fighting, one million injured, and up to twelve million—more than half of the total population of the country—displaced as they sought to escape from the violence and retribution. It was the worst of outcomes for an Arab Spring that began with such hope and promise in 2011–2012.

SUGGESTED READINGS

Akbarzadeh, S., & Baxter, K. (2018). *Middle East politics and international relations: Crisis zone*. London: Routledge.

Clark, J. H. (2017). Feminist geopolitics and the Middle East: Refuge, belief, and peace. *Geography Compass, 11*(2), e12304.

Del Sarto, R. A. (2017). Contentious borders in the Middle East and North Africa: Context and concepts. *International Affairs, 93,* 767–87.

Evered, K. T. (2017). Beyond Mahan and Mackinder: Situating geography and critical geopolitics in Middle East studies. *International Journal of Middle East Studies, 49,* 335.

Feldman, N. (2020). *The Arab Winter.* Princeton: Princeton University Press.

Finkel, C. (2005). *Osman's dream: The story of the Ottoman Empire, 1300–1923.* London: John Murray.

Hubbard, B. (2020). *MBS: The rise of a Saudi prince.* New York: Random House.

Kausch, K. (ed.). (2015). *Geopolitics and democracy in the Middle East.* Madrid: Fride.

Koch, N. (2017). Geopower and geopolitics in, of, and for the Middle East. *International Journal of Middle East Studies, 49,* 315–18.

Mahmood, S. (2012). Religious freedom, the minority question, and geopolitics in the Middle East. *Comparative Studies in Society and History, 54*: 418–46.

Morton, M. Q. (2017). *Empires and anarchies: A history of oil in the Middle East.* London: Reaktion.

Salloukh, B. F. (2013). The Arab uprisings and the geopolitics of the Middle East. *International Spectator, 48,* 32–46.

Seliktar, O. (2020). Iran's geopolitics and revolutionary export: The promises and limits of proxy empire. *Orbis, 65,* 152–71.

Spyer, J. (2019). Syria's civil war is now 3 civil wars. *Foreign Policy.* https://foreignpolicy.com/2019/03/18/syrias-civil-war-is-now-3-civil-wars/.

Yeşiltaş, M., and Kardaş, T. (eds.). (2018). *Non-state armed actors in the Middle East: geopolitics, ideology, and strategy.* Cham: Springer.

NOTES

1. Culcasi, K. (2010). Constructing and naturalizing the Middle East. *Geographical Review, 100,* 583–97, 583. See also Bonine, M. E., Amanat, A., & Gasper, M. E. (eds.). (2012). *Is there a Middle East? The evolution of a geopolitical concept.* Stanford: Stanford University Press.

2. Allen, L. (2005). *The Persian empire.* London: British Museum Press.

3. Daryaee, T. (2009). *Sasanian Persia: The rise and fall of an empire.* London: I. B. Taurus.

4. Dignas, B., & Winter, E. (2007). *Rome and Persia in late antiquity.* Cambridge: Cambridge University Press.

5. Bennison, A. (2009). *The Great Caliphs: The golden age of the Abbasid Empire.* New Haven: Yale University Press.

6. Kennedy, H. (2007). *The great Arab conquests: How they spread Islam and changed the world we live in.* Philadelphia: Da Capo.

7. Finkel, C. (2005). *Osman's dream: The story of the Ottoman Empire, 1300–1923.* London: John Murray.

8. Fromkin, D. (2009). *A peace to end all peace: The Fall of the Ottoman Empire and the creation of the modern Middle East.* New York: Holt; Quataert, D. (2005). *The Ottoman Empire 1700–1922.* Cambridge: Cambridge University Press.

9. Morton, M. Q. (2017). *Empires and anarchies: A history of oil in the Middle East.* London: Reaktion.

10. Kamrava, M., & Kamrava, M. (2013). *The modern Middle East: A political history since the First World War.* Berkeley: University of California Press.

11. Kamrava, M. (ed.). (2011). *The international politics of the Persian Gulf*. Syracuse: Syracuse University Press.

12. Hope, B., & Scheck, J. (2020). *Blood and oil: Mohammed bin Salman's ruthless quest for global power*. New York: Hachette; Hubbard, B. (2020). *MBS: The rise of a Saudi prince*. New York: Random House.

13. See https://web.archive.org/web/20210226180954/https://www.odni.gov/files/ODNI/documents/assessments/Assessment-Saudi-Gov-Role-in-JK-Death-20210226.pdf.

14. *The Battle of Algiers* (1966) was directed by Gillo Pontecorvo.

15. Lacoste, Y. (2011). The Sahara: Geopolitical perspectives and illusions. *Hérodote, 3*, 12–41.

16. Danielson, R. E. (2007). *Nasser and Pan-Arabism: Explaining Egypt's rise in power*. Monterey, CA: Naval Postgraduate School. https://apps.dtic.mil/dtic/tr/fulltext/u2/a470058.pdf.

17. Foliard, D. (2017). *Dislocating the Orient: British maps and the making of the Middle East, 1854–1921*. Chicago: University of Chicago Press.

18. Broich, J. (2019). Why there is no Kurdish nation. *The Conversation*. https://theconversation.com/why-there-is-no-kurdish-nation-126243.

19. Kinzer, S. (2008). *All the Shah's men: An American coup and the roots of Middle East terror*. Hoboken: John Wiley.

20. A vivid memoir poignantly describes some of the impacts on women: Nafisi, A. (2003). *Reading Lolita in Tehran: A memoir in books*. New York: Random House.

21. Seliktar, O. (2020). Iran's geopolitics and revolutionary export: The promises and limits of proxy empire. *Orbis, 65*, 152–71.

22. Kaya, S. (2009). The rise and decline of the Turkish "Deep State": The Ergenekon case. *Insight Turkey, 11*, 99–113. https://web.archive.org/web/20091123024450/http://www.derinsular.com/pdf/serdarkaya-insightturkey-fall2009.pdf.

23. Tharoor, S. (2020). A century-old treaty haunts the Mediterranean. *Washington Post*. https://www.washingtonpost.com/world/2020/08/10/treaty-sevres-erdogan-turkey/.

24. Lewy, G. (2005). *The Armenian massacres in Ottoman Turkey: A disputed genocide*. Salt Lake City: University of Utah Press.

25. Coru, A. (2020). Erdogan's micro-imperialism could prove disastrous for Turkey and its neighbors. *Armenia Mirror-Spectator*. https://mirrorspectator.com/2020/02/13/erdogans-micro-imperialism-could-prove-disastrous-for-turkey-and-its-neighbors/.

26. Gingeras, R. (2020). Blue homeland: The heated politics behind Turkey's maritime strategy. *War on The Rocks*. https://warontherocks.com/2020/06/blue-homeland-the-heated-politics-behind-turkeys-new-maritime-strategy/.

27. Fuller, G. (2019). *Turkey's new geopolitics: From the Balkans to western China*. London: Routledge.

28. International Crisis Group. (2020). *Turkey wades into Libya's troubled waters*. Report 257. https://www.crisisgroup.org/europe-central-asia/western-europemediterranean/turkey/257-turkey-wades-libyas-troubled-waters.

29. The New Humanitarian. (2020). A manufactured refugee crisis at the Greek-Turkish border. https://www.thenewhumanitarian.org/analysis/2020/03/04/refugees-greece-turkey-border.

30. Kirisci, K. (2018, February 14). The new geopolitics of Turkey, Syria, and the West. *Brookings*. https://www.brookings.edu/blog/order-from-chaos/2018/02/14/the-new-geopolitics-of-turkey-syria-and-the-west/.

31. Gordon. P. H., & Sloat, A. (2020). The dangerous unraveling of the U.S.-Turkey alliance. *Foreign Affairs*. https://www.foreignaffairs.com/articles/turkey/2020-01-10/dangerous-unraveling-U.S.-turkish-alliance.

32. Taylor, A. (2019). Five uncomfortable facts at the heart of the U.S.-Turkey relationship. *Washington Post.* https://www.washingtonpost.com/world/2019/10/15/uncomfortable-facts-heart-U.S.-turkey-relationship/.

33. Erşen, E., & Çelikpala, M. (2019). Turkey and the changing energy geopolitics of Eurasia. *Energy Policy, 128,* 584–92.

34. Partridge, D. (2018). Egypt's waning geopolitical position in the MENA region. *Inside Arabia.* https://insidearabia.com/egypts-waning-geopolitical-position-mena-region/.

35. Balfour, A. J. (1917). *The Balfour declaration.* London: British Foreign Office.

36. Avineri, S. (2013). *Herzl's vision: Theodor Herzl and the foundation of the Jewish State.* London: Weidenfeld and Nicolson.

37. Mearsheimer, J. J., & Walt, S. M. (2007). *The Israel lobby and U.S. foreign policy.* London: Macmillan.

38. Compare the organizations' respective websites, https://www.aipac.org and https://jstreet.org.

39. Shavit, A. (2013). *My promised land: The triumph and tragedy of Israel.* New York: Spiegel and Grau, xii.

40. Shafir, G. (2017). *A half century of occupation: Israel, Palestine and the world's most intractable conflict.* Berkeley and Los Angeles: University of California Press.

41. Booth, W., & Taha, S. (2017). A daily commute through Israel's checkpoints. *Washington Post.* https://www.washingtonpost.com/graphics/world/occupied/checkpoint/.

42. Teibel, A. (2020). Two-state solution. *Washington Post.* https://www.washingtonpost.com/business/two-state-solution/2020/01/27/e6bc438e-4135-11ea-99c7-1dfd4241a2fe_story.html.

43. Sinanoglou, P. (2020). *Partitioning Palestine: British policymaking at the end of empire.* Chicago: University of Chicago Press.

44. As one historian noted, "it will not be self-evident to future generations of Americans why the imperial might and international reputation of the United States are so closely aligned with one small, controversial Mediterranean client state." Judt, T. (2006, April 19). A lobby, not a conspiracy. *New York Times,* A21.

45. Cockburn, P. (2015). *The rise of Islamic State.* London: Verso.

46. Weiss, M., & Hassan, H. (2016). *ISIS: Inside the army of terror.* New York: Simon and Schuster.

47. Cole, J. (2014). *The new Arabs: How the millennial generation is changing the Middle East.* New York: Simon and Schuster.

48. World Bank. (2013). *Breaking the barriers to youth.* Washington, DC: World Bank. https://www.worldbank.org/content/dam/Worldbank/document/MNA/tunisia/breaking_the_barriers_to_youth_inclusion_eng_intro.pdf.

49. Amirali, A. (2019). *The "Youth Bulge" and political unrest in Iraq: A political economy approach.* London: UK Department for International Development. https://opendocs.ids.ac.uk/opendocs/handle/20.500.12413/14815; Mirkin, B. (2013). *Arab Spring: Demographics in a region in transition.* United Nations Development Programme: Regional Bureau for Arab States; Weber, H. (2019). Age structure and political violence: A re-assessment of the "youth bulge" hypothesis. *International Interactions, 45,* 80–112.

50. Massoud, T. G., Doces, J. A., & Magee, C. (2019). Protests and the Arab Spring: An empirical investigation. *Polity, 51,* 429–65.

51. Feldman, N. (2020). *The Arab Winter.* Princeton: Princeton University Press.

52. McKernan, B. (2020) War in Libya: How did it start, who is involved and what happens next? *The Guardian.* https://www.theguardian.com/world/2020/may/18/war-in-libya-how-did-it-start-what-happens-next.

53. Rigoulet-Roze, D. (2016). Geopolitics of Yemen at the dawn of the 21st century. *Hérodote, 1,* 159–76.

54. Amnesty International. (2020). *Yemen war: No end in sight.* https://www.amnesty .org/en/latest/news/2015/09/yemen-the-forgotten-war/.

55. Abouzeid, R. (2018). *No turning back: Life, loss and hope in wartime Syria.* New York: Norton; Glass, S. (2016). *Syria burning: A short history of a catastrophe.* London: Verso.

56. Spyer, J. (2019). Syria's civil war is now 3 civil wars. *Foreign Policy.* https://foreign policy.com/2019/03/18/syrias-civil-war-is-now-3-civil-wars/.

57. Halbfinger, D. M. (2018, December 20). Syria pullout by U.S. tilts Mideast toward Iran and Russia, isolating Israel. *New York Times.* https://www.nytimes.com/2018/12/20 /world/middleeast/syria-U.S.-withdrawal-iran.html/.

9

Africa

GEOPOLITICAL CONTEXT

Africa is home to the human race. Around one hundred thousand years ago, the first humans left the continent to populate the world. Africa is thus hugely significant in world history as a place in itself, but if we concentrate on current geopolitics, the story of Africa is dominated by the colonial experience. Over a relatively short period, from 1880 to 1940, most of the continent was divided up by European countries. Local economies were incorporated into the *core-periphery global economy* and local societies were subsumed under *colonial control*. There was the creation of *uneven development* as economies were structured to provide cheap raw materials for core economies. Imperial controls were less concerned with human development and more with gaining monopoly control over economic exploitation. This economic legacy has continued to deform African economic and political development and was a weak platform for economic independence as *neocolonial economic relations* persist.[1] The arbitrary colonial boundaries framed the postcolonial boundaries of nation-states and the artificial national boundaries, often cutting across and through complex ethnic and tribal allegiances, often created difficult conditions for states to generate legitimacy and exercise authority. In some cases, the new states were *unstable states*.

To write about Africa as a general theme on anything and especially geopolitics is fraught with difficulties. The continent contains fifty-four countries, forty-eight of them in sub-Saharan Africa. They differ in population size from the demographic giant of Nigeria with over 206 million people to Sao Tome and Principe with fewer than a quarter of a million. There are landlocked countries and others with long coastlines. There are Anglophone and Francophone, predominantly Arab and mainly Christian and some animist. There are hundreds of languages and thousands of dialects. Countries differ in political histories as well as in resource endowments, with some rich in minerals. Even those lucky to have rich endowments differ in how they navigate commodity booms and resource curses.

The geopolitics of the continent is dominated more by intersections with great power projections and the internal divisions and tensions within states than by conflicts between the different states. In recent years commodity booms have both helped and hindered social progress. Africa is now a complex pattern of zones of instability and stable states where social progress is being made and democracies are emerging. In such a vast continent these areas of stability garnish little attention. The fracture lines and hotspots attract the most attention. Africa is a trope for dislocation, collapse, and chaos for much of the outside world. There is, of course, a deeply racist tinge to this African imaginary. It is Africa as the dark continent, the Heart of Darkness.[2]

In this chapter, I look at Africa through the lens of wider geopolitical concepts of *settler societies*, *state stability*, and *state fragility*. I look at the *resource curse* caused by the *commodity booms and slumps*, ongoing areas of conflict, and emerging sites of stability. I note the growing though disparate roles of China and the United States.[3]

A note on geographical terminology. The chapter is entitled "Africa," but the observant reader will note that map 9.1 highlights only the areas south of the Sahara. The North African countries of Algeria, Egypt, Tunisia, Morocco, and Libya are in a liminal category: they are in Africa but so influenced by their history as part of the Arab and Turkish empires that they constitute also the Middle East. And yet, they are connected to the countries to the south. Trade, migration, and geopolitical conflicts spill out over the desert. We will use the more inclusive term Africa in this chapter rather than "sub-Saharan Africa" to highlight these connections.

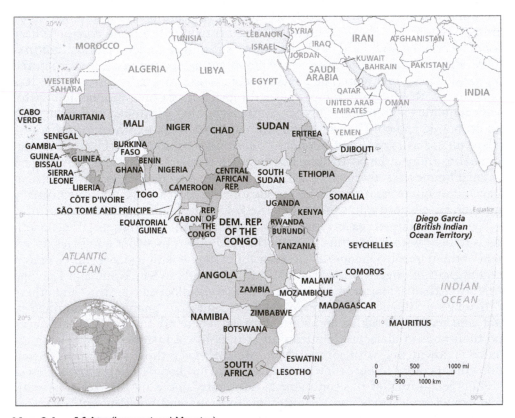

Map 9.1. Africa (International Mapping)

COLONIAL LEGACIES

Africa has a vibrant precolonial history, embracing the rise and fall of empires and the emergence of independent centers of civilization with contacts and trade across the Mediterranean, the Sahara, and the Indian Ocean. Africa has long connections with Europe and Asia and there were colonial ventures before the Europeans. The Arab Empire extended out from Arabia into the Horn of Africa and along the northern coast. Later, the Ottoman Empire held sway over a similar range of territory. But the coming of European colonialism was to squash all this cosmopolitan diversity into a punishing colonial frame.

The Portuguese made the first tentative incursions. Their ships sailed around the continent searching for trade routes to Asia. They extended control around strategic ports such as Mombasa, which came under discontinuous Portuguese control from 1593 until 1729 before it returned to sultanate rule. Dutch traders made forays to Asia. The shipwreck of a Dutch ship in March 1647 eventually led to the establishment of a Dutch settlement on the Cape of Good Hope in 1652. The early colonies were limited to ports or narrow coastal areas. The vast interior was difficult to reach. With few roads, erratic rivers, and unhealthy tropical climates, it did not attract much European attention in the seventeenth and eighteenth centuries. However, the African interior became a more inviting proposition as more of the rest of the world was being annexed and appropriated. By the end of the nineteenth century, the interior of Africa became the last prize for European imperialism.

The global depression of 1873 marked a turning point because it reinforced a sense of economic frailty in Europe. In order to compete against the dominant economic and military power of the UK, the other European powers sought to protect their growing industries and to stimulate their own industrial bases with the acquisition of colonies. The increased competition between the national economies was the essential ingredient of what has been termed *the age of imperialism*, which can be loosely dated twenty years either side of 1900.[4] It marks the extension of formal empires on a vast scale. The fusion of economic and political interests is most clearly shown in the case of Germany, which entered during the last three decades of the nineteenth century, lagging the UK. A strong school of *neo-mercantilist* thought began to promote protection for industry at home and possession of colonies overseas. Germany began an aggressive colonial annexation in Africa and in the South Pacific.

The race was now on as countries began to annex more territory. The UK announced unilateral control of Egypt in 1881. The king of Belgium claimed much of the central interior and Germany claimed territory throughout the continent. In this atmosphere of claims and counterclaims, open hostility and rivalry, a conference was called by the German leader Bismarck in 1884–1885. The Berlin-Africa conference, which defined the conditions for future claims, marked the beginning of the wholesale partition of Africa. Figure 9.1 depicts a scene where the all-male group of White politicians carve up the continent. By 1914, the whole of Africa, apart from Liberia and Ethiopia, was partitioned among the European powers. Map 9.2 shows the result of their deliberations. The older colonial powers expanded from their existing holdings. The French moved inland from Algeria and Senegal to claim much of the Sahel. The British laid down claims in south Africa and pushed into Botswana and north into Zimbabwe and Zambia. The British imperialist Cecil Rhodes used the phrase "from Cape Town to Cairo" to map out British ambitions for a rail line to link Britain's territories along the entire north–south axis of the continent. The Portuguese extended control from their early ports into what became known as Angola and Mozambique. The newer colonial power also made claims. Italy claimed Eritrea and Somalia. Belgium laid claim to the vast interior of the Congo and an upstart Germany held territory in the southwest, east, and west of Africa. The demarcation of the colonial boundaries paid scant attention to realities on the ground. The haphazard nature of the boundary led to continual need for readjustments and negotiations.[5]

Colonial annexation was both enforced and resisted. When the colonial yoke was imposed, there was collaboration by some tribal elites. The colonialists often played on tribal differences and if some chiefs were unwilling to bend the knee, they could always find another to play the role. There was also resistance, insubordination, and refusal. Ethiopians resisted Italy's attempted annexation by defeating Italian forces in 1896. In Uganda, armed resistance continued into the 1920s. Resistance was often met with violent punishment. In 1898–1899, a French military expedition laid waste to much of southern Niger. At the village of Birni n'konni on May 2, 1899, more than fifteen thousand people were mas-

Figure 9.1.   The Berlin Conference, 1884 (Wikimedia / Adalbert von Rößler [†1922])

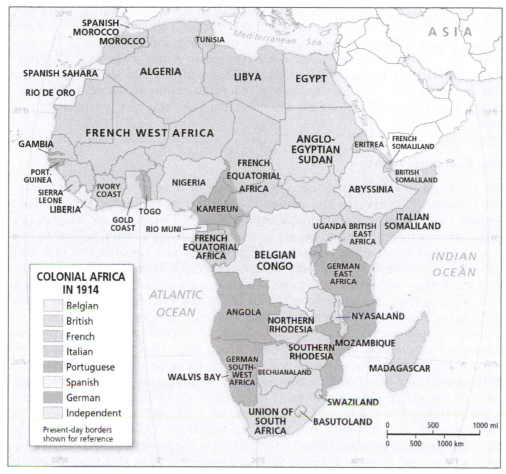

Map 9.2. Colonial Africa (International Mapping)

sacred by French troops. In what is now Namibia, between 1904 and 1908, three tribal groups rebelled against brutal German rule of using Africans as slave labor and of taking their land. A small group of rebels killed more than one hundred German men in January 1904, sparing the women and children. In retaliation, the German general, Lothar von Trotha, corralled thousands into camps in the desert. It was one of the twentieth century's earliest genocide campaigns. Between thirty thousand and one hundred thousand people died from starvation and exhaustion. The deaths were neither accidental nor unplanned. The general wrote before the encounter, "I believe that the nation as such should be annihilated."[6] In Kenya in the 1950s, the British killed thousands and created a gulag to lock up hundreds of thousands of Kikuyu who were fighting for independence.[7]

Even when some colonial powers were defeated in Europe, their colonies were simply seen as spoils to be divvied up among the winners. German territories were reallocated after World War I. German territory in East Africa was divided up between the UK (Tanzania) and Belgium (Rwanda and Burundi).

The former German territories were classified as League of Nation mandates, awarded to the respective countries. But the threefold nature of these mandates is interesting. Mandate A territories were to achieve independence in the very near future. There were no Mandate A territories in Africa: they were all former Ottoman territory in the Middle East. In Africa, all the mandates were either classified as B, defined as able to become independent only in the very long term, except South West Africa, which was classified as C, thought incapable of ever being independent.

The Economic Legacy

We can identify at least four legacies of the age of imperialism in Africa. First, there was an effective transfer of wealth from Africa to Europe that we have already highlighted in the dramatic exploitation of Congo by the king of Belgium. Almost twenty million people were brought under a brutal regime to provide slave labor for rubber plantations. The society was ripped apart, and local economies were destroyed in order to transfer wealth from the center of Africa to a small state in northwest Europe. Africa was linked to Europe through *uneven development*, the process by which cheap raw materials were sent to the metropoles. It was not so much that Africa was underdeveloped as it was *actively* underdeveloped in a system of *unequal exchange* with Europe. The most obvious transfer of wealth was the slave trade in which more than 12.5 million people were snatched from their homes and taken on ships to the New World. Two million died en route. People across west and west central Africa were shipped across the ocean to a life of slavery. It was, in hard, unblinking, economic terms, a forced transfer of human capital as people with strength and knowledge were taken from their homelands to work in the mansions, fields, and mines of the New World. Large parts of Africa were stripped of their human capital while the economies of the New World were valorized with the labor, skill, and ingenuity of enslaved Africans and their descendants.

Second, the economies of regions in Africa were oriented toward the exploitation and export of raw materials to the metropoles. Africa became a primary commodity-producer dependent on a narrow range of primary commodities subject to fluctuating world prices. The value-added work, such as turning cocoa into chocolate, or diamonds into gemstones, or rubber into tires was done in the metropole. This trading arrangement laid the basis for industrial growth and increased national wealth in the metropole while stripping wealth from the colonies. The commodity trade also oriented colonies to the colonial center with few other internal links. Transport routes linked the interior to coast ports rather than to other regions. This linearity and its lack of regional integration is a characteristic that still hampers Africa's development. Narrow corridors still link resources with ports and do not stimulate wider regional development. Colonial and neocolonial patterns of resource have few local multiplier effects; they were geared more toward transportation of raw material to the outside world. Consider the giant rubber plantation in Liberia. It was developed by the Firestone tire company to supply rubber for manufacturing into tires and goods. Almost 40 percent of all latex in the United States comes from the Firestone rubber plantation. It is a 220-square-mile enclave of between eight million and fifteen million rubber trees. Apart from cheap labor, it is largely unconnected to the rest of the Liberian economy: no manufacturing from rubber ever took place in Liberia.

Third, agriculture was transformed; cash crops such as cotton, rubber, groundnuts, and coffee were introduced into the smallholder farming system. With some of the best land appropriated in settler societies, an expanding number of smallholders were expected to produce more cash crops. The result was often soil degradation and long-term environmental damage.

Fourth, Africa was colonized on the cheap. There was little attempt to create self-sustaining economies and societies. It was not like Australia or Canada, where democratic societies were established as part of economic development. The emphasis was on cheap exploitation rather than long-term investment. Little money was spent on civil society, education, or creating conditions for long-term, self-sustaining growth. There was limited spending on policing or even large-scale military presence. The colonialists offset the administration cost through indirect rule, often exploiting local animosities to rule more effectively. Tribalism was reinforced as a way to maintain control and divide opposition. When Belgium took control of Rwanda in 1914 after Germany's defeat in World War I, the minority Tutsis were favored over the majority Hutus. Across the colonial landscape, some tribes were favored over others, and the more collaborative tribal chiefs were given additional power and authority. Indirect rule reinforced tribalism and hardened what were once more fluid ethnic identities.[8]

It is impossible to understand the contemporary state of Africa without consideration of the colonial experience. In summary, the postcolonial legacy meant an orientation toward primary commodity extraction, poor transport connections, environmentally damaging cash crops, and intensified tribal conflicts. Given this legacy, the question is not why Africa is so poor, but how it has managed to emerge so successfully from this crippling colonial experience.

The Geopolitical Legacy

Decolonization in Asia strengthened anticolonial forces in Africa. Sudan achieved independence in 1956, and thereafter independence for other British colonies followed with each new independent state increasing the weight of precedence. Ghana obtained independence in 1957, Kenya in 1963, and Tanzania in 1964. Most of the French colonies achieved independence in 1960. The last colonial power left Africa in 1975 when a revolution in Portugal, in large part caused by the costly colonial wars, resulted in overnight independence after years of struggle for Angola, Guinea Bissau, and Mozambique. It was another four years before Zimbabwe achieved independence, and Namibia did not achieve independence from South Africa until 1990.

Independence meant the end of colonial control, but the postcolonial states had a difficult time. In some cases, such as the Belgian Congo, withdrawal was so rapid that new countries emerged almost overnight with little political experience or administrative expertise. With very little commitment to education or to the creation of an educated workforce, European powers made it difficult for sub-Saharan Africa to create and staff a functioning state "from scratch," especially in those hasty colonial withdrawals.

The struggle for independence also took place within the territorial boundaries of colonial rule, which often lacked any geographic or cultural rationale. The idiosyncrasies of colonial demarcations became the geopolitical reality of postcolonial Africa. The present political map of Africa (see map 9.1) bears a striking resemblance to the boundaries of the formal empires depicted in map 9.2. National boundaries were the result of the machinations of competing colonial powers rather than any underlying national coherence. For example, the colonial legacy is clear in tiny Gambia in west Africa, which is three hundred miles long but only twenty miles wide in places. Its national boundary reflects French and British rivalry. Britain created a Gambia to give it control over the mouth of the Gambia River. British control was a block to French control of the interiors. Because of the national fragmentation, the river was not fully utilized by surrounding regions as a transport artery to stimulate regional economic growth. Another example of this "nationalized colonialism" is the long sliver of the Caprivi strip in Namibia. The shapes of Angola, Botswana, Namibia, Zambia, and Zimbabwe in this part of contemporary Africa all result from nineteenth-century demands by colonialist Germany for access to the Zambezi River.

The adoption and subdivision of colonial boundaries also led to a number of landlocked states such as Botswana, Burkina Faso, Burundi, Central African Republic, Chad, Eswatini, Malawi, Mali, Niger, Rwanda, South Sudan, Uganda, Zambia, and Zimbabwe. These landlocked countries have the added burden of increased transportation costs and the lack of maritime connections to add to their economic woes. Consider the case of Lesotho, an enclaved country, completely surrounded by the territory of South Africa. Lesotho has ethnic homogeneity—more than 90 percent of the two million population are Basotho—but lacks easy and independent access to the wider world. Even those technically considered "non-landlocked," such as Congo and the Democratic Republic of Congo (DRC), have only narrow, limited maritime access (see map 9.1).

The number of competing and geographically complex colonial claims meant that postcolonial Africa is a continent of fragmented states, with long borders that cut through cultural homelands.[9] Africa has 28,600 miles of boundaries. Most African states have more than one neighbor and twenty have four or more neighbors. The DRC shares borders with nine neighboring states, making national cohesion all that more difficult because of many, frequent, and relatively easy cross-border incursions by foreign armies and armed militias.

There is a vigorous debate about the role of national borders in hampering African development.[10] Artificial and porous, they are now a postcolonial reality that is reaffirmed and undermined, negotiated and contested by a range of actors, through numerous informal networks, legal and illegal. They also act as sites of regional integration.[11] The border between Niger and Nigeria passes through the Hausa region, so cross-border interactions are common.

The highly artificial borders of colonial Africa have been, by and large, respected by postcolonial Africa. In 1964, the Organization of African Unity upheld the principle of intangibility of borders. The integrity of states has persisted with some tragic exceptions. Nigeria achieved political freedom, but as had many other African nations, it remained a prisoner of political geography. There are three major tribes in Nigeria. The Hausa inhabit the north; the Yoruba populate the southern and central areas. The Igbo, who make up 18 percent of the country's population, are found mainly in the southeast of the country. They are Christians compared to the Muslim Hausa and the more syncretic religions of the Yoruba. In 1967, army officers of the Igbo tribe proclaimed the independent state of Biafra in eastern Nigeria. The resulting bloody civil war lasted three years. The war was pivotal in shaping the world's views of Africa because scenes of war and famine were broadcast widely just as television was becoming a more popular medium. Between a half-million and three million civilians died of starvation. The scenes of starving Biafran children left an indelible mark on Western perceptions of Africa: images of starving children were added to the usual tropes of lions in the savannah and apes in the jungle.

The Horn of Africa continues to be a zone of more actively disputed state borders. In the breakup of formerly Italian-held territory after World War II, Eritrea was federated with Ethiopia in 1950. It was not a match made in heaven. In 1961, the Eritrean liberation movement was established and waged a military campaign against the Ethiopian authorities. Eritrea won independence in 1993, but the boundary between Eritrea and Ethiopia remains in dispute: it was the basis for a conflict from 1998 to 2001. In that same postcolonial division, Ethiopia was given control over the Ogaden, a region populated by ethnic Somali Muslims. In 1977–1978, Somali forces invaded the Ogaden to take control over the territory and reunite the Somali peoples. With help from Cuba and the USSR, Ethiopia won the war. The Horn of Africa, with its border disputes exacerbated by simmering conflict among failed and failing states, remains an exception. Borders created by colonial regimes have survived in most of postcolonial Africa and now largely are taken for granted, persisting as porous and lightly policed (if at all).

Many postcolonial states emerged from a mosaic of tribal groupings or from a small number of tribal groups. The unifying influence of anticolonial liberation struggles sometimes splintered into postcolonial tribalism. A major problem for politicians in Africa is the formation of national cohesion since different tribal and ethnic groups often share a nation-state. The motto of Zambia is "One Zambia, one nation," as much a plea as an affirmation of reality.

In a number of states, tribal rivalries continue to undermine the coherence of the state. In South Sudan, the Nuer and Dinka compete for control of the state. In Zimbabwe, the oppressive rule of Robert Mugabe favored his tribal group, the Shona, over the Ndebele. In Burundi and Rwanda, the Hutu-Tutsi divide played major roles in civil-war and cross-border incursions. In Kenya, the conflict between the Kikuyu and Luo continues to plague national politics.

Independence sometimes exacerbated identity politics. Created and maintained in the colonial areas, tribal differences can become important when governments are in a position to allocate resources and benefits. When the spoils of the state become political currency, then tribal and ethnic differences become narratives to be encouraged, created, and promoted by ethnic-entrepreneurial politicians. One way to keep control is to ensure a tribal base. In much of sub-Saharan Africa, tribal identities became the bases of support, carefully managed and choreographed by politicians eager to solidify their control and power.

The result may be perpetual conflict, however, as in the case of Kenya, where one group stays in power by means of the creation and exploitation of ethnic and tribal differences. The result is polarization, political marginalization, and declining legitimacy of the state. When the state becomes a vehicle for exploiting rather than transcending ethnic and tribal differences used by one group to advance its interest over other groups, then the government loses its universal appeal. Things tend to be worse, as in the case of South Sudan or Kenya, where a small number of large groups compete with one another for the offices, payoffs, and benefits of the state. In countries with a large number of smaller groups, such as Tanzania, tribal politics play a very limited role.

SETTLER SOCIETIES

The term *settler society* generally refers to European White settlers taking control over the land and economy of indigenous peoples, although there are more recent settler societies with different binaries.[12] Algeria, Australia, New Zealand, Canada, Mexico, and the United States are examples of settler societies. The creation of these societies involved the forcible annexation of the land of indigenous people, the insertion of racialized rule, and the creation of racial categories that define differential access to power. Settler societies emerge with complex patterns of gender, race, and class.[13]

Africa has examples of settler societies. South Africa under the apartheid system, for example, embodies the politics of race in its more brutal forms. Liberia, in contrast, is a settler society that does not fit the typical racial pattern.[14] All settler societies, however, are characterized by the forcible annexation of land and the subjugation of indigenous peoples. The earliest were Dutch settlements in South Africa. Later, Black Americans moved to Liberia and White European settlers colonized parts of what are now Namibia, Zimbabwe, and Kenya.

South Africa is the most iconic settler society. The Dutch East India Company established Cape Town in 1652. Slaves were imported from Indonesia and Madagascar. The mixed race that resulted were known as "Colored." The Dutch farmers—the Dutch word for *farmer* is *Boer*—moved from the coast looking for land in the interior. They fought indigenous peoples for the prime land. From 1806, South Africa came under the control of the UK. There were tensions between the British and the Boers. The Boer Wars (1801–1881; 1899–1902) led to the assertion of British controls after vicious guerrilla war campaigns that included the British use of concentration camps to round up Boer families. Across South Africa, land was taken by the Whites, and racial segregation was maintained by pervasive methods of informal control. In 1931, South Africa became independent from the UK. In 1948, the National Party representing the conservative Dutch speakers came to power and instituted a legalized formalization of racial segregation known as *apartheid*, the Dutch word for *separation*. The population was formally divided into Blacks, Whites, and Colored and segregated into different areas of the cities and the country. From 1948 to 1994, the country upheld, with law and policing, a rigid separation between the races. Blacks could not live in the central cities, were forced to live in townships on the city's edge, and had to leave city centers before nightfall. Jobs, education, and housing were allocated and controlled according to this racialized system. There were huge disparities in income, employment opportunities, and education provision. The Whites lived in the First World, sustained by Black labor, while the Blacks were condemned to the Third World. Racial injustice and oppressive policing sustained the racial order.

Resistance to the system was strong. The rigid classification gave Blacks little hope for change within a system. The African National Congress (ANC) was the main, though not the only, movement that sought the end of racial restrictions. South Africa, very dependent on global trade, became a *cause célèbre* for liberal activists seeking racial justice. A successful disinvestment campaign played a role.[15] The international condemnation hardened the more reactionary forces in the country. But some White politicians in the National Party were forced to see how the old system had to change. In 1990, the National Party recognized the ANC and in the first open election held in 1994, the ANC won overwhelmingly. South Africa moved from a formal settler society to a functioning democracy. Problems remain. There are still legacies of the settler society embodied in the massive disparities in income, employment opportunities, and education and health of Black South Africans compared to Whites. The ANC's effective monopoly of power has now led to the creation of a Black political elite insulated from democratic accountability and consequently more open to corruption. But South Africa has press freedom, a judicial system largely independent from political influence, and a democratic polity. Despite all the problems, South Africa is an example of political reconciliation in postcolonial settler societies. The success owes a great deal to the moral authority and leadership shown by the first democratically elected President, Nelson Mandela. Despite being locked up in prison for twenty-seven years, he preached that reconciliation was not only possible but also necessary. South Africa was fortunate to have a politician of such incredible moral authority with a capacity of forgiveness to guide the country from one of the most racist systems in the world to a functioning democracy. The establishment of a Truth and Reconciliation Commission also allowed an opportunity for previous wrongs to be addressed and articulated.[16] In many ways, South Africa remains a model for what reconciliation can mobilize. Other countries, including the United States, could learn from the experience.[17]

The more fertile zones of southern and eastern Africa also had settler societies. In Kenya, White settlers were concentrated on the best land in the White Highlands. Many of them were rich and from the upper echelons of British society. Even a Danish baroness got in on the act. Isak Dinesen bought six thousand acres in 1913. Her memoir of her time in Kenya, *Out Of Africa*, first published in 1937, was made famous by the 1985 movie of the same name. The lush romantic epic does not, of course, raise the obvious question of how come she gets this land. There is no rendering of the brutal dispossession necessary for the author to write, as well as the character played by Meryl Streep to say, "I had a farm in Africa."

In 1917, the British government offered 999-year leases, free of any land tax, to White settlers. They were not the dirt-poor farmers of other colonies, but the well-connected with enough money to purchase large estates. On the eve of independence, there were approximately sixty thousand White settlers in a country with a population of ten million. After independence, much but not all the White-owned land was redistributed to the Kikuyu elite. There are now forty-one thousand Whites living in a country of fifty-three million. A few are farmers but most are now in the service sector. They belong to the wealthier sectors of society, but their social world now overlaps with the Black economic and political elite of the country.

White settlers in Zambia formed an important element in the colonial society. However, their numbers were small, only seventy-four thousand in 1963, and not powerful enough to resist independence. Thousands moved to South Africa after Zambian independence in 1963, and only around forty thousand remained by 2014, less than 0.3 percent of the country's population. It was a different case in neighboring Rhodesia. The cheap and available land, annexed from indigenous people, attracted Whites of course. Whites had the best land, the best jobs, and the best public-service posts. By 1965, Whites numbered around three hundred thousand, comprising a powerful economic and political elite. Faced with inevitable consequences of the loss of their privileged positions with the prospect of Black-majority rule, White politicians issued a unilateral declaration of independence in 1965 for Rhodesia. A civil war ensued with numerous liberation movements pitted against each other and the White-led government forces.[18] A deal was brokered in 1978, and universal suffrage in 1979 meant the end of White rule and White privilege. Under the corrupt regime and inept leadership of Robert Mugabe, who held onto power from 1980 to 2017, the land of the White farmers was confiscated, not for general redistribution but allocated mainly to allies and cronies of Mugabe. Most of the White farmers had their land expropriated, and by 2020, there were only around twenty-two thousand Whites left in Zimbabwe.

The dominant theories and descriptions of settler societies tend to pose the issue in terms of White settlers on the one hand and Black and Brown indigenous peoples on the other. This is clearly the predominant form. However, there is the case of Liberia, where Black Americans created a settler society. Freed and free-born Blacks started moving to Liberia in 1822. The Americo-Liberians formed a politically powerful economic elite. The country declared independence in 1847, and the first president was a free-born Black from Virginia. The colonists created a society that emulated the United States. The Liberian flag is modeled on the Stars and Stripes, and the capital, Monrovia, was named after a U.S. president, James Munroe, who supported the colonization of Liberia. The lighter-skinned, Americo-Liberians built Monrovia to look like buildings in the American South. They also brought similar racial prejudices, denying indigenous people political rights until the early twentieth century.[19] Liberia's racial politics grew from its U.S. roots. The country's main social ethnic fracture line ran between the Americo-Liberians and the indigenous peoples. A division took hold between the Americo-Liberian elite in the capital and the indigenous people who comprised at least fifteen different ethnic groups, including the Kpelle, Bassa, Greba, Gio, and Krahan. Referred to as the "bush" people, the population of these groups was forced into a form of compulsory labor that amounted to slavery. The stark divisions between a Black settler class living well in the city and the exploited people of the interior eventually led to social unrest. In a military coup in 1980, the Americo-Liberian president and cabinet were executed. This martial action was the start of a long road of misery for the country as coup and countercoup, ethnic tensions, and social breakdown led to civil wars from 1989 to 1997 and from 1999 to 2003, which killed around a half-million civilians in a total population of five million.[20] The conflict spilled over into Sierra Leone where an eleven-year civil war from 1991 to 2002 killed more than fifty thousand people. By 2005, normal elections were held in Liberia, and in 2006, a Truth and Reconciliation Commission along the lines of the South African model investigated the causes and crimes of the civil wars. Liberia remains one of the poorest countries in the world.

A CONTINUUM OF STATES

Africa is such a vast and diverse continent that it is difficult to generalize about state stability. It is more accurate to consider a continuum from failed to functioning states with the position of individual countries changing over time.

Failed and Failing States

The conditions for failed and failing states were mapped out in chapter 2. A state tends to be failed or failing especially when economic and political inequality is mapped onto racial, ethnic, or religious difference; it lacks national cohesion; the central authorities are failing to meet populous demands; and the government is faced with severe shocks such as disasters and rapid economic decline. Fragile and failed states are caused by numerous triggering elements, including but not limited to:

- environmental pressures, made more extreme in a time of global climate changes;
- very rapid population growth;
- government corruption and incompetence; and
- societal breakdown in the wake of famines, conflict, extreme endemic violence, and wars.

In reality, extreme triggering events can cluster in time and space in a cascading spiral of bad outcomes made worse as they fold into and feed off each other.

Each year the Fund for Peace produces an index of fragile states that measures risk and vulnerability in 178 countries. There are many criticisms of the index, so it is best used as a starting point rather than an endpoint.[21] Countries are ranked most fragile to least fragile. Among the least fragile are Australia, Canada, Finland, Norway, Switzerland, Denmark, Iceland, New Zealand, and Sweden. Of the twenty-five most fragile states, seventeen are in sub-Saharan Africa. Table 9.1 lists them in order of their global ranking in fragility. Let us consider three examples of countries that have been at the top of this ranking for at least a decade.

Table 9.1. Fragile States in Sub-Saharan Africa

Rank	Country
2	Somalia
3	South Sudan
5	Congo D.R.
6	Central African Republic
7	Chad
8	Sudan
10	Zimbabwe
11=	Cameroon
11=	Burundi
14	Nigeria
15	Guinea
16	Mali
18	Eritrea
19	Niger
21	Ethiopia
23	Guinea Bissau
24	Uganda
25	Congo Republic

Source: Data in Fragile States Index 2020: https://fragilestatesindex.org/data/

Somalia is for all intents and purposes a *failed state*. In 1977, Somali forces invaded Ethiopian territory to annex the Ogaden, a region populated by ethnic Somali Muslims. It was a bloody, expensive failure, and the military dictatorship ran out of popular support as various secessionist movements resisted central government control. Since the 1990s, the country has lacked a strong central state and is now dominated by powerful militias and the Islamic group al Shabaab. The weakness of the state created ungoverned spaces for criminal enterprises to flourish. This was brought to global attention when, from 2000, Somali pirates terrorized the busy shipping lanes of the Red Sea and Gulf of Aden by boarding and taking over ships, claiming ransoms from the shipowners. The Somali government was unable to halt the piracy and by 2011 there were 237 pirate attacks. The piracy was only reduced by 2017 after an international coalition of armed vessels provided an effective show of force. This modern-day piracy was a symptom of a failed state unable to control territory and activities within its borders and of the desperation of a people with few economic opportunities. To take to the sea on small boats and to capture the huge oil tankers required organization and cunning. But a long-term, sustainable business plan it was not.

Somalia has experienced a downward spiral as lack of effective government control has created spaces for the operation of clan-based militias and non-state actors such as al Shabaab in the south and separatists in the north. These groups often meet some of the welfare needs of local populations, garnering support and further weakening the power and legitimacy of the central government. The balkanization of power between different and often antagonistic forces often makes humanitarian aid difficult to deliver and makes recurring episodes of hunger and famine more frequent and more severe.

South Sudan is one of the newest independent states in the world. It became independent in 2011 after it broke away from Sudan. Decades of war with Sudanese forces have impoverished the landlocked country. Conflict emerged early in the life of the new state between two tribal groups, the Dinka and the Nuer. At its worst in 2017, when aid was blocked by soldiers and combatants from reaching the general population, 30 percent of the eleven million people were acutely malnourished, and four children were dying every day from hunger. More than 1.6 million fled the country and two million were internally displaced.

The Central African Republic (CAR) is a landlocked state in the middle of Africa that extends from the tropical rainforest through the savanna northward to the edge of the Sahel. It was a French colonial territory that gained independence in 1960. It is a majority Christian population with around 15 percent of Muslims out of the total population of 4.6 million. There are a variety of ethnic groups, but the division is mainly between a Muslim north and a Christian south. The religious division is overlain with differences in wealth; the Muslims tend to be wealthier. Since 2012, when Muslim groups captured its capital city and imposed a harsh rule, the country has been in the state of civil war—or *wars*, to be more accurate. A Christian militia fought back, and as it moved north, Muslims fled across the border to escape genocide. Soon millions were homeless. To stop the threat of genocide, UN peacekeepers arrived in 2014, joining the elements of the French Army and troops from the African Union. Their control, however, barely extended beyond the gates of the camps as the country fractured into fiefdoms with competing groups struggling to control valuable mineral resources. Despite the election of a president in 2016 eager to make peace with the various armed ethnic groups and actively promoting disarmament and reintegration of fighters back into normal society, the country remains a failed state with six hundred thousand living as internal refugees in a country of 4.6 million. Effective government rule does not extend much beyond the limits of the capital city, Bangui. Armed groups hold sway over most of the country, despite the 13,200 UN and UN-affiliated troop presence.

The CAR, Somalia, and South Sudan are all failed or failing states but with different reasons for failure. One study looked in detail at these perennial members of the "fragile state" category.[22] The authors found significant differences. In the CAR, it is the lack of a formal security apparatus that causes problems while in South Sudan, it is the very size of the (competing) security forces that creates conflict. There are also differences in the form of the factionalized elites. The CAR has a small, dispersed elite that rotates through regime change, while in South Sudan, two large and factionalized elite groups are locked into a perennial struggle to control the means of power. The three countries also differ in the role of extended intervention by outside forces; it is a much more important factor in Somalia. In other words, the study suggests that using a single index flattens out very subtle differences in the causes of state fragility and insecurity.

Zones of Instability

Failed and failing states do not exist in isolation. There tend to be clusters of state instability where environmental, political, and social issues combine to create the preconditions for state fragility. There are two main zones, one in east-central Africa and another in the region running along latitude 10-degree north, across the Sahel and into east Africa.

The zone of instability in east Africa includes the eastern provinces of the DRC and at various times Uganda, Rwanda, and Burundi. It is a region that is rich in minerals. It is also experiencing rapid population growth that strains existing resources and weak, failing, and failed states unable to provide welfare and security. It is a fertile ground for ethnic conflict. In 1994, a campaign of genocide in Rwanda by the Hutus against the Tutsi resulted in the deaths of almost eight hundred thousand people.[23] Hutu soldiers fled to eastern DRC, and Rwandan troops invaded the DRC and installed a new government. In 1996, the Rwanda-DRC agreement dissolved, and rebel groups backed by the different governments and various ethnically based militias fought for control of the valuable mineral deposits. Ugandan troops invaded Congo in 1998. They also fought against Rwandan troops and only pulled out in 2003. In the 1993–2006 civil war in Burundi, between Hutus and Tutsis, more than more three hundred thousand people were killed. In the ungoverned zones of failed and failing states, militias and paramilitary organizations can flourish. In 2000, a cult-like insurgency, the Lord's Resistance Army (LRA), emerged in the border regions of the CAR, South Sudan, and Uganda, kidnapping children and slaughtering villagers.

There have been some improvements: the civil war in Burundi was ended; Rwanda became a more peaceful society; and the LRA has been largely defeated. But conflicts simmer between Rwanda and Uganda, and eastern provinces of the DRC have yet to achieve a sustainable peace. The eastern DRC has seen multiple invading armies and competing militia groups. Since 1994, the results have been more than five million people killed, three million displaced, and one million raped. More than 2.7 million people are living as internally displaced refugees. This is an intense human tragedy, a bleeding wound in the global body politic.[24]

A second zone of instability is across the Sahel, where an environmental crisis is unfolding. Map 9.3 depicts the core region of the Sahel, defined as a zone of transition between desert and savannah. In a swath growing larger and migrating south, it runs across the continent in a belt that spans from five hundred to one thousand miles. Climate change is increasing desertification and leading to the loss of pastoral grazing and fertile agriculture. The climate is warming, rains are less frequent, and when they do come, they can cause flooding. When spring and summer rains fail, crop failures can push a vulnerable population from food insecurity through hunger to starvation. Desertification has extended infertility into the grazing and growing areas. This environmental disaster is the context for political instability from Eritrea through Sudan, Chad, Niger, and Mali.

Eritrea, South Sudan, and Somalia are failed or failing states for many reasons. They are all, for example, impacted by deteriorating environmental conditions that create conditions for hunger and famine, displacement and conflict. With the government unable to exert control outside the capital of Mogadishu, as in the case of Somalia, or humanitarian aid from outside is often blocked from reaching the vulnerable, as is the case for both Somalia and South Sudan, then political instability leads to hunger and famine. Eritrea is similarly impacted with climate change and still recovering from its war with Ethiopia. A one-party

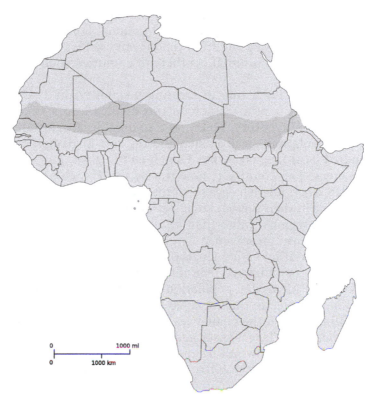

Map 9.3.   The Sahel (Wikimedia / Felix Koenig)

state imposes compulsory and harsh military service. Conditions are so harsh that many try to leave. Eritreans along with Somalis now constitute a significant part of the stream of migrants making their way to economic opportunities and political freedoms in Europe. Remittances now constitute one-third of gross domestic product. Climate change is just one more punishing turn of the screw to the people and the countries in this region.

Further west in the Sahel, climate change and desertification has led to a shrinkage in available grazing areas at a time of rapid population increase. Almost 50 percent of people in the region now live below the poverty line. It is against this backdrop of severe challenges and inadequate government response that Islamic militant groups have emerged to challenge the central government in Niger, Mali, and Chad. They often play an important role providing jobs, money, and security to people too often ignored by weak governments. The Islamic State in Greater Sahara formed in 2015 and operates in Burkina Faso, Mali, and Niger. It has a dominant base of Fulani, who are being hard pressed for grazing land by Zarma and Hausa peasants.

The instability across the region is caused also by the religious differences across this part of Africa where the Muslim north meets the Christian/animist southern zones. The jihadist insurgency Boko Haram operates in the borderland between different religious groups in Cameroon, Chad, and Nigeria.

The instability is heightened by the ability of non-state actors to quickly and easily cross the long, porous, poorly defended national borders. Militants moving south from northern Africa and from the Libyan civil war, for example, now play significant roles in the internal conflicts in countries such as Mali, Niger, and Chad.

Even language can play a role in creating instability. In 1916, the former German colony of what is now Cameroon was divided into a small UK- and a larger French-controlled territory. Today, as a colonial legacy, around 80 percent of the country's population speak French and the rest English. There are more than two hundred local languages, but French and English are *lingua franca* in the respective areas. The country is now run by the French speakers. Fighting broke out in 2018 when English speakers protested the increasing use of French language by officials in their region. French-speaking army troops raided separatist English-speaking regions. More than five hundred thousand were displaced and the conflict remains unresolved.

The cause of the conflict varies across the region—here ethnicity, there tribal grouping or language or religions. The different countries in the region share the same backdrop of increasing population pressure and deteriorating environmental conditions. People are finding it harder to get by and governments seem unable or unwilling to meet the challenges. The result is failed and failing states and desperate people. This leaves space and opportunity for the entry of non-state actors. In the context of a dwindling resource base and increasing population pressure, struggles can quickly mobilize around the politics of religion, language, or ethnic identity.

Changing States

The stability of states varies over time. A war, a famine, or the entry of outside forces can all turn a functioning state into a failed or failing state. Over a ten-year period, the Fund for Peace Index reveals movement in either direction. Since 2010, Mali, Mozambique, and Eritrea have become more fragile. Libya's collapse sent shockwaves of militias and jihadis into the countries of the Sahel, including Mali, Chad, and Niger. In 2020, a military coup in Mali replaced the seven-year rule of a civilian president after street protests against government corruption and the failure to defeat extremist militants.[25]

The opposite may also happen as stability returns with a more functioning state. There are also hopeful signs across the continent. In parts of west Africa, for example, the savage violence has subsided. The bloody civil wars in Liberia and Sierra Leone have ended. The civil war in Sierra Leone, for example, was marked by mass killings of civilians, mass rape, the use of children as combatants, and the displacement of two million people, which represented almost one-third of the population. But since 2002, a land wracked by horror has returned gradually to more peaceful ways. Regular elections are held, and while there were some clashes in 2019 when 5,500 people were displaced, the horrors of the 1990s are largely gone. Sierra Leone as well as Liberia continue to struggle with many problems, but the states have become more stable and functioning as the violence has receded. And of course, there is a symbiosis—as the violence recedes, then more normal politics and forms of governance can take hold.

There were also improvements across the continent. Sudan had a late Arab Spring in April 2019 when the long-term leader al-Bashir was overthrown after weeks of street protests against his brutal and authoritarian thirty-year rule. Al-Bashir had pursued an aggressive campaign in South Sudan and Darfur that led to major humanitarian crises. The new transitional government, still finding its feet after years of authoritarian military rule, promises to be more inclusive and less warmongering. Sudan is still faced with major problems, but few are sorry to see the end of the regime run by a corrupt war criminal and the architect of bloody campaigns against his own people.

Replacing corrupt leaders does not always bode major improvements. The long-term leader of Zimbabwe, Robert Mugabe, was overthrown by a military coup in 2017 after years of financial and economic mismanagement that brought the country to its knees. The new leader, alas, looks remarkably similar to the previous leader in terms of his limited capacity to allow opposition to his rule or to upset the cronyism of the political elite.

Ethiopia's inclusion in table 9.1 is a legacy of previous conditions that seemed out of date at the time I first wrote these lines in mid-2020. People in the Oromia and Amhara region had long resisted a government dominated by the Tigrayans. Land grabs by the government led to protests and when the government brutally suppressed them the conflict only heightened. Although there was sustained economic growth and an increase in foreign investment, the spoils were unequally shared. The Tigrayans dominated the business and political arenas; Oromia people, who make up around 40 percent of the one hundred million, saw their land taken away from them in official and unofficial land grabs by Amhara people around Addis Ababa. Conflict, protest, and government curtailment of civil liberties were most apparent in 2016. Then, things began to improve for the better. The election of a new prime minister in 2018 marked a major change. Political prisoners were released. The first female president was installed and the prime minister, Abiy Ahmed, was awarded the Nobel Peace Prize in 2019 for his efforts brokering a peace agreement with Eritrea. The signs of positivity seemed to herald a more stable state formation. One election and a new president and prime minister did not signal an end to enduring conflicts over land and resources. Tribal and ethnic differences remain. Tigray, a province in the north of the country, is home to around six million people. Tigrayans in the Tigray People's Liberation Front (TPLF) dominated the Ethiopian government for almost three decades, holding power from 1991 to 2018. When the TPLF lost the election, they resisted the central government's call for unity and kept control over military bases, armaments, and rocketry in the region. When TPLF forces attacked an Ethiopian army base on November 4, 2020, the government in Addis Ababa sent in troops, called in air strikes, and took back control of the main cities in the region. While many TPLF fighters were killed, others disappeared into the surrounding countryside. There were civil casualties. More than a thousand civilians were killed, 95,000 were displaced, and almost 50,000 fled across the border to Sudan; more are expected as food supplies run short. There are now real fears of a famine; more than one million people are in need of food aid. Another tragedy looks to be unfolding in the troubled Horn of Africa.

Stable States

At the other end of the continuum from South Sudan, Somalia, and the CAR are more stable, resilient states. If Finland is considered the most stable with a rank of 178 and Yemen the least stable with a rank of 1, then we get some idea of the relative position of the more stable African countries in table 9.2. Let us look at three examples.

Table 9.2. More Stable States in Sub-Saharan Africa

Country	Rank
Mauritius	153
Botswana	122
Namibia	105
Ghana	108
Gabon	90
South Africa	85
Benin	77

Source: Fragile States Index: https://fragilestatesindex.org /data/

The peace and stability of Botswana and Namibia were not a given. Both could have fallen to the resource curse. One emerged from a long guerrilla campaign for independence, which is often a prologue to extended, one party, one-man rule, as with Zimbabwe. Botswana became independent in 1966. Since then, continuous civilian governments have followed socially progressive policies and encouraged foreign investments, especially in the lucrative diamond mining industry. The civil peace has encouraged an influx of foreign tourists eager to see the wildlife.

Namibia covers territory annexed by Germany as South West Africa, which after 1915 then came under the control of South Africa. A resistance campaign was launched in 1960 by the Marxist-inspired South West People's Organization (SWAPO). Independence was only finally achieved in 1990. Governments dominated by SWAPO have ruled since then, and they pursue socially progressive policies and encourage foreign investors to exploit the diamond and uranium deposits. Both Namibia and Botswana have a heavy reliance on a narrow range of primary commodities thus vulnerable to global commodity prices fluctuations. Both have high rates of HIV/Aids infection. Yet both countries are stable.

In west Africa, Ghana stands out as relatively peaceful and stable. It emerged as the first independent state in 1957 but then experienced a series of military dictatorships. Since 1992, it has been ruled by the result of democratic elections. It is a free-market economy with a range of commodities, including gold and cocoa and more recently oil. As with Namibia and Botswana, the relative peace has ensured economic growth, while economic development generates political stability.

To say that Namibia, Ghana, and Botswana are stable states is not to imply they do not have problems. They face the same sort of fiscal and crisis issues as many other countries. But they do so from a platform of relative political stability. In comparison to Agamben's notion of state of exception, they inhabit a state of normalcy.[26]

THE RESOURCE CURSE

Africa is rich in resources. It holds half the world's supply of bauxite. It has long been exploited for its resources. Colonial annexation was driven primarily by the desire to monopolize these resources. Resource exploitation still goes on. Gas and oil, timber, minerals, and agricultural land currently are being exploited vigorously to meet global demand. Many national economies in sub-Saharan Africa are dependent on a few primary commodities for generating government revenue. This makes them very vulnerable to the *resource curse* that involves vulnerability to fluctuating global prices, the stunting of non-resource-based economic development, and the opportunities for corruption. It is much easier siphoning off revenues from one single stream of commodity revenues than it is from an economy with a varied range of firms, goods, and services. The resource curse means that despite the vast natural wealth of Africa, very little of the proceeds finds its way to improving the lot of ordinary people in many countries. Much of the wealth is siphoned by *predatory elites*.

A heavy reliance on primary commodities or a mineral-based economy does not necessarily lead to a resource curse. A counterexample is Botswana, where the resource base of diamond, nickel, and soda ash brought impressive and widely distributed growth. A strong effective state and a democratically elected government meant that resource exploitation has benefited the population of Botswana. There is still a gap between the very rich and the very poor, and the rich continue to get richer. Nevertheless, in large measure Botswana is a case study of successful exploitation of resources.

In contrast, the resource curse has been identified in countries across the continent, including Angola, Chad, Congo, Gabon, Guinea, Nigeria, and Zambia. The more commodities dominate exports, the more pronounced the curse tends to be. Mineral and energy resources account for more than 90 percent of exports for countries such as Angola, Chad, Guinea, Nigeria, and Sudan and constitute between 50 and 75 percent of all total export earnings in African countries.

Resource development can be an expensive proposition and many African countries are thus dependent on the operations and investments of large, multinational companies whose primary responsibility is to their shareholders, the majority of whom live in the First World. The asymmetry between powerful, rich corporations on the one hand and relatively impoverished countries on the other often leads to imbalance in negotiations and to a distribution of benefits, where a few politicians may reap tremendous rewards with very little trickle down.[27]

The resource curse of oil is evident in the case of Nigeria, which is sometimes characterized as a *rentier state* with oil revenues very much in the control of self-interested political elites. More than 92 percent of exports earnings in Nigeria are from oil. Another example is Guinea, where although the country has a high per capita income, calculated by dividing oil revenue by the total population: very little of the actual monies have percolated downward. There is an uneven distribution of resource revenues, as government ministers have amassed vast personal fortunes while the majority of the population remain desperately poor.[28]

Angola

A well-documented, recent case is Angola, where more than 97 percent of export earnings are from oil.[29] Angola achieved independence from Portugal in 1975, and peace only came to the country in 2002 after struggles between competing independence movements ended. Oil production had taken place since 1950 but on a relatively small scale. The political stability after 2002 meant that the long-term agreements between oil companies and the government could be structured and the valuable offshore oil revenues could be exploited. Many of the world's major multinational oil companies were involved, including BP, ExxonMobil, and Chevron. Angola soon emerged as the large oil producer in Africa capable of producing around two million barrels of oil a day, a capacity second only to Nigeria. Much of it was exported to oil-thirsty China. By 2012, after the great recession was ending, oil production ramped up to meet growing global demand. By 2014, when a barrel of oil was $100, Angola had moved from the standard resource curse of a kleptocracy to a *captured state*.[30] This is a state where the political elite and companies operate together to privatize the benefits of public resources.[31] You knew Angola was a captured state when each member of the Angolan parliament was given a new $100,000 Lexus to pass legislation. Or when the daughter of the president was made the sole owner of the monopolistic mobile phone company and appointed head of the state oil company. She is Africa's first female billionaire. Angola is not a *failed state*, but a captured state. The state is working well to enrich the political elite and selected private companies.

The sudden influx of oil revenues and the thousands of expatriates and locals paid by foreign companies spurred inflation in Angola and made it difficult for ordinary people to survive. In 2015, a bottle of coke averaged ten dollars. Government coffers filled as revenue increased from $32 billion in 2005 to $64 billion in 2015. But much of the government revenue from oil was siphoned off by the political elite or spent on prestigious megaprojects rather than improving social welfare. In 1975, the population of Luanda was a half million; today, it is more than six million. Luanda is one of the unequal cities in the world with the oil revenues providing an extravagant and luxurious life of few, while the majority get by on less than two dollars a day. The country became sharply divided, with marked inequality between a small, politically connected elite and the vast majority of poor people living in peripheral settlements. The cocooned life of expatriate oil workers and corrupt politicians living in exclusive, gated communities was set against a landscape of grinding poverty. Around half of the population is malnourished, and the country has the continent's lowest life expectancies and highest infant mortality; Angola has been characterized as the world's richest poor country.

The oil boom began to falter as a barrel of oil fell from $100 in 2014 to as low as $11 during the pandemic shutdown. As its economy crashed, Angola had difficulty getting aid, as the previous vast revenues meant that it was classified as an upper-middle-income country, making it ineligible for many aid programs. The government has slashed spending, even stopping purchasing malaria medicine and closing public hospitals. The crash in oil prices means a decline in the value of local currency. That makes it harder for local people with access only to local currency. The government refused to pay for garbage collection and the mounting rubbish led to an outbreak of yellow fever. Oil, while it enriched a few, was more of a curse than a blessing for the majority of the population.

WIDER CONNECTIONS

African Union

The countries of Africa are also tied together in various international organizations. The Organization of African Unity (OAU) was established by thirty-two states in 1963 to promote unity and create solidarity between the African states. As more countries achieved independence, membership grew. The OAU was superseded by the African Union (AU) in 1992, which now includes all independent countries in the continent. A principal aim is to foster the integration of African countries through trade agreements, to reduce the gender gap and inequality, and to "silence the guns." The AU plays an important role in providing a forum for African-wide discussions and for raising issues but currently lacks the policy tools to achieve these aims. Barriers to integration, for example, include an infrastructure that promotes exports rather than internal economic coherence and the vast differences between states in their ability to achieve shared economic and social objectives. However, there are plans to create an African Economic Union, similar in form to the EU with similar goals for a single, tariff-free, common market, a central bank, and a common currency by 2023. In 2018 the AU adopted a policy of free movement of people within the entire bloc.

The AU is also involved in peace-keeping missions. The AU has sent troops, recruited from member states, to intervene and stop genocide and war crimes. States receive some benefits for their participation in sending troops.[32] Since 2003, AU troops have been involved actively in Burundi, the CAR, Darfur, Somalia, and South Sudan. Some of the operational missions are noted in table 9.3. AU troops are often deployed as part of UN missions. They are an easier political choice for multinational peacekeeping missions because they are able to draw on local experience and with better racial optics. White troops in Africa as part of international missions are a reminder of colonial days. AU troop missions are often supported by troops from the UN as well as from individual countries, and are often transported by U.S. military or French military planes. Troops of these two nations also act as advisors on the ground. This raises tactical issues of the lack of integration between multinational forces.[33] There are also more strategic issues, such as when international peacekeeping becomes *coercive diplomacy*. One study looked at a threatened AU intervention in Burundi in 2015 that failed to materialize because of Burundi's successful diplomacy and the unwillingness of many African leaders to countenance AU intervention that could threaten national sovereignty.[34] Coercive diplomacy by the UN is used more often in the African context, not simply because of the scale of the threat, but also because of small African countries' relative lack of international power. There is an asymmetry in the use of internal policing and even of international criminal justice. African leaders are regularly hauled up to international courts for war crimes but no political or military leaders in the United States were ever indicted for war crimes in the invasion of Vietnam or Iraq.

Table 9.3.   Active Deployment of African Union Troops

Country	Troops	Opponents
Somalia	20,600	al Shabaab
CAR, Uganda	5,000	Lord's Resistance Army
Mali, Niger, Chad, Burkina Faso	5,000	Islamist rebel groups
CAR	3,500	Local militias

The War on Terror

The United States is an active economic partner with many African countries. While there is a long-standing history of trade and commerce with Africa, direct military interventions, unlike in Central and South America, are rare. The United States was never part of the partition of Africa and so had no colonies to defend. The United States did get involved during the Cold War when it installed and supported brutal dictators such as Mobuto in the Congo for his supposed anti-Communism. The United States saw liberation movements in Angola and Mozambique as a Communist-led front and worried that Ethiopia was turning toward the Soviet Bloc after the fall of Haile Selassie in 1974. But in general the United States tended to ignore Africa in favor of South America, East Asia, and Southeast Asia as strategically more important.

Attitudes began to change when the War on Terror became a guiding strategy. The United States was eager to suppress radical Islamicist movements just as they were becoming more active in Africa. A number of groups can be identified. Al Shabaab, allied to al Qaeda, has been active since 2006 and currently boasts between seven thousand and nine thousand members, recruiting in the West as well as in the Middle East and east Africa. Al Shabaab is active in Eritrea, Somalia, and north Kenya, has conducted terrorist attacks across the region, and controls large parts of rural areas of Somalia. Al Shabaab launched a terrorist attack in a mall in Nairobi, Kenya and killed sixty-seven innocent shoppers.

There are various groups active in the Sahel. In Mali in 2012, al Qaeda affiliates joined with Tuareg separatists to take over the north of the country. Sharia law was imposed.[35] In response, France sent troops and the UN authorized the deployment of AU troops. The Islamicists were routed; they melted away into the desert sand but still pose a serious security threat. Terrorist groups such as the Islamic State in West Africa Province (ISWAP) are active in Burkina Faso, Cameroon, Chad, Mali, Mauritania, and Niger.

France plays an important role in the region. French troops were significant in dismantling the Islamicist control of northern Mali, and they continue to operate in Burkina Faso, Chad, and Mali. The United States has also expanded its footprint. The United States has drone bases in Agadez in Niger and N'Djamena in Chad that can trace the movement of militants and provide information and intelligence in real time to local troops and allies. U.S. advisors and troops are also stationed in Burkina Faso, Mali, Niger, and Chad.

Africa is now such an important region for the U.S. War on Terror that the U.S. Africa Command, one of eleven commands of the U.S. Department of Defense, was established in 2007. There are only around seven thousand troops stationed in Africa, but this is a large increase over the last twenty years. The United States provides specialized support, air cover, logistical support, intelligence, and surveillance across the Sahel and the Horn of Africa. A major camp was established in 2001 in Djibouti, Camp Lemonnier, built on the grounds of an old Foreign Legion camp; it houses approximately one thousand U.S. special forces and numerous aviation units. Camp Lemonnier is a base for a vast drone campaign. A drone leaves the base every forty minutes.

The China Connection

While the United States has stepped up its military and security footprint in Africa, China has extended its economic influence. Photo 9.1 is a billboard in Nairobi, Kenya that is suggestive of the growing ties. China is one the biggest markets for primary commodities, including oil and gas, diamonds, and uranium. The economies of resource-rich African countries benefit from the growth of China's economy. China's trade with Africa was only $4 billion in 1990 but increased to $200 billion by 2010. Export increased 40 percent in a staggering rate of growth from 2000 to 2006, although exports declined after 2015 as China's growth slowed.

China is also a major investor in the continent. China invested $299 million from 2005 to 2018, building roads, dams, bridges, ports, and railways. It also allocated $130 billion in loans to African countries since 2000. Hundreds of thousands of Chinese have moved to Africa. There are more than ten thousand Chinese companies in Africa.

The United States still invests more in Africa than China, but it is the rate of growth of China's involvement that is striking. Between 2000 and 2014, China's investment in Africa increased from 2 percent of U.S. levels to 55 percent.[36] Chinese economic investment in Africa tends to be tied more closely to the Chinese state. British, French, and U.S. economic involvement tends to be between private companies and nation-states, while Chinese involvement engages government-owned companies and companies closely associated with the Chinese government. Chinese investment in Africa is knitted more closely into the geopolitical aims of the China state than the investment patterns of other countries. However, there are those who argue that Chinese investment fits in more closely to national economies' development strategies of adding value.[37]

Photo 9.1.   Sign in Nairobi, Kenya (John Rennie Short)

We should be careful of drawing too sharp a distinction between a United States dominated by geopolitical objectives with China's geoeconomic goals. The United States has major economic interests, and China has geopolitical objectives. U.S. direct investment in Africa is almost double that of China's, which is even eclipsed by France's and the UK's. So geoeconomics is still an important part of the U.S.-Africa relationship. The China-Africa connection is also more than just about economic development; it also comes with geopolitical consequences for Africa. China supported Al Bashir, the dictator of Sudan, for years in order to maintain the flow of oil. China even sent thousands of troops in 2000 to protect the Sudanese oil fields from the Sudan People's Liberation Army. When Robert Mugabe became a pariah in the West for his brutal rule in Zimbabwe, China helped to keep it in power with its bilateral ties. China purchased diamonds, tobacco, and uranium, and a state-owned company, China International Water and Electric, farmed 250,000 acres in southern Zimbabwe. Because of Zimbabwe's shortage of hard currency, trade was conducted by barter. In return for access to land and mineral resources, China supplied Zimbabwe with fighter planes, military vehicles, and radar systems. China also uses its economic stature and connections to influence voting in international forums such as the UN and in elections for international regulatory bodies.

The U.S. involvement in Africa is more than just the War on Terror, while China's involvement is more than just an economic transaction. In the future, Africa may become an arena for more direct competition between the two powers.

GEOPOLITICAL HOTSPOT: THE CONTEXT FOR BOKO HARAM

Boko Haram came to international prominence in 2014 when it kidnapped three hundred girls from a female boarding school in Chibok, in northern Nigeria, and took them away in the middle of the night on trucks and motorcycles. The event captured global media attention and the safe return of the girls became one of those issues that celebrities started to promote. It is useful to understand the context.[38]

Boko Haram stared as a nonviolent movement. Its origins lie in the relative poverty and political marginalization of northern Nigeria compared to the more affluent southern regions. Boko Haram was also an expression of discontent at the prevalence of corruption in Nigerian society. The country has valuable oil reserves but much of the wealth is siphoned off by a tiny political elite. Few benefits percolate to the ordinary people in northern Nigeria.

Boko Haram started its operations in 2002 in the Borno region of northern Nigeria.[39] The Nigerian north/south divide is also overlain with religious differences. The north is Muslim while the south is either Christian or animist. The Muslims of the north long felt marginalized. The name, Boko Haram, can be translated as either "Western education is forbidden," or "Western education is unclean." At first hearing it sounds like a backward-looking, almost premodern slogan. There is a deeper meaning. Education in the north paid no attention to the cultural sensibilities of the Muslim population; it was also like much of the Nigerian public services, where bribes and kickbacks are common. Students can get better grades by paying for them. Since students in the north were poorer, they performed less well and were less able to get employment. The education system, rather than leveling social and religious differences across the country, magnified and exacerbated them. Even those who did well on their exams often could not find employment. So public education in much of northern Nigeria was associated with an imposed alien culture and poor outcomes that did not lead to employment. One study found that those in northern Nigeria most against the education system and more favorable to Boko Haram were not the uneducated but those with more direct experience of the system.[40] The education system was perceived widely as corrupt and as a force of cultural marginalization.

From 2009, Boko Haram morphed into a more violent organization and started to attack public buildings. Nigerian police and military, with a well-deserved reputation for corruption and brutality, responded in a violent crackdown. More than eight thousand villagers were killed by military forces between 2009 and 2015. The military's violence and extra-judicial killings hardened support for Boko Haram. The presidential election in 2011 of a Christian from the south, Goodluck Jonathan, added to the sense of marginalization in the north. Jonathan treated Boko Haram as a northern issue, not a national problem. While the state's response was brutal, it was not very successful. Boko Haram expanded its operations in a region that stretched across the very porous and poorly policed borders of Nigeria, Cameroon, Niger, and Chad, where it sometimes acted as the only functioning state, providing legal and health services.

The election of the ex-military man Muhammadu Buhari as Nigeria's president in 2015 led to a more direct confrontation with Boko Haram. He had pledged to defeat the organization, and in new offensives, the Nigerian military retook control over some territory. The military campaigns did not defeat Boko Haram, which continues to operate in the liminal border zone of three countries and is still able to mount attacks.

Boko Haram changed over time with young cadres replacing killed and captured leaders. Internal power struggles led to a split in 2016, and the creation of the Islamic State in West Africa. The organization boasts fifteen thousand soldiers. In contrast to its origins as a nonviolent movement, Boko Haram now has an appetite for violence and kidnapping. Boko Haram has lost territory since 2015 with the renewed campaigns of the Nigerian state, but that loss now appears as only a brief lull in another round of attacks on infrastructure and public buildings. Boko Haram still controls significant territory in the more rural areas of northern Nigeria and nearby countries. Its core base is now in an area around Lake Chad.[41] In its operation, Boko Haram had displaced more than two million people and killed thousands.

In the wake of the Chibok kidnappings, the United States and other nations pledged to help in the recapture of the young women. There were problems. First, the only way to get rid of Boko Haram involves collaboration with Nigerian forces, widely seen as a serial violator of human rights. Some aid was still given, and some girls were recaptured and returned to their homes. Second, Nigeria, despite being a weak state, is Africa's largest economy and most populous country with enough regional and global influence to preclude the necessary international intervention.[42] Even weak states, if they have international leverage, can resist international pressure for action.

SUGGESTED READINGS

Abrahamsen, R. (2017). Africa and international relations: Assembling Africa, studying the world. *African Affairs, 116*, 125–39.

Baaz, E. M., & Verweijen, J. (2018). Confronting the colonial: The (re) production of "African" exceptionalism in critical security and military studies. *Security Dialogue, 49*, 57–69.

Browning, C. S., & de Oliveira, A. F. (2017). Reading brand Africa geopolitically: Nation branding and competitive identity in world politics. *Geopolitics, 22*, 481–501.

Diallo, I. (2019). *Geopolitics of French in Francophone sub-Saharan Africa: Attitudes, language use, and identities*. Newcastle: Cambridge Scholars Publishing.

Foucher, M. (2020). African borders: Putting paid to a myth. *Journal of Borderlands Studies, 35*, 287–306.

Grant, R. (2015). *Africa: Geographies of change*. New York and Oxford: Oxford University Press

Heffernan, A. (2019). Africanizing the state: Globalizing the discipline. *Nokoko, 7*, 203–40.

Kapuscinski, R. (2001). *The shadow of the sun*. New York: A. A. Knopf.

Kornega, F., & Mthembu, P. (eds.). (2020). *Africa and the world: Navigating shifting geo-politics*. Johannesburg: Mapungubwe Institute for Strategic Reflection.

Mailey, J. R. (2015). The anatomy of the resource curse: Predatory lending in Africa's extractive industries. *Special Report No. 3*, Africa Center for Strategic Studies. https://africacenter.org/publication/the-anatomy-of-the-resource-curse-predatory-investment-in-africas-extractive-industries/.

Walker, A. (2016). *Eat the heart of the infidel: The harrowing of Nigeria and the rise of Boko Haram*. London: Hurst and Co.

NOTES

1. One astute observer used an African proverb as his book title to situate an understanding of Africa's development: Amoako, K. Y. (2020). *Know the beginning well: An inside journey through five decades of African development.* Trenton, NJ: Africa World Press.

2. The phrase is the title for Joseph Conrad's 1899 novel, *The Heart of Darkness*, based on the Belgian Congo. It was the basis for the 1979 movie directed by Francis Ford Coppola, *Apocalypse Now*. Interesting to note that the "dark hearts" in both the novel and the movie belong to the White interlopers, not the indigenous people.

3. In this chapter I draw heavily from two excellent textbooks: Grant, R. (2015). *Africa: Geographies of change*. New York and Oxford: Oxford University Press; Stock, R. (2013, 3rd ed.). *Africa south of the Sahara*. London and New York: Guildford.

4. Hobsbawm, E. J. (1987). *The age of empire, 1875–1914*. London: Weidenfeld and Nicholson.

5. Butlin, R. (2009). *Geographies of empire: European empires and colonies c. 1880–1960*. Cambridge: Cambridge University Press.

6. Mamdani, M. (2001). *When victims become killers: Colonialism, nativism, and the genocide in Rwanda*. Princeton, NJ: Princeton University Press, 11.

7. Elkins, C. (2005). *Imperial reckoning: The untold story of Britain's gulag in Kenya*. New York: Henry Holt.

8. One of the best analyses of Rwanda and of recent events in Africa in general is Kapuscinski, R. (2001). *The shadow of the sun*. New York: A. A. Knopf.

9. Nugent, P., & Asiwaju, A. (eds.). (1996). *African boundaries: Barriers, conduits and opportunities*. London: Pinter/Caswell.

10. Foucher, M. (2020). African borders: Putting paid to a myth. *Journal of Borderlands Studies, 35*, 287–306. See the response: Walther, O. (2020). Comment on "African borders: Putting paid to a myth." *Journal of Borderlands Studies, 35*, 311–12.

11. Moyo, I. (2018). Theorising borders in Africa—What are the implications for African integration? *Africa Insight, 48*, 29.

12. Haklai, O., & Loizides, N. (eds.). (2015). *Settlers in contested lands: Territorial disputes and ethnic conflicts*. Stanford, CA: Stanford University Press.

13. Stasiulis, D., & Yuval-Davis, N. (eds.). (1995). *Unsettling settler societies: Articulations of gender, race, ethnicity and class*. London and Thousand Oaks: Sage.

14. Ginsburgh, N., & Jackson, W. (2019). Settler societies. In Worger, W. H., Ambler, C., & Achebe, N. (eds.), *A companion to African history*. London: Wiley, 77–91.

15. MacAskill, W. (2015, October 20). Does disinvestment work? *New Yorker*. https://www.newyorker.com/business/currency/does-divestment-work.

16. Republic of South Africa Truth and Reconciliation Commission. https://www.sahistory.org.za/article/truth-and-reconciliation-commission-trc-0.

17. Verdeja, E. (2017). Political reconciliation in postcolonial settler societies. *International Political Science Review, 38,* 227–41.

18. Moorcraft, P. L., & McLaughlin, P. (2010). *The Rhodesian war: A military history.* Mechanicsburg, PA: Stackpole Books.

19. Akpan, M. B. (1973). Black imperialism: Americo-Liberian rule over the African peoples of Liberia, 1841–1964. *Canadian Journal of African Studies, 2,* 217–36.

20. Johnston, P. (2008). The geography of insurgent organization and its consequences for civil wars: Evidence from Liberia and Sierra Leone. *Security Studies, 17,* 107–37.

21. Ferreira, I. A. (2017). Measuring state fragility: A review of the theoretical groundings of existing approaches. *Third World Quarterly, 38,* 1291–309.

22. Glawion, T., De Vries, L., & Mehler, A. (2019). Handle with care! A qualitative comparison of the Fragile States Index's bottom three countries: Central African Republic, Somalia and South Sudan. *Development and Change, 50,* 277–300.

23. Mamdani, *When victims become killers.*

24. Van Reybrouck, D. (2015). *Congo: The epic history of a people.* New York: Ecco/Harper Collins.

25. Devermont, J. (2020). *The Malian military ousts a wayward government.* Washington, DC: Center for Strategic and International Studies. https://www.csis.org/analysis/malian-military-ousts-wayward-government.

26. Agamben, G. (2004). *State of exception.* Chicago: University of Chicago Press.

27. Mailey, J. R. (2015). The anatomy of the resource curse: Predatory lending in Africa's extractive industries. *Special Report No. 3,* Africa Center for Strategic Studies. https://africacenter.org/publication/the-anatomy-of-the-resource-curse-predatory-investment-in-africas-extractive-industries/.

28. Human Rights Watch. (2020). *Equatorial Guinea: Why poverty plagues a high-income nation.* https://www.hrw.org/news/2017/01/27/equatorial-guinea-why-poverty-plagues-high-income-nation#.

29. Bassett, V., Landau, K., & Glandorf, J. (2020). *A master class in corruption: The Luanda leaks across the natural resource chain.* Washington, DC: Brookings. https://www.brookings.edu/blog/up-front/2020/07/23/a-master-class-in-corruption-the-luanda-leaks-across-the-natural-resource-value-chain/.

30. Africa Center for Strategic Studies. (2020). *The challenges for reform in Angola.* https://africacenter.org/spotlight/the-challenges-of-reform-in-angola/.

31. Hellman, J. S., Jones, G., & Kaufmann, D. (2000). *Seize the state, seize the day: State capture, corruption, and influence in transition.* Policy Research Working Paper 2444. Washington DC: World Bank. http://documents1.worldbank.org/curated/en/537461468766474836/125525322_20041117154552/additional/multi-page.pdf.

32. Williams, P. D. (2018). Joining AMISOM: why six African states contributed troops to the African Union Mission in Somalia. *Journal of Eastern African Studies, 12,* 172–92.

33. Carayannis, T., & Fowlis, M. (2017). Lessons from African Union–United Nations cooperation in peace operations in the Central African Republic. *African Security Review, 26,* 220–36.

34. Wilén, N., & Williams, P. D. (2018). The African Union and coercive diplomacy: The case of Burundi. *Journal of Modern African Studies, 56,* 673–96.

35. Anderson, J. L. (2013, July 1). State of terror: What happened when an al Qaeda affiliate ruled in Mali? *The New Yorker,* 36–47.

36. Pilling, D. (2019, March 27). The other side of Chinese investment in Africa. *Financial Times.* https://www.ft.com/content/9f5736d8-14e1-11e9-a581-4ff78404524e.

37. Manda, S. (2020). China's investment in Africa. *The Conversation.* https://theconversation.com/chinas-investments-in-africa-a-fresh-lens-offers-more-balanced-insights-121396.

38. Campbell, J., & Page, M. T. (2018). *Nigeria: What everyone needs to know*. New York: Oxford University Press.

39. Walker, A. (2016). *Eat the heart of the infidel: The harrowing of Nigeria and the rise of Boko Haram*. London: Hurst and Co.

40. Afzal, M. (2020). *From "Western education is forbidden" to the world's deadliest terrorist group*. Washington, DC: Brookings. https://www.brookings.edu/research/from -western-education-is-forbidden-to-the-worlds-deadliest-terrorist-group/.

41. Idika-Kalu, C. (2020). The socioeconomic impact of the Boko Haram insurgency in the Lake Chad Basin region. In *Terrorism and Developing Countries*. IntechOpen. https:// www.intechopen.com/books/terrorism-and-developing-countries/the-socioeconomic-im pact-of-the-boko-haram-insurgency-in-the-lake-chad-basin-region.

42. Mickler, D., Suleiman, M. D., & Maiangwa, B. (2019). Weak state, regional power, global player: Nigeria and the response to Boko Haram. *African Security, 12*, 272–99.

10

South Asia

GEOPOLITICAL CONTEXT

The geopolitics of South Asia has more than just regional significance. With two nuclear powers in permanent conflict, a long civil war in Afghanistan, simmering border issues, and endemic ethnic and religious tensions, this is a major hotspot on the world political map. The largest geopolitical rupture in the region is the continuing conflict between India and Pakistan. Since the two countries became independent from the UK in 1947, they have fought three wars, engaged in numerous proxy campaigns, and spawned an enduring standoff over Kashmir. There are also growing tensions along the China-India border as these two emerging powers compete for regional hegemony.

IMPERIAL LEGACIES

As one of the hearth areas of world civilization, this region experienced a substantial measure of imperial activity, from the rise of city-states such as Mohenjo-Daro and Harappa almost five thousand years ago, to the Mughal Empire (1528–1857) that diffused Islam into the subcontinent, to the more recent entry and then withdrawal of the British in the middle of the twentieth century. Let us concentrate on the most recent.

Initially the English then British involvement was strictly commercial. In the seventeenth century the East India Company established trading ports along the coast in such places as Madras (Chennai) and Bombay (Mumbai). In order to achieve greater control over trade, more inland territory was effectively annexed, and a large private army was established. The rebellion of 1857–1858 against East India Company rule led to the company's dissolution. The trade was so large and the geopolitical consequences so weighty that the British government took control and by 1859, India was a British colony.

Britain's vast Indian empire was a cash cow. Commodities from India fueled the British industrial revolution while the huge Indian market was an important and guaranteed site for the sale of British manufactured goods. There was an unequal exchange as the value-added work, and hence profits, accrued to British interests. India was an important force behind the "Great" in Great Britain.

Imperial management employed a variety of methods. There was direct control. The British administered two-thirds of the country and four-fifths of the population of close to 180 million. But elsewhere, Britain governed indirectly through local rulers. There were over 560 autonomous potentates, including the Maharajah of Bangalore, the Nizam of Hyderabad, the Rajah of Denkannal, and the Nabob of Oudh, whose armies could be called upon by the British. There was a patchwork of small princely states, such as Assam, Baluchistan, Bhutan, Hyderabad, Kashmir, Mysore, Sikkim, and Nepal, whose rulers owed allegiance to the British Crown.

There were limits to imperial expansion. The balance of power between Britain, competing powers, and local resistance defined the edges of empire. In the east, for example, British designs on Assam were contested by the Konbaung Dynasty of Burma in three Anglo-Burmese wars (1824–1885). Britain's ultimate military success meant that by 1885 Burma was a British colony. On the other side of the subcontinent, in the northwest frontier zone, British power butted up against the shadow of the Russian Empire and obstinate local resistance. A sense of the British geopolitical imagination is shown in figure 10.1. It depicts a bird's eye view of the border region around 1900. Two British soldiers, at the edge of a boundary line marked in red, look across the mountainous terrain of

LETTS'S BIRD'S EYE VIEW OF THE APPROACHES TO INDIA.

Figure 10.1. The British look north. "Letts's bird's eye view of the approaches to India," c. 1900 (Library of Congress, Geography and Map Division.)

Afghanistan. In the far distance is "Russian Territory." The British fought two wars—the First Afghan War (1839–1842), the Second Afghan War (1878–1880)—and led numerous military expeditions (1847–1908) all of which failed to discipline the Afghans. In 1903, the British delimited their control with the Durand Line, which pushed British control up into the mountains as a buffer against any possible Russian threat yet far enough away from the vulnerable and important settlements in the downriver valleys to provide some measure of security. The Durand Line went through the Pashtun cultural region. Imperial boundaries paid scant regard to cultural regions or ethnic loyalties. The contemporary border between Pakistan and Afghanistan closely follows this line. In the demarcation, the British recognized the local autonomy of the North-West Frontier Provinces. Later, under an independent Pakistan they were renamed the Federally Administered Tribal Areas.

IMPERIAL BREAKUP AND NEW NATION-STATES

There always was resistance to British imperialism. Anticolonialism waxed and waned but was a source of constant anxiety for the British ruling class. There was the Indian Rebellion of 1857–1858—sometimes referred to as the First War of Independence—and from 1915 to 1947, Mahatma Gandhi led a nonviolent campaign against British rule.[1]

The easy victories of the Japanese Army in Southeast Asia in World War II undermined the legitimacy of colonial rule and British authority. Across Southeast Asia independence movements were emboldened by the quick defeat of the prewar colonial powers of France, Netherlands, and UK. The postwar push for independence in the British colonies gained influence because a Labour government at home wanted to abandon Britain's imperial posture abroad. The postcolonial breakup of the British Empire in South Asia created newly independent states (see map 10.1), and in most of them, the nation-state comprises different and often competing ethnic and religious groups.[2] In 1947, India and Pakistan declared independence and a year later Burma and Sri Lanka gained independence.

British India split into the independent states of India and Pakistan. Muslim activists worried that they could lose power to an overwhelming Hindu majority in a postcolonial, unitary India. Muslims had been protected under the British raj, part of a policy to maintain religious differences in order to rule more effectively: "divide and rule" was a common technique across Britain's empire in Africa and Asia. With communal violence rising in intensity, the British drew up maps under the Radcliffe Commission to create two new states. It was a hasty and ill-conceived division, paying little heed to realities on the ground.[3] The boundary between Pakistan and India cut through the provinces of Punjab and Bengal, and the new Pakistan comprised two territories, East and West, both with Muslim majorities but separated by different languages, ethnicities, and over one thousand miles of Indian territory. Partition was enmeshed in communal violence between Muslims and Hindus with the figures ranging from two hundred thousand to two million deaths, and a vast exodus of people as Muslims in India moved to Pakistan, and Hindus in what is now Pakistan moved to India.

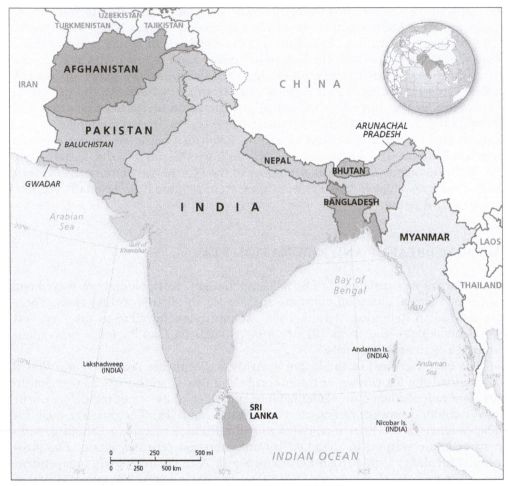

Map 10.1.   South Asia (International Mapping)

Tensions were high. A Hindu nationalist assassinated Gandhi for being too accommodating to Muslims. Partition, as it turned out, cemented the religious nature of the countries: Pakistan became more Muslim while in India a significant Muslim minority often felt under threat. Pakistan became an Islamic republic while Hindu nationalism, embodied in the Bharatiya Janata Party (BJP), later came to dominate Indian political life. When its leader, Narendra Modi, became prime minister in 2014, he used his power to create a Hindu state.

THE INDO-PAKISTAN CONFLICT

The two countries emerged from the bloodbath of partition to become implacable enemies. The tension between the two is marked by outbreaks of war, gray zone activity, and constant competition.[4]

The first Indo-Pakistan War of 1947 took place immediately after partition. Some princely states were allowed to join either India or Pakistan or to remain independent. Kashmir (together with Jammu) was a majority Muslim state but with a Hindu ruler, Maharajah Hari Singh. Pakistan, fearing he would declare for India, sent troops to back up local tribal forces. The maharaja called on India for support. The final battle lines established a Line of Control (LOC) agreed upon in 1949. Under the cease-fire, India gained control of two-thirds of Kashmir, Jammu and Ladakh (see map 10.2). The border along the LOC remains a constant source of irritation between the two countries. The second Indo-Pakistan War of 1965 also arose in the contested region of Kashmir. Pakistan aided an insurgency, and India responded with a full-scale invasion of West Pakistan. The seventeen-day war was a bloody affair with thousands killed.

The Indo-Pakistan War of 1971 was prompted by East Pakistan's breakaway from West Pakistan. Pakistan at that time was one state with two very different parts. Although both were majority Muslim, West Pakistan was predominantly Urdu speaking while East Pakistan was Bengali. Urdu speakers from the West dominated the Pakistan Army. Atrocities in East Pakistan by the Pakistan armed forces, including mass rape, led to deaths estimated at between three hundred thousand and three million, and ten million Bengalis were forced to flee to India. Indian forces joined with Bangladeshi irregulars to defeat the Pakistani Army and Bangladesh became an independent country in 1971. When Pakistani forces attacked along the western frontier with India, they were defeated. The war was another loss for Pakistan. Bangladesh achieved independence, and almost one hundred thousand Pakistani soldiers were taken prisoner. The Indian military exerted significant damage on the Pakistan army, air force, and navy.

The contested region of Kashmir was the scene of the next Indo-Pakistan War of 1999, when Pakistani forces moved across the LOC, and India responded with a military and diplomatic offensive and regained control. Thousands of Pakistani soldiers were killed in what was yet another defeat for Pakistan.

There is both direct confrontation and gray zone activity. The Pakistani military intelligence organization, Inter-Services Intelligence, known as ISI, is often described in Pakistan newspapers as the "invisible government" because of its outsized and secretive role in Pakistan foreign policy. ISI is thought to be a major funder and supporter for terrorist organizations such as Lashkar-e-Taiba, responsible for the attack on Mumbai in 2008 that killed 164 people. In that attack, armed terrorists landed by boat and then fired indiscriminately into a hospital, two hotels, a railway station, and a popular café. Pakistan's tacit support of such terrorist organizations undercuts attempts at rapprochement with India.

The conflict between the two countries makes it difficult for the United States to navigate between them. The U.S. government would like more economic connections with India—a huge market with an expanding middle class —yet requires military and strategic assistance from Pakistan as a geopolitical ally in its war against terrorist organizations in the region.

The two adversaries are locked and loaded with nuclear weapons.[5] Both countries possess around one hundred nuclear warheads, and in 2014 Pakistan test-fired a new ballistic missile, Shaheen III, that can carry a nuclear warhead up to 1,900 miles. The conflict seems embedded into the fabric of each society with both seeing an existential threat in the other. In India a rising Hindu nationalism sees Islamic Pakistan as a political and religious rival. And in Pakistan the powerful military that controls large parts of the economy as well as much of the direction of foreign policy tends to see things from the military perspective.[6] Pakistani support for the Taliban was in part due to desire to have a strategic redoubt in case of invasion by India. Pakistan's often conflicting policy toward Islamic groups in Afghanistan can only be understood in terms of a strategy to deal with conflict with India. The fact that Pakistan has been so roundly defeated in each of its major encounters seems to generate extra animosity among the powerful Pakistani military. A rising Hindi nationalism in one country and a powerful military in the other, combined with religious fundamentalism in both, do not provide much confidence in the countries reverting to normal politics any time soon. And Kashmir is the open sore that refuses to heal.

Kashmir

The contested region of Kashmir continues to be the site of tensions.[7] We have already noted that it is divided between a Pakistani- and Indian-administered Kashmir (see map 10.2). It remains a significant source of conflict, a flashpoint always liable to burst into conflagration. In August 2019, tensions were heightened when the Indian government abolished Indian-administered Kashmir's autonomy without any consultation with local people, stripped it of statehood, and partitioned it into two federally administered territories. In the Kashmiri capital of Srinagar, a heavy troop presence kept people at home in an aggressive lockdown with a tightly enforced curfew. While India's grip on Kashmir tightened, its local support weakened. Observers of the troop mobilization noted more signs that read "Go India, go back."[8] Modi's predecessors used the narrative of inclusion to weaken Kashmiri separatism. Modi's current rhetoric of Hindu domination, in contrast, may strengthen local support for separatism.

BORDER DISPUTES

Common to other regions of the postcolonial world, South Asia has a number of border issues that are the legacy of imperial boundaries carried into the postcolonial world of new nation-states. The hasty and awkward partition led to numerous and ongoing disputes. It was only in 2015 that Bangladesh finally settled its forty-one-year border dispute with India when both countries agreed on the disposition of 110 border enclaves. There is the 1,510-mile-long border between Pakistan and Afghanistan that bisects the ethnic Pashtun region. This border region is often beyond the effective reach of both national governments' control and hence is a space vulnerable to control by nongovernment agencies and terrorist groups such as al Qaeda. But perhaps the most explosive border conflict is between China and India.

Map 10.2. Kashmir (International Mapping)

India and China

China and India share a long 2,167-mile border. The boundary was fixed by British imperial officials. There are various disputed areas.[9] Arunachal Pradesh in the eastern Himalayas is now part of India but is claimed by China. The McMahon Line, drawn in 1914 between Tibet and Britain, gave Arunachal Pradesh to India and annexed 25,000 square miles of territory that previously belonged to China. It is a remote area only connected to India by a narrow land corridor that China describes as "South Tibet." Today, China claims 32,000 square miles of Arunachal Pradesh.

In the Indian state of Sikkim, tightly squashed between Bhutan, Nepal, and China, more than one hundred soldiers were injured in recent clashes between Indian and Chinese troops.

There is also a proxy dispute in Bhutan over the disputed region of Doklam. When the Chinese recently started to build roads in the region, India—a close ally of Bhutan—sent troops to protect Bhutan's claim. This border dispute pits China against India rather than the tiny state of Bhutan.

In the western Himalayas, the border between China and India were never clearly demarcated (see map 10.2). The border dispute led to the high-altitude Indo-China war of 1962. China gained control over 14,000 square miles of Aksai Chin. Occasional skirmishes followed but after a 1988 meeting between the Indian prime minister and Deng Xiaoping, things quieted down. Both sides agreed to ban firearms along the border zone to lessen the tension. A poorly defined line of control, agreed in principle by both countries, follows an erratic course across rivers, 14,000-foot-plus snowcapped peaks, and a glacier. Confrontation along this line heated up as China constructed highways along the border and more Chinese troops moved into the area. In response, India built roads close to the line of control to service a new air base, and a more nationalist Indian government spoke openly of taking back all of Kashmir, including Aksai Chin. In June 2020, it was reported that twenty Indian troops were killed in a confrontation with Chinese troops in the Galwan Valley (see map 10.2). It was the first deadly encounter in the border region in almost fifty years. As tensions mounted, troops from both sides have flooded into the region.

The tension is made more acute because the events take place in the context of contested Kashmir and China's Belt and Road Initiative (BRI) expansionary policy. Aksai Chin sits close to both Pakistan- and Indian-administered territories. As part of the BRI, China has an economic corridor with Pakistan in the Karakoram Highway through Pakistan-administered Kashmir and close to the Indian-administered Kashmir.[10]

The dampening of conflict that was possible in the past is less easy now. Xi in China and Modi in India both use aggressive rhetoric of nationalism in their foreign policy. Modi plans to build more than sixty roads close to the Chinese border. Meanwhile Xi promotes an expansionist China that will not back down. Watch this border space in the years to come; it is a potential conflict zone for two emerging powers eager to advance their claim to major-power status.[11] The Sino-Indian border dispute, once only an irritant, now has the possibility of engaging two growing powers in more direct confrontation.[12]

NATIONS AND STATES

The postcolonial states created from the breakup of Empire rarely were homogeneous. Most of them comprised different ethnic and religious groups. In a number of states the diverse groups make national integration a problematic affair. A common theme in the region is the attempt by states to create a religious political space that is more homogeneous. In some states, there is a shift from an inclusive secular state to a more theocratic state dominated by the religious majority. Pakistan and Bangladesh have steadily moved to a more fundamentalist Muslim national identity. Buddhist nationalists in Sri Lanka long have railed against the Hindi Tamil minority. In Myanmar, Buddhist nationalists are part of the long-standing resentment against the Rohingya Muslim minority. Let us briefly review a number of these multiethnic states experiencing conflicts.

Sri Lanka

In Sri Lanka, the two main groups are divided by religion and language. Photo 10.1 shows a stone plaque in Kandy that celebrates the multilingual nature of the new state with words in English, Sinhala, and Tamil. The Buddhist Sinhalese constitute about 85 percent of the population. The remaining 15 percent are Hindu Tamils, who are concentrated around Jaffna and along the northeast coast. There are also Tamils in central plantation areas of Nuwara Eliya, descendants of indentured plantation laborers brought over from India in the nineteenth century. After independence in 1948, the state became a vehicle for Sinhalese interests, often at the expense of the Tamils. Tamil alienation led to resistance against the Sri Lankan state. A Tamil separatist group, the Liberation Tigers of Tamil Eelam, known popularly as the Tamil Tigers, fought an insurgency campaign from 1983 to 2009. The north and east of the island came under Tamil control. The civil war was deadly. More than one hundred thousand people died. The civil war halted economic development; it made the country too dangerous for large-scale investment. The civil war was only ended in 2009 with the final defeat of separatist forces.[13] Close to one hundred thousand Sri Lankan Tamils remain in refugee camps in the southern Indian state of Tamil Nadu. A more recent rise of Sinhalese nationalism often fueled by Buddhist clergy and the "postwar triumphalism" of certain politicians has increased tensions in recent years.[14]

Photo 10.1. Independence commemoration in Kandy, Sri Lanka (John Rennie Short)

Bhutan

In Bhutan, the majority of the country's 733,000 population are Buddhist, with around 25 percent Hindu. Ethnic Nepali, who constitute around one-third of the population, face discrimination; many were forced out and there are now 23,000 refugees in camps in Nepal.

Pakistan

In Pakistan, there are also a variety of distinct and different regions. Different regional languages, for example, include Baluchi (southwest), Sind (southeast), Punjabi (along the eastern border) and Pashtun (in the northwest). In the northwest, the Pashtuns have more cultural affinity with fellow Pashtuns in neighboring Afghanistan than with people in the south of Pakistan. The Pakistan Taliban gained control of the northwest in 2007; they introduced sharia law, banned dancing and music shops, and destroyed four hundred schools. In 2009 the Pakistan Army launched a campaign against Taliban control on Swat Valley, only a four-hour drive from Islamabad and hence vulnerable to Taliban takeover. Pakistan's military offensive against the Taliban pushed farmers out of the Tirah Valley, where more than one hundred thousand people make a living by growing marijuana. In 2014, the Pakistan Army launched a major campaign against the Pakistani Taliban in North Waziristan. More than a half-million people were evacuated or left the region. Over the past decade, Pakistan has lost fifty thousand soldiers and civilians by taking on these militant groups, once supported and now challenged. The Pakistani Taliban slaughtered 150 students at Peshawar in December 2014.

Baluchistan was a separate kingdom until incorporated into Pakistan in 1947. A separatist movement gained momentum in the 1960s, but was quashed in the 1970s, and reemerged in recent years around demands for increased royalties for natural resources. The province is rich in resources but remains one of the poorest provinces in the country. A tiny elite is very wealthy; there is a small middle class and a vast majority of poor people. The poor and the middle class are more supportive of greater autonomy. Baluchistan, as well the North West areas, highlight a feature of Pakistan geography. Pakistan emerged from separate and distinct regions, some of which, such as Baluchistan, Punjab, and North West, had greater links with similar regions in neighboring countries, respectively Iran, India, and Afghanistan.

Bangladesh

Bangladesh is populated predominantly by Muslim Bengalis. The Chittagong Hill Tracts, however, is home to hill tribes known as the Jumma. When the Bangladeshi government tried to settle the region with Bengalis, these tribal peoples formed a resistance movement that was successful in gaining more autonomy for the state. A land grab of indigenous land for commercial plantations continues to provoke resistance, and more than one-third of the Bangladesh Army is deployed in this small region of the country.

Myanmar

Various ethic religious groups inhabit Myanmar. The Burmese dominate demographically and politically. During British rule, the other minorities were favored, but under an independent Burma, they have not fared as well. A major issue concerns the Rohingya, a Muslim minority living in Rakhine province.

During World War II, the Rakhine fought with the British while Buddhists sided with the Japanese. After Burma gained independence, the Rohingya were denied citizenship and remained vulnerable. A consequent separatist movement fought government forces.

It was assumed that the introduction of a more democratic government in Myanmar would inaugurate a less punitive attitude toward the Rohingya. Myanmar was long ruled by a military dictatorship. From 1962 until 2010 a repressive military elite ran the country. There were periodic uprisings and embargoes, but the junta persisted in their quixotic and brutal rule. The state was on a permanent war footing against ethnic minorities. In 2010, things began to change. A very popular figure, Aung San Suu Kyi, was released from house arrest and allowed to take control of her party, the National League for Democracy (NLD), and play a significant role in governance. The military still held onto power with an assured parliamentary representation and with guaranteed control of the key ministries of defense, interior, and border affairs. However, the change in government did not mean changed attitudes toward the Rohingya. The NLD and Kyi supported the army's military campaign of ethnic cleansing. When Rohingya separatists attacked border posts in 2016, the Burmese Army responded with deliberate attempts to expel the Rohingya, egged on by Buddhist nationals eager to have a unitary Buddhist state. From 2017, the military pursued a policy of ethnic cleansing. Consequently, over one million Rohingya left for neighboring Bangladesh, where many of them remain in refugee camps.

Kyi's power increased and her NLD party won the November 2020 election in a landslide. However, personal animosities with a military leader and the military elites' fear of being sidelined even further prompted a military coup in February 2021. Myanmar, it seems, is again sliding into military dictatorship.[15]

Elsewhere in Myanmar, while the Burmese dominate the central part of the country and especially the area around Yangon and the Irrawaddy valley, hill tribes continue to occupy the higher, more inaccessible border areas. The British encouraged ethnic minorities, such as the Chin, Kachin, Kayin, Shan, and Wa, through indirect rule and through policies that favored them over the Burmese. For example, the British used the hill tribes for paid military service but denied entry to the Burmese. Some of these hill tribes have resisted incorporation into the Burmese state and continue to fight against the Burmese Army. Only in 1993 did the Kachin Independence Organization sign a cease-fire with the government, ending their year-long war. But renewed fighting in 2018 caused thousands to be displaced. Many of the liberation movements persist over the years because they can generate the necessary funds from the lucrative drug trade. The Golden Triangle of Laos, Thailand, and Myanmar is a hub in Southeast Asia's opium trade. Proceeds have funded Shan armed forces.

Creating a Hindu State in India

More recently, a fundamentalist Hindi vision of India has emerged after decades of a secular, more inclusive form of politics. Muslims constitute 14 percent of the 1.3 billion people. The vast majority of people are Hindu, but there is a substantial Muslim population in a belt running from Kashmir through the Great

Plains to the border area surrounding Bangladesh, a legacy of the Mughal Empire. There is also a significant Muslim population in the region around Mumbai. Sikhs are concentrated in the Punjab. There have been periodic outbreaks of communal violence since partition. In 1992, for example, more than two thousand people were killed, mostly Muslim, in sectarian violence.

The BJP under Modi pursues a vision of India as a Hindu/national political space. He was minister of the state of Gujarat in 2000 when communal violence broke out. He was deemed partially responsible, denied a visa into the United States, and boycotted by the EU. His Hindu nationalism is fiercely anti-Muslim, constructing a narrative of historical Hindu subjugation by the Mughal Empire. Since he was elected prime minister in 2014, he has encouraged explicit demonstrations of Hindu nationalism. This agenda, reinforced when he won reelection in 2019, involves the suppression of interfaith marriage between Hindus and Muslims and new citizenship rules that discriminate against Muslims. The young Muslim couple shown in photo 10.2, walking along a promenade in Mumbai, are seen by the more fervent Hindu nationalist as less than full Indian citizens. In 2019, the India Supreme Court allowed the construction of a Hindu temple on a disputed site in Ayodhya. The recent display of Indian power in Kashmir is part of the long-standing Hindu nationalist agenda to bring the predominantly Muslim Kashmir under more formal Indian government control.

Photo 10.2. Young people in Mumbai (John Rennie Short)

CHINA AND SOUTH ASIA

China has a huge influence in the area. From west to east, China has borders with Afghanistan, Pakistan, India, Nepal, Bhutan, and Myanmar.[16] The British created many of the borders with these states as they extended their empire at the expense of a weakening Qing Dynasty. A resurgent China has reactivated old claims along these borders and especially the Indian border.

As a major economy, China exerts tremendous power, especially in its asymmetrical relations with much weaker countries in the region. China's economic role is most obvious in the BRI. The BRI comprises four major projects in the region, which are the China-Pakistan Economic Corridor (CPEC), the Bangladesh-China-India-Myanmar Economic Corridor (BCIM), the Trans-Himalaya Corridor, and China's cooperation with Bangladesh, Sri Lanka, and the Maldives under the twenty-first-century Maritime Silk Road. Together, these projects represent a significant investment of almost a quarter of a trillion dollars in infrastructure that ties China to the regions of the rest of the world through South Asia.

The $62 billion CPEC, for example, hinges on making the Pakistani port of Gwadar a vital hub of maritime, air, and overland routes and on the expansion of Sri Lanka's deep-water port in Kandy as a low-cost transit point (see photo 10.3). However, Chinese involvement in Sri Lanka has raised issues of the BRI as a form of "debt-trap diplomacy."[17]

Only India is a sort of match for China. Their interaction shapes geopolitics across the region.[18] There are obvious areas of cooperation between two of the two most populous countries in the world. Then there is the long-term Chinese vision of constructing a China-Pakistan India-Iran-Afghanistan-Kazakhstan Corridor—a multination mega-connectivity project that will dominate the heartland of Central and South Asia and even the Eurasian continent. There is also competition.[19]

Photo 10.3.   Deep water harbor in Sri Lanka (John Rennie Short)

China seeks military capability beyond the South China Sea and to resist confinement to East Asia. But many in India see China's expansion of influence into the Indian Ocean as a possible threat.[20] In response, Indian military is upgrading its naval, coast guard, and air capabilities in the Indian Ocean, expanding military ties with other major players in the Indo-Pacific. A memorandum of agreement, signed with the United States in August 2016, aligns the sharing of military facilities for refueling and replenishment. Since 2018, India has also gained greater access to French-controlled Reunion, Singapore's Changi Naval Base, and the port of Duqm in Oman. All of these are attempts to counter a rising Chinese presence in the Indian Ocean.

The major players now see the Indian Ocean as a vital region and are hurrying to get access to ports and bases and to connect with local and regional actors in bilateral, strategic arrangements to advance their interests and block those of possible competitors.

GEOPOLITICAL HOTSPOT: AFGHANISTAN

Geography is not kind to Afghanistan. Situated in the heart of Asia, it was long the stage for imperial designs from Alexander the Great to the rivalry between Britain and Russia in the nineteenth century as well as between the United States and Muslim fundamentalists in the twenty-first century. Afghanistan is a war-torn land and the setting for the longest U.S. war.[21]

Some recent history is in order. In 1978, a small, urban-based, Communist Party overthrew the existing government. The new socialist neighbor was appreciated by the Soviets, who stepped up aid. The new regime was thuggish and deeply factionalized. It forced its policies too quickly and brutally on the Afghans, and when it faced extreme resistance, it jailed and killed opposition members. The growing repression whittled away most of the remaining support, and soon most of the rural areas were in open revolt. In the summer of 1979, President Carter had authorized funding of anti-Communist guerrillas in the country. The government in Kabul appealed for Soviet aid. On November 26, 1979, the ruling elite of the Soviet Union—the Politburo's inner circle—decided to invade Afghanistan. The Soviet, and before them, the pre-Soviet Russian governments were long interested in the country situated close to its southern border. Soviet troops entered the country, killed the existing President Hafizullah Amin, and established Babrak Karmal as president. Soon, there were more than one hundred thousand Soviet military personnel in the country.

The U.S. response was muted. The Soviet invasion increased tension, but the United States was not going to initiate a direct confrontation with the USSR and perhaps risk a nuclear exchange for the sake of a faraway, dusty, mountainous country whose strategic importance was limited. In January 1980, President Carter announced a new doctrine, the *Carter Doctrine*, stating that outside force used to gain control of the Persian Gulf region would be considered an assault on the vital interests of the United States.[22] The Carter Doctrine was a warning against any further southern penetration by the Soviets. The Pentagon believed that Soviet expansion in the region was motivated by a search for warm-water ports. The doctrine was the official seal on the U.S. commitment to protect Gulf oil supply, and it also committed the United States to maintaining existing governments in the region.

Aiding the guerrillas was seen as a way to drain the power and prestige of the Soviet Union. Afghanistan was a wound that could be deepened to bleed the Soviet Empire. The United States joined Saudi Arabia and Pakistan in funding and training resisters to Soviet occupation. There were diverse groups such as Tajiks and Pashtuns and competing warlords. The insurrection also caught the imagination of Islamicists who saw the struggle as jihad, a holy war between the followers of Islam and the godless Communists. "Mujahedeen," roughly translated from Arabic, means "people undertaking jihad." Saudis such as Osama bin Laden joined the fight.

Under the *Reagan Doctrine* (the U.S. Empire often is formulated as a series of doctrines—immediate responses to pressing events that can solidify into longer-term, strategic goals), the United States sought to provide direct and covert aid to anti-Communist forces across the world.[23] The Mujahedeen qualified for assistance under this doctrine. U.S. aid supported the use of their favored weapons against Soviet troops' land mines. The Saudis also helped, especially with religious education for refugees. Madrassas, schools that taught the severe Saudi form of Islam, proliferated along the Afghan-Pakistan border. The land mines employed, and the religious zealots encouraged by the United States against the Russians, were decades later to come back to haunt the United States.

The resistance to Soviet rule was successful. The Soviets paid a heavy price for their occupancy and finally left in 1989, the same year Communism collapsed. The war ravaged Afghanistan. Afghan deaths are estimated at between one and two million. Millions more fled and towns were reduced to rubble. In the ensuing civil war, further damage was inflicted on the country and its people. In 1996, the Taliban, with support from Pakistan and Saudi Arabia, emerged as the eventual victors, proclaiming an Islamic Emirate of Afghanistan. They were funded by the Gulf States, eager to see an Islamic theocracy along strict Sunni lines, and supported by a Pakistan eager to have a strategic redoubt in their ongoing conflict with India. By 2000, the Taliban had control over most of the territory. The Taliban gave comfort and support to Osman bin Laden.

Immediately after the terrorist attack against the United States on 9/11—in late September 2001—the United States began a campaign to overthrow the Taliban; it found lots of local allies disenchanted with the Taliban's brutal rule. Within two months, local allies and U.S. forces overthrew the Taliban. It was not a simple victory; the Taliban retained strongholds in villages especially in the east and south of the country, and al Qaeda operatives still moved between Pashtun areas in Afghanistan and Pakistan. While the United States was successful in toppling the rule of the Taliban, they were not able to eradicate support for the Taliban.

The recent history of Afghanistan is a complex and often sordid tale as murderous factions try to annihilate each other and neighboring states fan ethnic tensions and religious differences in order to promote their own interests: Saudis, for example, to promote a strict form of Islam or the Pakistani intelligence agencies eager to back warlords in Afghanistan as part of their strategic maneuvering against India.

The United States fought in Afghanistan for longer than World War I, World War II, Korea, and Vietnam combined. It is the longest war in U.S. military history. After the U.S. invasion of Afghanistan and the fall of the Taliban, the United States was committed to establishing a government in Kabul. No government had effective control, and so the United States began to send troops. In order to buttress their positions, more troops were sent. Then even more. By 2009, there were almost one hundred thousand U.S. troops after a surge from 68,000 (see photo 10.4). Troop withdrawals only began in 2011 after a decade that included 2,300 U.S. troop deaths, more than twenty thousand wounded, and a total bill close to $500 billion. In 2020, an agreement to pull out the remaining 12,000 U.S. troops was realized. The Taliban will return as the U.S. presence fades from view. Yet another costly war failed to achieve long-term objectives of returning Afghanistan to normal politics. Afghanistan remains a hugely factionalized nation with a deeply corrupt state.

Photo 10.4. U.S. troops in Kandahar, Afghanistan, 2019 (Maj. Thomas Cieslak, U.S. Army)

The United States, and the British and Soviets before them, learned the hard way that Afghanistan is the graveyard of empires.[24] Its tough physical geography makes occupancy and movement difficult. The prime minister is referred to as the "Mayor of Kabul" from the limited ability to influence events outside the capital. It also has a tough social geography. There are tribal enmities, murderous ethnic differences, and history governance marked more by corruption than national integration.

U.S. intervention did little to improve the lot of the average Afghan. It remains one of the poorest countries in the region. Corruption is rife. There is little to show for the billions of dollars of foreign aid. It is an authoritarian kleptocracy where the elite overwhelmingly benefit from the foreign aid and development funds. The one sector that does work well in Afghanistan is the narcotics trade of poppy growing and opium production: it is now worth close to $2 billion. Afghanistan is now the world's largest producer of opium. It could be described as a "narcostate." Most of the heroin consumption in Europe derives from Afghanistan.

SUGGESTED READINGS

Adeney, K. (2015). A move to majoritarian nationalism? Challenges of representation in South Asia. *Representation, 51,* 7–21.

Ahmad, P., & Singh, B. (2017). Sino-Pakistan friendship, changing South Asian geopolitics and India's post-Obama options. *South Asia Research, 37,* 133–46.

Basrur, R. (2018). India-Pakistan rivalry: Endless duel? *Asian Security, 14,* 100–5.

Bhat, S. A. (2019). The Kashmir conflict and human rights. *Race & Class, 61,* 77–86.

Chapman, G. P. (2009, 3rd ed). *The geopolitics of South Asia.* Burlington: Ashgate.

Chung, C. P. (2018). What are the strategic and economic implications for South Asia of China's Maritime Silk Road initiative? *Pacific Review, 31,* 315–32.

Cons, J., & Sanyal, R. (2013). Geographies at the margins: Borders in South Asia—an introduction. *Political Geography, 35,* 5–13.

Ganguly, S. (2019). *The origins of war in South Asia: Indo-Pakistani conflicts since 1947.* London: Routledge.

Lintner, B. (2015). *Great game east: India, China, and the struggle for Asia's most volatile frontier.* New Haven: Yale University Press.

Pant, H. V. (2016). Rising China in India's vicinity: A rivalry takes shape in Asia. *Cambridge Review of International Affairs, 29,* 364–81.

Pillalamarri, A. (2017). Why is Afghanistan the "Graveyard of Empires"? *The Diplomat.* https://thediplomat.com/2017/06/why-is-afghanistan-the-graveyard-of-empires/.

Ranjan, A. (2017). Public interest and private gain in Pakistan: Managing the state despite predictions of failure. *South Asia Research, 37,* 296–314.

Smith, P. J. (2013). The tilting triangle: Geopolitics of the China–India–Pakistan relationship. *Comparative Strategy, 32,* 313–30.

Turner, O. (2016). China, India and the US rebalance to the Asia Pacific: The geopolitics of rising identities. *Geopolitics, 21,* 922–44.

Wagner, C. (2016). The role of India and China in South Asia. *Strategic Analysis, 40,* 307–20.

Weihua, W. (2015). The trends of geopolitics in South Asia in the changing world and their influences on the construction of China-Pakistan Economic Corridor. *Indian Ocean Economic and Political Review, 2,* 54–73.

NOTES

1. Metcalf, B. D. (2011). *A concise history of modern India.* Cambridge: Cambridge University Press.

2. Chapman, G. P. (2009, 3rd ed). *The geopolitics of South Asia.* Burlington: Ashgate.

3. Chester, L. P. (2009). *Borders and conflict in South Asia.* Manchester: Manchester University Press.

4. Ganguly, S. (2019). *The origins of war in South Asia: Indo-Pakistani conflicts since 1947*. London: Routledge.

5. Hagerty, D. T. (2020). *Nuclear weapons and deterrence stability in South Asia*. London: Palgrave Macmillan; Sagan, S. D. (2009). *Inside nuclear South Asia*. Palo Alto: Stanford University Press.

6. Lieven, A. (2011). *Pakistan: A hard country*. New York: Public Affairs; Sha, A. (2014). *The army and democracy: Military politics in Pakistan*. Cambridge, MA: Harvard University Press.

7. Behera, N. C. (2016). The Kashmir conflict: Multiple fault lines. *Journal of Asian Security and International Affairs, 3*, 41–63; Bhat, S. A. (2019). The Kashmir conflict and human rights. *Race & Class, 61*, 77–86.

8. Masih, N. (2019, August 15). Kashmir's calm belies seething resentment of India. *Washington Post*, A7.

9. Lintner, B. (2015). *Great game east: India, China, and the struggle for Asia's most volatile frontier*. New Haven: Yale University Press.

10. Khurana, G. S. (2019). India as a challenge to China's Belt and Road initiative. *Asia Policy, 14*, 27–33; Saraswat, D. (2016). Geoeconomic resurgence of Silk Road and India's Central Asian strategy. *Journal of Central Asian Studies, 23*, 83–104.

11. Ethirajan, A., & Pandey, V. (2020). China-India border: Why tensions are rising between the neighbours. *BBC News*. https://www.bbc.com/news/world-asia-52852509.

12. Taylor, A. (2020). A border clash between the world's biggest nations. What could go wrong? *Washington Post*. https://www.washingtonpost.com/world/2020/05/28/china-india-border-standoff/.

13. Klem, B. (2014). The political geography of war's end: Territorialisation, circulation, and moral anxiety in Trincomalee, Sri Lanka. *Political Geography, 38*, 33–45.

14. Mashal, M. (2019). For Sri Lanka, a long history of violence. *New York Times*. https://www.nytimes.com/2019/04/21/world/asia/sri-lanka-history-civil-war.html.

15. Polling. G. (2021). *Myanmar's military seizes power*. Washington, DC: Center for Strategic and International Studies. https://www.csis.org/analysis/myanmars-military-seizes-power.

16. Thant, M-U. (2011). *Where China meets India: Burma and the closing of the great Asian frontier*. London: Faber.

17. Singh, A. (2019). China's vision for the Belt and Rod in South Asia. *The Diplomat*. https://thediplomat.com/2019/03/chinas-vision-for-the-belt-and-road-in-south-asia/.

18. Freeman, C. P. (2018). China's "regionalism foreign policy" and China-India relations in South Asia. *Contemporary Politics, 24*, 81–97; Pant, H. V. (2016). Rising China in India's vicinity: A rivalry takes shape in Asia. *Cambridge Review of International Affairs, 29*, 364–81; Siddiqi, F. H. (2012). India-China relations in the 21st century: Impact on regional and global politics. *Pakistan Horizon, 65*, 59–72; Wojczewski, T. (2016). China's rise as a strategic challenge and opportunity: India's China discourse and strategy. *India Review, 15*, 22–60.

19. Boon, H. T. (2016). The hedging prong in India's evolving China strategy. *Journal of Contemporary China, 25*, 792–804.

Chand, B. (2019). Dynamics of rivalry between geographically contiguous regional powers: The case of Sino-Indian competition. *Asian Politics and Policy, 11*, 122–43.

Turner, O. (2016). China, India and the US rebalance to the Asia Pacific: The geopolitics of rising identities. *Geopolitics, 21*, 922–44.

Macaes, B. (2018). China and India: The struggle for mastery in Eurasia. *Insight Turkey, 20*, 13–23.

20. Palit, A. (2017). India's economic and strategic perceptions of China's Maritime Silk Road initiative. *Geopolitics, 22*, 292–309.

21. Council on Foreign Relations. (2020). The U.S. war in Afghanistan 1999–2020. https://www.cfr.org/timeline/us-war-afghanistan.

Jones, S. G. (2009). *In the graveyard of empires: America's war in Afghanistan*. New York: Norton.

Lyn, D. (2009). *In Afghanistan: Two hundred years of British, Russian and American occupation*. New York: Palgrave. Tanner, S. (2009). *Afghanistan: A military history from Alexander the Great to the war against the Taliban*. Philadelphia: Da Capo.

22. Leffler, M. P. (1983). From the Truman Doctrine to the Carter Doctrine: Lessons and dilemmas of the Cold War. *Diplomatic History, 7*, 245–66.

23. Pach, C. (2006). The Reagan Doctrine: Principle, pragmatism, and policy. *Presidential Studies Quarterly, 36*, 75–88.

24. Pillalamarri, A. (2017). Why is Afghanistan the "Graveyard of Empires"? *The Diplomat.* https://thediplomat.com/2017/06/why-is-afghanistan-the-graveyard-of-empires/.

Central and South America

GEOPOLITICAL CONTEXT

A recent report on Latin America described it as

> a nuclear-free zone with no hot or cold wars, minor frozen conflicts, minimal advanced arms competition, limited terrorism, and a policy of constructive engagement from Washington.[1]

This remarkably upbeat assessment would have been impossible to imagine in the 1970s and 1980s when terrorist groups were active across the region, military juntas were in power, civil unrest was common, and revolution was in the air. Over the past fifty years, the region has experienced a wave of democratization and marked declines in absolute poverty. From a distance, the region appears as a stable geopolitical area. But the variation is enormous. Parts of Central America remain a scene of political instability and significant issues persist across South America. We will discuss these in some detail, but it is important to begin with a discussion of the *imperial shadow*.

IMPERIAL SHADOW

Empire casts a heavy shadow over Central and South America. It started with the indigenous empires, including the Aztecs, Incas, and Mayans, which extended their reach across regions of South and Central America. Consider, as just one example, the Inca (also known as Inka).[2] The Inca built on the imperial gains of previous powers to turn their ethnic state into a vast empire. In a relatively short period, from roughly 1438 to 1533, the Inca controlled territory stretching over 2,500 miles along the spine of the Andes Mountains. Only when the empire came up against the organized Mapuche tribe did the empire reach its southern limit in present-day central Chile. At its peak no more than sixth thousand ethnic Inca ruled over twelve million people. It was the largest pre-Columbian empire in South America. Based in Cuzco, the empire was linked by a complex road network. Roads were policed to prioritize the work of the empire. Imperial power varied from direct control to indirect control. Some polities lobbied to join the empire in order to avoid conflict with the Inca or to escape possible annexation by neighbors. The Inca used collaborative elites. Control was maintained through the patronage of local elites and defense was left to local allies with the promise of Inca support in the event of conflict. This strategy allowed the Inca to extend their control more widely while minimizing costs. Tribute was paid to supporters in the form of agricultural produce, textiles, and workers. The Inca moved work parties all over the empire to minimize their ability to organize resistance. The state owned most things, including land. With only one control city for a vast empire, the Inca reached imperial overstretch. They were in decline even before the Spanish arrived in 1532. A succession struggle splintered an empire weakened by diseases. All these factors rendered the Inca Empire vulnerable to a small group of no more than two hundred Spaniards. Even today, however, around nine million Andean people still speak variants of the basic language of the Inca Empire, Quechan.

European Colonialism

In 1492 the Spaniards first landed in the islands of the Caribbean and later extended their reach onto the mainland. In a stunning series of victories, they soon brought most of Central and South America under their control.[3] Their victories were in large part due to their superior armaments but also due to the invisible but deadly power of viruses. People moving across the North American land bridge and icy seas from Northeast Asia settled the New World. The migration occurred before the advent of settled agriculture. Living with their animals, the people of the Old World eventually came to develop resistance to diseases such as smallpox, measles, and influenza. The indigenous populations of the New World, in contrast, were susceptible to these diseases and they died in the millions. The population of the entire region declined by around 90 percent between 1500 and 1700. It was a demographic holocaust. Consequently, slave labor was brought from Africa to work the plantations and mines. Almost twelve million people were shipped from Africa to the New World. Slaves were first sent to the Spanish and Portuguese colonies and then later to the colonies of the British, French, and Dutch. More than half died during the sea crossing, while 20 percent died within the first year of work. The fear and reality of slave revolts became a constant threat to the White elites in the region.

The two dominant European powers in the early years were Spain and Portugal. Under the Treaty of Tordesillas, signed in 1494, the pope divided South America into Spanish and Portuguese spheres of influence. The divide remains as a linguistic legacy. Brazil is still primarily Portuguese speaking, while the rest of South and Central America is largely Spanish speaking. Later, the English, French, Dutch, Danish, and even the Scots all annexed territory across the region. These other European powers arrived later, only able to grab slivers of continental territory, but they were more effective in the islands of the Caribbean, which were difficult for Spain to police. By 1600 the Spanish were entrenched in the western region of South America and the Portuguese along the coast of Brazil.

In the coastal area between the Orinoco and the Amazon, the English, then British, French, and Dutch all laid claim to territory and annexed selected islands in the Caribbean for plantation economies.

European colonial appropriation of land and the subsequent dispensation into vast estates had major impacts on the region. Power, land, and wealth were concentrated into the hands of a small elite. The deep polarization of societies along lines of class and ethnicity continue to impact the economic and political development of the region. Domestic politics were often bitterly fought struggles between the landed elites and the urban bourgeoisie and later between established elites on the one hand and landless peasants and underpaid workers on the other. This division reinforced racial and ethnic disparities. The struggle between these groups continues to inform internal politics throughout the region. In the more tropical areas with plantation economies and a history of slave labor, a Black underclass emerged to add another element to domestic politics. In the more inaccessible areas such as the tropical forest or mountain areas, indigenous people managed to survive.

There was the partial replacement of indigenous religions with Roman Catholicism. In some cases, hybrid forms of Christianity emerged that mixed indigenous belief systems into the folds of Catholicism. The Catholic Church became an important player, sometimes siding with the wealthy, but at other times and in specific places articulating a liberation theology for social justice and racial equality.

There was also the legacy of colonies economically structured to provide primary products for the global market. This put the region onto a path of dependency on primary products. The national economies of the region were precariously balanced on a narrow range of commodities whose price could fluctuate widely on the global market.

In summary: the imperial legacy created deeply divided societies and economies based on the export of primary products. These internal political conflicts and economic crises were to shadow the region for decades to come.

Rising Nationalism

The imperial yokes were always resisted, not only by indigenous peoples but also by local Hispanic elites.[4] The geographic location of the New World in a time of sail meant that the relationship between Spain and its New World colonies was always tempered by the tyranny of distance. The region was at the far reaches of imperial control and, despite the centralizing tendencies of the Spanish Crown, the colonies developed a measure of separate identity. Colonial local economies were structured so as to enrich Spain. Trade with foreign countries was forbidden, and only the Spanish-born could plant grapes, grow tobacco, or own a mine. Manufacturing was banned and punitive taxes made their way back to Spain with little local investment. Creoles, those with Spanish ancestry but born in the New World, chafed at these political and economic restrictions. Creoles were denied access to the highest levels of political office, reserved for those born in Spain. Even their economic power as large landowners was limited by taxation by Spain and trade restrictions that tied them to the Spanish imperial system rather than the expanding markets of the UK and the United States. The American Revolution (1776) and French Revolution (1780) inaugurated a new era. Distant, absolute power was questioned, and old colonial ties were severed.

The invasion of Iberia by Napoleon and the overthrow of the king of Spain in 1808 gave new hope to the Creole elites of Latin America, eager to loosen the bonds to Spain. Napoleon's resounding victory demonstrated that the imperial center was vulnerable, a spent rather than ascendant force. Brazil peacefully separated from Portugal in 1822 to establish a new kingdom. It was not so easy for the Spanish possessions. Spain was a failing power eager to maintain its colonies for the wealth and the prestige, especially because its relative position was deteriorating in comparison with the dynamic colonial and commercial empire of the UK. The result was a bitter military struggle that began in isolated uprisings immediately after Napoleon's invasion of Spain but grew in the subsequent decade. The insurrections eventually wrested control sway from Spain. The Argentine Republic was declared in 1816 and forms of independence were achieved in Chile (1818), Colombia (1819), Venezuela (1821), Mexico (1821), Ecuador (1822), Peru (1824), and Bolivia (1825). They are the basis of the current states depicted in map 11.1.

POSTIMPERIAL GEOPOLITICAL UNCERTAINTIES

The new states of Central and South America emerged from vast sprawling empires with ill-defined territorial boundaries. The early states were born in this state of territorial confusion. Lacking any historical *raison d'être*, nationalism had to be constructed. The heroes of the liberation movement became important national figures. Statues of nationalist figures are an important part of the urban iconography in villages, towns, and cities throughout the region. Photos 11.1 and 11.2 represent only a small sample. Photo 11.1 is a commemoration of General San Martin in Puerto Madryn, Argentina. Photo 11.2 commemorates Jose Gervasio Artiga, known as the father of Uruguayan nationhood, in Montevideo, Uruguay.

The immediate postimperial era was one of territorial flux as nations were constructed and reconstructed. In 1821, Gran Colombia was established. It included Colombia and present-day Panama-Ecuador and Venezuela. By 1830 the confederation had split into three separate parts. Later Panama, with U.S. encouragement, finally broke away from Colombia in 1903. In 1823, Central America seceded from Mexico, and only seven years later the breakaway territory further splintered into five separate republics. Peru achieved independence in 1824. As with other South American countries, there was territorial ambiguity and confusion. A Peru-Bolivian confederation was a short-lived affair from 1836 to 1839 after rival neighbors Chile and Argentina invaded. Later, in the War of the Pacific (1879–1884), Peru lost mineral-rich territory to Chile.

Mexico had major territorial ruptures after it obtained independence in 1821 as separate republics of Central America split off in 1823. In 1824 Mexico annexed what is now the state of Chiapas, and most of the Yucatan in 1848. In the north, there were boundary disputes with its expansionist neighbor. In 1836, Texas, with encouragement from the United States, declared independence. A

Map 11.1. Central and South America (International Mapping)

border dispute erupted into the U.S.–Mexican War of 1848. It was a major victory for the United States but a disaster for Mexico. Under the 1848 Treaty of Guadalupe Hidalgo, Mexico lost almost half of its national territory.

The territorial uncertainty created conflict and resulted in wars. Let us consider the case of Chile as a representative example: it is one of the longest and thinnest countries in the world (see map 11.1). Why? Chile emerged from the Viceroyalty of Peru, a long sliver of Spanish-claimed land on the Pacific side of the Andes. From this Spanish imperial spatial organization emerged the distinctive shape of both Peru and Chile. But effective territorial control of the new

Photo 11.1. Statue in Puerto Madryn, Argentina (John Rennie Short)

republic was limited and contested. In the south, the Mapuche kept up resistance until the 1880s, and precise national boundaries remained ill defined. In 1881 a deal was reached between Chile and Argentina in which Chile gained control of the Strait of Magellan, but Argentina obtained eastern Patagonia. Some of the contested land in the north was rich in minerals and resources. Things came to head in the War of the Pacific (1879-1884) between Chile and Peru-Bolivia. Chile won and wrested considerable territory from Peru and Bolivia, effectively cutting off Bolivia's access to the sea and dooming it to its present-day landlocked status. Bolivia has continued to seek redress. The Chileans have offered access but not sovereignty while Bolivia continues to assert sovereignty. The border between Chile and Peru was only settled in 1929, and Peru's access to the Chilean port of Arica was only finally settled in 1999. Territorial disputes continue to cause friction in Chile-Argentina relations. Argentina has long claimed jurisdiction over three small islands in the Beagle Channel, and in 1978, during the military junta, Argentina threatened war. Under the old adage that "the enemy of my enemy is my friend," the Chilean government and military provided valuable assistance to the UK during the Falklands War in 1982.

Continuing Boundary Disputes

Boundary disputes between nation-states reflected the uncertain nature of territorial formation in the wake of Spain's withdrawal. They lingered over the years, sometimes breaking out into direct conflict.

A territorial dispute between Ecuador and Peru led to outright war in 1941 and remained a simmering source of resentment for many years. Another round of conflict flared up in 1981 and again in 1995. Over time, the disputes became brief military clashes rather than full-blown wars. Peace was finally achieved with a border agreement in 1998. A brief war between El Salvador and Honduras erupted in 1969 after a football (soccer) match between the two countries. It is

Photo 11.2. Statue in Montevideo, Uruguay (John Rennie Short)

known as the Football War (La Guerra del Futbol), but its real origins lie in the border disputes and tension caused by immigration from El Salvador to Honduras. The war lasted less than one hundred hours. The two countries signed a peace treaty, and the International Court of Justice demarcated the border, with most of the disputed territory going to Honduras.

Since 1990, territorial disputes between Argentina and Chile, Ecuador and Peru, Chile and Peru, and Brazil with all its neighbors have been arbitrated, but unresolved issues still remain. Venezuela claims land west of the Essequibo River, almost two-thirds of the entire territory of Guyana. Guatemala has long made claims to parts of Belize. And Argentina continues to claim sovereignty over the Falklands. While most of the land border disputes are either settled or in the process of adjudication, maritime boundaries are an emerging site of interstate relations in the region. The Caribbean is a relatively small body of water where thirty-six states (twenty-two independent countries and seventeen territories) lay claim to what is essentially a closed sea. The United Nations Convention of the Law of the Sea, ratified in 1994, allows states to claim up to two hundred nautical miles of their coast as an Exclusive Economic Zone (EEZ). This extends the reach of small island states, such as Barbados, which claims up to ten times more maritime than terrestrial space. These claims become increasingly important as oil, gas, and valuable mineral deposits are discovered offshore. In 2001, Nicaragua took Colombia to the International Court of Justice over a disputed maritime boundary. In 2012, the court granted Nicaragua an EEZ that shifted the previous maritime boundary eastward, roughly along the 82-degree meridian. This effectively meant a transfer of 30,000 square miles from Colombia to Nicaragua. A maritime dispute between Chile and Peru over 14,600 square miles of maritime territory first arose in the mid-1980s. By 2008 there was still no resolution; Peru took its claims to the International Court of Justice. In 2014, the Court ruled in favor of Peru.[5]

EL NORTE: THE ROLE OF THE UNITED STATES

Just as independent nation-states were beginning to be established in South and Central America, throwing off the yoke of imperial Spain, a new power was emerging in the north. Just as the North Star is a constant in the northern night sky, so does the United States play a similarly signal role for Latin America. It is a constant presence at the center of a shifting scene. Although many of the nations in the region are south of the equator—rendering this metaphor less than accurate—the United States remains the polestar of the region. The United States aggressively asserted its primacy in the *Monroe Doctrine*, which was proclaimed in 1823 and laid claim to geopolitical influence in the region. This edict stated that while existing boundaries would be honored, the United States would not allow any further European incursions into the region. The doctrine only came into effect after 1850 when the UK—the unrivalled global superpower of the time—agreed. Issued like a blank check at a time when the military power of the United States was severely limited, the Monroe Doctrine has been cashed in continually as the United States has grown in military dominance.

The United States has exerted a huge influence in the region. Cuba was invaded, and Puerto Rico was permanently annexed. The United States backed a revolution that broke off Panama from Colombia in exchange for $10 million dollars to the new Panamanian government. The United States gained control—from 1904 to 2000—over a ten-mile-wide Canal Zone that ran through the middle of the new country. In 1916, the United States purchased from Denmark what is now the U.S. Virgin Islands. The Monroe Doctrine became a rationale for numerous interventions over the years. In some cases, the military intervened as it did in Honduras a number of times from 1903 to 1925. In other cases, there was outright occupation, including of Nicaragua from 1912 to 1933 and of Haiti from 1915 to 1934. There were also more covert actions of regime change and attempted regime change, including Guatemala in 1954, Cuba in 1959, and the Dominican Republic in 1961. In 1973, a military junta under General Pinochet overthrew Salvador Allende's democratically elected government of Chile with help from the United States, inaugurating almost twenty years of repression and a harsh neoliberalism.

From 1946 until 1990, the United States considered the region as a potential battleground of the Cold War. It used direct and indirect power to undermine left-wing governments and to support right-wing and military juntas in Argentina in the 1970s, Bolivia in 1964, Brazil in 1964, Ecuador in 1960–1963, and Uruguay in 1964–1970. At the time, military juntas, conservative governments, and political elites could easily persuade the United States that peasant uprisings or workers' movements were all part of a global Communist conspiracy, rather than national movements protesting against inequality and repression. El Salvador's civil war, fought from 1979 to 1992 between leftists and U.S.-backed government forces, devastated the country. Almost 75,000 people died. Many people fled, and now one in five citizens lives abroad. In Guatemala, where Hispanic elites have long dominated the indigenous Maya, a thirty-six-year civil war ended only in 1996. More than two hundred thousand people died, and one million were displaced, especially in the Mayan region of the country where the U.S.-backed government forces burned villages and removed people to punish the insurgency.[6] In 1979, leftists overthrew a U.S.-backed dictatorship in Nicaragua. The United States then funded a guerrilla movement for over a decade, and the ongoing conflict weakened the economy.

Most of the U.S. interventions during the Cold War era deposed and undermined leftist governments and regimes, supporting the landowning class and U.S. corporate interests. However, the end of the Cold War and domestic revulsion at U.S. actions meant a recalibration. The United States still has enormous economic investments in the region, and these play a role in guiding international relations. But the direct involvement of the Cold War era is passing from view, and domestic political issues can no longer be ascribed so insistently to external forces.

Since the 1980s, the United States has been more often associated with the promotion of neoliberalism. The *Washington Consensus*, a term widely used in the region, refers to the politics and practices of the World Bank and International Monetary Fund, which are both located in Washington, DC, only blocks from the White House. Both organizations stressed free trade, the lifting of tariffs that support domestic industries, cuts in social welfare spending, reductions in the tax rates of the wealthy, opening up national economies to foreign investments, and tight control of government spending. The implementation of these policies in the 1980s and 1990s—as so many countries needed to borrow money on these terms—led to declines in living standards, increasing inequality, and a perception that the region was still under the shadow of the U.S. policy. It was widely seen as a form of economic neocolonialism.

Bolivarism

There was a counter geopolitical narrative to the U.S. economic and geopolitical dominance: Bolivarism.[7] Simon Bolivar (1783–1830) played an important part in the liberation of Venezuela in 1811. With others, he helped Bolivia and Peru achieve independence. From 1819 to 1830 he was president of the Republic of Gran Colombia. His name lives on, not only in the names of countries, such as Bolivia and the Bolivarian Republic of Venezuela and numerous streets, plazas, and monuments across the region, but also in the political idea of Bolivarism, an anti-imperialist rhetoric that promotes income redistribution, national sovereignty, and an antipathy toward the power of the United States in the region. Bolivarism existed as a counterpoint to U.S. hegemony in the region. Some countries, such as Cuba and Venezuela, successfully resisted U.S. hegemony.

Cuba was a former Spanish colony that became independent in 1902 but with a constitution that gave the United States the right to intervene and run its national finances and foreign relations. A U.S. governor ruled the country from 1899 to 1906. A permanent U.S. naval station was also established at Guantanamo and still exists as a detention center for suspected terrorists. When Fidel Castro came to power in 1959 and redistributed all landholdings over one thousand acres, the United States saw Castro as a leftwing threat in a U.S.-dominated region. Their worst fears were confirmed when the USSR exported missiles to the islands, a little over one hundred miles from the U.S. mainland. The Cuban

Missile Crisis of 1962 was arguably the closest that the Cold War came to turn-ing into a hot war with nuclear weaponry. Cuban exiles in Florida played a major part in generating anti-Castro sentiment in the United States, and the political importance of Florida in presidential elections assured them a receptive audience at the highest levels of government. U.S. sanctions against Cuba persist after a brief thaw under the Obama administration. Most other countries now trade with Cuba, and more than 2.6 million tourists visit the island annually, mainly from Canada and Europe.

Venezuela's rich oil reserve gave it a special place as one of the more afflu-ent countries in South America. The Orinoco River basin is estimated to have deposits of at least 1.2 trillion barrels of oil. Previously, wealth was unevenly distributed among a small rich elite, leaving behind a small middle class and a large, impoverished mass of people in poverty. A military dictatorship in the 1950s created massive public works programs, helping to lift many out of pov-erty and to grow the middle class. For years Venezuela was a pro-U.S. ally. The Rockefellers owned much of the country's oil reserves as well as vast tracts of land. Things changed radically with the election of Hugo Chavez in 1999. In an example of contemporary Bolivarism, he established close ties with Cuba and espoused an explicitly anti-U.S. rhetoric. He also embarked on an ambitious program of wealth redistribution and encouraged the more active participation of people in society that included the encouragement of the "invasion" of occupied buildings by squatters. His immediate successor, Nicolas Maduro, also followed a more distinctly anti-U.S. posture. But economic mismanagement, a decline in oil prices, and political corruption led to an economic collapse. The "Maduro diet" was an enforced reduction in food intake, mass emigration, and a loss of skilled workers. The Bolivarist state lingers on. But for how long?

A Shift to the Left

Cuba and Venezuela were the most obvious examples of anti-U.S. resistance, but many political movements in Central and South America were schooled in the basic tenets of Bolivarism. Today, there is no longer a simple binary between pro-U.S. and Bolivarism. Now we can imagine a continuum from neoliberalism to Bolivarism. In the past twenty years, there has been a shift across the region to the more Bolivarist end of the continuum.[8] In Uruguay, Presidents Vazquez (2005–2010) and Mujica (2010–2015) introduced a more progressive set of poli-cies. Evo Morales was the first indigenous person to become president of Bolivia and held the position from 2006 to 2019. Rafael Correa, during his term as presi-dent of Ecuador from 2007 to 2017, introduced more progressive measures. In Brazil, in 2002, Luiz Inacio Lula da Silva, popularly known as Lula, was elected and subsequently introduced policies of social and income redistribution. Chile's President Bachelet governed from 2006–2010 and again from 2014 to 2018. She and her family were arrested, detained, and tortured during the U.S.-backed Pinochet regime.

A commodities boom fueled by China's meteoric growth rates since the 1990s aided the shift to the left. As commodity prices rose, politicians had more money to spend on social welfare. No longer so dependent on U.S. markets and companies, many countries could move beyond the Washington Consensus of neoliberalism.

The leftward shift in turn created a countercurrent from the right that became more obvious by 2018. Voters expressed their displeasure with rampant corruption, poor public services, and a decline in commodity prices that created a fiscal crisis.[9] A right-wing businessman was voted back into office in Chile in 2018. Evo Morales, the first indigenous person to become president of Bolivia, was deposed in 2019. A member of the traditional political elite became president of Uruguay in 2019. And after years of the Workers' Party in power, the right-winger Jair Bolsonaro, the self-styled Trump of the Tropics, became president of Brazil in 2019. The situation remains in flux as the balance between Bolivarism and neoliberalism continues to shift and twist. When billionaire businessman Sebastian Pinera was elected to the presidency of Chile in 2018 and inaugurated a return to neoliberalist policies, he was soon faced with popular protests that swept across the country in October 2019. He was criticized heavily for deploying the army and in the wake of continual popular protests, he canceled fare increase for public transport and promised a commission to consider major constitutional reforms, including the right to education, healthcare, and social security.

CHINA

A significant player in the region is China.[10] This region is connected still to the global economy, mainly as a source of primary products. This has meant a roller coaster for national economies as the price of primary products, such as oil, can fluctuate widely. Without substantial diversification, many economies in the region are subject to the vagaries of global market prices. Wildly fluctuating government revenues often were smoothed out with reductions in welfare spending. Yet by the late 1990s and early 2000s, a global commodity boom driven in large part by China's rapid and large-scale industrialization created spectacular rates of growth throughout much of the region, replacing several decades of recession, hyperinflation, and political turmoil. China's growth sucked in raw materials. Oil, copper, beef, palm oil, and soybeans now found their major market in China. Almost 90 percent of Ecuador's oil exports end up in China. Most of Chile's copper is exported to China. Chile is not only hypersensitive to the price of copper on the global market, but as with many other countries in the region, is dependent on the health and dynamism of the Chinese manufacturing sector. To secure its supplies and strengthen its ties, China also has embarked on an ambitious program of investments.[11]

In an echo of the U.S. construction of the Panama Canal, China is aiming to build a new canal across Nicaragua. Under the plan, Lake Nicaragua will be dredged, existing rivers widened, and locks built, to enable huge ships to move from the Atlantic to the Pacific. It is a massive undertaking that involves the building of roads, towns, ports, and airports. The estimated cost is $40 billion. The project is to be financed and built by the China Railroad Construction Corporation, which will pay the government of Nicaragua $10 million a year for the first decade of operations and subsequently a share of the endeavor's profits. Almost fifty thousand jobs will be created by this construction; most of them are to be allocated to Chinese workers.

A new canal is just one element in the emerging economic and geopolitical power of China in the region. Consider the case of Ecuador. The relationship is simple. China needs oil; Ecuador has oil. Lots of it. Ecuador is relatively poor while the Chinese government can mobilize huge amounts of money. Since 2009, China has given $43 billion in loans to the government of Ecuador. Many of the loans are to be repaid in barrels of oil. Under the agreement, if Ecuador fails to repay, the Chinese government legally can seize Ecuadorian assets, including oil reserves. The Chinese government has prompted oil exploration and drilling into the ecologically sensitive Amazonia area, threatening biodiversity and the lives of indigenous communities. The case of Ecuador highlights the compromised sovereignty of relatively small primary producers doing deals with China.

While China is very active in the region, its rise there is not seen as a threat to U.S. interests. Although both powers seek to maximize advantages—China, for example, uses its economic relations to create allies in international organizations—there is little direct antagonism between them. Rather, there is a shared interest in reducing internal conflicts and securing peace, property, and economic development, especially if it coincides with U.S. corporate and Chinese national interests. U.S. oil companies are just as eager to develop the oil fields of Ecuador as Chinese companies. There is low conflict in China's meteoric rise in the region; it does not harm core U.S. national interests. While in the short to medium term their interests may seem shared and non-antagonistic, in the longer term, there is the possibility of geoeconomic conflict.

THE CARIBBEAN BASIN SHATTER ZONE

The Caribbean basin was a site of contest. The old cannons overlooking the main harbor in Grenada, shown in photo 11.3, are a reminder of the contested nature of the Caribbean between competing imperial powers among the colonial powers. While Spain ruled much of the mainland territory of Central America, it found

Photo 11.3. Cannons in Grenada (John Rennie Short)

it difficult to retain effective control over the scatter of islands in the Caribbean. There were too many of them too widely scattered to police effectively. From 1600 to 1800, other European powers moved into the Caribbean to establish sugar plantations.

With no singular power authority, small islands changed hands frequently. Dominica was under French control from 1632 to 1761, then British control, then French control again from 1778 to 1783, and then British again until it achieved independence in 1978. Most of the small island nations of the Caribbean have similarly complex histories. Trinidad was under Spanish control from 1532 to 1797, when it became a British territory until achieving independence in 1962. In its complex colonial history, St. Lucia was held by the French nine separate times and by the British six times. The end result is that in the wake of decolonization, much of the basin comprises a number of relatively small independent nations (see map 11.1). It is shatter zones of small, vulnerable nation-states that face not only the problems of economies still heavily dependent on a mere few commodities and industries, such as tourism, but also on the environmental hazards of volcanoes and hurricanes. The small size of the island nations makes them especially vulnerable. Powerful hurricanes in small Caribbean nations can devastate the entire national economy. The smaller island states have a difficult time generating enough revenue to provide infrastructure for economic and social development. As a result, educational and employment opportunities are very limited, and many people have left, and continue to leave, the islands in search of jobs in Britain, Canada, and the United States.

There is an asymmetry between small island governments on the one hand and powerful outside interests on the other. Major corporations have greater bargaining power than the state while criminal elements such as gangs and drug cartels can often wield greater muscle than government forces. Small island governments are vulnerable in a world of mobile giant corporations and powerful and ruthless cartels. Jamaica, for example, is a significant transit point for cocaine being shipped from South to North America. With a large coastline, weak enforcement, geographic proximity to both supply and demand points, and porous borders, this island nation is a significant hub in the international drug trade. This weakens civil society, fuels political corruption, and contributes to a high rate of violence. Jamaica has the fifth-highest murder rate in the world.

It is not just geopolitical history to blame. The Dominican Republic (DR) and Haiti share the small island and have similar histories, but their paths diverged as the DR moved into middle-income status, while Haiti remains one of the poorest countries in the region with a poverty level of close to 80 percent and a life expectancy of only sixty-three. When Haiti gained independence from France in 1804, there was factional infighting, especially between Blacks and mulattos—a divide that still persists today. The political instability created a condition of *predatory elites* in which any group that came to power sought not to develop the country but to enrich themselves and their supporters. The result was a slow, steady spiral downward. The United States occupied the island from 1915 to 1934 in order to protect its economic interests. Later, the political dictatorship of the Duvalier family, from 1971 to 1986, did little to aid the country and in fact led to further impoverishment through outright corruption and gross mismanagement. The mass of people remains poor and illiterate. The 2010 earth-quake was a catastrophe for an already impoverished nation.

THE DRUG CORRIDOR: STRUGGLING STATES, FAILED STATES, AND NARCOSTATES

The relative weakness of the states in the Caribbean and Central America makes them vulnerable to the pernicious effects of the drug trade that flows through the region, connecting suppliers of narcotics in Central and South America to the world's biggest market. Along this corridor we can find struggling states, failed states, and narcostates. The impact is most severe in small and vulnerable states, especially where the isthmus narrows, and the drug trade casts a large and very dark shadow. This can be found in the nexus of Belize, El Salvador, Guatemala, Honduras, and Mexico.[12]

Today high mass unemployment, high levels of violence, pervasive power of criminal gangs, and the corrupting influence of the narcoeconomy mark these countries. Border security is weak, and police enforcement is lax and often cor-rupt. The derisive term "banana republics" was used to describe these countries because they based their economies on primary tropical commodities such as bananas. The term had other more specific connotations because the U.S. United Fruit Company played an outsized role in the economy and policies of the region. For many years, these narcostates were republics but certainly not democracies; wealthy elites and army officer corps dominated economic and political power. The result was small, poor states where government often lacked legitimacy. There was a weak rule of law and a poorly developed civil society. A recent his-tory of political violence further undermined the rule of law and weakened civil society. El Salvador's civil war, fought from 1980 to 1992 between leftists and U.S.-backed government forces, devastated the country. Almost 75,000 people died. In Guatemala, a thirty-six-year civil war only ended in 1996. More than two hundred thousand people died and one million were displaced, especially in the Mayan region of the country where government forces burned villages and removed people to punish the insurgency. In 1978–1979, leftists overthrew the Somoza dictatorship in Nicaragua. The country became the site of a proxy Cold War. The United States funded a guerrilla movement, the Contras, for over a decade. More than thirty thousand people were killed before peace was achieved in 1990. Before leaving office in 1990, leaders of the leftist government appropri-ated property and millions of dollars from the state treasury. Honduras, unlike the other republics, did not have a civil war but was a haven for military forces, guerrillas, and insurgents fighting in Nicaragua and El Salvador.

We can define a *narcostate* as one controlled and essentially corrupted by drug-trade organizations (DTOs).[13] Rather than a simple binary of narcostate/non-narcostate, it is more accurate to envision all the countries in this drug corridor as situated closer to the narcostate than the non-narcostate end of the continuum. The criminal nature of DTOs and the high profits that can be made generate the potential for violence as police fight the cartels, and competing car-tels fight it out in the most violent ways. The breakdown of the social order also provides a fertile ground for criminal gangs with the resulting violence against members of the public in coercions, shakedowns, and wanton acts of sheer thuggery. The endemic violence fuels the migrant movement northward to the United States.[14]

The lack of democratic accountability and endemic corruption make these countries particularly vulnerable to DTOs. In some cases, the cartels also provide public services, becoming, in effect, a shadow government more powerful and sometimes more sensitive and responsive to local needs than the official state. Guatemala is a producer as well as a transit route for illegal drugs. The mountainous areas are ideal for poppy cultivation. A large mass of poor people is easily recruited into the earning opportunities provided by the drug trade. Drugs also move through the country from Bolivia, Colombia, and Peru en route to Mexico and ultimately to the United States. The country shares a long border with Mexico and is situated in the heart of the drug corridor triangle of Belize, Guatemala, and Honduras. The Guatemalan army is reputed to be in alliance with some of the cartels. The DTOs are now an integral part of Guatemala's economy with proceeds from drug sales used to buy legitimate businesses. DTOs also fund local politicians and can easily afford to corrupt the political, military, and judiciary establishment. Guatemala is a weak state further weakened by its location on the drug corridor.[15]

Ninety percent of the cocaine refined in Colombia for the U.S. market passes through Honduras. It is part of the Northern Triangle of El Salvador and Guatemala, where drugs are trafficked into Mexico. The region's coastline and national borders are only lightly policed, and the resources of the small state have difficulty controlling powerful rich cartels. Tons of cocaine pass through the Honduran bridge that was established through that country in the 1970s between Mexican and Colombian cartels. Turf wars between competing cartels and gang violence makes Honduras a crime-ridden land with the second-highest murder rate in the world.[16] Rival gangs commit grisly murders to send intimidating messages. Many of the gangs originated in Los Angeles. When gang members were deported back to Honduras and other Central American countries, they became the muscle for DTOs. Gang violence is one of the principal reasons pushing migrants toward safer havens. With weak law enforcement and few formal employment opportunities for young people, working for the cartels seems a smart choice in the short term. The vast amount of money from the drug trade circulates throughout the country, polluting the normal rule of law and undermining civil society. In 2019 the brother of the president of Honduras was convicted in a U.S. court of drug trafficking and in 2021 U.S. prosecutors made public their criminal investigation of the president of Honduras for bribes in return for protecting drug traffickers shipping tons of cocaine to the United States.[17]

As an index of civil disorder, we can note that some of these countries have the highest murder rates in the world, with El Salvador ranked first (82.8 homicides per 100,000 in 2021), Honduras second (56.5), Venezuela third (56.3), U.S. Virgin Islands fourth (49.2) and Jamaica fifth (47.1). The Caribbean basin is the location for seventeen of the top twenty countries with the world's highest murder rates.[18] Across the world, murder kills more people than wars or terrorism combined. The main motivations for murder are organized crime, inequality, gender stereotypes, unemployment, political instability, and easy access to guns and drugs. So murder rates are like the pulse of the polity: high rates indicate something seriously wrong.

Drugs flow through Nicaragua, but in contrast to its neighbors, there is much less violence. Its most violent city has a homicide has rate lower than that of Detroit, Michigan. There is one main criminal gang, and this monopoly means no major turf wars, and unlike other states, Nicaragua has tended to manage the drug trade rather than antagonize the drug cartel.[19] The resulting lack of violence in the country is less the result of a lack of a drug trade than of a well-organized trade with deep ties to the ruling party.[20]

Mexico is a transition point for drugs entering the United States from further south as well as a production site for heroin and methamphetamines. When cartels were targeted by U.S. law enforcement in Colombia, and the Medellin cartel was eradicated around 2007, the drug flows to Florida were dismantled. These involved individual carriers, known as "mules," on commercial flights to New York City and Miami. But police interdiction became so successful in the United States that the drug flow shifted to the Central American corridor. Mexican cartels then emerged as the distribution agents for cocaine made in South America and consumed in North America.

The legalization of marijuana in certain U.S. states has suppressed its price, but heroin, cocaine, and amphetamines remain high value and continue to be produced and moved along this Central America drug corridor. This creates corruption, gang violence, and social instability that in turn are causing mass emigration as migrants seek to escape the poverty and violence.

Photo 11.4. Federal police in Guadalajara (John Rennie Short)

In 2006, the Mexican government launched a war on organized crime and the drug trade. The war on drugs militarized the nation. Military and federal police were dispatched to states around the country, an acknowledgment of the endemic corruption of local police. Photo 11.4 shows a federal officer deployed in the city of Guadalajara in Jalisco state. Over the next ten years, at least 45,000 troops were deployed. But in the carnage of the War on Drugs more than 60,000 people have "disappeared" with over 31,000 people murdered in 2019 alone.[21]

The wealth made from the drug trade is invested in legitimate organizations and businesses such as restaurants, farms, and day-care centers. In some Mexican states such as Sinaloa, more than two-thirds of the state's economy is intertwined with drug money. In some cases, the cartels provide a range of public services that the state is unable to provide, binding local institutions to the cartels. With the election of a new president, Andrew Manuel Lopez Obrador in 2018, there was a step back from the war. His stated policy was "Abrazos, no balazos" (Hugs, not bullets). The emphasis was to shift the focus from a War on Drugs to health and social policy. While the policy shift has yet to see positive returns, many in the country believe that the War on Drugs created more violence and eroded human rights without ridding the country of the pervasive influence of DTOs and their corrupting effect on the society.

The narcoeconomy has an insidious, corrupting influence undermining the rule of law, effective policing, and non-corrupt judiciary. All the normal workings of a society and the democratic expressions of a polity are weakened as the narcoeconomy turns the polity into a narcostate. But it is not simply that the narcoeconomy corrupts the polity. Corrupt polities enable the narcoeconomy to gain a foothold, flourish, and dominate. The cartels easily outmatch the limited resources of municipal government and local police. It is not only that crime creates corruption, but also that the corruption of public institutions facilitates crime.

Some states have reversed the trend. Colombia is only just emerging from a crippling fifty-year internal insurgency. The Revolutionary Armed Forces of Colombia (FARC) emerged in the 1960s as an insurgency that used violence to call attention to the vast inequalities in the country. By the early 1990s, it had control of more than 50 percent of the country, with 18,000 fighters in seventy different areas. The money to fund its organization came from the drug trade, extortion of companies, castle rustling, and kidnapping. The drug trade was a major source of funding for gangs, FARC, and the paramilitaries. In 1982, when a group of wealthy industrialists, landowners, and DTOs, such as the Medellin cartel, funded rival paramilitary units, it set the scene for cycles of violence. Close to six million people were displaced and up to 250,000 were killed over the course of the long conflict. The weakening of FARC's popular appeal and its dwindling capability allowed the government to be involved in peace talks that began in Havana in 2012. A peace treaty marking the end of the conflict came into full force in 2017. Colombia remains one of the more unequal societies, but now with the insurgency at an end and the power of the drug cartels blunted, there may be a peace dividend. However, the relative peace has enabled drug cultivation and distribution to prosper without the fear of civil war violence. Today the bulk of cocaine produced in the Colombia highlands is exported to Europe as well as the United States.

Stable States

There are more stable states in the region. Costa Rica has long been an island of relative stability. It is one of the richest countries in Central America, in part because of a long period of stable democracy. Political stability and economic growth feed off each other; the country can afford to create a more educated workforce that in turn attracts companies seeking more skilled labor. Manufacturing, service industries, and tourism have created more job opportunities that in turn attract migrants, especially from Nicaragua.

Panama is also relatively peaceful, apart from the invasion by U.S. forces in 1989. The construction and operation of the Panama Canal was done with U.S. dollars, and Panama City developed as a dollar-friendly banking site. The country has become an important provider of banking and financial services. Its banking secrecy and lack of transparency makes Panama City a global hub for finance. Panama has long been known as a "gray area" for encouraging tax avoidance; the 2016 publication of the *Panama Papers* revealed publicly that the Panamanian banking system was a favored place for wealthy individuals seeking to hide and/ or launder their money.[22] The scheme was part of a global network that linked rich individuals in China, Russia, Switzerland, and the UK with shell companies registered in Panama, British Virgin Islands, Bahamas, and Seychelles with financial agents in Hong Kong, Switzerland, and London. Panama acts as a wormhole for the shadowy world of the global rich seeking to avoid taxes, evade scrutiny, and maintain secrecy. The well-heeled and manicured bankers of Panama move as much illegal money as Mexican cartels or Colombian drug lords and far more than the poor peasants of Bolivia struggling to make a living from their coca crop or the coca pickers in Andean Colombia, who make roughly $75 a month for backbreaking work.

BRAZIL, ARGENTINA, AND GRANDEZA

The largest country in the region is Brazil. With a population of 211 million and an area of thirty-two million square miles, it occupies an important geopolitical position. It has long held visions of regional hegemony and world prominence, sometimes summed up in the word *Grandeza*, which can be translated as "greatness," "grandeur," or "enormity."

Brazil is part of the group known by the acronym *BRICS* (short for Brazil, Russia, India, China, and South Africa), designating large and emerging economies. Together, they represent over three billion people, more than one-third of the people in the world, and are responsible for almost a quarter of the world's gross domestic product. Since 2009, they have met in annual summits to discuss mutual interests. In the early 2000s they were seen as part of a new world order, embodying a marked shift away from the dominance of North America and Europe in the global economy. They were widely touted in the financial press as a profitable source of investment, outperforming the traditional economic heavyweights. But by 2020, their collective star had dimmed, even before the COVID-19 pandemic. While China and India maintained high growth rates, although beginning to slip as well, the others have had a more fluctuating experience. BRICS as a collective does not yet constitute a credible coherent geopolitical force but individually their size and economic heft make them candidates as regional hegemons.

Brazil is the giant of South America, by far the largest country in South America both by population and area. Its population of over 211 million is four times larger than the region's next largest population, and at thirty-two million square miles, it is four times larger than the next largest country of Argentina. The population of Brazil constitutes almost 50 percent of the total population of all of South America. Colombia is the second largest country with more than fifty million, but decades-long insurgency and drug war has weakened its projection of power. The case of Argentina, with forty-five million people, is interesting because it shows the rise and fall of a possible rival to Brazil. In 1900, Argentina was estimated to be the seventh-richest country in the world. Exports of beef, wheat, and other primary commodities to growing markets in Europe and North America led an economic boom that lasted from around 1880 to the early 1930s. The city of Buenos Aires is filled with beautiful buildings and elegant streetscapes from that era. But the Great Depression marked the beginning of decline as commodity prices fell and continuing political instability—the first military coup occurred in 1930—restricted the rise of the country to a regional hegemon. Political crises were often expressed in a succession of high-spending populist regimes alternating with military juntas and neoliberal agendas. The result was a long series of fiscal and political crises. It was a perfect storm of reduced revenues and cuts in the social wage followed by overspending, hyperinflation, and runs on the currency. Bouts of severe inflation, recurring recessions—from 1964 to 1990 and 1998 to 2002—and the collapses of the currency all weakened a country that in 1900 was favorably compared to Canada and Australia. But by 2014, Argentina had to be bailed out by the IMF. In the first six months of 2018, while the Mexican peso basically held its own against the U.S. dollar, the Argentina peso declined by more than 30 percent. The resource base and educated workforce could only lift the country up so far against the weight of endemic fiscal and political crisis. Crisis and protest now seem endemic. As one observer noted,

> It's an Italian car of a country; on its surface, graceful and sleek. But under the hood, it keeps breaking down. In short, Argentina looks great but just doesn't work.[23]

The geopolitical result was that Brazil grew more dominant in the region as Argentina grew relatively weaker. The military dictatorship of 1976–1982 was the last gasp of geopolitical significance for Argentina. While democracy returned in 1983, the state continues to be racked by economic and fiscal crisis. Photo 11.5 shows a political rally in Buenos Aires against President Macri, the IMF, and capitalists. The decline of Argentina and the fracturing of Colombia mean that there are no serious regional rivals to Brazil.

Brazil became a republic in 1889, but military rule was common. The generals were in power from 1934 to 1945 and again from 1965 to 1984. A military-dominated geopolitical discourse is apparent.[24] Army officers developed geopolitical strategies in the 1950s. Generals such as Golbery do Couto e Silva developed ideas of economic growth with territorial and social coherence as a form of national security against Communism.[25] It was a Brazilian version of Manifest Destiny with emphasis on a strong military, the rise of Brazil as an industrialized society, and the transformation of Amazonia from a jungle to "productive traversed space." Their rule is associated with the so-called Brazilian Miracle from approximately 1965 to 1980 that involved rapid urbanization and industrialization. People flocked from rural areas to the rapidly growing cities to build their accommodations. The favelas of modern-day Brazil are an offshoot of the miracle.

When a military dictatorship took control of the country in 1964, they pursued policies of rapid industrialization, tightening of internal security, a buildup

Photo 11.5.   Protest in Buenos Aires, Argentina (John Rennie Short)

in arms, and pursuit of regional hegemony. In 1965 for example, a border conflict with Paraguay over a dam project was used by Brazil, with the backing of the United States, to defeat Paraguay, lay the basis for Brazil's rapid industrialization, and to marginalize Argentina.[26] The development of the Amazon was seen as a project vital to ensure continued economic growth and to show the effective power of the state to achieve the transformation from jungle to developed country.

There was also a competing geopolitical discourse to the militarization of geopolitics, one put forward by socially progressive political geographers arguing for a more inclusionary understanding of the role of the state.[27]

The new democratic governments that first came to power in 1985 were initially dominated by a neoliberalism that failed to improve living standards. Rising resentment eventually led to the presidential election in 2002 of the Worker Party's candidate, Luiz Inacio Lula da Silva, popularly known as Lula. He placed more emphasis on social reforms and income redistribution. However, the military still played an important role. Lula sent thirty thousand troops to Haiti in 2004, and the military continued to play a major role in internal surveillance and social control. Military officers occupied ministerial positions. The Worker's Party did soften inequalities with income redistribution policies and direct subsidies. More than sixty million people escaped absolute poverty from 2002 to 2014. Economic and political elites continued to do well, and the military was firmly entrenched in the state and the national imagination. Because the Worker's Party stressed personal consumption over investments in public service, major problems arose when the economy imploded and the precarity of the newly created middle class became more obvious.[28] There was dissatisfaction with the hosting of the World Cup in 2014 and the Olympic Games in 2016, prestige projects to project and to embody *Grandeza*. Mass protests over bus fares in 2018 revealed the critical lack of public services and rising social discontent.

In 2018, a former army officer and right-wing politician, Jair Bolsonaro, was elected president as Brazilians voted against the ruling party now widely seen as both corrupt and incompetent. In some ways he carried on the geopolitical aims of the post-military government with its shared aim of economic and ultimately political leadership in South America and with an expanded role in multilateral trade talks, peace-keeping missions, and international forums. But in other ways, Bolsonara represented a return to the thinking of the army officers of the 1950s. He praised the rule of the generals. He promoted the buildup of internal surveillance and the military and did little about a mounting ecological crisis in Amazonia. Similar to the military geopoliticians of earlier decades, he thought Brazil's national destiny lay in defeating and transforming the Amazonia rather than saving or protecting it. Many international observers find it difficult to understand his antipathy to environmental arguments. His attitude only makes sense from the ideas of Brazil's military geopolitical past and the continuing commitment to a certain form of Grandeza. Bolsonaro harks back to the "good things" that the military junta achieved and shares the view of earlier military geopoliticians: that the development of the Amazon is vital to national economic development and to the notion of a form of Grandeza.

GEOPOLITICAL HOTSPOT: THE FALKLANDS ISLANDS/ISLAS MALVINAS

Sovereignty of the Falkland Islands, known as Islas Malvinas in Argentina, is a source of continuing disputes between the UK and Argentina. There was no indigenous settling of this cluster of two main island groups close to the tip of South America (see map 11.2). They became a sheltering port for early whalers sailing the southern oceans and numerous countries laid claim to them, including France, Spain, Argentina, and the United States. They came under effective British control in 1833, which Argentina protested at the time and has never stopped. When it joined the new body of the United Nations in 1945, Argentina again raised its claim to what it refers to as "Las Malvinas."

By the late 1970s and very early 1980s, the Falklands became enmeshed in national and international politics. The Argentinian military junta, then in power, used the issue of taking the islands to rally nationalist sentiment at a time of intense economic and political pressure. Argentinian trade unions were in open opposition; there was rising concern about the military and their human rights violations, especially the "disappearance" of dissidents. It was a crisis of legitimacy that the military leaders felt could be handled by taking Las Malvinas. There was widespread popular support for the idea that the islands belonged to Argentina. It could have been handled in a more diplomatic way. It was not a key UK asset, few in the UK really cared or even knew about the islands, and some sort of deal could have been struck. But military men tend to see military solutions. The military junta had good relations with the United States; it presented itself as a bulwark against Communism at a time of Cold War hostilities. In retrospect, the junta overplayed its hand by overestimating its military capabilities and its relations with the United States and underestimating the UK's resolve. The Argentinian military leaders thought that a quick invasion against a country

Map 11.2.   Location of Falklands (Wikimedia / Rob)

in decline with neither the will nor ability to respond would be a *fait accompli*. In their calculus they thought they could take back the islands with little or no cost and the dominant power, the United States, would not intervene. On April 2, 1982, Argentinian paratroopers invaded the islands and claimed control.

In Britain, the Prime Minister Margaret Thatcher was faced with her own economic and political crisis. Mass unemployment had undermined her party's election promises of getting people back to work. In the first years of her government, unemployment reached more than a million people for the first time since the Great Depression. Like the Argentinian generals, she also appealed to a sense of nationalism. The Falklands as a territory generated little support, more general claims were invoked, the idea of fairness, British pride, and resolve. Postwar British politicians had effectively managed to extricate the country from most of the empire. There was little support for a global military presence. The humiliation of Suez in 1956, when Britain, along with France and Israel, sought to play power politics with the invasion of Egypt and were reprimanded by the United States, revealed the real source of power in the world. A postimperial posture was emerging but the Argentinian invasion of the islands, even islands so far away, was too much of a provocation for Thatcher, who believed that the country still had a major role in the world. Allowing the Argentinians to unilaterally and forcibly take control of the Falklands would damage the nation's image. She ordered an immediate response.

A wannabe regional hegemon facing off against a weakened, fading world power: military junta against democracy. The stage was set. The Argentinian writer Jorge Luis Borges described it as "a fight between two bald men over a comb."

On April 5, 1982, the Royal Navy dispatched two aircraft carriers, HMS *Invincible* and *Hermes* and a task force of 124 vessels to retake the islands. The war had some popular support, but it was not universal. Thatcher was too much of a polarizing figure. A popular UK newspaper, the *Sun*, pursued a jingoistic line supporting Thatcher and the troops as a single representation of a united Britain taking on a military junta. British forces landed on East Falkland on May 21. From their bases in Port San Carlos and Goose Green, troops were marched, ferried, and helicoptered across the island. By June 14 they had taken control of the islands when Argentinian forces surrendered Port Stanley, the main town. The fight to retake the islands proved difficult and costly, although relatively quick. At least 650 Argentinians were killed and more than 11,000, mainly young and starving recruits, taken prisoner. The British lost 258 men.

The victory catapulted British Prime Minister Margaret Thatcher into higher approval ratings. The image of the Iron Lady was born. She won the 1983 general election on the back of the victory against Argentina. In Argentina when news surfaced of the defeat and stories of their underfed, undertrained young conscripts being overwhelmed by superior British forces, the discontent against the junta increased. It collapsed in 1983. What's the point of a military junta if they cannot even run a military campaign, especially one so close to the national shores while the UK had to send a task force thousands of miles across the Atlantic? The junta had misjudged their own power and the willingness and ability of Britain to reclaim the islands. Argentinian power was shown up as bluster, the rulers were a military that could only intimidate its own peoples but could not intimidate a fading power on the other side of the ocean. The gamble to gloss over economic incompetence and rising social discontent with a previously popular irredentism backfired. In Argentina, the defeat dented popular support not only for the junta but also for the military and strengthened cynicism about the authorities' use of territorial claims as a form of dodging more serious domestic issues. Even today in Argentina while many, but not all, believe that the islands should belong to Argentina, few think that war is the answer.[29] Argentinian forces have been much reduced; cynicism about the military in general and bitterness over the war in particular provides no support for military endeavors.

While the United States helped the UK, their support was confused and variable. President Ronald Reagan did not want to jeopardize the reputation of the United States in Argentina and Latin America. However, the "special relationship" proved more decisive; the United States did provide some support. Britain received direct and enthusiastic support from Chile. The UK did not reclaim its status as a world power with the successful retaking of the islands, but it did show that it would not depart from the world stage. The victory did not lead to major changes in the country's geopolitical trajectory. The defense forces were too chronically undefended to achieve global status. But Thatcher's critics could see the positive impacts of replacing a junta with a democratically elected government. And who knows if the victory in the Falklands may have persuaded subsequent British prime ministers to commit troops in their seemingly eternal support of U.S. ventures to maintain the global status and world power credibility that flickered so briefly on the South Atlantic.[30]

After the war, the islanders were made British citizens, military garrisons on the islands were strengthened, and the Falkland Islands, along with South Georgia and South Sandwich Islands, became a distinct British overseas territory, joining the British Virgin Islands, Gibraltar, the Cayman Islands, and eleven other fragments of empire. Britain and Argentina restored diplomatic relations in 1989 but Argentina continues to make the return of the Falklands to Argentina sovereignty an important priority of foreign relations as well as a part of its constitution. An official sign in the Argentinian port of Ushuaia, shown in photo 11.6, makes the point very clear, while a more personal sign on a vehicle in Port Stanley, photo 11.7, the capital of the Falklands, makes an equally clear though very different point. The almost three thousand permanent residents continue to

Photo 11.6.   Official sign in Ushuaia, Argentina (John Rennie Short)

Photo 11.7.   Sign in Port Stanley, Falklands (John Rennie Short)

want to remain British while the existence of oil and deposits in the surrounding seas add an extra dimension to competing territorial claims. Possession of the Falklands gives the UK major territorial claims to energy reserves in the South Atlantic and even in the Antarctic if and when commercial exploitation is allowed. The Falklands still have geopolitical and geoeconomic significance.

SELECTED READINGS

Arana, M. (2020). *Silver, sword, and stone: Three crucibles in the Latin American story.* New York: Simon and Schuster.

Barrios, M. Á. (2009). *Diccionario Latinoamericano de Seguridad y Geopolítica.* Buenos Aires: Editorial Biblos.

Franchi, T., Migon, E. X. F. G., & Villarreal, R. X. J. (2017). Taxonomy of interstate conflicts: Is South America a peaceful region? *Brazilian Political Science Review, 11.* https://doi.org/10.1590/1981-3821201700020008.

Kelly, P. (2010). *Checkerboards and shatterbelts: The geopolitics of South America.* Austin: University of Texas Press.

Martínez, Ó. (2016). *A History of violence: Living and dying in Central America.* London: Verso.

Montoya, M. A., Lemus, D., and Kaltenecker, E. (2019). The geopolitical factor of Belt and Road Initiative in Latin America. *Latin American Journal of Trade Policy, 2,* 6–21.

Nolte, D., & Wehner, L. E. (2016). Geopolitics in Latin America: Old and new. In D. R. Mares and A. M. Kacowicz (eds.), *Routledge Handbook of Latin American Security* (33–43). Abingdon: Routledge.

Piccone, T. (2016). *The geopolitics of China's rise in Latin America.* Washington, DC: Brookings, 20. http://chinhnghia.com/the-geopolitics-of-chinas-rise-in-latin-america_ted-piccone.pdf.

Puntigliano, A. R. (2011). "Geopolitics of integration" and the imagination of South America. *Geopolitics, 16,* 846–64.

Puntigliano, A. R. (2019). The geopolitics of the catholic church in Latin America. *Territory, Politics, Governance,* 1–16. https://doi.org/10.1080/21622671.2019.1687326.

Radcliffe, S. A. (2007). Latin American indigenous geographies of fear: Living in the shadow of racism, lack of development, and antiterror measures. *Annals of the Association of American Geographers, 97,* 385–97.

Torres, R. M. (2018). A crisis of rights and responsibility: Feminist geopolitical perspectives on Latin American refugees and migrants. *Gender, Place & Culture, 25,* 13–36.

Van Ramshorst, J. P. (2019). Laughing about it: Emotional and affective spaces of humour in the geopolitics of migration. *Geopolitics, 24,* 896–915.

NOTES

1. Piccone, T. (2016). *The geopolitics of China's rise in Latin America.* Washington, DC: Brookings, 20. http://chinhnghia.com/the-geopolitics-of-chinas-rise-in-latin-america_ted-piccone.pdf.

2. Alconini, S., & Covey, R. A. (eds.). (2018). *The Oxford Handbook of the Incas.* Oxford: Oxford University Press.

3. Arana, M. (2020). *Silver, sword, and stone: Three crucibles in the Latin American story.* New York: Simon and Schuster.

4. Blaufarb, R. (2007). The western question: The geopolitics of Latin American independence. *American Historical Review, 112*, 742–63.

5. International Court of Justice. (2014). *Maritime dispute (Peru v. Chile)*. The Hague. https://web.archive.org/web/20140202143900/http://www.icj-cij.org/docket /files/137/17928.pdf.

6. An official account of the violence of the civil war was produced by the Catholic Church. The four-volume report of the *Recovery of Historical Memory* is a heartbreaking account of the atrocities, the vast majority committed by the military. A shortened English version is available: Archdiocese of Guatemala (1999). *Guatemala: Never again*. New York: Orbis.

7. Dykmann, K. (2008). The antagonism between Pan-Americanism and Bolivarism in Inter-American relations. In Thies, S., & Raab, J. (eds.), *E Pluribus Unum? National and transnational identities in the Americas* (129–40). https://www.unibi.de/ZIF /FG/2008Pluribus/publications/index_pluribus_unum_2008.pdf.

8. Ellner, S. (ed.). (2020). *Latin America's pink tide: Breakthroughs and shortcomings*. Lanham: Rowman & Littlefield.

9. Vivares, E. (ed.). (2018). *Regionalism, development and the post-commodities boom in South America*. Cham: Palgrave Macmillan.

10. Vadell, J. A. (2019). China in Latin America: South-south cooperation with Chinese characteristics. *Latin American Perspectives, 46*, 107–25.

11. Gonzalez-Vicente, R. (2011). China's engagement in South America and Africa's extractive sectors: New perspectives for resource curse theories. *Pacific Review, 24*, 65–87; Malacalza, B. (2019). What led to the boom? Unpacking China's development cooperation in Latin America. *World Affairs, 182*, 370–403.

12. Carpenter, T. G. (2012). Drug mayhem moves south. *National Interest, 117*, 32–37; Trejo, G., & Ley, S. (2018). Why did drug cartels go to war in Mexico? Subnational party alternation, the breakdown of criminal protection, and the onset of large-scale violence. *Comparative Political Studies, 51*, 900–37.

13. For an alternative viewpoint, see Chouvy, P. A. (2016). The myth of the narco-state. *Space and Polity, 20*, 26–38.

14. Martínez, Ó. (2016). *A History of violence: Living and dying in Central America*. London: Verso.

15. Brands, H. (2010). *Crime, violence, and the crisis in Guatemala: A case study in the erosion of the state*. Carlisle, PA: Strategic Studies Institute.

16. World Population Review. (2021). Murder rate by country 2021. *World Population Review*. https://worldpopulationreview.com/country-rankings/murder-rate-by-country.

17. Palmer, E., & Malkin, E. (2019, October 18). Honduran president's brother is found guilty of drug trafficking. *New York Times*. https://www.nytimes.com/2019/10/18/world /americas/honduras-president-brother-drug-trafficking.html; de Cordoba, J. (2021, February 8). U.S. prosecutors investigate Honduras president for taking drug-related bribes. *Wall Street Journal*. https://www.wsj.com/articles/u-s-prosecutors-investigate-honduras -president-for-taking-drug-related-bribes-11612840848.

18. World Population Review. (2021). Murder rate by country 2021. *World Population Review*. https://worldpopulationreview.com/country-rankings/murder-rate-by-country.

19. Peralta, E. (2014, October 26). Nicaragua follows its own path in dealing with drug traffickers. *NPR: National Public Radio*. https://www.npr.org/sections/parallels /2014/10/26/357791551/nicaragua-follows-its-own-path-in-dealing-with-drug-traffickers.

20. Asmann, P. (2019). Nicaragua government's alleged drug trade ties deepen with arrest. https://www.insightcrime.org/news/brief/nicaragua-governments-alleged-drug -trade-ties-deepen-arrest/.

21. BBC News. (2020). Mexico's war on drugs: More than 60,000 people "disappeared." https://www.bbc.com/news/world-latin-america-51015791.

22. Harding, L. (2016, April 5). What are the Panama Papers? A guide to history's biggest data leak. *The Guardian.* https://www.theguardian.com/news/2016/apr/03/what-you-need-to-know-about-the-panama-papers.

23. Faiolo. A. (2018, December 28). A plummeting peso, fears of default—it's *déjà vu* in Argentina. *Washington Post,* A6.

24. da Costa, W. M. (2017). The Brazilian geopolitics and its influence on national strategic thinking. *L'espacepolitique.* https://journals.openedition.org/espacepolitique/4117.

25. Hepple, L. W. (1986). Geopolitics, generals and the state in Brazil. *Political Geography Quarterly, 5,* S79–90.

26. Blanc, J. (2018). Itaipu's forgotten history: The 1965 Brazil–Paraguay border crisis and the new geopolitics of the Southern Cone. *Journal of Latin American Studies, 50,* 383–409.

27. Ferretti, F. (2018). Geographies of internationalism: Radical development and critical geopolitics from the northeast of Brazil. *Political Geography, 63,* 10–19; Ferretti, F., & Pedrosa, B. V. (2018). Inventing critical development: A Brazilian geographer and his northern network. *Transactions of the Institute of British Geographers, 43,* 703–17.

28. Anderson, P. (2019). *Brazil apart: 1964–2019.* London: Verso.

29. Benwell, M. C., & Dodds, K. (2011). Argentine territorial nationalism revisited: The Malvinas/Falklands dispute and geographies of everyday nationalism. *Political Geography, 30,* 441–49.

30. Berbéri, C., & Castro, M. O. B. (eds.). (2015). *30 years after: Issues and representations of the Falklands War.* Farnham: Ashgate.

IV

NEW GLOBAL CHALLENGES

12

Global Challenges and the State

Traditional geopolitical thinking has its limits. Its traditional focus on nation-states tends to ignore or marginalize those thorny issues that interlace the global and the national. There is, of course, an international system of treaties, organizations, and practices. The World Health Organization and the United Nations are just two examples of advisory and regulatory bodies that cohere a world order. In chapters 2 and 3, we discussed the ideas of an emerging new world order. Orders is probably a more accurate word. In this final chapter, however, I return to this general theme to examine how new threats and challenges slice and dice the global with the national in complex and myriad ways. I want to explore the global nexus beyond these formal arrangements to consider global challenges faced by nation-states. I will focus on three main issues: pandemics, climate change, and in the Hotspot section, the global commons of the polar regions.

PANDEMICS

A new virus, first observed in the Chinese city of Wuhan in December 2019, spread across the globe. In only a few months, the virus spread, causing a new respiratory disease, COVID-19, that left some untouched while killing others. COVID-19 spread easily and quickly among people, although many of its precise mechanisms are still not fully known at the time of this writing. As I write these lines, the global death total is approximately 3.38 million with some estimates as high as 6.93 million. In the United States alone, the number of deaths is more than 586,000, with some estimates as high as 900,000.[1] Much already has been written about the virus, the disease, and the debilitating impact of the enforced lockdowns. Here, I want to highlight just three implications for the global-national nexus.[2]

First, globalization has made international travel cheaper, easier, and more prevalent. Within months, perhaps weeks, of the first outbreak, the disease seeded and spread around the world. Globalization has "smoothed" the world, making disease transmissions, especially one spread by person-to-person contact, all that more rapid and virulent. Globalization is an accelerant capable of turning outbreaks into epidemics and epidemics into pandemics. Resistance to globalization and calls for national biosecurity likely will be strengthened by this pandemic.

Second, the pandemic has reinforced a sense of national uncertainty. The response of closing borders to halt the spread reinforces a sense of individual nations' acting in opposition to global threats. The lockdowns are a form of "global distancing" between nations, matching the "social distancing" between persons within the nation-states. By revalorizing the national in contrast to the global, this pandemic secures nationalist narratives, which likely will remain strong even when there is return to a semblance of "normal." This pandemic does not spell the end of globalization but nonetheless reinforces the rhetoric of nationalism and undermines global narratives.

Third, in contrast to the other two trends, to meet the challenge of the pandemic requires some form of global coordination and global cooperation. We will need the work of scientists from around the world to develop future vaccines, and these will have to be tested and to be administered globally. While the pandemic weakens some forms of globalization, such as international travel, it strengthens the need for global cooperation. At the individual and national levels where social distancing is recommended, a global distancing will sever further the worldwide networks of science and information, policy and practice that might help solve future pandemics. Risk of new diseases increases as we extend commercial exploitation into wild lands and ecosystems. As we cut down more rainforest, for example, we expose the world's population to diseases for which we have no immunity. Future disease outbreaks are not only possible but certain. A world fragmented into nation-states offers little help against such looming threats.

CLIMATE CHANGE

The world is warming, and our climate is changing: the evidence is indisputable.[3] Human activity such as oil, gas, and coal burning as well as continued deforestation is leading to increasing levels of carbon dioxide. The level of carbon dioxide in preindustrial times was 280 ppm (parts per million); now it is 415 ppm, and the world has warmed 1.8°F on average above preindustrial levels. We are likely to face even more devastating temperature increases. Recent estimates suggest a temperature rise of at least 3.5°F within a hundred years, with upper estimates as high as 8.6° if no substantial progress is made in reducing emissions.

The impact of climate change is already visible in the melting of polar ice sheets, the bleaching of coral reefs, and rising sea levels. There are also the greater probabilities of more extreme weather events, such as heat waves, tropical storms, flooding, and wildfires: their impacts are felt across the globe. Vanuatu is sinking, California is burning, small island nations in the Caribbean are seeing more destructive hurricanes, pastoralists in the Horn of Africa are pushed to the edge of survival, and people in European cities are experiencing record-breaking, sweltering summers.

There are various geopolitical challenges. The first is the uneven nature of resiliency. Climate change adaptation and mitigation are expensive propositions whose enactment reveals the vast differences in the abilities of states to meet the challenges. The *global commons* have been trashed by the richer countries of the world, their wealth due in part to growth based on environmental destruction and rapid industrialization, causing greenhouse gases. The impacts, in contrast, are most heavily felt by the poorest countries in the world. Tiny Pacific nations, such as Vanuatu, are sinking under seas swamped by the heavy carbon footprint of the rich world. In 2020, torrential rains submerged more than a quarter of Bangladesh, following from a cyclone two months previously. Climate change caused severe cyclones and extreme flooding. The rains inundated over a million homes. There is an uneven distribution of costs and benefits with most of the costs shouldered by the poor and the benefits reaped by the rich world.

Second, climate change raises the issue of individual states and of the global commons. While nation-states refer to the interests of particular people in particular territory, the global commons is the idea that we all share the physical resources of the world. If economic nationalisms take greater hold, some countries may become more committed to national growth rate than to reducing the global carbon footprint. And while many countries sign on to international agreements on limiting and preventing further climate change, their commitment always is hedged by nationalist considerations. Climate change is also an example of the *tragedy of the commons*, by which individual countries acting in their own self-interest produce a sub-optimal outcome. It is rational that individual states "carry on as usual," while allowing other countries to make necessary yet expensive improvements to the global commons. While the optimal solution for each country is to gain the benefits of a carbon economy while others reduce their carbon footprint, collectively the result is suboptimal as the commons deteriorate. The challenges of climate change are real and growing in all countries. The evidence is so overwhelming, except to the most committed climate change deniers, that more people around the world can see that the global solution is to reduce carbon emission and embark on massive investment in climate change adaptation and mitigation.

Finally, there are the more geopolitical concurrences of climate change. This can take a variety of forms. We already discussed in chapter 9 the possible connections among desertification, civil unrest, and state fragility in the Sahel area, where 65 percent of arable land is now degraded. One study found that around the globe, the habitable niche that people can reasonably inhabit will shrink, leaving 1.3 billion in barely livable conditions.[4] Rising tides could displace at least another 150 million people by mid-century. Climate change is the likely driving force in population displacement and in mass migration that destabilizes states.[5] In countries such as Guatemala, for example, climate change–induced deterioration of agricultural productivity has led to mass migration. More people are forced to leave the land and to move to cities or to opportunities elsewhere. The result could be cities that become home to millions of displaced people and thus fertile ground for extremist groups, especially in areas with weak, failed, and failing states. The fate of individual countries and their people increasingly will be shaped by global climate change. A new world is emerging with climate change as a causal factor in geopolitics. This is not to propose a crude form of environmentalism but rather a more sophisticated understanding that geopolitics will be shaped by the impacts of and responses to global climate change. In turn, these impacts and responses to climate change will be guided by geopolitics. The biggest geopolitical concern of the twenty-first century will be climate change.

Map 12.1.   The Arctic (CIA World Fact Book)

GEOPOLITICAL HOTSPOTS: THE POLAR REGIONS

Global warming varies across the globe. The polar regions are some of the most rapidly warming places with temperatures, since the 1990s, rising three times faster than the global average.[6]

While sharing a similar environmental change, the two polar regions vary in the form of governance. They do have regime similarities: both are subject to international agreements, the Arctic Council and the Antarctic System of Treaties; both represent institutional innovations outside the UN system; and both are in the frontline of scientific cooperation in measuring global climate change. They differ, with the Arctic more reliant on nonbinding instruments and being inhabited and so raising issues of indigenous peoples' rights. Fundamentally, however, the Arctic's governance is primarily nation-states with an advisory Arctic Council, while the Antarctic is an example of international governance.[7] The comparisons and contrasts provide us with an interesting pair of case studies.

The polar regions have changed in the global geographical imagination. The uninhabited Antarctic, as well as the Arctic region, while home to many people, have long been imagined as empty zones easily filled with imaginings and longings. Early voyagers depicted them as wastelands, barren icy deserts or as examples of gothic sublime, majestic and empty. This "emptiness" became full of other possibilities from around 1820 when they began to enter the popular imagination. "Arctic fever" took hold from around 1820 to a peak in 1911.[8] The polar regions became the scene of nationalist enterprises, scientific endeavors, and an insecure masculinity at a time of the ending of "wilderness." All these are embodied in the life of Roald Amundsen (1872–1928).[9]

In Britain, Amundsen sometimes exists as a counterpoint to his contemporary, the English naval officer R. F. Scott. Scott's fatal attempt to reach the South Pole contrasts with Amundsen's success. For the British, Scott was an epitome of Edwardian amateurism: his failure a sign of heroism and dignity, while Amundsen's success seemed too easy and too professional. Scott and Amundsen in this telling are both cardboard cutout figures, one representing the British love of amateur failure in contrast to the grubby professionalism of the successful foreigner.

Roald Amundsen's achievements in the polar regions are worth noting. From 1903 to 1926, he completed both the North West Passage and the North East Passage and reached both the North and South Poles. Amundsen developed his expedition skills over many years. He was a member of the Belgian Antarctic expedition from 1897 to 1899. His bitter experience of a winter in Antarctica made him prepare with great care for subsequent journeys. In 1903, he sailed from Norway, escaping just in time from pressing debts and angry creditors, to find a way through the icy reaches of northern Canada. The North West Passage had long been a goal of many a doomed explorer. In a small ship that wintered in Inuit villages, he reached Nome in 1906. His sensitivity to cultural difference allowed him to see how the indigenous people coped with the extreme cold, and that knowledge guided his planning for the next expedition. His inability to cash in on the adventure—the news was widely leaked before he could sell his story—also made him acutely aware of controlling tightly the news of his subsequent explorations. Amundsen's exploits were widely publicized. He was feted and honored and began world lecture tours. In 1910, he set off for another polar expedition. He told everyone he was headed for the North Pole, but after leaving Norway, he headed south. Using skis and dog sleds and carefully placing supply depots along the route, he managed to reach the South Pole on December 14, 1911. Scott's poorly equipped team—they had ponies rather than dogs, and few could ski well enough—made it, but they died in the return. The British press was bitter in their criticism. In Norway, his status as national hero was confirmed. In the United States, he became a popular celebrity, embarking on successful lecture tours and never-ending fund-raising trips. In 1918, he set sail from Norway north and east in a small ship, *Maud*. After numerous delays, the ship made the North East Passage. In 1925, Amundsen with the backing of a rich American, Lincoln Ellsworth, made an attempt to fly to the North Pole. They did not make it, but the next year, as part of an Italian airship expedition, Amundsen was probably one the first people to pass over the North Pole.

Amundsen was exploring when there was nothing much else to explore. The polar ice caps and the icy seas of the North Pole were all that was left. The explorations had to be funded and financed, and so the story is as much about the emergence of celebrity culture and the concurrent making of national folk heroes as the revealing of new geographical realities. Amundsen, arguably the last real explorer, was definitely the first global celebrity explorer.

The Arctic

The Arctic became a battleground during the Cold War. Less than sixty miles separated Alaska from the USSR, and the quickest missile flight path between Moscow and Washington was across the North Pole (see map 12.1). Iceland became a key member of NATO in 1949 and home to a U.S. base. Denmark's membership gave U.S. military access to Greenland and with Norway provided a curtain of encirclement around the northern edges of the USSR. The Arctic was ringed with U.S. and USSR bases, military installations, and early warning systems. Canada and the United States became closer military allies against what they saw as a Soviet threat across the polar icefields. On the other side, the USSR saw the NATO arc as a noose around its northern neck. The Arctic was a site of nuclear testing. The United States tested bombs on the Aleutian island of Amchitka, while the USSR exploded a massive bomb on Novaya Zemlya.[10]

Scientific research was also conducted by both sides. This has remained even after the end of the Cold War as the Arctic became an important scientific testing site. This work has provided a rich body of evidence to show the existence and impacts of global climate change.

In the past thirty years, the Arctic has seen a resource boom. It is home to around 15 percent of the world's oil reserves and holds between 20 and 30 percent of natural gas reserves. More sophisticated technology allows exploitation even in these cold and inhospitable reaches. Warmer temperatures have melted the frozen seas, at least for part of the year, allowing greater accessibility and the possibility of northwest and northeast passages due to longer ice-free summer months.

A number of issues face the Arctic. The first is the environmental pollution. Air and water pollution from industrial military and resource exploitation activities impact a fragile ecosystem. Hazardous waste and pollution from mining and the military are problems incapable of being solved by just one nation. The second issue is determining national sovereignty in a complex and changing environment of melting ice sheets, possible new sea routes and rich oil and gas reserves.[11] The Arctic fuses issues of national sovereignties and international rights over issues such as fishing, maritime access, and exploitation of oil and gas reserves. Norway's oil exploration, for example, has shifted from the North Sea off the west coast of Norway to even further north into the Arctic waters of its northern borders.

The Arctic Council was established in 1996 as an intergovernmental forum. Membership includes Canada, Denmark, Finland, Iceland, Norway, Russia, Sweden, and the United States. It functions as a forum for these nations to discuss shared problems and to seek solutions. Some indigenous groups, such as the Aleut and Saami, are permanent participants. There are also permanent observer states. Although it lacks real power, the council, when it articulates clear strategies as in the case of ensuring biodiversity, has impacted behaviors of both Arctic and non-Arctic states.[12]

As a steward for the Arctic, the council acts as a general forum for Arctic nations as well as a specific security arrangement.[13] Military and security issues traditionally were off the table at the Arctic Council but have emerged as the Arctic opens up. The Arctic is being militarized more heavily than at any time since the end of the Cold War. Russia sees the Arctic as central to both its economic and military plans; NATO increasingly is more active to guard against perceived Russian threats. China, with active involvement in Russian oil and gas and big plans for Greenland, now considers itself a near-Arctic nation. We are on the verge of a new polar power struggle.[14]

Climate change, especially the rapid increase in temperatures, is having major impacts on the Arctic aside from igniting a new power politics in the region. Melting ice sheets and rising sea levels generate severe risks for wildlife and indigenous peoples. Drier, warmer conditions have led to massive forest fires in Alaska and Siberia and the release of methane and the melting of permafrost. Climate change provides opportunities as well as costs. Maritime transits are now possible between July and October. As depicted in map 5.2, the Chinese BRI also now includes a northern Arctic route.

The costs as well as opportunities are perhaps most evident in the case of Russia, which has embarked on a Far North Strategy as an important domestic priority. In 2020, the Kremlin published a fifteen-year plan to target more development investment in the Arctic, encouraging resource exploitation and building new towns. The Far North was described as an Arctic frontier, opening up economic and geopolitical opportunities for Russia. A strategic goal is to use the northern sea route to export more oil and gas.[15] However, the same warming that opens up the Arctic also liquifies the Arctic. Permafrost, the layer of permanent ice below the surface, provides the solid support for a range of vital infrastructure, including pipes, roads, and buildings. With warming, the permafrost is melting. In late May 2020, melting permafrost shifted the foundations of the Norilsk Nickel mine fuel storage tank, releasing pollutants into the ecosystem. More than 21,000 tons of diesel washed into the rivers and wetland.[16] Melting permafrost undermines, in some cases literally, the proposed surge in northern development. More than 90 percent of Russian gold and diamond mines and 30 percent of its oil are located on areas of permafrost.

The Antarctic

The warming of the Arctic raises new issues over territorial claims, mining rights, and ownership of new sea routes. While Antarctica faces similar climate concerns facing the Arctic of warming and consequent ice-sheet collapse and sea-level rise, it does so from a different geopolitical context. The Antarctic, in contrast, is one of the few examples of the triumph of the commons. Effective collective agreement over demilitarization and scientific research has made this region technically owned by no one but managed by many. It is an international, demilitarized space with governance without a government.[17]

Antarctica was uninhabited and until relatively recently inaccessible. It was not, however, unclaimed. The British, French, and Norwegian governments made early claims to sections of the continent. By the mid-twentieth century, Australia, Argentina, Chile, New Zealand, Norway, France, and the UK all had territorial claims (see map 12.2).

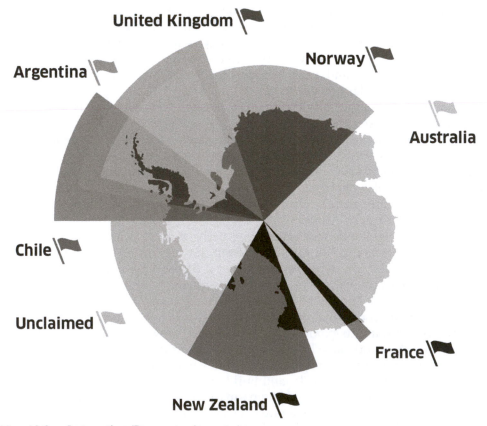

Map 12.2.   Antarctica (Discovering Antarctica)

A landmark treaty signed by twelve countries in 1959—the countries making claims as well as Belgium, Japan, South Africa, the United States, and the USSR—became effective from 1961. Under the treaty, all the existing claims were put to one side, neither renounced nor abandoned—and no new claims were permissible. Under the agreement, Antarctica was to be used for peaceful purposes as a natural reserve devoted to peace and science. There were ten main points:

- No military uses
- Freedom of scientific investigation
- Free exchange of scientific plans and data
- Any territorial claims to be put on hold
- Nuclear-free zone
- All stations to be open to inspection by other nations
- National laws applied to citizens, not areas
- Any modification of treaty requires unanimous consent of all signatories
- All nations to ensure compliance

The Antarctic Agreement was widened and deepened in what is now referred to as the Antarctic Treaty System, which has added conservation measures and environmental protection. There are now more than forty-five signatories and a series of research stations that are open to international observers (see photo 12.1). Argentina, Australia, Chile, China, Germany, India, Japan, Russia, South Africa, South Korea, the UK, the United States, and the USSR all have research stations that provide information on global warming.

In many ways, the Antarctic Treaty System is a great success. It has ensured the freedom of scientific investigation and provided high quality data on global climate change. It was data from Antarctica that allowed scientists to note the thinning of the protective ozone layer and ultimately to the banning of hydro-fluorocarbons in 1987—a measure that was responsible for two million fewer cases of skin cancer. The Vostok research site, located above the deepest part of the continental ice sheet, provides climate data from ice cores for the past four hundred thousand years. The treaty has prohibited military activity and is a rare example of international harmony. There are lots of examples of the tragedy of the commons or of the suboptimality of the commons. Antarctica is a rare example of the triumph of the commons.

Photo 12.1.   Research station on Deception Island, Antarctica (John Rennie Short)

The future will present problems for Antarctica. With ten thousand scientists and fifty thousand visitors on average visiting the continent in summer, extra pressure will be placed on the fragile ecology and delicate ecological balance. The greatest threat is climate change and especially rapid warming, especially in the western region. Ice shelves are breaking off, now lubricated by the water at their base. The sea ice is thinning with the possibility of positive feedback. More open water means less reflected light and more heat absorption. Ice reflects 90 percent of sunlight, while open water reflects only 6 percent. The result is that more warming will lead to more open water than sea ice, which leads to even more warming. The Antarctic holds 70 percent of the earth's fresh water and 90 percent of its ice. A warming Antarctica will have global impacts with sea-level rise and trillions of tons of cold water dumped into global, oceanic circulation systems. The long-term consequences could be dire.

The Antarctic Treaty ends in 2030, and we may see a return to territorial claims to bolster rights to rich fishing grounds and to valuable oil and gas deposits. For the moment, however, we should remember how international cooperation has created a place for scientific research, free from resource exploitation and military conflict—a good place to end a book on geopolitics and perhaps an instructive way to consider solutions to our collective futures.

SELECTED READINGS

Barry, T., Daviðsdóttir, B., Einarsson, N., & Young, O. R. (2020). The Arctic Council: An agent of change? *Global Environmental Change, 63*, 102099. https://doi.org/10.1016/j.gloenvcha.2020.102099.

Hemmings, A. D., Dodds, K., & Roberts, P. (eds.). (2017). *Handbook on the politics of Antarctica.* Cheltenham and Northampton: Edward Elgar.

McCannon, J. (2012). *A history of the Arctic.* London: Reaktion.

Oliva, M. (2017). Arctic cold war: Climate change has ignited a new polar power struggle. https://theconversation.com/arctic-cold-war-climate-change-has-ignited-a-new-polar-power-struggle-107329.

Young, O. R. (2016). Governing the antipodes: International cooperation in Antarctica and the Arctic. *Polar Record, 52*, 230–38.

NOTES

1. See https://coronavirus.jhu.edu.

2. In this lecture I discuss the pandemic in relation to space-time compression, globalizations, and environmental change in the Anthropocene: https://vimeo.com/416056090.

3. Sherwood, S., et al. (2020). An assessment of Earth's climate sensitivity using multiple lines of evidence. *Reviews of Geophysics.* https://doi.org/10.1029/2019RG000678.

4. Xu, C., Kohler, T. A., Lenton, T. M., Svenning, J. C., & Scheffer, M. (2020). Future of the human climate niche. *Proceedings of the National Academy of Sciences, 117,* 11350–55.

5. Lustgarten, A. (2020). The great climate migration. *New York Times Magazine.* https://www.nytimes.com/interactive/2020/07/23/magazine/climate-migration.html?searchResultPosition=1.

6. Clem, K. R., Fogt, R. L., Turner, J., et al. (2020). Record warming at the South Pole during the past three decades. *Nature Climate Change, 10,* 762–70.

7. Young, O. R. (2016). Governing the antipodes: International cooperation in Antarctica and the Arctic. *Polar Record, 52,* 230–38.

8. Robinson, M. F. (2010). *The coldest crucible: Arctic exploration and American culture.* Chicago: University of Chicago Press.

9. Bowen, S. (2012). *The last Viking: The life of Roald Amundsen.* Boston: Da Capo Press.

10. McCannon, J. (2012). *A history of the Arctic.* London: Reaktion.

11. Drewniak, M., Dalaklis, D., Kitada, M., Ölçer, A., & Ballini, F. (2018). Geopolitics of Arctic shipping: The state of icebreakers and future needs. *Polar Geography, 41,* 107–25; Young, O. R. (2016). The shifting landscape of Arctic politics: Implications for international cooperation. *Polar Journal, 6,* 209–23.

12. Barry, T., Daviðsdóttir, B., Einarsson, N., & Young, O. R. (2020). The Arctic Council: An agent of change? *Global Environmental Change, 63,* 102099. https://doi.org/10.1016/j.gloenvcha.2020.102099.

13. Wilson, P. (2016). Society, steward or security actor? Three visions of the Arctic Council. *Cooperation and Conflict, 51,* 55–74.

14. Oliva, M. (2017). Arctic cold war: Climate change has ignited a new polar power struggle. https://theconversation.com/arctic-cold-war-climate-change-has-ignited-a-new-polar-power-struggle-107329.

15. Laruelle, M. (2020). Russia's arctic policy: A power struggle and its limits. *Nei Visions,* 117. https://www.ifri.org/sites/default/files/atoms/files/laruelle_russia_arctic_policy_2020.pdf.

16. Khurshudyan, I., & Freedman, A. (2020). An oil spill in Russia's Arctic exposes risks for Moscow's far north plans. *Washington Post.* https://www.washingtonpost.com/climate-environment/2020/07/28/an-oil-spill-russias-arctic-exposes-problems-moscows-big-plans-far-north/?arc404=true.

17. Hemmings, A. D., Dodds, K., & Roberts, P. (eds.). (2017). *Handbook on the politics of Antarctica.* Cheltenham and Northampton: Edward Elgar.

Index